Law in the Time of Oxymora

What do different concepts like *true lie*, *bad luck*, *honest thief*, *old news*, *spacetime*, *glocalization*, *symplexity*, *sustainable development*, *constant change*, *soft law*, *substantive due process*, *pure law*, *bureaucratic efficiency* and *global justice* have in common? What connections do they share with innumerable paradoxes, like the ones of happiness, time, globalization, sex, and of free will and fate?

Law in the Time of Oxymora provides answers to these conundrums by critically comparing the apparent rise in recent years of the use of rhetorical figures called "essentially oxymoronic concepts" (i.e. oxymoron, enantiosis and paradox) in the areas of art, science and law. Albeit to varying degrees, these concepts share the quality of giving expression to apparent contradictions. Through this quality, they also challenge the scientific paradigm rooted in the dualistic thinking and binary logic that is traditionally used in the West, as opposed to the East, where a paradoxical mode of thinking and fuzzy logic is said to have been cultivated.

Following a review of oxymora and paradoxes in art and various scientific writings, hundreds of "hard cases" featuring oxymora and a comprehensive review of the legal literature are discussed, revealing evidence suggesting that the present scientific paradigm of dualism alone will no longer be able to tackle the challenges arising from increasing diversity and complexity coupled with an apparent acceleration of change. *Law in the Time of Oxymora* reaches the surprising conclusion that essentially oxymoronic concepts may inaugurate a new era of cognition, involving the ways the senses interact and how we reason, think and make decisions in law and in life.

Rostam J. Neuwirth is Professor of Law at the University of Macau (China) where he also serves as the Program Coordinator of Master of International Business Law (IBL) in the English Language. He received his Ph.D. degree from the European University Institute (EUI) in Florence (Italy) and also holds a Master's degree in Law (LL.M.) from the Faculty of Law of McGill University in Montreal (Canada). His undergraduate studies he spent at the University of Graz (Austria) and the Université d'Auvergne (France). Previously, he taught at the West Bengal University of Juridical Sciences (NUJS) in Kolkata (India) and the Hidayatullah National Law University (HNLU) in Raipur (India). Prior to that, he worked for two years as a legal adviser in the Department of European Law in Department I.4 (European Law) of the *Völkerrechtsbüro* (International Law Bureau) of the Austrian Federal Ministry for Foreign Affairs.

Neuwirth has authored more than 70 articles in international journals around the world. His research interests focus strongly on interdisciplinarity and include the legal areas of international economic law, WTO and EU law, the creative economy, intellectual property, cultural diversity, comparative law, as well as various "law and . . ." issues.

Juris Diversitas

Rooted in comparative law, the *Juris Diversitas* series focuses on the interdisciplinary study of legal and normative mixtures and movements. Our interest is in comparison broadly conceived, extending beyond law narrowly understood to related fields. Titles might be geographical or temporal comparisons. They could focus on theory and methodology, substantive law, or legal cultures. They could investigate official or unofficial 'legalities', past and present and around the world. And, to effectively cross spatial, temporal, and normative boundaries, inter- and multi-disciplinary research is particularly welcome.

"Professor Rostam J. Neuwirth has produced a scholarly work of real excellence that will be certain to test the concept of law. In the vanguard of research, his work re-conceptualises the perception and reality of law. Its contribution is more than important. It is fundamental."

Professor Gonzalo Villalta Puig, The University of Hull, UK

"*Law in the Time of Oxymora*, like its title, brings together fields and thoughts that are often considered opposites, to present a well-reasoned and compelling argument about the durability and applicability of western binary approaches across many disciplines. Regardless of your field of expertise – from science to law to art – this book should be read for its original and imaginative insights that are delightfully well written and presented, and which are likely to make you rethink some of your accepted 'truths'."

Colin B. Picker, University of Wollongong, Australia

"Rostam J. Neuwirth's study of the oxymoron – the word itself represents an oxymoron – in literature, art and science, and, dependent on these, law, shows that binary logic and universal principles without irreconcilable contradictions are difficult to maintain in a globalised world. Not only will the lawyer look differently at law after having read this fascinating book on oxymoronic concepts, the researcher will be delighted by the rich source material the author provides from literature, philosophy, science, law and politics."

Andreas Rahmatian, University of Glasgow, UK

"Rostam Neuwirth's book *Law in the Time of Oxymora* is a thoughtful and complex investigation of the varying uses of this fascinating figure of speech and its impact on our thought. While Professor Neuwirth focuses on the oxymorons of law, he also examines their use in science and the arts. He takes us on an exciting and informative journey through many areas of knowledge, leaving us more informed and more intrigued about the world and the many ways that we think about it."

Christine A. Corcos, Louisiana State University Law Center, USA

Other titles in this series:

Stateless Law
Evolving Boundaries of a Discipline
Edited by Helge Dedek and Shauna Van Praagh

The Diffusion of Law
The Movement of Laws and Norms Around the World
Edited by Sue Farran, James Gallen, Jennifer Hendry and Christa Rautenbach

Indigenous Rights in Scandinavia
Autonomous Sami Law
Edited by Christina Allard and Susann Funderud Skogvang

Law Between Buildings
Emergent Global Perspectives in Urban Law
Edited by Nisha Mistry and Nestor M. Davidson

For more information about this series, please visit:
www.routledge.com/Juris-Diversitas/book-series/JURISDIV

Law in the Time of Oxymora

A Synaesthesia of Language, Logic and Law

Rostam J. Neuwirth

Routledge
Taylor & Francis Group
LONDON AND NEW YORK

First published 2018 by Routledge

2 Park Square, Milton Park, Abingdon, Oxfordshire OX14 4RN
52 Vanderbilt Avenue, New York, NY 10017

Routledge is an imprint of the Taylor & Francis Group, an informa business

First issued in paperback 2019

British Library Cataloguing-in-Publication Data
A catalogue record for this book is available from the British Library

Library of Congress Cataloging-in-Publication Data
Names: Neuwirth, Rostam J., author.
Title: Law in the time of oxymora : a synesthesia of language, logic and law / Rostam J. Neuwirth.
Description: New York, NY : Routledge, 2018. | Includes index.
Identifiers: LCCN 2017059167 | ISBN 9780815346692 (hardback)
Subjects: LCSH: Law–Language. | Semantics (Law) | Oxymoron.
Classification: LCC K213 .N485 2018 | DDC 340/.14—dc23
LC record available at https://lccn.loc.gov/2017059167

ISBN: 978-0-8153-4669-2 (hbk)
ISBN: 978-0-367-89364-4 (pbk)

Typeset in ITC Galliard Std
by Swales & Willis Ltd, Exeter, Devon, UK

For Holger S. Neuwirth

Engineer, Painter, Architect, and . . . Father

Contents

Preface

The initial idea for *Law in the Time of Oxymora* gradually concretized as the result of diverse educational and professional experiences gained over the past two decades all around the world. Throughout these years, every new research question or experience at large appeared to invite the sole conclusion that a strongly dualistic conception of law as of life – expressed in a binary logic and in language through an infinite number of dichotomies, antagonisms or dualistic pairs – poses a serious obstacle to successfully tackling the problems caused by the increasingly complex and rapidly changing world in which we live. In this world, the complexity and the accelerated pace of change equally threaten – like a new pandemic global disease – to undermine law, especially the rule of law as an instrument providing legal certainty and predictability. These factors seem to contribute to the failure of law to meet expectations and to solve the great problems faced by the global governance debate today.

The apparent failure of the present international legal order, which is characterized by the absence of a coherent body of global law, is what invited the association with the book *Love in the Time of Cholera* written by Gabriel García Márquez, which provided more than the phonetical inspiration for the title of this book. By showing that love can flourish even in a time of pandemic disease, Márquez provided, in my view, encouragement to try to find ways for law to function as a "social medicine" as described so well by Pierre Lepaulle. To successfully do so, however, law must carefully address the prospects for global governance in the future, which James N. Rosenau described as the ability "to discern powerful tensions, profound contradictions, and perplexing paradoxes". In law, however, contradictory language mostly causes a malaise, given the law's strongly dualistic conception, which holds that a contract is either void or valid, an act legal or illegal, or a person innocent or guilty, but – usually – never both at the same time.

The possibility of a cure for this malaise of the law is what prompted my inquiry into the language and logic of the rhetorical figures of the oxymoron, the enantiosis and the paradox, or the so-called "essentially oxymoronic concepts", as I described them in an article published in 2013 as a homage to the notion of "essentially contested concepts" coined by Walter B. Gallie in 1956. *Law in the Time of Oxymora* departs from the premise of a possible shift from contested to oxymoronic concepts to an examination of the likely trend of an increase in the use of essentially oxymoronic concepts. Subsequently, it assesses the extent to which this linguistic trend is a harbinger of more profound changes, which could eventually pave the way to deeper cognitive and possibly genetic changes. The reason is that cognitive changes are urgently needed if the objectives of a drastic institutional and legal reform of the present system and the establishment of a coherent global legal order are to be accomplished. In trying to show how oxymora and paradoxes may trigger such changes in cognition and possibly genetics, synaesthesia provides an adequate metaphor for a greater unity of perception, whether it is applied to the different senses themselves, to language, logic and law, or to art, science and law. In sum, a greater unity of the senses, and in perception as a whole, is expected to form the basis for overcoming the global fragmentation of laws and possibly many other serious problems, the solution of which may have been prevented so far by a neglect of the fact that contradictions are only apparently absurd, however, they may in fact be or turn out to be true.

It is certainly true that this book would never have been possible without all the creators of the different artistic, scientific, legal and other works cited throughout this book, which are too numerous to be listed in a separate bibliography. They have all made the research for this book not only an exciting synaesthetic journey but have also provided many missing links and great intellectual support for a topic which has not yet been addressed in such a comprehensive way. In this task, great inspiration has come from the many people with whom I was so privileged to study and research at different places. The journey began with my studies at the law faculties of the Université d'Auvergne in Clermont-Ferrand (France) and the Karl-Franzens University in Graz (Austria). It continued at McGill University, where so many important insights were received during my postgraduate studies, notably in the classes by my supervisor Prof. H. Patrick Glenn, who sadly passed away too early and without being able to comment critically on my book as he had promised. His teaching and supervision were a true eye-opener to the rich and diverse world of law and the essential role of the comparative method for law and legal reasoning across the world's different legal traditions. At the same time, more inspiration came from Armand De Mestral, Rabbi Joshua Shmidman, El Obaid A. El Obaid and Stephen Toope, who all reinforced my interest in the various foundations of the unity in the diversity of law in a global context. I would equally like to acknowledge the many interesting seminars or courses delivered by my supervisor, Bruno de Witte, as well as Giuliano Amato, Philip Alston, Gráinne de Búrca, Pierre-Marie Dupuy, Claus-Dieter Ehlermann, Christian Joerges, Karl-Heinz Ladeur, Neil Walker and Jacques Ziller during the time I spent at the European University Institute.

For my legal formation and later academic career, an indispensable professional experience was provided by my work in the regional courts in Styria, as well as the International Law Bureau of the Austrian Federal Ministry of Foreign Affairs in the context of the Austrian EU presidency in 2006. Following the work in the Foreign Ministry, I moved on to teach at two National Law Schools in India, the Hidayatullah National Law School (HNLU) and the National University of Juridical Sciences (NUJS) in Kolkata (India). Here, all my gratitude goes to Mahendra P. Singh, the former Vice-Chancellor of NUJS, for his unique mentorship, great intellect and kind support over all those years.

As a unique Eastern-Western place, my special thanks go to the Macau SAR and the University of Macau for providing such an interesting research environment in legal, economic, historical, cultural and culinary terms. Equal thanks go to my colleagues and students at the Faculty of Law for providing support for so many ideas through related research and teaching activities. Equally important were my various stays as a visiting professor at the University of New South Wales, the Eduardo Mondlane University, Hokkaido University, the European University Institute, the Pan-European University, Kobe Law School, the University of Life Sciences in Vienna and the Universidad Andina Simón Bolívar in Quito. Although there are too many to list, every single conference was a rich source of ideas, and I would like to especially mention the Juris Diversitas annual conferences in 2016 and 2017, which provided an open-minded platform for the presentation of the principal ideas underlying this book.

Finally, I also thank the following friends and colleagues who directly or indirectly contributed to the realization of this book: Irene Calboli, Ignazio Castellucci, Christine A. Corcos, Christiaan De Beukelaer, Denis De Castro Halis, Yvonne Donders, Iris Eisenberger, Rai Ekraj, Francesco Francioni, Miguel Goede, Christoph Beat Graber, Peter Griss, Sonei Griss, Véronique Guèvremont, Frank Hammel, Lilian Hanania-Richieri, Daniel and Brigitte Hollegha, Andrew Johnston, Martin Kleiner, Michael Kratzer, Arno Kreilhuber, Andreas Kumin, Lee Keun-Gwan, Li Shiqiao, Michel Levi Coral, Bing Ling, Esther Lorenz, Salvatore Mancuso, Stefan Meyer, Gu Minkang, Olivier Moréteau, Colin B. Picker, Andreas Rahmatian, Akira Saito, Robert Schuetze, Martina Spernbauer, Alexandr Svetlicinii, Yoshiyuki Tamura, Gonzalo Villalta Puig, Wang Heng, Richard H. Weisberg, Peter K. Yu, Zhao Yun, and Lorenzo Zucca.

Beyond words, a true *conditio sine qua non* for the realization of the book is the strong support from my closest family, in the context of which I want to mention my father Holger, to whom this book is dedicated, as he laid the foundations to it in more than a dozen ways and provided important critical feedback on an earlier draft. To my mother Eva, I am grateful for her belief in me and for having, from the very beginning, truly set the foundations for me to pursue my career globally. Similarly, I acknowledge my grandparents, who continue to provide essential support, guidance and hope, even from the life after life. Further acknowledgements go to Iris P. Neuwirth, Mohammed M. Abderrahmane and Harald "Harry" Neuwirth, Gösta Neuwirth and Olga Neuwirth, who also provided great support to this book, far beyond the mention or explanation of specific oxymora. At last, my special gratitude and love goes to my wife Pui Mang and my very favourite "oxymora", our two children Elam J. and Lea J.

Rostam J. Neuwirth, Macau, October 10, 2017

1 Prologue

The quest for light

Dunkel wars, der Mond schien Helle!
(It was dark, the moon shone bright!)

Proverb

It may be best called an "open secret" that the best hiding places are right before us, where we least expect them. Such may be the case with a large number of experiences we are all exposed to, i.e. experiences captured by concepts and rhetoric we all use and are used to, without duly understanding their impact on our mind and their role in our future. Artists, scientists, lawyers and all citizens – literally no one is spared from the creeping effects of this rhetoric. From Shakespeare's "honourable villain" to Orwellian doublethink and Faulkner's "peaceful despair", from the pianoforte to free jazz and other sounds of silence, from architecture as the "art of construction" (*Baukunst*) or "petrified music" to paintings by Escher and Magritte – all the art forms thrive on these concepts. In science too, physicists formulate the "uncertainty principle", biologists study "cognitive genetics", like economists analyse competition through "creative destruction", computer experts develop a "memristor", or physicians diagnose an "anaesthesia dolorosa" or "noninflammatory arthritis". In social science, critical theorists are occupied with the culture industry, and political scientists try to measure "soft power" in a world of glocalization. In law too, attorneys write "lengthy briefs", judges hear cases on "welcome sexual harassment", while scholars debate "intellectual property", "substantive due process" or "binding policies" adopted by the government. Or else, we may just order a *frappuccino* while enjoying a gourmet pizza, drive a sports utility vehicle (SUV) to a nearby cinema to watch the movie *True Lies*, or wear a "skort" with a "real fake" knockoff luxury handbag.

Literally, there appears to be no end to the kind of experiences referred to here. These experiences can also be transformed into manifold questions, like the following: Is there or can there be "global justice"? Can someone lie and tell the truth or be guilty and innocent at the same time? How can we realize the global goals of "sustainable development"? Is it possible to be happy and sad, or happy and poor, as well as sad and rich, at the same time? Do we all want to live in developing countries? What do "global justice", "sadomasochism" and the "creative economy" have in common? Is clean coal a reality or an alternative fact? Do we learn from history, and is logic innate? Is there life after death, do genes transmit experiences? Can words change the way we think, our mind, or even us and the reality around us? Is there a free will or only fate or "kismet"?

These experiences and questions all share as a common element the rise of so-called "essentially oxymoronic concepts" in contemporary discourses, artistic, scientific, legal and otherwise. The numerous experiences related to these concepts also share the paradox of the obvious, namely that, usually, the answers to the most complex questions may be hidden where we least expect them. This is also reflected in an old allegory regarding the human quest for "light" as a metaphor for the fundamental three questions of human evolution: "Where do we come from? What are we? Where are we going?" taken from the title of a painting by Paul Gauguin. The quest for light thus refers to efforts to discard the darkness obstructing a greater understanding and awareness of the direction that human evolution will or is supposed to take. By analogy, the quest for light is also closely related to the quest of law for truth and justice and the solution of serious problems on the way there. Metaphorically, the struggle of this quest is reflected in an old allegory which goes as follows:

> There was a time in the history of the race when the gods stole from man his divinity, and, meeting in a high conclave, sought to decide where to hide that which they had stolen. One god suggested that they hide it on *another planet*, for there man could not find it, but another god arose and said that man was innately a great traveler and they had no guarantee that, eventually, he might not find his way there. "Let us," he said, "hide it in the *depths of the sea*, at the bottom of the ocean for there it will be safe." But again a dissenting voice was heard, and it was pointed out that man was a great natural investigator and that he might some day succeed in penetrating to the deepest depths as well as the greatest heights.[1]

Evidently, this allegory invites the question of what causes the current darkness and where, in the end, the light guiding humans was hidden. If the reader has not already guessed it, to find out, law can play a useful role in its rediscovery. In the following pages, therefore, the attempt will be made to show that it is, most likely, in the same place from which the phenomenon of the rise of oxymoronic concepts is taking its origin.

1 See Foster Bailey, *The Spirit of Masonry*, 3rd ed (New York: Lucis Publishing, 1979) at 106–107 [*Italics* added].

Introduction

In the beginning was the Word, and the Word was with God, and the Word was God. The same was in the beginning with God. All things were made by him; and without him was not any thing made that was made. In him was life; and the life was the light of men. And the light shineth in darkness; and the darkness comprehended it not.[1]

Law in the Time of Oxymora is essentially concerned with the role of law in an age of a seemingly accelerating pace of change or at least the perception of change. It is a time where so-called "essentially oxymoronic concepts" appear to be on the rise globally. Put briefly, these essentially oxymoronic concepts are rhetorical figures that display varying degrees of intrinsic contradictions or consist of apparently conflicting and logically irreconcilable propositions. Most of all, their contradictory nature appears to be incompatible and clash with the dominant mode of binary or bivalent logics as used in dualistic thinking and classical logic. Linguistics has defined several of these figures, such as oxymoron, enantiosis (or *contradictio in adiecto*) and paradox. However, in their usage the borders distinguishing them are often blurred both in linguistics and in other scientific contexts. Therefore, the present book condenses them into the new category of essentially oxymoronic concepts, which I have deliberately created in homage to an article by Walter B. Gallie, titled "Essentially Contested Concepts", published in 1956.[2] Gallie's seminal article is often used as a means to communicate better the meaning of numerous vague concepts that dominate our multiple discourses, like art, health, justice or the rule of law. All these mentioned and most other concepts we frequently use are, in fact, contested concepts, namely those of which we share the terminology but not necessarily the same meaning.

Important for the role of concepts and language in law as a means of organizing life and governing societies, the idea underlying this book is that essentially oxymoronic concepts evolved from their contested counterparts. Generally speaking, they mark a shift of human culture from contestation and conflict to contradiction

1 John 1:1–5 AV.

2 Walter B. Gallie, "Essentially Contested Concepts" (1956) 56 *Proceedings of the Aristotelian Society* 167 and Rostam J. Neuwirth, "Essentially Oxymoronic Concepts" (2013) 2(2) *Global Journal of Comparative Law* 147.

and convergence. It is a shift symbolizing the changing way humans perceive reality, conceive their thoughts based on ideas and communicate them to others so as to foster their understanding of the phenomena around and within them. The central difference is thus that, in an era of contestation, the process of understanding proceeded primarily by way of conflicts – solved by contest between persons, groups, companies or countries – which still dominate large parts of our lives, from education and sports, to economics, politics, war and the law. By contrast, the dawning era of contradiction and convergence inaugurated by oxymoronic concepts may be one where the conflicts are simultaneously present in every person exposed to these concepts. Put differently, essentially oxymoronic concepts elevate conflicts from the external and interpersonal to the internal and intrapersonal level of the mind.

If this premise is confirmed and essentially oxymoronic concepts do have an impact on the way we perceive, think and subsequently act, then it may be of great relevance for all areas of life. It may allow us to formulate new ideas for the efficient tackling and proper solution of all kinds of problems, both individual and collective or local and global. Eventually, they may inaugurate a new mode or even organ of cognition, which may be born out of the contradictions they carry. This potential impact is best highlighted in the context of law. The reason is that law nowadays pervades all areas of life such that it can easily be termed a universal science. At the same time, all these areas of life are changing at unprecedented and truly breakneck speeds, as reflected in the pace of technological innovation and scientific progress. Additionally, due to the continuing and irreversible globalizing trends, law is gradually being transformed, and, most of all, called upon to evolve, from a system of many separate national legal systems to an emerging coherent system of global law. In view of a rising number of serious global problems and threats, law still has a long way to go to that end.

The necessity of establishing a global law supported by a more efficient and just global institutional framework is recognized by the global governance debate. The main challenges related to global governance were outlined by James N. Rosenau in the following lines:

> To anticipate the prospects for global governance in the decades ahead is to discern *powerful tensions, profound contradictions, and perplexing paradoxes.* It is to search for order in disorder, for coherence in contradiction, and for continuity in change. It is to confront processes that mask both growth and decay. It is to look for authorities that are obscure, boundaries that are in flux, and systems of rule that are emergent. And it is to experience hope embedded in despair.[3]

Global governance thus meets with serious paradoxes. Its most important one consists in the difficulty of creating a truly global legal framework without

3 James N. Rosenau, "Governance in the 21st Century" (1995) 1(1) *Global Governance* 13 at 13 [*Italics* added].

having a truly global legal platform in which the necessary deliberations can take place. These conditions are presently not met. First, this is because the present international legal order established mainly after World War II does not reflect the political, economic and other realities of the twenty-first century. Second, the main international organizations are fragmented and inefficient and cannot provide a platform for a much needed reform.

So how to proceed in the face of this global governance paradox? As in the past, if the necessary changes do not come from within the system, they will have to come from somewhere else. The idea pursued here is that institutional changes will follow only when significant cognitive changes have taken place. In view of many divisions and borders, law and its noble goals of pursuing justice can provide a common ground for tracking possible sources of cognitive changes. One track may be provided by language, as language is a way to make visible the underlying cognitive processes. In this regard, Andrew Halpin and Volker Roeben also suggested the development of a "common language" as the way to overcome the present international discord that characterizes both "the different legal provisions and perspectives found within the societies of the world".[4]

Another useful piece of advice for addressing the current paradox of global governance was given by George P. Fletcher when he wrote that "if we wish to avoid disabling contradictions, we must reach a deeper understanding of the legal premises that guide our thinking".[5] This implies that usually solutions to problems have to be found at levels adequate to the causes that created them. In other words, the solution of a paradox, which is contradictory within a system of binary logic and dualistic thinking, must be sought beyond the constraints imposed by such logic.

For the many unsettling questions related to both tasks, namely developing a common language and trying to unveil the deeper causes of many apparent contradictions, essentially oxymoronic concepts may hold a key to the answers. This is what this book is aiming to contribute to, namely a better understanding of the cognitive challenges that law in the time of oxymora faces. It means to decipher the codes hidden in essentially oxymoronic concepts, especially to enquire into the causes leading to their rise and to comprehend the impact they have on cognition in general and decision making in particular. Ultimately, it seeks to assess their role in evolution and the contribution they can make in the process of the formation of a new global legal order of the future.

4 See Andrew Halpin and Volker Roeben (eds), *Theorising the Global Legal Order* (Oxford: Hart, 2009) at 6.

5 George P. Fletcher, "Paradoxes in Legal Thought" (1985) 85(6) *Columbia Law Review* 1263 at 1292.

3 From essentially contested to oxymoronic concepts

Duality is the condition of our perception of the phenomenal (three-dimensional) world; it is the instrument of our perception of phenomena. But when we come to the perception of the noumenal world (or the world of many dimensions), this duality begins to stand in our way, to become an obstacle to knowledge.[1]

If currently there is an important shift of cognitive modes of thought taking place, from essentially contested to oxymoronic concepts, then what is the difference between them? How does their difference affect the way we perceive, think and act, if at all? This question means to understand how essentially oxymoronic concepts may affect our decision making in general and in the area of law and legal reasoning in particular. To this end, the differences between contested and oxymoronic concepts need to be outlined by looking at the phenomenon of change, as perhaps and paradoxically the sole constant of life. The look at change entails first an attempt to understand the perception of change, as change may be constant but our perception of change, or perception alone, is not. Second, to be able to verify the impact, namely whether essentially oxymoronic concepts may play a certain role in the advancement of human understanding, it is also important to consider how perception itself may have changed during human evolution. This includes the search for evidence of how the shift from contested to oxymoronic concepts started to materialize.

3.1 Essentially contested concepts: contestation and conflict

Contest is a part of human life everywhere that human life is found. In war and in games, in work and in play, physically, intellectually, and morally, human beings match themselves with or against one another.[2]

1 Peter D. Ouspensky, *Tertium Organum: The Third Canon of Thought – A Key to the Enigmas of the World*, 2nd ed (New York: Alfred A. Knopf, 1922) at 265–266.

2 Walter Ong, *Fighting for Life: Contest, Sexuality, and Consciousness* (Ithaca: Cornell University Press, 1981) at 15.

What are "essentially contested concepts"? And what is their role in our life and, subsequently, also in law? To begin with, the notion of "essentially contested concepts" was introduced by Walter B. Gallie in an article published in 1956. In the article, he defined concepts which are essentially contested by calling them "concepts the proper use of which inevitably involves endless disputes about their proper uses on the part of their users".[3] Practically, this may render every word "contested" because one may dispute the meaning of every word. This is also related to an overarching problem of communication between people, namely the distinction between a word and its meaning or – as John Rawls distinguished – concepts from conceptions (of justice).[4] This distinction means that while two (or more) people may agree on the existence of a word its invocation does not necessarily (or possibly ever) create an identical association in the mind of another person. More so, the meaning associated with a word may even differ in the same person from one moment to another. This is where the role of perception in general and in particular of the perception of change in our framework of time and space comes into play.

In his article, Gallie used the word "art" and also democracy, social justice and the adherence to a particular religion as examples to show how the meaning and use of concepts may be contested between different persons. Shortly thereafter, in a second article, he further elaborated on art as a contested concept, with which he sought to "unravel the puzzles and paradoxes with which art-criticism is constantly beset".[5] Gallie's articles soon inspired many more authors from different scientific backgrounds to use this terminology for other contested concepts. For instance, "nature", a very broad term of many different associations, was termed an essentially contested concept;[6] so was "love".[7] Similarly "freedom" was critically discussed from the perspective of it being essentially contestable.[8] Even logic, often understood as an immutable law of thought, has been listed as being an essentially contested concept among others, like morality, the novel, nature, rationality, culture, science and philosophy.[9] Equally, health has been discussed as a contested concept, because it "cannot be defined by appeal to something that is genuinely objective (which is to say, existing independently of the observing subject)".[10]

3 See Walter B. Gallie, "Essentially Contested Concepts" (1956) 56 *Proceedings of the Aristotelian Society* 167 at 169.

4 John Rawls, *A Theory of Justice* (Cambridge: Belknap Press, 1971) at 5.

5 See Walter B. Gallie, "Art as an Essentially Contested Concept" (1956) 6(23) *The Philosophical Quarterly* 97 at 97.

6 See Franklin Ginn and David Demeritt, "Nature: A Contested Concept" in Sarah L. Holloway, Stephen P. Rice and Gill Valentine (eds), *Key Concepts in Geography* (London: SAGE, 2003) 300.

7 See Richard P. Hamilton, "Love as a Contested Concept" (2006) 36(3) *Journal for the Theory of Social Behaviour* 239.

8 See Patrick Day, "Is the Concept of Freedom Essentially Contestable?" (1986) 61(235) *Philosophy* 116.

9 See John Kekes, "Essentially Contested Concepts: A Reconsideration" (1977) 10(2) *Philosophy & Rhetoric* 71 at 71.

10 See A. Edgar, "Health Care Allocation, Public Consultation and the Concept of 'Health'" (1998) 6(3) *Health Care Analysis* 193 at 197 [footnote omitted].

Closely related to health, medicine too has been examined under the terms of essentially contested concepts.[11] Various economic concepts, both broad and narrow or generic and specific, such as "globalization",[12] both "development"[13] and "sustainable development",[14] "market",[15] and "corporate social responsibility"[16] and have been investigated from this perspective. So has "power"[17] and, unsurprisingly, again "democracy".[18] For democracy, a highly disputed term in international politics, its qualification as a contested concept was explained by the following argument:

> This is so because democracy is an essentially contested concept: there is not just one, but rather a plurality of competing conceptions of democracy, each of which emphasizes a different good commonly associated with democratic political regimes.[19]

Many political and social concepts have been classified as contested concepts.[20] Similarly legal concepts have been included in the list of essentially contested concepts, including those of "law",[21] "justice",[22] the "rule of law",[23] "hard

11 See C. McKnight, "Medicine as an essentially contested concept" (2003) 29(4) *Journal of Medical Ethics* 261.

12 See Jonathan R. Strand, Tina F. Mueller, and Jessica A. McArthur, "The Essentially Contested Concept of Globalization" (2005) 1(1) *Journal of International Political Theory* 45.

13 See Björn Hettne, *Thinking about Development: Development Matters* (London: Zed Books, 2009) at 1.

14 See Michael Jacobs, "Sustainable Development as a Contested Concept" in Andrew Dobson (ed), *Fairness and Futurity: Essays on Environmental Sustainability and Social Justice* (Oxford: Oxford University Press, 2002) 21 and Steve Connelly, "Mapping Sustainable Development as a Contested Concept" (2007) 12(3) *Local Environment: The International Journal of Justice and Sustainability* 259 at 260 and 262.

15 See Eckehard F. Rosenbaum, "What is a Market? On the Methodology of a Contested Concept" (2000) 58(4) *Review of Social Economy* 455.

16 See Adaeze Okoye, "Theorising Corporate Social Responsibility as an Essentially Contested Concept: Is a Definition Necessary?" (2009) 89(4) *Journal of Business Ethics* 613.

17 See Steven Lukes, *Power: A Radical View*, 2nd ed (Basingstoke: Palgrave Macmillan, 2005) at 30, 62, and 164 and K. I. MacDonald, "Is 'Power' Essentially Contested?" (1976) 6(3) *British Journal of Political Science* 380.

18 See *e.g.* Howard A. Doughty, "Democracy as an Essentially Contested Concept" (2014) 19(1) *The Innovation Journal* 1.

19 See Dan M. Kahan, "Democracy Schmemocracy" (1999) 20(3) *Cardozo Law Review* 795 at 795–796.

20 See *e.g.* Christine Swanton, "On the 'Essential Contestedness' of Political Concepts" (1985) 95(4) *Ethics* 811 at 811; see also John N. Gray, "On the Contestability of Social and Political Concepts" (1977) 5(3) *Political Theory* 331.

21 See also Kenneth E. Ehrenberg, "Law Is Not (Best Considered) an Essentially Contested Concept" (2011) 7(2) *International Journal of Law in Context* 209.

22 See Steven Lukes and W. G. Runciman, "Relativism: Cognitive and Moral" (1974) 48 *Proceedings of the Aristotelian Society, Supplementary Volumes* 165 at 184 and 191.

23 See *e.g.* Jeremy Waldron, "Is the Rule of Law an Essentially Contested Concept (in Florida)?" (2002) 21(2) *Law and Philosophy* 137; see also J. A. Goguen, "The Logic of Inexact Concepts" (1969) 19(3) *Synthese* 325; Gallie, "Essentially Contested Concepts", *supra* note 3 at 180.

cases",[24] "equality"[25] or "equal protection",[26] and "legitimacy"[27]. Equally, the European Union, which has been steadily working towards the goal of greater European integration or an ever closer union among its peoples, has been called a "contested project".[28]

These few concrete examples seem to suggest that, as a matter of fact, every concept is and can potentially be "contested". This is because it lies in the nature of humans to contest, compete and even to "crush" the opponent in order to "convince". When you come to think of it, it is no coincidence that "to convince" shares the same origin as "to conquer" or "to be victorious". This inclination for contest may also be caused by a strongly dualistic conception of life, of reality or of everything. The same dualism is also strongly ingrained in the nature of most languages, where it surfaces in the use of negation, which is used to reverse "truth and falsity" and has been qualified as "a conditio sine qua non of every human language".[29] As for the main use of negation, it was said that negative sentences are mainly "to contradict and to point a contrast".[30] It is thus a contest between an affirmative and a negative proposition, which is best represented by the dualistic distinction between "yes" and "no".[31] Yes-and-no answers best reflect the dualistic conception or classical logic underlying reasoning, for their opposition marks a conflict by which "we automatically reject one limb as false when we accept the other as true, and conversely".[32] But even "yes" or "no" appear to be contestable concepts, the meaning of which is not always clear. This is why we may at times answer a question with "yes" but mean "no" or vice versa. Or else, we may choose to answer with the oxymoronic "YO" or "*Jein*" in German, meaning "maybe", especially when the evidence or information available is not sufficient for a decisive YES or NO, i.e. to accept or reject a hypothesis.[33] Such a strategy of hesitation allows one to stall for time in order to learn more or make further observations before taking a decision or action.

24 See generally Thomas D. Perry, "Contested Concepts and Hard Cases" (1977) 88(1) *Ethics* 20.

25 See George Rutherglen, "Disparate Impact, Discrimination, and the Essentially Contested Concept of Equality" (2006) 74(4) *Fordham Law Review* 2313.

26 See James M. O'Fallon, "Adjudication and Contested Concepts: The Case of Equal Protection" (1979) 54(1) *New York University Law Review* 19.

27 See Achim Hurrelmann, Steffen Schneider and Jens Steffek, "Conclusion: Legitimacy – Making Sense of an Essentially Contested Concept" in Achim Hurrelmann, Steffen Schneider und Jens Steffek (eds), *Legitimacy in an Age of Global Politics* (Basingstoke: Palgrave Macmillan, 2007) 229.

28 Zenon Bañkowski and Emilios Christodoulidis, "The European Union as an Essentially Contested Project" (1998) 4(4) *European Law Journal* 341.

29 See Laurence R. Horn, "Introduction" in Laurence R. Horn (ed), *The Expression of Negation* (Berlin: De Gruyter, 2010) 1 at 1.

30 See Otto Jespersen, *Negation in English and Other Languages* (København: A.F. Høst, 1917) at 4–5.

31 See also Ian Rumfitt, "'Yes' and 'No'" (2000) 109(436) *Mind* 781.

32 Gottlob Frege, "Logic" in Hans Hermes, Friedrich Kambartel, and Friedrich Kaulbach (eds), *Gottlob Frege: Posthumous Writings* (Oxford: Basil Blackwell, 1979) 1 at 8.

33 See Ya. I. Khurgin, *Yes, No Or Maybe (Science for Everyone)* (Moscow: Mir Publishers, 1985) at 47–48.

In sum, dualism and dualistic thinking mark a strong simplification of the reality perceived. The simplification of a complex phenomenon by dividing it in two has clear benefits. At the same time, though, it leaves ample room for contesting interpretations. These leave doubts whether a dualistic conception is capable of dealing with more complex issues.

It is precisely due to this quality of human nature expressed through language that the notion of essentially contested concepts is so important. It is the need to look beyond the literal meaning of a word and to try to transcend the nature of contest and lead it towards a more cultured form of reaching a consensus. Consensus, again from its Latin origin, may be interpreted as meaning to have common sensory information, which in practice appears to be always impossible to realize, as no two perceptions in time or space ever seem to be the same. This is where Gallie's contribution comes into play, namely, where there is a problem with the confusion caused by a lack of universal agreement about the concepts that interlocutors would invoke and the conceptual confusion that might ensue. Such confusion poses a serious problem in the social sciences, for which Gallie thus provided useful insights into the problem of understanding of contested concepts.[34]

The conditions Gallie listed for a concept to be essentially contested have been outlined as follows. First, such a concept needs to be "appraisive, not purely descriptive (nonevaluative)".[35] Second, it needs to be "controversial" in the sense that "disputes about its proper use are endless".[36] Third, the disputes are nevertheless sustained by respectable arguments (as opposed to mere "bullshit").[37] Fourth, the disputing parties must adhere to divergent views but also understand that their own view is contested. This requirement could perhaps also be explained by the need for the disputing parties to be ready to accept the other person's viewpoints. Fifth and last, the disputing parties also accept "the notion that the concept in question does have a correct or proper use" or that there may be "truth" after all.[38]

The last point means that finding a universal meaning of the concept in question by transcending the confusion associated with the meaning of the concept is at least theoretically possible. Such transcendence of conceptual confusion is highly relevant for the field of law, notably in the processes of law making, the interpretation and application of laws as well as their implementation.[39]

In sum, the insights resulting from Gallie's initial work contain at least one valuable fundamental insight, viz. the realization of the duality of human nature expressed in the form of contest and contestation. Contest, whether carried out

34 See also David Collier, Fernando D. Hidalgo and Andra O. Maciuceanu, "Essentially Contested Concepts: Debates and Applications" (2006) 11(3) *Journal of Political Ideologies* 211 and Eugene Garver, "Rhetoric and Essentially Contested Arguments" (1978) 11(3) *Philosophy and Rhetoric* 156 at 168.

35 See Thomas D. Perry, *supra* note 24 at 24.

36 *Ibid.*

37 See Harry G. Frankfurt, *On Bullshit* (Princeton: Princeton University Press, 2005).

38 See Perry, *supra* note 24 at 24.

39 See also Brian Bix, "Conceptual Questions and Jurisprudence" (1995) 1(4) *Legal Theory* 465.

as competition or conflict, necessarily involves opposing views between a minimum of two disputing parties. In all kinds of areas, contest and contestation serve as the dominant ways of finding meaning or of convincing by different means so as to establish a universal truth. This in itself is an important realization. A second important element of contested concepts is the encouragement they provide for the further search for new approaches to various fact- and truth-finding missions. Such new approaches to finding consensus or universal meaning it is hoped will be born from essentially oxymoronic concepts, to which we shall now turn.

3.2 Oxymoron, enantiosis and paradox: contradiction and convergence

In Oxymoron contradictions meet,
And jarring epithets and subjects greet.
Enantiosis poiseth diff'rent things;
And words and sense as into balance brings.
Synceceiosis to one subject ties
Two contraries, and fuller sense supplies.[40]

In line with the mysterious nature of language, in particular its relation to thoughts, words and concepts seem vested with an almost magical power; a power that law also often makes use of.[41] It is in line with change being perhaps the sole constant that language also changes constantly. This change happens in many ways, but mainly through semantic change or the creation of new words, so-called "neologisms". In this regard, literature, poetry and other forms of literary expression keep any language developing, often through a highly creative way of combining existing words, syllables, morphemes or the like. The main challenge related to language appears to be connecting the imaginary with the real, the world of ideas and the world of facts, so as to communicate and construct the reality that one perceives. The artful use of language is also known as "rhetoric", which also helps to classify several different forms of rhetorical figures. For the present purpose, the three main central rhetorical figures used and summarized under the term "essentially oxymoronic concepts" are: oxymoron, enantiosis (or *contradictio in adiecto*) and paradox.

A first reason why these three figures have been selected and combined in one group is that their mutual use in particular in the English language is not always clear. It often happens that an oxymoron is used for a term that is more an

40 See John Stirling, *A System of Rhetoric, in a Method Entirely New; Containing All the Tropes and Figures Necessary to Illustrate the Classics, Both Poetical and Historical* (New York: James Ryan, 1824) at 15 [the order of their listing was changed by the author].

41 See generally Christopher Hutton, *Language, Meaning and the Law* (Edinburgh: Edinburgh University Press, 2009); see also Loren A. Smith, "Law and Magic: An Introduction Out of a Hat" in Christine E. Corcos (ed), *Law and Magic: A Collection of Essays* (Durham: Carolina Academic Press, 2010) 3 at 3.

enantiosis or a paradox and vice versa. This is why it is necessary to look at their definitions individually before elaborating more on their commonalities.

To begin with the *oxymoron*, as usual, the best way to define a term is to look at its etymological origin. In this case it is ancient Greek, where the meaning of oxymoron not only describes but also constitutes an oxymoron. This is because it combines in one word the Greek words "*oxus*", meaning "sharp or pointed", and "*mōros*", meaning "dull or foolish".[42] This has also earned it the Latin denomination as "acutifatuum" or "wise-folly" in English.[43] Put simply, it is a contradiction in terms but expressing two opposite meanings, like both "smart and stupid", in one single word, which is at times more difficult to achieve in English than in the German language. This is why strictly (and etymologically) speaking, an oxymoron should be one word only. More literally, the Oxford English Dictionary defines it as "a figure of speech or expressed idea in which apparently contradictory terms appear in conjunction".[44] In this definition, the omission of the requirement of an oxymoron being only one word may explain the occasional confusion with its other peers.

Oxymora can also be "stretched in reference to ad hoc and unthinking juxtapositions of words which create a contradiction in terms".[45] This leads to the second rhetorical figure, i.e. *enantiosis*, which derives from the Greek and literally means "opposition".[46] Enantiosis has been defined as the "expression of an opposition of meaning in such a manner that the words also stand opposed to each other".[47] Equally, it has been defined as a figure, "by which things very different or contrary are compared or placed together, and by which they mutually set off and enhance each other".[48] Or they were said to describe a concept where the "most heterogeneous ideas are yoked by violence together".[49] In its Latin expression, an enantiosis is called a *contradictio in adiecto* (contradiction through adjunction or "in what (adjective) is added (to a noun)").[50] In sum, they both mark a contradiction created by the connection between two opposite terms, where an adjective meets with a noun to be precise, for example, in *discordia concors* (harmonious discord).

42 See Catherine Soanes and Angus Stevenson (eds), *Concise Oxford English Dictionary*, 11th ed (Oxford: Oxford University Press, 2008) at 1024.

43 See E. W. Bullinger, *Figures of Speech Used in the Bible: Explained and Illustrated* (London: Eyre and Spottiswoode, 1898) at 816.

44 See Soanes and Stevenson, *supra* note 42 at 1040.

45 See Pam Peters, *The Cambridge Guide to English Usage* (Cambridge: Cambridge University Press, 2004) at 402.

46 See John Holmes, *The Art of Rhetoric Made Easy: Or, the Elements of Oratory* (London: C. Hitch & L. Hawes, 1755) at 53.

47 See Samuel Neil, *The Elements of Rhetoric; A Manual of the Flaws of Taste, Including the Theory and Practice of Composition* (London: Walton and Maberly, 1854) at 183–184.

48 See Thomas Gibbons, *Rhetoric; or, a View of its Principal Tropes and Figures* (London: J. and W. Oliver, 1767) at 248.

49 See Samuel Johnson, *The Lives of the Most Eminent English Poets* (London: John Murray, 1854) at 20.

50 Literally translated the Latin phrase *contradictio in adiecto* means "*Widerspruch durch Beifügung*" (contradiction by adjunction).

The third and last rhetorical figure is the *paradox*, which also derives from Greek, where it means "beyond thought", from "*para*" (beyond/against) and "*doxa*" (opinion) or "*dokein*" (thought).[51] It extends the contradiction from one or two words, respectively, to a sequence of words which express a proposition or statement that is seemingly absurd or self-contradictory but "may in fact be true".[52] Additionally, it refers to "an apparently sound statement or proposition which leads to a logically unacceptable conclusion".[53] Paradox is also described as a "sentence bringing in something strange and unexpected".[54] A paradox can thus be expressed in a few words, an entire sentence or even a story. In sum, the various definitions outlined are:

> *paradox, n.* Statement contrary to received opinion; seemingly absurd though perhaps really well-founded statement; self-contradictory, essentially absurd, statement; person, thing, conflicting with preconceived notions of what is reasonable or possible.[55]

As an example of a paradox, one may consider the statement that "babies are larger than their parents". This apparently contradictory and thus paradoxical statement, however, turns out to be true for a South American frog aptly named *Pseudis paradoxa*. It is a frog that grows from an egg into a tadpole, or a "giant baby frog" so to speak, which is four times larger than the adult frog it eventually becomes.[56]

The three figures of speech outlined thus stand in a kind of order from one word (i.e. oxymoron) or two (i.e. enantiosis or *contradictio in adiecto*) to three or more words (i.e. paradox). From this angle, the oxymoron is the highest form of expression of contradiction as it merges two antonyms into one word. This is why the oxymoron was also termed the "show-off among figures of speech", because it is "a paradox compressed into a single self-contradicting phrase".[57] But, contradicting any hierarchical and linear ordering, one can say that even a single word constitutes a paradox. Thus, essentially oxymoronic concepts appear to be linked in an order which defies the usual linear mode of thinking. It seems more suitable to apply a mode of circular thinking instead. To give examples of the respective differences between these three figures by the same term, one can think of "smartass" for oxymoron, an "ignorant savant" for enantiosis (or *contradictio in adiecto*) and the phrase "I know that I know nothing" for a paradox. Similarly, the

51 See *Webster's II New College Dictionary*, 3rd ed (Boston: Houghton Mifflin, 2015) at 815.
52 See Soanes and Stevenson, *supra* note 42 at 1037.
53 *Ibid.*
54 See Holmes, *supra* note 46 at 60.
55 See H. W. Fowler and F. G. Fowler (eds), *The Concise Oxford Dictionary of Current English* (Oxford: Clarendon Press, 1919) at 593.
56 See John L. Behler and Deborah A. Behler, *Frogs: A Chorus of Colors* (New York: Sterling, 2005) at 114.
57 See Helen Vendler, *The Music of What Happens: Poems, Poets, Critics* (Cambridge: Harvard University Press, 1988) at 242.

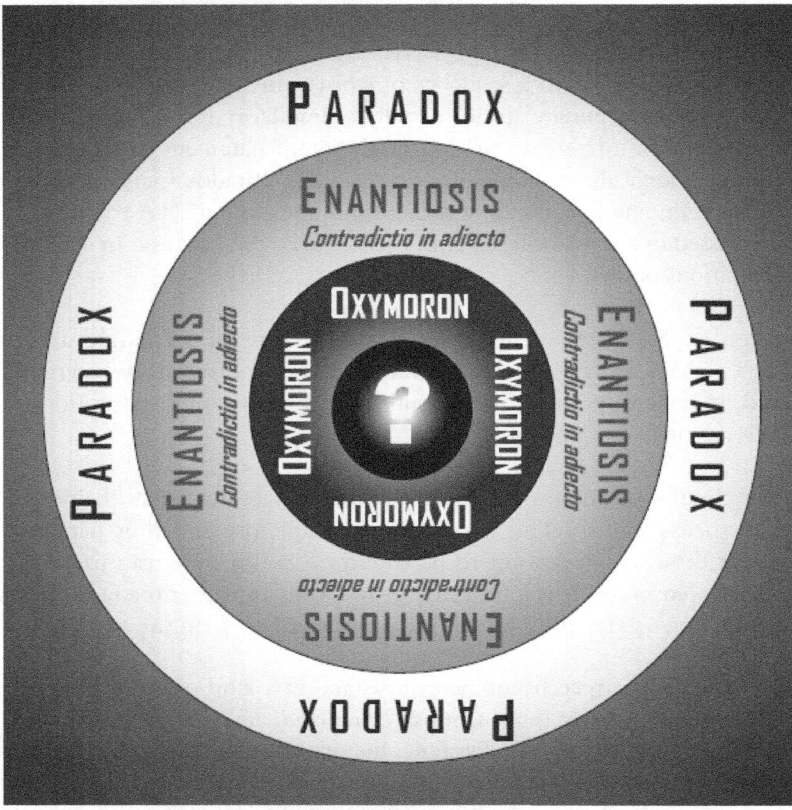

Figure 3.1 Essentially oxymoronic concepts

German term "*Kulturindustrie*" (English culture industry), which was deliberately coined as an oxymoron, transforms into a *contradictio in adiecto* of "cultural industry".[58] Finally, expressed as a paradox, the cultural industries have been defined as being paradoxically of "both an economic and a cultural nature".[59]

From these clarifications the core element binding these three rhetorical figures emerges. The core element that they all share is an inherent contradiction or apparent logical conflict, especially in light of the laws underlying the dominant modes of bivalent or binary logic and dualistic thinking. These modes of thought and logic derive from three traditional laws of thought, i.e. the "laws by which or in accordance with which valid thought proceeds".[60] These three laws have been explained by Bertrand Russell as follows:

58 Cf. Art 2012 Canada-United States Free-Trade Agreement (CUSFTA), (1988) 27 I.L.M. 281.

59 See Recital 18 of the Preamble and Art. 4(5) UNESCO Convention on the Protection and Promotion of the Diversity of Cultural Expressions (CDCE), 2440 UNTS.

60 See Robert Audi (ed), *Cambridge Dictionary of Philosophy*, 2nd ed (Cambridge: Cambridge University Press, 1999) at 489.

1 The law of identity: "Whatever is, is."
2 The law of non-contradiction: "Nothing can both be and not be."
3 The law of excluded middle: "Everything must either be or not be."[61]

These laws are also the axioms of classical or standard logic, which – as opposed to fuzzy or polyvalent logic – is essentially bivalent or dualistic. Related to the laws of thought is also the principle of bivalence, which states that "every sentence of a language is either true or false but not both and not neither, i.e. each and every sentence has exactly one of the two truth-values *true* or *false*".[62]

Thus, oxymoron, enantiosis and paradox are three different categories of rhetorical figures which share the same inherent but apparent contradictions. They merely differ in the intensity of the clash of opposites and the number of words they use to express the contradiction or logical conflict. As a last remark, it is also important to stress that, in spite of their evident contradiction and conflict with classical logic, they may still be true. This has been stated for the oxymoron by describing them as "sense in the masquerade of folly"[63] and for enantiosis by the addition that even the combination of very different or contrary terms can still result in an understanding where "they may mutually set off and illustrate each other".[64] Similarly, the paradoxical frog has provided a living example of a paradox being not only apparently but also really true.

To summarize briefly, there seems indeed to be a shift taking place from essentially contested concepts to their oxymoronic cousins. As a matter of fact, for all the individual contested concepts cited above, such as development, power, equality, freedom, democracy, globalization, law and justice, such a shift can be noted. A few selected examples of their oxymoronic counterparts include the concepts of "sustainable development",[65] "the paradox of power and weakness",[66] "gender equality",[67] "the paradox of freedom",[68] "democratic dictatorship"[69]

61 See Bertrand Russell, *The Problems of Philosophy* (London: Williams & Norgate, 1912) at 113.

62 See Paul Tomassi, *Logic* (London: Routledge, 1999) at 389.

63 See Gibbons, *supra* note 48 at 240.

64 See also John Walker, *A Rhetorical Grammar* (London: T. Cadell, 1829) at 206.

65 See *e.g.* Wolfgang Sachs, "Sustainable Development and the Crisis of Nature: On the Political Anatomy of an Oxymoron" in Frank Fischer and Maarten A. Hajer (eds), *Living with Nature: Environmental Politics as Cultural Discourse* (Oxford: Oxford University Press, 1999) 21 at 38, Esther Njiro, "Introduction: Sustainable Development an Oxymoron?" (2002) 52 *Agenda* 3 and Michael Redclift, "Sustainable Development (1987–2005): An Oxymoron Comes of Age" (2005) 13(4) *Sustainable Development* 212.

66 See George Kunz, *The Paradox of Power and Weakness: Levinas and an Alternative Paradigm for Psychology* (Albany: State University of New York Press, 1998) at 13.

67 See also Muna Jawhary, *Women and False Choice: The Truth about Sexism: How to Fight Sexism in the Workplace* (Bloomington: Balboa Press, 2014) and Keally DeAnne McBride, *Postliberal Politics: Feminism, Communitarianism, and the Search for Community* (Berkeley: University of California, 1999) at 68.

68 See *e.g.* Karl R. Popper, *The Open Society and Its Enemies: The High Tide of Prophecy: Hegel, Marx and the Aftermath*, vol 2 (London: Routledge, 1947) at 42.

69 See Recital 6 of the Preamble of the Constitution of the People's Republic of China, adopted at the Fifth Session of the Fifth National People's Congress and promulgated for implementation by the Proclamation of the National People's Congress on December 4, 1982.

or the "democratic paradox",[70] "glocalization",[71] "soft law"[72] or the "paradox of justice".[73]

If there is indeed a shift from contested to oxymoronic concepts, it is interesting to know how the two categories of concepts differ. In the past, essentially contested concepts seem to have brought to light the power of contestation in human nature. The power of contestation is possible because of an inherently dualistic conception of language, reasoning and perception. By contrast, the rhetorical figures known as oxymoron, enantiosis and paradox seem to perform precisely the opposite role – they tend to tie together apparently conflicting, incompatible or contradictory concepts, also known as antonyms (words characterized by opposite meanings). Similarly, contest has given rise to many conflicts, often bloody and lethal ones, whereas it was said that "no one has ever died from contradictions".[74] Perhaps, it is still valid to say that many have died and continue to die because of not taking contradictions seriously. Yet, science and law still seem to despise and avoid at all costs contradictions and conflicts of logic.

3.3 Perceptions of change

> *I do not perceive the steady continuance of this because of (the mind's) instability.*[75]

If indeed a shift in language from essentially contested to oxymoronic concepts is occurring, then how can it be best tracked and assessed? Such possible change in language needs, first, a closer look at "change" and, second, the perception and communication of change. In this regard, "change" can be regarded as a contested concept, because it can give rise to endless disputes. Additionally, change certainly poses serious problems in many areas of life. Thinking of time, change is a fact, at least according to the watch on your wrist. Changes in time are the

70 See Chantal Mouffe, *The Democratic Paradox* (London: Verso, 2000); see also David Held, *Democracy and the Global Order: From the Modern State to Cosmopolitan Governance* (Stanford: Stanford University Press, 1995) at 21.

71 See *e.g.* Jin Y. Park, "Introduction: Rethinking Philosophy in a Time of Globalization" in Jin Y. Park (ed), *Comparative Political Theory and Cross-Cultural Philosophy: Essays in Honor of Hwa Yol Jung* (Lanham: Lexington Books, 2009) 1 at 4; see also Rostam J. Neuwirth, "Governing 'Glocalisation': A View from the Macau Special Administrative Region of China" (2011) 3(1) *City University of Hong Kong Law Review* 89 at 90.

72 See *e.g.* John F. Murphy, *The Evolving Dimensions of International Law: Hard Choices for the World Community* (Cambridge: Cambridge University Press, 2010) at 20 and Anthony C. Arend, *Legal Rules and International Society* New York: Oxford University Press, 1999) at 25.

73 See Charles Handy, *The Age of Paradox* (Boston: Harvard Business School Press, 1995) at 39–41 and 195.

74 See Gilles Deleuze and Felix Guattari, *Anti-Oedipus: Capitalism and Schizophrenia* (Minneapolis: University of Minnesota Press, 1983) at 151.

75 See Christopher Key Chapple (ed), *The Bhagavad Gītā (Twenty-fifth-Anniversary Edition)* (Albany: State University of New York Press, 2009) at 304.

sine qua non for the distinctions between past, present and future. Yet, is it possible to measure precisely when a moment in time has changed from the past to the present or to the future? Change is also a serious problem in decision making when the uncertainty of the future looms. You may decide to leave your umbrella at home on a sunny day but a little later it starts to rain. Or you may read about the bullish stock market in the morning and later place your order but, sooner rather than later, the market turns bearish and your investment has shrunk. There appears to be an infinite number of decisions that we take where success or failure depends on change happening or not. It is no surprise then that in the area of law, where decision making or "judging" is a primary concern, change also poses a serious problem. In fact, the issue of change coupled with uncertainty is even elevated to a fundamental problem for law in the following paragraph:

> The omnipresence of change throughout all human experience thus creates a fundamental problem for law; namely, how can law preserve its integrity over time, while managing to address the newly emerging circumstances that continually arise throughout our history.[76]

The problem with change resides in the claim that for law "to be considered law, it must be based on its repeated applicability".[77] In a changing environment, however, this becomes impossible. Since we expect the law, by way of the rule of law, to provide certainty and predictability, there may be cases where change happens too suddenly or too unexpectedly. The problems that "change" poses in decisions and in law require an understanding of change and the tools for the perception of change.

What then is the major problem with the nature of change? The answer may lie in our perception of change, which is said to be caused essentially by one important element, viz. contrasts, or a dualistic conception based on opposites. In line with the duality of human nature, as expressed by contestation outlined before, change in perception is caused by the contrasts created by the rapid succession of sensory data pulsating between two extreme opposites. Depending on the different senses, these opposites can be the "changing" and the "unchanged", i.e. a dynamic or a stable reference point. They can also be the loud and the silent, the sweet and the sour (taste), the warm and the cold, the stabilizing or destabilizing. Visually, a car is therefore only perceived as in motion when it is related to the ground, which remains immobile. In hearing, sound or silence are distinguished by their mutual variation or contrast. The same applies to taste where extremes, such as bitter or sweet, are contrasted with each other, the same way as in olfaction and touch, where we distinguish stench or perfume, bruises or kisses, in typical pairs of opposites.

76 See Mark L. Johnson, "Mind, Metaphor, Law" (2007) 58(3) *Mercer Law Review* 845 at 845.
77 See Reinhard Koselleck, *Zeitschichten: Studien zur Historik* (Frankfurt a. M.: Suhrkamp, 2000) at 352.

This is true for the five known senses (sight, hearing, touch, smell and taste), the total number of which, however, is contested.[78] For instance, some argue there is a sixth or "lost sense" (and not the one in the sense of an intuitive or paranormal meaning), which is that of balance (equilibrioception). Usually, the sense of balance helps to prevent us from falling but it has also been defined as "the action of not moving".[79] There is another sense called "proprioception", which is defined as "awareness of the spatial and mechanical status of the musculoskeletal framework", i.e. basically providing information about the position of one's body in space.[80] Another candidate for a sense would be the vomeronasal system, which detects pheromones but is separate from the olfactory system.[81] Others have listed up to 12 different senses, including the "sixth" or paranormal sense of "extrasensory perception" (ESP).[82] As for the development of new senses in the future, science fiction writers have mentioned X-ray vision, mind-reading sense, sixth sense (as the ability to perceive the future) or infrared perception, to mention but a few.[83]

Be that as it may, the taxonomy of the senses may vary and, depending on the criteria applied, accordingly also their number. This also includes the important question about the relations between the individual senses and whether there exists a "common sense", but not in the sense of "judgmental common sense" like "fire is hot", but in the sense of an "observational common sense" (the classical *sensus communis*)[84] or a "unity in the diversity of senses".[85] This "*sensus communis*" is concerned with

> the collection and coordination of the deliverances of our external senses with special reference to those features of things that are accessible to more than one of our senses (as, for example, the shape or size of objects discernible by both sight and touch, while their colour is discernible by sight alone).[86]

This question assumes great importance as an individual sense and at least a few more or all of our senses may betray us and we may, at times, find ourselves in

78 See also Constance Classen, *Worlds of Sense: Exploring the Senses in History and Across Cultures* (London: Routledge, 1993).

79 See Scott McCredie, *Balance: In Search of the Lost Sense* (New York: Little, Brown and Company, 2007) at 264.

80 See Barry C. Stilman, "Making Sense of Proprioception: The meaning of proprioception, kinaesthesia and related terms" (2002) 88(11) *Physiotherapy* 667 at 667.

81 See Fiona Macpherson, "Taxonomising the Senses" (2011) 153(1) *Philosophical Studies: An International Journal for Philosophy in the Analytic Tradition* 123 at 125.

82 See Andreas Riener, *Sensor-Actuator Supported Implicit Interaction in Driver Assistance Systems* (Wiesbaden: Vieweg+Teubner, 2010) at 14.

83 See Fiona Macpherson, "Individuating the Senses" in Fiona Macpherson, *The Senses: Classical and Contemporary Philosophical Perspectives* (Oxford: Oxford University Press, 2011) 3 at 21–22.

84 See Nicholas Rescher, *Common-Sense: A New Look at an Old Philosophical Tradition* (Milwaukee: Marquette University Press, 2005) at 12.

85 See Lawrence E. Marks, *The Unity of the Senses: interrelations Among the Modalities* (New York: Academic Press, 1978).

86 See Rescher, *supra* note 84 at 12.

a situation of life-threatening dimensions where we have to choose between the information provided by different senses.

For the sense of sight only, such betrayal can be observed when we are sitting in a train that is stationary in a railway station and the train on the next line starts to move, which leaves us for a moment in doubt as to who is moving now – the train you are on or the one that was previously stationary next to you. Another confusion happens from the sense of balance when we step onto the pier after a long boat trip and continue, for some time, to feel the rocking of the boat. Other cases of sensory deception are reported from aviation medicine. Pilots flying in clouds may experience spatial disorientation with serious risks for the safety of the plane and passengers.[87] Numerous more cases of spatial disorientation, like so-called "Leans", are known in aviation medicine.[88]

Generally, the reliability of the senses individually and collectively becomes even trickier with changing conditions, for instance, when we put a cold or warm hand into lukewarm water, we will arrive at different conclusions as to the true temperature of the water. These variations in contrast effects are also known from various other contexts, such as sales tactics, where the contrast effects may manipulate our sensation of price to influence our decisions to purchase items. Sales practices using contrast effects to sell products may consist in sales people showing a poor quality product alongside one that they want you to buy (because the contrast between the poor quality product and another product enhances the apparent quality of the latter).[89] The very same effects may influence the way we perceive temperature, colours, weight or even the aesthetic quality of music.[90]

In law it is no different, as the same contrast effects may also play a significant role in our judgement of legal problems, of serious matters deciding between justice or injustice.[91] In this regard, it is interesting to add that, in line with the duality of perception, contrast effects are opposed to assimilation effects, which means that changing reference points may either move a person further away from her initial position or entrench her more strongly in her original position.[92]

At this stage, however, it suffices to state that most sensory information is processed by the brain and mind in a dualistic way, as exemplified by so-called

87 Gary L. Drescher, *Good and Real: Demystifying Paradoxes from Physics to Ethics* (Cambridge: MIT Press, 2006) at 11.

88 See *e.g.* Jörg Draeger and Jürgen Kriebel (eds), *Praktische Flugmedizin* (Landsberg: ECOMED, 2002) at 82–83; see also the examples of "vestibular illusions", listed in Federal Aviation Administration (FAA), *Spatial Disorientation*, at 4; available at: http://www.faa.gov/pilots/safety/pilotsafetybrochures/media/SpatialD.pdf (accessed 1 October 2017).

89 See Namrata Palta, *The Art of Effective Communication* (New Delhi: Lotus Press, 2007) at 21.

90 See *e.g.* Charles Crawford and Dennis L. Krebs (eds), *Handbook of Evolutionary Psychology: Ideas, Issues, and Applications* (Mahwah: Lawrence Erlbaum, 1998) at 504, Michel E. Chevreul, *The Principles of Harmony and Contrast of Colours*, 2nd ed (London: Longman, 1855), Vincent Di Lollo, "Contrast Effects in the Judgment of Lifted Weights" (1964) 68(4) *Journal of Experimental Psychology* 383, and Scott Parker et al., "Positive and Negative Hedonic Contrast With Musical Stimuli" (2008) 2(3) *Psychology of Aesthetics, Creativity, and the Arts Copyright* 171.

91 See *e.g.* Barry Markovsky, "Anchoring Justice" (1988) 51(3) *Social Psychology Quarterly* 213.

92 See Muzafer Sherif, Daniel Taub, and Carl I. Hovland, "Assimilation and Contrast Effects of Anchoring Stimuli on Judgments" (1958) 55(2) *Journal of Experimental Psychology* 150.

"contrast effects", or the oscillation between opposite extremes. In other words, change is perceived only in relation to a reference point, which remains stable because if all reference points change at the same time it will be impossible for us to perceive the change. Regarding the sensation of sight, Arthur Zajonc wrote: "stabilize images perfectly on the retina and they disappear" which is why we only see "change, movement, life".[93] Thus, change and perception are very closely related, as is exemplified by "contrast effects", which appear to dominate all our senses, or possibly only the mind which interprets the sensory data accordingly. For the moment, what is most interesting to consider is the role of senses for the perception of change and, in turn, also the role of change for the senses. Our current senses are said to be retraceable to "a single primitive sense, a simple undifferentiated responsiveness to external stimulation",[94] so it is safe to assume that during evolution the senses and modes of perception have also changed.[95] And, most likely, they will keep changing in the future. In this regard, it is interesting to inquire about past developments that related to the shift from essentially contested to oxymoronic concepts and what may be their role for perception and the mind in the future.

3.4 Changes of perception

Photography is truth, and cinema is truth twenty-four times a second.[96]

In line with the culture of contestation as restated by the significance of essentially contested concepts, duality is the point of departure for our perception of change. Duality seems to be the starting point for everything else too, like knowledge, logic, scientific verification or justice. But perception and likely the sensory organs have changed in the past and will continue to change time and again. The principal question is how perception may have changed already so as to explain an increasing rise of essentially oxymoronic concepts. The measurement of changes in perception is a difficult task. This difficulty exists in both directions of time. This means that it is as hard to imagine how a Roman legionary soldier may have perceived the world around the year 30 BCE as it is to imagine the perception of a person born in the year 2100 CE. The related problem is that we tend to judge the past by the standards of its distant future, namely the present. By the same token, we also tend to imagine a future by the old standards that we apply now in the present. Good indicators for the perception of change and changes in

93 See Arthur Zajonc, *Catching the Light: The Entwined History of Light and Mind* (Oxford: Oxford University Press, 1993) at 107.

94 See Marks, *supra* note 85 at 182.

95 See also Ian Stewart and Jack Cohen, *Figments of Reality: The Evolution of the Curious Mind* (Cambridge: Cambridge University Press, 1997) at 136.

96 A phrase uttered by one of the characters in Jean-Luc Godard's film "Le Petit Soldat" (1963); see also Christiane Schönfeld, "Modern Identities in Early German Film: The Cabinet of Dr. Caligari" in Tim Cresswell and Deborah Dixon (eds), *Engaging Film: Geographies of Mobility and Identity* (London: Rowman & Littlefield Publishers, 2002) 174 at 174.

perception, however, are provided by language as well as technology as applied in the fields of art, science as well as law.

As for the arts, we may just compare the technical skills in artworks depicting a lion by Villard de Honnecourt sketched between the years 1230 and 1235 (*The Lion and the Porcupine*) and by Albrecht Dürer in 1520 (*Lying Lion*). Or more generally, one can compare paintings before and after the use of linear perspective as described by Leon Battista Alberti (1404–1472) in his *Della pittura* (On Painting) first published in 1435.[97] Linear perspective basically tackled the challenge of representing three-dimensional objects upon two-dimensional surfaces.[98] Surrealist paintings may have carried that process even further. Technologies too give an important idea about perception in the past and, as exemplified by the works of Jules Verne as a "visionary nostalgic",[99] possibly about perception in the future as well. This is largely due to the fact that there exist close metaphorical connections between prominent technologies and conceptions of the mind.[100] As for visual perception in particular, different stages include the invention of the camera obscura, still photography, cinematography and computers with related new technologies allowing for the visualization of augmented realities. All these also carry an important message as to how the mind works.

As for the transition from essentially contested concepts to oxymoronic concepts, the critical stage to consider is the one around the period of the invention of cinematography, usually dated shortly before the turn of the twentieth century.[101] The reason for the relevance of cinematography is that it can be said to have inaugurated the technological age of paradox or of essentially oxymoronic concepts even though the effects started to unfold only much later. The reason for the relevance of cinema for the rise of essentially oxymoronic concepts is, first and foremost, that "cinematography" literally set "pictures in motion", viz. the terms "motion picture", which can be regarded as an oxymoron of stasis and motion. In this quality of films rests already a first paradox of perception, namely that single static images or still photographs, when projected onto a wall by light at a certain successive speed, create the "illusion" of motion. A similar phenomenon was observed long before cinema, namely by Plato in his allegory of the cave.[102] With this allegory, Plato had practically anticipated the technology of cinema (if one replaces the bright fire by the light generated by a projector). The common element between the allegory of

97 Leonbatista Alberti, *Della pittura e della statua* (Milano: Dalla Società Tipografica dei Classici Italiani, 1804).
98 See Kirsti Andersen, *The Geometry of an Art: The History of the Mathematical Theory of Perspective from Alberti to Monge* (New York: Science+Business Media, 2007) at 2.
99 See Timothy Unwin, "Technology and Progress in Jules Verne, Or Anticipation in Reverse" (2000) 93(1) *Journal of the Australasian Universities Language and Literature Association* 17 at 31.
100 See Norm Friesen, "Mind and Machine: Ethical and Epistemological Implications for Research" (2010) 25(1) *Artificial Intelligence and Society* 83 at 83.
101 See generally Wheeler Winston Dixon and Gwendolyn Audrey Foster, *A Short History of Film* (New Brunswick: Rutgers University Press, 2008).
102 Plato, *The Republic* (Cambridge: Cambridge University Press, 1866) at 235 (Book VII).

the cave and cinema is that as long as one does not know the original source of signals received by the senses, the question about whether what we perceive is reality or illusion persists. Or, seen from another angle, there may always be another reality behind the reality as we perceive it. In both cases, it highlights the fascination with perception, as perception forms the basis for our orientation in the world we live in.

This is a first indicator that the technology of cinematography created a dilemma for the dominant dual conception of perception by contrasts. Second, it indicates an acceleration of the speed with which perception of change occurs. It was said that we have reached now the "epoch of the nanosecond", where everything goes "faster" and everything seems to be in a state of acceleration.[103] The same observation of an accelerating pace of change was also confirmed by Paul Nora when he spoke about the "acceleration of history" to mean "a rupture of equilibrium" or an "increasingly rapid slippage of the present into a historical past that is gone for good, a general perception that anything and everything might disappear".[104] A similar trend is also found to dominate the current epoch of the Anthropocene, which means that "human activities are significantly influencing Earth's environment", many of which have been found to be accelerating.[105] Called the "Great Acceleration of the Anthropocene", the beginning of which is dated to 1945, the "human enterprise" is said to have "suddenly accelerated" in many ways, ranging from population growth to oil consumption and the increasing interconnectedness of cultures.[106] In sum, acceleration of perception of change through time is a phenomenon that – under the notion of "social acceleration" – is noticeable in all areas of life.[107]

These recorded trends of an acceleration of the perception of change also have a significant effect on the understanding and description of change itself. Since ancient times, change has been recognized as an important factor in life. For instance, Heraclitus is widely accredited with the statement that "[E]verything is in flux and nothing abides everything flows and nothing stays fixed everything is constantly changing and nothing stays the same".[108] Heraclitus exemplified this

103 See James Gleick, *Faster: The Acceleration of Just About Everything* (New York: Vintage Books, 2000) at 6.

104 Paul Nora, "Between Memory and History: Les lieux de mémoire" (1989) 26 *Representations* 7 at 15.

105 See Eckart Ehlers and Thomas Krafft, "Managing Global Change: Earth System Science in the Anthropocene" in Eckart Ehlers and Thomas Krafft (eds), *Earth System Science in the Anthropocene* (Berlin: Springer, 2006) 5 at 5.

106 See Will Steffen, Paul J. Crutzen and John R. McNeill, "The Anthropocene: Are Humans Now Overwhelming the Great Forces of Nature?" (2007) 16(5) *Ambio* 614 at 617.

107 See also Hartmut Rosa and William E. Scheuerman (eds), *High-Speed Society: Social Acceleration, Power and Modernity* (University Park: Pennsylvania State University Press, 2009) and Hartmut Rosa, *Social Acceleration: A New Theory of Modernity* (New York: Columbia University Press, 2013).

108 See Samuel Babatunde Jegede, "Heraclitean Flux as a Philosophy of Social Change" (2014) 3(6) *International Journal of Humanities and Social Science Invention* 41 at 42; see also G. S. Kirk (ed), *Heraclitus: The Cosmic Fragments* (Cambridge: Cambridge University Press, 1954) at 14.

statement by the metaphor of a person being unable to "step into the same river twice".[109] This statement includes perhaps a first hint at an accelerating trend since Plato appears to have challenged this assumption by stating that it may not even be possible to step into the same river even once.[110]

We may speculate about the reasons for this possible perception of change, such as humanity growing older and accumulating a greater amount of collective data.[111] Be that as it may, it is certain that such an increasingly rapid pace of change also requires a more appropriate language of change. Hence, with the modes of visual perception changing, it is also likely that we need to adapt our language to the newly perceived phenomena. In brief, to describe change adequately also requires an adequate language of change. This is where the growing appeal of essentially oxymoronic concepts comes into play, namely that they may be better prepared to communicate statements that are valid over a longer period of time than are their contested counterparts. The reason is that an oxymoron already includes the continuous process of the oscillation between two extreme poles described by apparently antagonistic concepts, as opposed to a single contested concept, which must proceed by endless disputes. Paradoxically, it may mean that, by these new rhetorical figures, we are blurring or converging the lines of distinction and lose some accuracy in the short term but gain a better understanding of the trends in the long term.

The change in perception is matched by a shift in language from essentially contested to oxymoronic concepts. In other words, it parallels the shift from "change" being a contested concept to the enantiosis of "constant change".[112] Thus, the rise in essentially oxymoronic concepts may be closely related to an acceleration of the perception of change. It is noteworthy that previously the use of oxymora and related rhetorical figures was mainly reserved to poetry, literature or mysticism. Now, by contrast, they seem to have entered the realm of science and daily life. This not only testifies to the prophetic quality of the arts, but also these essentially oxymoronic concepts seem to build upon and further enhance the insights into human nature and the world of human cognition as gained from essentially contested concepts.

Essentially oxymoronic concepts are basically three types of concepts on the gradient scale of rhetorical devices indicating a possible change in perception and cognition. They may also be the harbingers of further drastic and accelerating change, as is mirrored in the qualification of the current epoch as both the age of paradox and the Anthropocene era. These changes in perception also bring important changes to language, both as a tool to bring about change and to

109 See Kirk, *ibid* at 366; see also Plato, *Against the Atheists* (New York: Harper & Brothers, 1845) at 161 and Jegede, *ibid* at 42.

110 See Francesco Ademollo, *The Cratylus of Plato: A Commentary* (Cambridge: Cambridge University Press, 2011) at 203.

111 See Douwe Draaisma, *Why Life Speeds Up As You Get Older: How Memory Shapes Our Past* (Cambridge: Cambridge University Press, 2004) at 201–225.

112 Isaac Asimov, "My Own View" in Robert Holdstock (ed), *The Encyclopedia of Science Fiction* (Octopus, London 1978) 5.

tackle change by describing and communicating its effects accurately. Symbolized by the invention of cinematography, the current changes in perception have also creepingly infiltrated the area of law. For instance, the perception of "law as being not a thing but a process",[113] or "legal practice as an unfolding political narrative"[114] seem to follow the trend inaugurated by cinematography. The link between change and language and the law is also reflected in Benjamin N. Cardozo's writing about both the links between law and literature and between paradoxes and legal science.[115] The same paradoxical relation between language and change also governs law and language and change. This paradox was well formulated in the statement that "law changes as language changes – perhaps because language changes".[116]

113 "Law is not a thing but a process" is a phrase attributed to Michael I. Sovern, quoted in Reimer von Borries, "Einleitung" in Max Rheinstein, *Einführung in die Rechtsvergleichung*, 2nd ed (München: C. H. Beck, 1987) 1 at 5; see also David M. Trubek, "Toward a Social Theory of Law: An Essay on the Study of Law and Development" (1972) 82(1) *The Yale Law Journal* 1 at 9, Sally Falk Moore, *Law as Process: An Anthropological Approach* (Boston: Routledge & K. Paul 1978) and James MacLean, *Rethinking Law as Process: Creativity, Novelty, Change* (Oxon: Routledge, 2012).

114 See *e.g.* Ronald Dworkin, *Law's Empire* (Cambridge: Harvard University Press, 1986) at 225.

115 Benjamin N. Cardozo, "Law and Literature" (1939) 48(3) *Yale Law Journal* 489 (first published in 1925) and Benjamin N. Cardozo, *The Paradoxes of Legal Science* (New York: Columbia University Press, 1928).

116 See the Foreword by Adolph S. Oko in Nathan S. Isaacs, *The Law and the Change of Law* (Miami: Hardpress, 2012) at 6.

4 Essentially oxymoronic concepts in art and science

> *The mystical experience has in its history with language applied specific modi loquendi, namely primarily paradox, oxymoron, negation etc., which are all rhetorical figures expressing a kind of swoon, which ought to express the superior power of the experience, the ineffability of the experienced.*[1]

Art and science both qualify as contested concepts and both have and continue to lead to endless disputes. One such dispute may also include the question of their mutual relation, whether they are really one field or two different fields of human efforts. It is also possible that they may share many goals but differ in other aspects or are similar and dissimilar at the same time. It is noteworthy that one important aspect in which they are said to differ is in their acceptance and use of essentially oxymoronic concepts:

> Yet there is a sense in which paradox is the language appropriate and inevitable to poetry. It is the scientist whose truth requires a language purged of every trace of paradox; apparently the truth which the poet utters can be approached only in terms of paradox.[2]

Whether this difference in the use of oxymoronic language is in line with the present paradigm or *Zeitgeist* and generally still holds true today needs to be assessed. There are overlaps and, especially, overlaps in terms of the cognitive and mental processes underlying artistic creations and scientific discoveries, which are worth noting. Linguistically, these overlaps surface in the contradictions in terms reflected by the enantiosis of genius and madness (*Genie und Wahn*) that has been applied to persons engaged not only in art[3] and science,[4] but also

1 Alois M. Haas, *Sermo mysticus: Studien zu Theologie und Sprache der deutschen Mystik* (Freiburg: Universitätsverlag, 1989) at 27–28 [translation from German by author].

2 See Cleanth Brooks, "The Language of Paradox" in Cleanth Brooks, *The Well Wrought Urn: Studies in the Structure of Poetry* (London: Dobson Books, 1949) 3 at 3.

3 See *e.g.* Jean Clair et al. (eds), *Mélancolie: Génie et folie en Occident* (Paris: Editions Gallimard, 2008).

4 See *e.g.* John Monahan, *They Called Me Mad: Genius, Madness, and the Scientists Who Pushed the Outer Limits of Knowledge* (New York: Berkley Books, 2010).

philosophy[5] and politics[6].[7] Yet it is interesting to know whether there exist also more substantial overlaps between art and science that a linguistic analysis of oxymoronic concepts in art and science may reveal.

4.1 Essentially oxymoronic concepts in art

> *Oxymora like* bright smoke, lead feathers, *and* sick health, *do not simply represent figures of speech but also reflect poetic schemes for conceptualizing human experience and the external world.*[8]

Since time immemorial, rhetorical figures like oxymoron, enantiosis (*contradictio in adiecto*) and paradox, in other words "essentially oxymoronic concepts", have held an extraordinary fascination in the minds of creators of poetry, literature, music and the fine arts in general. For the mystery that often concealed their deeper meaning, they were frequently applied in creative and notably literary works. In terms of literary works, we may, for instance, think of the *Metamorphoses* by Ovid (43 BCE–17 CE) who lets Narcissus exclaim with hope embedded in despair "*inopem me copia fecit*" ("my plentie makes me poore") when he realizes that he himself is the unattainable object of his desire.[9] The opposite is also expressed by way of a paradox, namely that "giving will not make you poor", in the Bible verse: "He that giveth unto the poor shall not lack".[10]

William Shakespeare's writings are not only replete with essentially oxymoronic concepts, such as "Fair is foul, and foul is fair", "parting is such sweet sorrow", "O brawling love! O loving hate!" or "A damned saint, an honourable villain!", but have even been qualified as expressing a "culture of paradox".[11] Hence it hardly comes as a surprise that one of his most famous works, that is *Romeo and Juliet*, has been considered to be an oxymoron.[12] Similarly, the title of the collection of poems by Johann Wolfgang Goethe (1749–1832) "West-Eastern Divan" is oxymoronic, as is the concept of an "open secret" ("*Offenbar Geheimnis*") that he refers to in his allusion to the mysteries voiced by the Persian

5 See *e.g.* Almos Csongár (ed), *Nietzsche light: Zwischen Genie und Wahn* (Berlin: Patchworldverlag 2010).

6 See *e.g.* Theodor Kissel, *Kaiser zwischen Genie und Wahn. Caligula, Nero, Elagabal* (Düsseldorf: Artemis & Winkler, 2006).

7 See generally Dean Keith Simonton, "Are Genius and Madness Related? Contemporary Answers to an Ancient Question" (2005) 22(7) *Psychiatric Times* 21.

8 See Raymond W. Gibbs, *The Poetics of Mind: Figurative Thought, Language, and Understanding* (New York: Cambridge University Press, 1994) at 395.

9 Ovid, *Shakespeare's Ovid: Being Arthur Golding's Translation of the Metamorphoses* (London: At the De la More Press, 1904) at 74.

10 See Proverbs 28:27; see also Harold V. Cordry, *The Multicultural Dictionary of Proverbs: Over 20,000 Adages from More Than 120 Languages, Nationalities and Ethnic Groups* (Jefferson: McFarland, 2005) at 37 (Entry 2478).

11 See Peter G. Platt, *Shakespeare and the Culture of Paradox* (Abingdon: Ashgate, 2009).

12 See *e.g.* Webster Wheelock, "'Not Life, but Love in Death': Oxymoron at the Thematic Heart of 'Romeo and Juliet'" (1985) 74(2) *The English Journal* 70.

poet Hafez.[13] George Orwell prolifically uses contradictions expressed through multiple "doublethink" expressions of his Newspeak language, such as "War is Peace", "Freedom is Slavery" and "Ignorance is Strength".[14] The same is true for the work of William Faulkner (1897–1962), who uses a large number of essentially oxymoronic concepts, such as "beautiful, young, ugly body", "without hope, yet still optimistic", or "her pretty unpretty face", "peaceful despair", or "furious calm".[15] Faulkner has also formulated paradoxical phrases, such as "so the purpose of war is to end the war".[16] Showing their close connection, Faulkner used both oxymora, like "dynamic static", and paradoxes, like "motion in stasis", to express contradictions also as means of achieving static effects in the description of dynamic events.[17]

A related literary device is the so-called "hysteron proteron", which is an oxymoron itself deriving from Greek and meaning "latter before". Combining two opposite concepts, here the contrast is not necessarily created between two opposite meanings per se but instead by a temporal reversal of the logical order of the ideas expressed by it.[18] As a rhetorical device the hysteron proteron can be found in the verse of the Greek poet Homer where it has been used as a "twofold instruction, proposal, or question and in a subsequent passage reversing the original order of presentation".[19] Shakespeare and Goethe have also been credited with its use. In the case of Shakespeare, it has given rise to the qualification as the "Shakespearean preposterous". "Preposterous" has been defined as the English equivalent to the hysteron proteron, namely a manner of "disordered speech, when we misplace our words or clauses and set that before which should be behind".[20] An example of a preposterous by Shakespeare is, for instance, the following from *A Winter's Tale* where he writes: "I was a gentleman born before my father".[21] In Goethe's case, it is in Faust that Mephistopheles conveys greetings sent to Martha by her husband in the following words: "Your husband's dead, and sends a greeting" ("*Ihr Mann ist tot und lässt Sie grüßen*").[22] These quotes, as well as sayings like "putting on one's shoes and socks", confirm that the hysteron proteron is not only used in literature but also in everyday talk.[23] A similar situation in real life recently happened (again) in Austria, where – in the course of a

13 Johann Wolfgang von Goethe, *West-Eastern Divan* (London: J. M. Dent & Sons, 1914) at 28.

14 George Orwell, *Nineteen Eighty-Four* (London: Penguin Books, 2000) at 156.

15 See Susanne Frohriep, *Innovation und Tradition. Stilistische Kreativität in der Erzählkunst William Faulkners* (Würzburg: Königshausen & Neumann, 1999) at 124.

16 *Ibid* at 124.

17 *Ibid* at 88–89.

18 See also Herbert C. Nutting, "Hysteron Proteron" (1916) 11(5) *The Classical Journal* 298.

19 See Elizabeth Minchin, "How Homeric Is 'Hysteron Proteron?'" (2001) 54(6) *Mnemosyne* 635 at 644.

20 See George Puttenham, *The Arte of English Poesie* (London: Bloomsbury, 1869) at 181.

21 See Patricia A. Parker, *Shakespeare from the Margins: Language, Culture, Context* (Chicago: The University of Chicago Press, 1996) at 22.

22 See Johann Wolfgang von Goethe, *Faust: A Tragedy – The First Part* (Leipzig: F. A. Brockhaus, 1872) at 114.

23 See also Minchin, *supra* note 19 at 644.

recruitment proceeding for the Austrian broadcasting corporation (ORF) – the "recruit was hired and presented to the press weeks before the vacancy notice was published in the gazette".[24]

In short, these few examples serve as evidence for the significance of oxymoronic concepts for literature. It has been qualified as a "common device, closely related to antithesis and paradox, especially in poetry, and is of considerable antiquity".[25] In literature, oxymora and paradoxes are hence stylistic devices that are frequently used. Perhaps as a further sign of their rising significance, oxymora have been recently honoured by a series of books on the subject.[26] The same is true for paradoxes as well.[27]

In other art forms, like the visual arts, contradictory effects on the senses similar to those of essentially oxymoronic concepts are also in use. Famous examples of such visual oxymora can be found in the mind-challenging designs by Dutch graphic designer Maurits Cornelis Escher (1898–1972), such as the "Moebius Strip", "Relativity", or his interpretation of the "Tower of Babel", which ought to remind us of the origins of the confusion caused by language. Finally, the work of René François Ghislain Magritte (1898–1967) provides an equal amount of interesting works, such as his famous painting, *The Treachery of Images* (*La trahison des images*) (1929) to mention but one.[28] On a general level, the visual arts also create a particular paradox, called the "paradox of painting" (or paradox of pictures), which was explained as lying in the fact that "a visual array on a two-dimensional surface is seen as a depiction of three-dimensional objects or scenes" or that what is "really" two dimensional

24 See *e.g.* the article written by the uncle of the sa(i)d recruit, Anton Pelinka, "ORF Falsche Häme: Die Struktur des ORF verlangt politischen Gehorsam. Das ist der Skandal. Nicht die Bestellung eines bestimmten Büroleiters", *Die Zeit* (5 January 2012); available at: http://www.zeit.de/2012/02/A-ORF (accessed 1 October 2017).

25 See John A. Cuddon, *The Penguin Dictionary of Literary Terms and Literary Theory*, 3rd ed (London: Penguin Books, 1992) at 669.

26 See *e.g.* Mardy Grothe, *Oxymoronica: Paradoxical Wit and Wisdom from History's Greatest Wordsmiths* (New York: Harper Collins Publishers, 2004), Jon Agee, *Who Ordered the Jumbo Shrimp? And Other Oxymorons* (New York: Harper Collins, 1998), Laine Vilensky, David R. Holmes and Jeff MacNelly, *Freezer Burn: Oxymorons and Other Contradictions of Everyday Life* (New York: Ballantine Books, 1991), Warren S. Blumenfeld and Lisa Amoroso, *Pretty Ugly: More Oxymorons and Other Illogical Expressions That Make Absolute Sense* (New York: Perigee Books, 1989), and Warren S. Blumenfeld, *Jumbo Shrimp & Other Almost Perfect Oxymorons: Contradictory Expressions that Make Absolute Sense* (New York: Putnam, 1986).

27 See *e.g.* Margaret Cuonzo, *Paradox* (Cambridge: The MIT Press, 2014), Roy T. Cook, *Paradoxes* (Cambridge: Polity Press, 2013), R.M. Sainsbury, *Paradoxes*, 3rd ed (Cambridge: Cambridge University Press, 2009), Harty Field, *Saving Truth from Paradox* (Oxford: Oxford University Press, 2008), Roy Sorensen, *A Brief History of the Paradox: Philosophy and the Labyrinths of the Mind* (Oxford: Oxford University Press, 2003), Doris Olin, *Paradox* (Bucks: Acumen, 2003), Michael Clark, *Paradoxes from A to Z*, 3rd ed (London: Routledge, 2012) and Nicholas Rescher, *Paradoxes: Their Roots, Range and Resolution* (Chicago: Open Court, 2001).

28 See Gisele Ollinger-Zinque and Frederik Leen, *René Magritte (1898–1967): Catalogue du centenaire* (Gand: Ludion, 1998); see also Michel Foucault and Richard Howard, "Ceci n'est pas une pipe" (1976) 1 *October* 6.

can "appear" three dimensional.[29] Nowadays, several paradoxical illustrations are popular, like the Rubin Vase,[30] or, more recently a dress that appears to some as white and gold and to others blue and black, apparently depending on the eye of the beholder.[31]

Equally, the relationship between literature and painting, or text and image, may serve as the point of departure for a critical review of our dominantly analytical or literal mode of thinking and reasoning. Especially, the frequent use of figures of speech in common language may serve as a means to overcome their separation. We know the proverb "a picture is worth a thousand words", which reflects the mnemonic quality of images and metaphors.[32] Generally, figures of speech are defined as including any unusual way of using words to refer to something, especially those which stimulate the imagination.[33] As such they are said to work by establishing a likeness between two unlike things. Figures of speech also include metaphors and essentially oxymoronic concepts, which help to transcend the limitations of words. The limitation imposed by words stands in contrast to figurative thought as it is often but not exclusively expressed by poets. As a matter of fact, Raymond W. Gibbs provides ample evidence in his book entitled *The Poetics of Mind* that figurative thought may influence ordinary language use and understanding.[34] In fact, Gibbs was quoted as suggesting that "poets make the twilight clear, seeing things not readily available to others, perhaps by organizing less-than-conscious or nonverbal information into a meaningful whole".[35] More concretely and in his own words, he restates as follows:

> Recent advances in cognitive linguistics, philosophy anthropology, and psychology show that not only is much of our language metaphorically structured, but so is much of our cognition. People conceptualize their experiences in figurative terms via metaphor, metonomy, irony, *oxymoron*, and so on, and these principles underlie the way we think, reason, and imagine.[36]

This quote confirms that cognition and thought is not only literal but is open to wider sources of information. It also confirms the assumption underlying this book that essentially oxymoronic concepts, as a variant of figures of speech, are on the rise.

29 See Marx W. Wartofsky, "The Paradox of Painting: Pictorial Representation and the Dimensionality of Visual Space" (1984) 51(4) *Social Research* 863 at 865–866.

30 See Edgar Rubin, *Visuell wahrgenommene Figuren: Studien in psychologischer Analyse* (København: Gyldendalske Boghandel, 1921) at 249.

31 See "Is That Dress White and Gold or Blue and Black?" (27 February 2015); available at: https://www.nytimes.com/interactive/2015/02/28/science/white-or-blue-dress.html?_r=0 (accessed 1 October 2017).

32 See also Robert R. Verbrugge and Nancy S. McCarrell, "Metaphoric Comprehension: Studies in Reminding and Resembling" (1977) 9 *Cognitive Psychology* 494.

33 See Pam Peters, *The Cambridge Guide to English Usage* (Cambridge: Cambridge University Press, 2004) at 206.

34 See Gibbs, *supra* note 8.

35 See Geraldine Shaw, "The Multisensory Image and Emotion in Poetry" (2008) 2(3) *Psychology of Aesthetics, Creativity, and the Arts* 175 at 175.

36 See Gibbs, *supra* note 8 at 5 [*Italics* added].

This suggests that the apparent contradiction between the visual arts and literature is artificial and rooted more in educational prejudice and the present scientific paradigm than in factual phenomena or reality as we perceive and live it. Reality, especially as we perceive it, is itself enigmatic, if not paradoxical. This is well reflected in the concepts of surrealism and magical realism. Surrealism literally means "beyond realism", similar to the concept of "beyond thought" underlying the term "paradox". In this sense, "surrealism" can be understood as a paradox, because of its mysterious quality of combining the real and the dreamlike, or the real and unreal. As a literary genre also used in the visual arts and film, "magical realism", on the other hand, builds on the dichotomy of magic and reality. Magical realism has been identified as an oxymoron and translated into the phrase "lies that tell the truth"[37] or describing the forced relationship of the irreconcilable terms "magical" and "realist".[38] Or else, it serves as a reminder that "magic may be real, reality magical".[39] Put differently and applied in a wider societal context, it can also be said that "magic is often given as a cultural corrective, requiring readers to scrutinize accepted realistic conventions of causality, materiality, motivation".[40] For sure, it poses a challenge to our accepted modes of perception and cognition.

In the digital age today, these pairs of apparent opposites are also found combined in the equally essentially oxymoronic concept of *virtual reality* which, similar to the poetic world view, describes the computer-generated simulations of an imaginary world. By the same token, the term "reality TV" has been described as a "misnomer, perhaps even an oxymoron".[41] Perhaps, reality is more (or less) virtual than we expect, depending on the viewpoint. Recalling the role of poets in clearing the twilight as mentioned above, the painter Paul Klee (1879–1940) also once explained that "art does not reproduce the visible; rather it makes visible".[42] Or similarly, Paul Valéry wrote that the "painter should not paint what he sees, but what will be seen".[43] From such a perspective, surrealism, magical realism, reality TV and virtual reality may not merely be essentially oxymoronic concepts denominating various but separate contradictory forms of expressions aimed at describing an imaginary reality but rather provide, in fact, the basis for a reality in the becoming. Or, they speak the language of the future by describing a reality which is not yet perceived.

37 See Anne C. Hegerfeldt, *Lies that Tell the Truth: Magic Realism Seen through Contemporary Fiction from Britain* (Amsterdam: Rodopi, 2005) at 11.

38 See Maggie Ann Bowers, *Magic(al) Realism: The New Critical Idiom* (London: Routledge, 2004) at 1, 3, 63 and 79.

39 See Lois Parkinson Zamora and Wendy B. Faris, "Introduction: Daiquiri Birds and Flaubertian Parrot(ie)s" in Lois Parkinson Zamora and Wendy B. Faris (eds), *Introduction to Magical Realism: Theory, History, Community* (Durham: Duke University Press, 1995) 1 at 3.

40 *Ibid.*

41 See Mark Andrejevic, *Reality TV: The Work of Being Watched* (Lanham: Rowman & Littlefield Publishers, 2004) at 16.

42 See Paul Klee, "Schöpferische Konfession", first published in Kasimir Edschmid (ed), *Tribüne der Kunst und Zeit: Eine Schriftensammlung* (Berlin: Erich Reiß Verlag, 1920) 28 at 28.

43 See Paul Valéry, *Analects*, vol XIV (Princeton: Princeton University Press, 1970) at 509.

Architecture is yet another interesting field in the quest for the use of essentially oxymoronic concepts. Called "petrified music" by Goethe,[44] architecture itself conceals an oxymoronic quality. This becomes more obvious in German language, where it is termed *Baukunst*, literally translated as "the art of construction". The term *Baukunst* thus unites the apparently divergent areas of craftsmanship and the arts, or construction and design, masonry or carpentry and creativity, as well as statics and aesthetics. This is reflected, inter alia, in the definition of architecture as rendered by the Danish architect Arne Jacobsen (1902–1971), who is reported to have said that "architecture is knowledge around the technology, susceptibility in relation to the artistic side of the affair".[45] In his book *Complexity and Contradiction in Architecture*, published in 1966, Robert Venturi draws on similar tensions manifest in literature or painting and describes the contradictions that derive from the many tensions created by the dualities inherent in architecture.[46] He extracts these contradictions from numerous examples of various architectural works from all times and from all over the world, all of which bear traits of contradictions caused by dualities. Such dualities include the tensions between simplicity and complexity, as also expressed by Mies van der Rohe's equally paradoxical credo "less is more", or between many more pairs of opposites, such as form or function, abstract and concrete, structural and ornamental, or evolutionary and revolutionary, to mention but a few.[47] In one interesting example, Venturi classifies the degree of contradiction (and complexity) in three basic stages, namely "ambiguity", "contradiction adapted" and finally "contradiction juxtaposed", which he defines as ending "*in a whole which is perhaps unresolved.*"[48] In this regard, a similar analogy could, in fact, be established between his architectural classification of contradictions and the linguistic ones underlying the essentially oxymoronic concepts used in this book. According to this analogy, "ambiguity" corresponds to "paradoxes", "contradiction adapted" to "enantioses" ("*contradictiones in adiecto*"), and "contradiction juxtaposed" to "oxymora".[49] This analogy is further supported by Venturi's reference to the level of cognition or logic, when he writes that he prefers "'both-and' to 'either-or,' black and white, and sometimes gray, to black or white.[50] In short, Venturi speaks of the "pastness of the present" or states that the "future is inherent in the reality of the present".[51]

Like literature and architecture, music too has a close connection with essentially oxymoronic concepts. These often surface through the dichotomy of sound

44 For "petrified music", see John Oxenford (ed), *Conversations of Goethe with Eckermann and Soret* (London: George Bell & Sons, 1875) at 378 (23 March 1829).

45 See Michael Paninski, "Erfahrende Erkenntnis" (2010) 1 *SYN* 10 at 14–15.

46 Robert Venturi, *Complexity and Contradiction in Architecture* (New York: Museum of Modern Art, 1966).

47 *Ibid* at 16, 17, 19–20, 36, 44, 50 and 62.

48 *Ibid* at 45 [*Italics* added].

49 *Ibid* at 20–22, 45–55, and 56–69.

50 *Ibid* at 23.

51 *Ibid* at 13–14.

and silence. Generally, it appears that this dichotomy is at the centre of our auditory perception, which is based upon the alteration between sound and silence. This fact was also noted by Aristotle when he wrote that "sound and silence are discriminated by mutual contrast".[52] In this regard, there seems to be a strong link between language and the way we perceive music.[53] Another example is provided by the musical instrument known as the "piano", which is an abbreviation of the oxymoron "*pianoforte*", deriving from the Italian words for silent (*piano*) and loud (*forte*). It is also known in the reverse order as "*fortepiano*", which denotes an earlier version of a piano. Similarly, the notion of "resounding pianissimo" would also constitute an oxymoron.[54] Another such musical oxymoron could be that of "atonal music", when music is understood as being tonal and melodious, even though it technically describes music that is not in any key.[55]

More drastically, the musical composer often plays with effects of the sound of silence and the silence of sound, which are achieved through the composition of different layers, one in the foreground and one in the background.[56] The same was made explicit in the title of the song "The Sound of Silence" (1964) by Paul Simon or in John Cage's (1912–1992) composition *4'33"* (*Four, thirty-three*), a three-movement composition instructing the performer not to play the instrument during the entire duration of the performance.

Therefore, contradictions in music not only derive from the opposite concepts of sound and silence but also of composition and improvisation. This can be seen from the concept of "aleatoric (or chance) music", denoting a compositional method by which some element of composition is left to chance or to the determination (and less to the interpretation) of the performer. The fact that composition and improvisation are somehow contradictory can be highlighted by reference to the musical genre of jazz.[57] In jazz music, the term "free jazz" (or "creative music") has also been characterized as an oxymoron.[58] The reason is that "free jazz" challenged the relation between composition and improvisation with the intention to bring the improviser "back to the original intention of all great music: to create and express original ideas without being inhibited by certain prescribed forms".[59] Nonetheless, the oxymoron "free jazz" is just exemplary

52 Aristotle, *On the Heavens (De caelo)* (J. L. Stocks, trans.) (Oxford: Clarendon Press, 1922) at 59.

53 See Diana Deutsch, "The Tritone Paradox: An Influence of Language on Music Perception" (1991) 8 *Music Perception* 335 at 335.

54 See Simon Mold, "Reviews" (1992) 76(12) *Organists' Review* 57 at 58.

55 See Michael Kennedy, *The Oxford Dictionary of Music* (Oxford: Oxford University Press, 2001) at 36 ("atonal").

56 See Eva-Maria Houben, *Die Aufhebung der Zeit: zur Utopie unbegrenzter Gegenwart in der Musik des 20. Jahrhunderts* (Stuttgart: Steiner, 1992) at 83.

57 See generally Stanley Sadie (ed), *The New Grove Dictionary of Music and Musicians*, 2nd ed, vol 12 (Oxford: Oxford University Press, 2001) at 903–926.

58 See Robert L. Taylor, *Cultures on a Collision Course: An Introduction to the History of Jazz* (Beijing, 2004) [on file with author].

59 See Eric Porter, *What Is This Thing Called Jazz?* (Ewing: University of California Press, 2002) at 258.

of many more paradoxes or contradictions in jazz.[60] Paradoxes in jazz include those of tradition and originality, or of artistic and commercial goals.[61]

As a last musical oxymoron, the counterpoint (*punctus contra punctum*) immediately comes to mind. Counterpoint may not read like an oxymoron, but it has been defined as music's unique ability to "say two things at once comprehensibly".[62] This is an ability akin to that of oxymora in spoken or written language or else the experiences derived from our different senses. This ability highlights the link between music and language given that "tone, rhythm and cadence, and lyricism" are the property of both.[63] To cut a long story short, it is time to track this ability in science.

4.2 Essentially oxymoronic concepts in science

> ***Paradoxes abound in nature and in the realm of the human condition. Paradoxes have been evident in fields of science – from plant biology to human biology to physics – and in areas of human endeavour, ranging through political, literary and social activities.***[64]

In art, essentially oxymoronic concepts were said and confirmed to be a defining feature for a long time. In science, however, one would expect them to rather play a minor role, at least when one understands science as generating knowledge by discerning the true from the false or fact from fiction based on dualistic thought and Aristotelian (binary) logic. Paradoxically though, science itself has been called a contested concept, as there is no consensus about what it is.[65] And one of the biggest challenges to science comes from an oxymoron that reflects one major truth of life, which is the one of "constant change". This essentially oxymoronic concept is synonymous with the term "*panta rei*" or "all things are in flux" as used by Heraclitus of Ephesus (535–475 BCE) but has been described by Isaac Asimov as follows:

> The only constant is change, continuing change, inevitable change, that is the dominant factor in society today. No sensible decision can be made any longer without taking into account not only the world as it is, but the world as it will be.[66]

60 See Paul Rinzler, *The Contradictions of Jazz* (Lanham: The Scarecrow Press, 2008).

61 See William Bruce Cameron, "Sociological Notes on the Jam Session" (1954) 33(2) *Social Forces* 177 at 179 and 181 and Robert Francesconi, "Art vs. the Audience: The Paradox of Modern Jazz" (1981) 4(4) *Journal of American Culture* 70.

62 See Kennedy, *supra* note 55 at 198.

63 See Barry Wallenstein, "Poetry and Jazz: A Twentieth-Century Wedding" (1991) 25(3) *Black American Literature Forum* 595 at 595.

64 See Narinder Kapur et al., "The Paradoxical Nature of Nature" in Narinder Kapur (ed), *The Paradoxical Brain* (Cambridge: Cambridge University Press, 2011) 1 at 1.

65 See George Ritzer and J. Michael Ryan (eds), *The Concise Encyclopedia of Sociology* (Malden: Wiley-Blackwell, 2011) at 517.

66 Isaac Asimov, "My Own View" in Robert Holdstock (ed), *The Encyclopedia of Science Fiction* (Octopus, London 1978) 5 at 5.

The same idea has also been formulated by way of the Lampedusa paradox which states that "*se vogliamo che tutto rimanga come è, bisogna che tutto cambi*" ("if we want things to stay as they are, things will have to change").[67] Thus, change, combined with an acceleration of the perception of change,[68] is therefore a serious challenge for science in trying to discover the objective and immutable truth behind various phenomena. The same challenge also finds expression in the so-called "paradox of scientific authority", which was described by the following dilemma: "The cases in which scientific advice is asked most urgently are those in which the authority of science is questioned most thoroughly".[69] This paradox is also related to various essentially oxymoronic concepts, such as "science policy", "risk assessment" and "risk management".[70] Generally, the assumption about the role of science and technology as instruments of progress has been contested.[71] Moreover, progress also gives rise to at least one paradox, if we recall Blaise Pascal's words that "[A]ll that is brought to perfection by progress perishes also by progress".[72] Ultimately, the progress paradox is rooted in the mystery of the perception of time or the unresolved relationship between past and future events.

Difficulties with attempts to prove knowledge and truth are also reflected in the paradoxical statement "I know that I know nothing" (*scio nescio*), the origin of which is usually attributed to Socrates.[73] In a modern expression the adage is known as the "complexity paradox", which holds that when "complex systems become better defined, they are understood less: paradoxically, progress means more questions than answers".[74] A similar thought has been expressed through the oxymoron of "*simplexity*".[75]

67 See Giuseppe Tomasi di Lampedusa, *Il Gattopardo* (Milan: Feltrinelli, 2005) at 32; Guiseppe Tomasi Di Lampedusa, *The Leopard* (London: Vintage Books, 2007) at 19.

68 See *e.g.* Paul Nora, "Between Memory and History: Les lieux de mémoire" (1989) 26 *Representations* 7 at 15, Jean Gebser, *Ursprung und Gegenwart: Erster Teil*, 2nd ed (Schaffhausen: Novalis, 1999) at 107, James Gleick, *Faster: The Acceleration of Just About Everything* (New York: Vintage Books, 2000) at 6, Will Steffen, Paul J. Crutzen and John R. McNeill, "The Anthropocene: Are Humans Now Overwhelming the Great Forces of Nature?" (2007) 16(5) *Ambio* 614 at 617, Hartmut Rosa and William E. Scheuerman (eds), *High-Speed Society: Social Acceleration, Power and Modernity* (University Park: Pennsylvania State University Press, 2009) and Hartmut Rosa, *Social Acceleration: A New Theory of Modernity* (New York: Columbia University Press, 2013).

69 See Wiebe E. Bijker, Roland Bal and Ruud Hendriks, *Paradox of Scientific Authority: The Role of Scientific Advice in Democracies* (Cambridge: MIT Press, 2009) at 1 [footnote omitted].

70 See also Sheila S. Jasanoff, "Contested Boundaries in Policy-Relevant Science" (1987) 17(2) *Social Studies of Science* 195.

71 See Maximilian Mayer, Mariana Carpes, and Ruth Knoblich, "The Global Politics of Science and Technology: An Introduction" in Maximilian Mayer, Mariana Carpes and Ruth Knoblich (eds), *The Global Politics of Science and Technology: Concepts from International Relations and Other Disciplines*, vol 1 (Berlin: Springer, 2014) 1 at 4.

72 See Blaise Pascal, *The Thoughts of Blaise Pascal* (London: Kegan Paul, Trench & Co., 1885) at 57.

73 See Gail Fine, "Does Socrates Claim to Know that He Knows Nothing?" (2008) 35 *Oxford Studies in Ancient Philosophy* 49 at 49.

74 See Kenneth L. Mossman, *The Complexity Paradox: The More Answers We Find, the More Questions We Have* (Oxford: Oxford University Press, 2014) at xii and 3.

75 See Jeffrey Kluger, *Simplexity: Why Simple Things Become Complex (and How Complex Things Can Be Simple)* (New York: Hyperion, 2008).

For the present era in general, this impact of oxymora and paradoxes in science is well exemplified in Charles Handy's book, *The Age of Paradox*.[76] Starting from the angle of business and commerce but expanding to various related areas, Handy identifies several contradictions which he calls the paradoxes of our time, such as the paradoxes of intelligence, of work, of productivity, of time, of riches, of organizations, of ageing, of the individual, and of justice.[77] In short, his analysis reveals the rise in essentially oxymoronic concepts and shows different pathways for their enhanced management. Perhaps one of the core oxymoronic concepts is that of "coopetition", a deliberate juxtaposition of the two dominant and yet apparently antagonistic features of economic behavioural processes, namely cooperation and competition. *Coopetition* (or co-opetition) has also been defined as a new and revolutionary mindset or new paradigm, not only in the way we conduct business but with much wider implications for the organization of our present societies.[78] In this regard it is also closely related to new forms of business practices, such as "crowdsourcing", which may lead to new roles for both consumers and producers by their fusion into the oxymoron of a *prosumer*.[79] The concept of *coopetition* also invites associations with the concept of "creative destruction" introduced by Joseph A. Schumpeter.[80] He used creative destruction to describe the process of competition by which some firms would perish so that new ones can emerge in the pursuit of the goal of perfect equilibrium or perfect competition.[81]

Overall, the language of economics is replete with dichotomies, such as those of supply and demand, inflation and deflation, or growth and recession. These dichotomies invariably give rise to several paradoxes and oxymora alike. For instance, the supply and demand paradox asks if demand creates supply or supply creates demand.[82] Similarly, for the relation of price and demand it was said that counter to the general assumption, there may be goods the demand for which rises with their price (the Giffen or Gray paradox).[83] One can also mention the notion of "job security", which in times of globalization, outsourcing and other

76 See Charles Handy, *The Age of Paradox* (Boston: Harvard Business School Press, 1995).

77 *Ibid* at 17–41.

78 See also Adam M. Brandenburger and Barry J. Nalebuff, *Co-opetition: A Revolution Mindset That Combines Competition and Cooperation: The Game Theory Strategy That's Changing the Game of Business* (New York: Doubleday, 1996); see also Said Yami et al. (eds), *Coopetition: Winning Strategies for the 21st Century* (Cheltenham: Edward Elgar, 2010).

79 See Jeff Howe, *Crowdsourcing: Why the Power of the Crowd Is Driving the Future of Business* (New York: Crown Business, 2008) at 4 and Georg Ritzer and Nathan Jurgenson, "Production, Consumption, Prosumption: The Nature of Capitalism in the Age of the Digital 'Prosumer'" (2010) 10(1) *Journal of Consumer Culture* 13.

80 See Joseph A. Schumpeter, *Capitalism, Socialism and Democracy* (New York: Harper, 1942).

81 *Ibid* at 90.

82 See Byron Fisher, *The Supply and Demand Paradox: A Treatise on Economics* (North Charleston: BookSurge Publishing, 2007) at 2.

83 See Simon Gray, *The Happiness of States: Or An Inquiry Concerning Population, The Modes of Subsisting and Employing It, and the Effects of All on Human Happiness* (London: Hatchard, 1815) at 509–510; see also Etsusuke Masuda and Peter Newman, "Gray and Giffen Goods" (1981) 91(364) *The Economic Journal* 1011.

changes has come to be described as an oxymoron.[84] In a breath, labour is also no longer what it used to be, as many labour services are nowadays performed for free, from the many unpaid internships to the users of social media creating and uploading content for free.[85]

As another example, in the wake of the financial crisis of 2008 and the resulting controversial debate about austerity or "growth in the time of debt",[86] the euphemistic but equally oxymoronic concept of "negative growth" (*Minuswachstum*) has been frequently invoked.[87] Related oxymoronic concepts are those of "deflationary inflation"[88] and "inflationary deflation".[89] By the same token, "stagflation", as a simultaneous occurrence of economic slump or stagnation and inflation,[90] has also been named as an oxymoron together with "global Keynesianism".[91] John Maynard Keynes himself is said to have contributed to at least one paradox in economics, known as the "paradox of thrift",[92] which he derived from an allegorical poem called "The Fable of the Bees" written by Bernard Mandeville in 1704.[93] Proving perhaps the kinship between poetry and economics or art and science, the paradox of thrift consists in the counterintuitive result that "when people attempt to save more, this will not necessarily result in more saving for the nation as a whole" or not every "penny saved is a penny earned".[94]

84 See Stuart G. Walesh, "Job Security is an Oxymoron" (1997) 67(2) *Civil Engineering* 62 at 62.

85 See José van Dijck, "Users Like You? Theorizing Agency in User-Generated Content" (2009) 31(1) *Media, Culture & Society* 41.

86 See *e.g.* Carmen M. Reinhart and Kenneth S. Rogoff, "Growth in a Time of Debt" (2010) 100(2) *American Economic Review* 573; but see Thomas Herndon, Michael Ash and Robert Pollin, "Does High Public Debt Consistently Stifle Economic Growth? A Critique of Reinhart and Rogoff" (2014) 38 *Cambridge Journal of Economics* 257.

87 See *e.g.* Tatyana P. Soubbotina, *Beyond Economic Growth: Meeting the Challenges of Global Development.* (Washington: The World Bank, 2000) at 25 and 31–32 and Serge Latouche, "Minuswachstum: Die falsche Kritik der Alternativökonomen", *Le Monde Diplomatique (German Edition)* (12 November 2004) at 14–15.

88 See Paul Mattick, "Economics, Politics, and The Age of Inflation" (1978) 8(3) *International Journal of Politics* I at 40.

89 See Elmar Altvater, "The Growth Obsession" (2002) 38 *Social Register* 73 at 75 and 84 and Elmar Altvater, "The Local and the Global in Financial Crises" in Valeria Gennaro Lerda (ed), *Which "Global Village"?: Societies, Cultures, and Political-Economic Systems in A Euro-Atlantic Perspective* (Westport: Praeger, 2002) 9 at 15.

90 See Paul Krugman, *The Return of Depression Economics and the Crisis of 2008* (New York: W. W. Norton & Company, 2009) at 15.

91 See Christopher L. Connery, "Pacific Rim Discourse: The U. S. Global Imaginary in the Late Cold War Years" (1994) 21(1) *Asia/Pacific as Space of Cultural Production* 30 at 42.

92 See Robert T. Nash and William P. Gramm, "A Neglected Early Statement of the Paradox of Thrift" (1969) 1(2) *History of Political Economy* 395; see also John M. Keynes, *The Collected Writings of John Maynard Keynes,* vol 7, 3rd ed (Cambridge: Cambridge University Press, 2013) at 84

93 Bernard Mandeville, *The Fable of the Bees: or, Private Vices and Publick Benefits,* 3rd ed (London: T. Tonson, 1724).

94 See Paul A. Samuelson and William D. Nordhaus, *Economics,* 16th ed (New York: McGraw-Hill, 1998) at 464.

A similar paradox can be found in the context of the commonly but uncritically used and, most of all, logically and philosophically flawed dichotomy of so-called "developing" versus "developed countries". First, the dichotomy is flawed logically because the antonym of a developed country is not a developing but a non-developed or least developed country, whereas the antonym of a developing country would be a stagnating or even receding country.[95] Philosophically, on the other hand, all countries ought to be "developing" because – as we know from the proverb "a rolling stone gathers no moss" – we all need to change, especially, and paradoxically, if we want things to stay the same and live on, as Mandeville put it, like "a spacious hive well stock'd with Bees, that lived in luxury and ease".[96] At the same time the so-called "developed countries" are more deeply indebted than their so-called "developing counterparts", which means that when you spend more money than you have, paradoxically you are considered more "developed".[97] This was also noted by Thomas Piketty, stating that "Europe is the most extreme case: it has both the highest level of private wealth in the world and the greatest difficulty in resolving its public debt crisis—a strange paradox".[98]

Related to economics and wealth is especially "money", which together with prices gives rise to many more paradoxes.[99] For instance, in Renaissance poetry, money was described by a paradox, namely that poets use "imagery of gold, money, trade, hoarding, etc. to express not only what is 'gaudy', 'trash', 'poison to men's souls' but also what has the highest value, even the highest spiritual value".[100] A similar contradiction lies in the "Mandeville's paradox" derived from the "The Fable of the Bees",[101] which lies in the assertion that "private economic 'lusts' or 'vices' lead to public virtues".[102]

Related to money, the statement "that money does not buy happiness, contrary to the widespread illusion that it does", was also elevated to a paradox.[103]

95 See also Rostam J. Neuwirth, "Global Law and Sustainable Development: Change and the 'Developing-Developed Country' Terminology" (2016) 29(4) *European Journal of Development Research* 911 at 921.

96 Mandeville, *supra* note 93 at 1.

97 See also Rostam J. Neuwirth, "A Constitutional Tribute to Global Governance: Overcoming the Chimera of the Developing-Developed Country Dichotomy" (2010) *European University Institute (EUI) Working Paper* LAW 2010/20 at 15.

98 See Thomas Piketty, *Capital in the Twenty-First Century* (Cambridge: Belknap Press, 2014) at 540.

99 See *e.g.* Jehan Cherruyt De Malestroict, *Les paradoxes du Seigneur Malestroict* (Paris: Martin Le Jeune, 1578) at 4 and 9; see also Agnieszka Steczowicz, "Renaissance Monetary Paradoxes: The Malestroit-Bodin Controversy" (2005) 2(4) *Renaissance Journal* 1.

100 See Irving D. Blum, "The Paradox of Money Imagery in English Renaissance Poetry" (1961) 8 *Studies in the Renaissance* 144 at 154.

101 See Mandeville, *supra* note 93.

102 See the quote of Mandeville in Carl Menger, *Investigations into the Method of the Social Sciences* (Auburn: The Ludwig von Mises Institute, 2009) at 18.

103 See Mike W. Martin, "Paradoxes of Happiness" (2008) 9(2) *Journal of Happiness Studies* 171 at 177.

Happiness too is being associated with many paradoxes, which go along the following lines: "To get happiness forget about it; then, with any luck, it will come as a by-product in pursuing meaningful activities and relationships".[104] This has also been termed the "hedonistic paradox".[105] John Stuart Mill expressed a similar thought by writing that paradoxically only those are happy "who have their minds fixed on some object other than their own happiness".[106] The paradox of happiness was also said to find expression in the sad paradox that "the more we try to eradicate suffering, the more it proliferates and multiplies".[107] In other words, and against the common credo, the harder you try, the more you will be likely to fail.

The same meaning is also reflected in the paradoxes related to "happy peasants and miserable millionaires or frustrated achievers".[108] Similarly, when money is seen as tied to happiness, then sadly "everything done to achieve happiness can also drive it away".[109] Refined, this kind of happiness paradox was also tied to economic growth and named the paradox of "unhappy growth", which seems to show a negative correlation between economic growth and happiness.[110] The same paradoxical correlation was also found to apply to states, where it was said that the "more expensive the style of living of a nation [...] the richer will it be".[111] This finding is perhaps related to another economic paradox, called the "Lucas paradox", which holds that, contrary to neoclassical economic predictions, in reality capital does not flow from richer to poorer countries.[112] Similarly, the Easterlin paradox holds that "economic considerations are very important to people, though by no means the only matters of concern" and that "higher income is not systematically accompanied by greater happiness".[113]

Various problems captured by paradoxes or oxymora related to various dichotomies in economics, such as saving or spending, power and weakness, growth or recession, are currently addressed by the term "sustainable development".

104 *Ibid* at 171.

105 See Lawrence H. White, "Introduction" in Carl Menger, *Investigations into the Method of the Social Sciences with Special Reference to Economics* (Auburn: The Ludwig von Mises Institute, 2009) 1 at 13.

106 John Stuart Mill, *Autobiography*, 2nd ed (London: Longman, Greens, Reader, and Dyer, 1873) at 142.

107 See Pascal Bruckner, *Perpetual Euphoria: On the Duty to Be Happy* (Princeton: Princeton University Press, 2000) at 37.

108 See Carol Graham, *Happiness Around the World: The Paradox of Happy Peasants and Miserable Millionaires* (Oxford: Oxford University Press, 2009).

109 See Bruckner, *Perpetual Euphoria*, *supra* note 107 at 173.

110 See Graham, *supra* note 108 at 146.

111 See Gray, *supra* note 83 at 5 and 151.

112 See Robert Lucas, "Why doesn't Capital Flow from Rich to Poor Countries?" (1990) 80(2) *American Economic Review* 92 at 92.

113 See Richard A. Easterlin, "Does Economic Growth Improve the Human Lot? Some Empirical Evidence" in Paul A. David and Melvin W. Reder (eds), *Nations and Households in Economic Growth: Essays in Honor of Moses Abramovitz* (New York: Academic Press, 1974) 89 at 118 and 120.

"Sustainable development", which was introduced in the context of a growing ecological awareness during the late 1980s, has also been called an essentially contested concept as well as an oxymoron.[114] Equally, the term "sustainable growth" was called a "bad oxymoron—self-contradictory as prose, and unevocative as poetry" when applied to the economy.[115] Additional oxymora are found in the context of research on the so-called "creative economy",[116] which evolved from the notion of culture industry and hence can also be understood as an apparent contradiction in terms.[117] This is primarily because artistic creativity and economic activity were for long periods of time separated and divided into pecuniary (for profit) and non-pecuniary (not for profit) activities, whence the stereotype of the "creative but poor artist".

Finally, new economic products too are becoming more oxymoronic given they often bear some sort of contradictory statements, such as the following portmanteau words: *motion picture*, *iced tea*, *iced coffee*, *frappuccino*, *gourmet pizza*, *SUV* (sports utility vehicle, a combination between a truck and a sports car). These creative products hint at a larger trend, which is the convergence of various industries, aptly described as follows:

> Boundaries are increasingly fading among hi-tech industries (for example, the ICT) as well as among hi-touch and hi-tech industries: nutriceutics (also called the 'functional food' industry), edutainment, cosmeceutics and genetics diagnostics are just a sample of the emerging convergent markets.[118]

This trend of convergent markets indicates that firmly established product categories tend to converge, such as fruit juices and vegetable soups that become "vegetable (or multivitamin) drinks" and "fruit soups". For the future, many more

114 See Michael Jacobs, "Sustainable Development as a Contested Concept" in Andrew Dobson (ed), *Fairness and Futurity: Essays on Environmental Sustainability and Social Justice* (Oxford: Oxford University Press, 2002) 21 and Steve Connelly, "Mapping Sustainable Development as a Contested Concept" (2007) 12(3) *Local Environment: The International Journal of Justice and Sustainability* 259 at 260 and 262; see also Wolfgang Sachs, "Sustainable Development and the Crisis of Nature: On the Political Anatomy of an Oxymoron" in Frank Fischer and Maarten A. Hajer (eds), *Living with Nature: Environmental Politics as Cultural Discourse* (Oxford: Oxford University Press, 1999) 21 at 38, Esther Njiro, "Introduction: Sustainable Development an Oxymoron?" (2002) 52 *Agenda* 3 and Michael Redclift, "Sustainable Development (1987–2005): An Oxymoron Comes of Age" (2005) 13(4) *Sustainable Development* 212.

115 See Herman E. Daly and Kenneth N. Townsend, *Valuing the Earth: Economics, Ecology, Ethics* (Cambridge: The MIT Press, 1993) at 267.

116 See Rostam J. Neuwirth, "Global Market Integration and the Creative Economy: The Paradox of Industry Convergence and Regulatory Divergence" (2015) 18(1) *Journal of International Economic Law* 21 at 32.

117 See Theodor W. Adorno and Max Horkheimer, *Dialectic of Enlightenment* (New York: Verso, 1997); see also Theodor W. Adorno, *The Culture Industry* (London: Routledge, 1991) at 98.

118 See *e.g.* Fabio Ancarani and Michele Costabile, "Coopetition Dynamics in Convergent Industries: Designing Scope Connections to Combine Heterogeneous Resources" in Said Yami et al. (eds), *Coopetition: Winning Strategies for the 21*st *Century* (Cheltenham: Edward Elgar, 2010) 216 at 216 [references omitted].

such creative products with surprisingly overlapping features can be expected to flood the market using equally creative neologisms. In sum, economics is replete with essentially oxymoronic concepts or "myths and paradoxes".[119] This fact was aptly summed up by Carl Menger, when he wrote that "real phenomena of human economy, as paradoxical as it may sound at first, are to no small extent of an uneconomic nature".[120]

The relation of economics to other areas of human activities is reflected in another important oxymoron, which was born out of the business environment and is found in the term *glocalization*. Originally derived from the Japanese concept *dochakuka*, which referred to the adaptation of farming practices to local needs in Japan,[121] later it was successfully used for Japanese business strategies to sell products globally while still respecting and paying attention to local needs. The strategy is best summarized in the formula and advertising slogan "think global, act local". Similar to the oxymoronic term "global village" coined by Marshall McLuhan,[122] it has, in the meantime, also advanced and by way of its merger with a greater cultural sensitivity helped to render the understanding of even the political processes underlying globalization within the context of the global governance debate more sophisticated.[123] Thus, glocalization is the oxymoron used to describe the various challenges experienced by the local levels in the context of the process of globalization, which were also found to give rise to one or more paradoxes.[124]

A similar transition from the economic to the political sphere can be observed in the case of *fragmegration*, another significant oxymoron formed by the merger of the antagonistic trends of fragmentation and integration.[125] Coined in the context of political economy, which in some ways might also qualify as an essentially oxymoronic concept, *fragmegration* can be applied to the description of the dynamics of modern societies as captured by Karl Polanyi's paradoxical concept of "double movement", i.e. the continuous expansion of the market and a countermovement checking the expansion in definite directions.[126]

119 See Paul Bairoch, *Economics and World History: Myths and Paradoxes* (Chicago: University of Chicago Press, 1995).

120 Menger, *supra* note 102 at 218.

121 See Habibul H. Khondker, "Glocalization as Globalization: Evolution of a Sociological Concept" (2004) 1(2) *Bangladesh e-Journal of Sociology* 1 at 4.

122 Marshall McLuhan, *The Gutenberg Galaxy: The Making of Typographic Man* (Toronto: University of Toronto Press, 1962) at 31.

123 See Habibul H. Khondker, "Globalisation to Glocalisation: A Conceptual Exploration" (2005) 13(2) *Intellectual Discourse* 181 at 187–188.

124 See *e.g.* Helena Hirata and Hélène Le Doaré, "Les paradoxes de la mondialisation" (1998) 21 *Cahiers de Gedisst* 5.

125 See James N. Rosenau, *Along the Domestic-Foreign Frontier: Exploring Governance in a Turbulent World* (Cambridge: Cambridge University Press, 1997) at 99–117.

126 See Karl Polanyi, *The Great Transformation: The Political and Economic Origins of Our Time* (Boston: Beacon Press, 2001) at 136 and 223.

Another oxymoronic concept is found in that of "systemic chaos" which apparently joins together order and disorder. Systemic chaos has been defined merely as "a situation of severe and seemingly irremediable systemic disorganization" and as a "situation that arises because conflict escalates beyond the threshold within which it calls forth powerful countervailing tendencies".[127] A related problem was described by Jeremy Rifkin as the "entropy paradox", which highlights the strange fact that in our perception the history of the universe appears to be shifting from a perfect state towards decay and chaos, while our notion of history follows the opposite course, that is to say, it seemingly evolves from a state of chaos to a progressively more ordered world.[128] In international law, the same contradiction is found in the quest for international peace or "law and order". In this quest, the political reality of international relations has seen the rising importance of the apparently contradictory concept of *soft power*, which is a power using values, educational institutions and the products produced by the cultural industries to change political behaviour as opposed to sanctions imposed by hard military power.[129]

Equally, Albert Einstein characterized the struggle for the objective of a more peaceful and secure world, as laid down in the United Nations Charter, by means of an oxymoron when in an interview he declared himself to be a *militant pacifist* who is willing to fight for peace.[130] By the same token the concept of a *clash of civilizations*, as coined by Samuel P. Huntington,[131] can be understood as a contradiction in terms, as civilizations, if they were truly civilized, would not "clash" but instead find more peaceful and constructive ways to define the boundaries with other civilizations. Such reading qualifying the clash of civilizations as an oxymoron can also be derived from another statement by Albert Einstein:

> If the believers of the present-day religions would earnestly try to think and act in the spirit of the founders of these religions then no hostility on the basis of religion would exist among the followers of the different faiths.[132]

127 See Giovanni Arrighi and Beverly J. Silver, *Chaos and Governance in the Modern World System* (Minneapolis: University of Minnesota Press, 1999) at 33 and Giovanni Arrighi, *The Long Twentieth Century: Money, Power and the Origins of Our Time* (London: Verso, 1994) at 31.

128 Jeremy Rifkin, *Entropy: A New World View* (London: Paladin, 1985) at 57.

129 See Joseph S. Nye, Jr., *Soft Power: The Means to Success in World Politics* (New York: Public Affairs, 2004).

130 See Albert Einstein, "Für einen militanten Pazifismus" in Albert Einstein and Sigmund Freud: *Warum Krieg? Ein Briefwechsel* (Zürich: Diogenes, 1972) at 7 [English translation from Bernard T. Feld, "Einstein and the Politics of Nuclear Weapons" in Gerald James Holton and Yehuda Elkana (eds), *Albert Einstein: Historical and Cultural Perspectives* (Princeton: Princeton University Press, 1982) 369 at 377].

131 Samuel P. Huntington, "The Clash of Civilisations" (1993) 72(3) *Foreign Affairs* 22.

132 See Helen Dukas and Banesh Hoffman (eds), *Albert Einstein, The Human Side: New Glimpses from His Archives* (Princeton: Princeton University Press, 1979) at 96.

Therefore Huntington's arguments appear more like policy objective rather than the basis for a scientific theory of explanatory value.[133] In other words, Huntington's thesis is better qualified as a self-fulfilling policy instead of a sound scientific theory.

Another fertile ground for essentially oxymoronic concepts are the tensions arising from the relationship between the individual and the collective mass. As example one can name the concept of "crowd intelligence", which can be considered an oxymoron from a historical perspective, whereby mass behaviour was believed to be the opposite of acting intelligently. This belief was well described in the book *Extraordinary Popular Delusions and the Madness of Crowds* written by Charles Mackay in 1841.[134] Mackay locates the madness of crowds in various areas, such as crusades, witch-hunts, fortune-telling, or most relevant, for today, in the formation of economic bubbles. A similar belief in the folly of crowds, was expressed later by Gustave Le Bon in his book, *The Crowd: A Study of the Popular Mind*, published in 1896.[135] Against a historical backdrop, "crowd intelligence", therefore, appears oxymoronic when contrasting it with the title of James Surowiecki's book, *The Wisdom of Crowds*, which he deliberately coined in contrast to Mackay's book.[136] Surowiecki picks up on the popular imagination, according to which "groups tend to make people either dumb or crazy, or both", but argues that "under the right circumstances, groups are remarkably intelligent, and are often smarter than the smartest people in them".[137]

Another concept related to the individual–collective dichotomy is the one of the *zoon politikon* (political animal). The concept was used by Aristotle's *Politics*, in which he wrote that man is by nature a political animal – a term that was later questioned as an oxymoron.[138] The term *zoon politikon* is related to the concept of "democracy" which has already been mentioned above as an essentially contested concept. Etymologically, democracy can also be qualified as an oxymoron because it combines the two Greek words *demos* (people) and *kratos* (rule). A more explicit conception of democracy as an oxymoron is found in the term "representative democracy", which has been called "as paradoxical an oxymoron as our political

133 See also Chiara Bottici and Benoît Challand, "Rethinking Political Myth: The Clash of Civilizations as a Self-Fulfilling Prophecy" (2006) 9(3) *European Journal of Social Theory* 315 and Rostam J. Neuwirth, "The Governance of Religion and Law: Insights from the Prohibition of Usury" (2014) 2 *International Review of Law* 1 at 10.

134 See Charles Mackay, *Memoirs of Extraordinary Popular Delusions and the Madness of Crowds* (London: Robson, Levey & Franklin, 1852).

135 Gustave Le Bon, *The Crowd: A Study of the Popular Mind* (New York: The Macmillan Co., 1896) at 2.

136 See James Surowiecki, *The Wisdom of Crowds: Why the Many Are Smarter Than the Few and How Collective Wisdom Shapes Business, Economies, Societies and Nations* (New York: Doubleday, 2004).

137 *Ibid* at xiii.

138 See Aristotle, *The Politics and Economics of Aristotle* (London: Henry G. Bohn, 1853) at 6; see also Johannes Thumfart, *Ist das Zoon Politikon ein Oxymoron? Zur Dekonstruktion des Begriffs von Biopolitik bei Giorgio Agamben auf der Grundlage einer Wiederlektüre des Aristoteles* (Saarbrücken: VDM Verlag Dr. Müller, 2008).

language has produced".[139] With regard to the functioning of democracy, another paradox was circumscribed by Joseph de Maistre in the phrase "*Le peuple est un souverain qui ne peut exercer la souveraineté*" ("the people is a sovereign that cannot exercise sovereignty").[140] As a strongly contested concept, democracy's main problem remains to find the proper balance between the one and the many, or the individual and society as a whole. For a single individual representing one polar extreme, the identity of the ruler with the state was expressed by the phrase "*l'état, c'est moi*", which may be called a paradox as it implies a conjunction of the impersonal with a person.[141] This may also explain why "President Trump" was called an oxymoron.[142] Towards the other end of the spectrum, a range of constitutional constructs exist which are expressed by various oxymoronic notions, such as "people's democratic dictatorship",[143] "representative democracy"[144] or "anarchist organization".[145] In the end, even political science has been termed an oxymoron.[146]

The interdisciplinarity of various concepts also surfaces in the next paradox, the so-called "paradox of power", which is made of two, namely the "paradox of the power of weakness" and "the paradox of the weakness of power".[147] Combined into one, it describes the paradoxical relationship between the only apparently opposite terms of power and weakness. Indeed, in the book *The Paradox of Power and Weakness*, George Kunz shows that these two terms are not always opposites and that the "illogical (oxymoronic) relationship between power and weakness, found so frequently in the lives and events of power and weak persons, underlies the political, economic, familial, and societal ironies, conflicts and happy surprises of daily life".[148] Furthermore, he writes that "power can be the very basis of power's weakness as well as its power; and weakness, still weak, can be the power of the weak".[149]

139 See Benjamin R. Barber, *Strong Democracy: Participatory Politics for a New Age* (Berkeley: University of California Press, 2003) at xxxiv.

140 See Joseph de Maistre, *Against Rousseau: "On the State of Nature" and "On the Sovereignty of the People"* (Montreal: McGill-Queen's University Press, 1996) at 45.

141 See Harvey C. Mansfield, *Machiavelli's Virtue* (Chicago: The University of Chicago Press, 1966) at 282.

142 See Howard Fineman, "Why 'Trump Administration' is an Oxymoron", *The Huffington Post* (19 March 2017); available at: http://www.huffingtonpost.com/entry/why-trump-administration-is-an-oxymoron_us_58cb1996e4b00705db4dd6ae (accessed 1 October 2017).

143 See Recital 6 of the Preamble of the Constitution of the People's Republic of China, 4 December 1982; available on Westlaw China.

144 See *e.g.* Nadia Urbinati, *Representative Democracy: Principles and Genealogy* (Chicago: The Chicago University Press, 2006) at 4.

145 See *e.g.* Michael Herzfeld, "Embarrassment as Pride: Narrative Resourcefulness and Strategies of Normativity Among Cretan Animal-Thieves" in Charles L. Briggs, *Disorderly Discourse: Narrative, Conflict, & Inequality* (Oxford: Oxford University Press, 1996) 72 at 78.

146 See Howard P. Greenwald et al., "Polling and Policy Analysis as Resources for Advocacy" (2003) 13(2) *Journal of Public Administration Research and Theory* 177 at 188.

147 See George Kunz, *The Paradox of Power and Weakness: Levinas and an Alternative Paradigm for Psychology* (Albany: State University of New York Press, 1998).

148 *Ibid* at 13.

149 *Ibid* at 14.

It is possible that the frequent occurrence of essentially oxymoronic concepts is not tied to the specific scientific field but rather to the subjects engaged in it. This would explain why even "human nature" was considered an oxymoron.[150] In medical science, the medieval Swiss scientist Paracelsus, otherwise known as Philippus Aureolus Theophrastus Bombastus von Hohenheim (1493–1541), expressed another paradox by stating that "All things are poison, and nothing is without poison; only the dose permits something not to be poisonous".[151] Hence, according to Paracelsus, paradoxically it is not the quality of the substance itself but the dose that determines whether a substance is poisonous or harmful to health or, in fact, healthy and a medical cure. This is, for instance, said about red wine and the same idea was later applied under the concept of the "poison paradox".[152] Generally, many medical oxymora were detected, like "noninflammatory arthritis", and found to be "pretty ugly".[153]

For biology, the tension between egoism and altruism has been elaborated by Richard Dawkins in the book, *The Selfish Gene*.[154] The term "selfish gene", however, could also be construed as a contradiction in terms because it contrasts the self with the hereditary information received by others, namely usually the parents. A similar contradiction is inherent in the concept of intergenerational equity, given that different generations will likely not be identical but are entitled to fairness in terms of the resources they have access to in society.[155] Intergenerational equity is also related to the so-called "paradox of future individuals", which asks whether the present world population is under a moral obligation to future people to pursue controlled growth policies in order to promote their well-being.[156] The paradox arises from the strongly counterintuitive conclusion that "we have no moral obligation to future generations beyond, at most, the next few to promote their well-being".[157] Basically, the paradox (also known as non-identity problem)[158] consists in the conflict of deciding on moral grounds whether someone should or should not exist and at the same time determine whether s/he would be better off or not (in a less overcrowded world).

150 See Claire McEachern (ed), *The Cambridge Companion to Shakespearean Tragedy* (Cambridge: Cambridge University Press, 2003) at 177.

151 See Heinrich A. Preu (ed), *Das System der Medicin des Theophrastus Paracelsus* (Berlin: G. Reimer, 1838) at 232 [translation by author].

152 See John A. Timbrell, *The Poison Paradox: Chemicals as Friends and Foes* (Oxford: Oxford University Press, 2005) at 209 and 250.

153 See Peter M. Ronai, "Medical Oxymorons Can Be Pretty Ugly" (1993) 161(4) *American Journal of Roentgenology* 816 at 816.

154 Richard Dawkins, *The Selfish Gene* (New York: Oxford University Press, 1976).

155 See *e.g.* Edith Brown Weiss, *In Fairness to Future Generations: International Law, Common Patrimony and Intergenerational Equity* (Tokyo: The United Nations University, 1989) at 95.

156 See Gregory Kavka, "The Paradox of Future Individuals" (1982) 11(2) *Philosophy and Public Affairs* 93.

157 *Ibid* at 93.

158 See *e.g.* David Boonin, "How to Solve the Non-Identity Problem" (2008) 22(2) *Public Affairs Quarterly* 127.

There are more oxymoronic concepts related to the duality of human nature, namely to sexuality and the way we procreate in particular. The duality underlying the two different sexes itself gives rise to a vast amount of contradictions and conflicts expressed through essentially oxymoronic concepts. To begin with, one can cite love as both a contested concept[159] and a source of higher sensual expression of sexuality,[160] which has led to several oxymoronic concepts. For example, Erich Fromm wrote about it that "in love the paradox occurs that two beings become one and yet remain two".[161] As another oxymoron, love was called a "tender force" (*zärtliche Kraft*).[162] Perhaps less sophisticated, an American actor used another oxymoronic concept in his autobiography to describe his love by calling the woman he was married to twice "an eternal one night stand".[163]

One may also think of the oxymoronic term "sadomasochism", which is a portmanteau of the two separate and opposite concepts of "sadism" and "masochism". Originally, sadomasochism was coined from the last names of the French writer Marquis de Sade (1741–1814) and the Austrian writer Leopold von Sacher-Masoch (1836–1895).[164] It describes a combination of the expression of sadistic and masochistic, or dominating and submissive, elements at the same time. The common legalized arrangement of sexual intercourse in the form of marriage has also been described satirically by the oxymoronic expression of "marital bliss".[165] Similarly, the term "gay marriage" could then also be considered an oxymoron, even in its double meaning of "gay".[166] Often contrasted with marriage, the concept of "free love" has even been called the oxymoron par excellence.[167] Sexuality in general has been described by a paradox, equalled to a "cosmic principle spanning the widest realms, from physics, through biology to our social futures – an ultimate tension between contraries and complements".[168]

Similar paradoxes occur in the distinction between woman and man. At their origin are the dichotomous distinction of woman from man, or "the sex" from what is – tellingly in view of our dualistic thinking – equally called "the opposite sex". Scientifically, the distinction was certainly changing or may not have existed at all in the earliest days of life. The theoretical approach to gender has also shifted

159 See also Richard P. Hamilton, "Love as a Contested Concept" (2006) 36(3) *Journal for the Theory of Social Behaviour* 239.

160 See Niklas Luhmann, *Love as Passion: The Codification of Intimacy* (Cambridge, MA: Harvard University Press, 1986) at 45.

161 Erich Fromm, *The Art of Loving* (New York: Harper, 1956) at 19.

162 See Alexander Kluge, *Das Labyrinth der zärtlichen Kraft: 166 Liebesgeschichten* (Frankfurt a. M.: Suhrkamp, 2009).

163 See Richard Burton, *The Richard Burton Diaries* (New Haven: Yale University Press, 2012) at 287.

164 See Marquis de Sade, *The 120 Days of Sodom and Other Writings* (New York: Grove Press, 1966); and Leopold von Sacher-Masoch, *Venus in Furs* (New York: Penguin, 2000).

165 See Joel Kohl, *Marital Bliss and Other Oxymorons* (Los Angeles: CCC Publications, 1994).

166 See also Ronald Dworkin, *Justice in Robes* (Cambridge: The Belknap Press, 2006) at 10.

167 See Pascal Bruckner, *The Paradox of Love* (Princeton: Princeton University Press, 2012) at 3.

168 See Christine Fielder and Chris King, *Sexual Paradox: Complementarity, Reproductive Conflict and Human Emergence* (Lexington: Lulu.com, 2006) at 1.

from a "one-sex" to a "two-sex" model.[169] Apparently, for thousands of years, the common approach was that women were identical to men and had the identical genitals as men.[170] Language too reflected this view as Claudius Galenus (Galen) and others even used the same word for the female and male genitals.[171] It was only during the eighteenth century that a gradual shift from this "one-sex" model occurred and became replaced by a "two-sex model".[172] Finally, it was stated that, in the world of a "two-sex" model, the term "one-sex body" became an oxymoron.[173]

More recently though, the scientific and legal limitations intrinsic to a binary distinction of gender have surfaced again. For instance, the preference to a binary sex paradigm, which is based on "the assumptions that only two biological sexes exist and that all people fit neatly into either the category male or female", was found to ignore the millions of people who are intersexed.[174] Anthropological research has collected evidence of various individuals or groups, such as the *Berdaches* in South America or *Hijras* in India, which are perhaps neither man nor woman but definitely challenge a binary conception of gender or even institutionalize a third sex or third gender.[175] The binary conception of gender has also been visually and literally challenged by the Austrian singer called "Conchita Wurst" who won the 2014 Eurovision Song Contest as a man disguised and dressed like a woman but with a full beard. Additionally, the artist's name "Conchita Wurst" is, in fact, an oxymoron, combining – like the Chinese *yin* and *yang* – the two seemingly opposite female and male genitals as "*Wurst*" is the German word for "sausage" and "*conchita*" the diminutive form of "*concha*" meaning "seashell", which, read imaginatively, both may carry sexual connotations.[176]

Against the background of a binary idea of gender even the term "gender equality" can be understood as an oxymoron when one considers the distinctiveness of the sexes and its implications for the attempt to make them equal.[177] The qualification of gender equality as an oxymoron is based on the violation of the

169 See Thomas Laqueur, *Making Sex: Body and Gender from the Greeks to Freud* (Cambridge: Harvard University Press, 1992) at 8.

170 See Nemesius, "A Treatise on the Nature of Man" in William Telfer (ed), *Cyril of Jerusalem and Nemesius of Emesa* (London: SCM Press, 1955) 224 at 369.

171 See Laqueur, *supra* note 169 at 4–5.

172 *Ibid* at 8.

173 *Ibid* at 19.

174 See Julie A. Greenberg, "Defining Male and Female: Intersexuality and the Collision between Law and Biology" (1999) 41(2) *Arizona Law Review* 265 at 275 [footnotes omitted].

175 On the Berdache, see Brian Schnarch, "Society Neither Man nor Woman: Berdache – A Case for Non-Dichotomous Gender Construction" (1992) 34(1) *Anthropologica* 105; on the Hijras, see Serena Nanda, *Neither Man nor Woman: The Hijras of India*, 2nd ed (Belmont: Wadsworth, 1999), Vinay Lal, "Not This, Not That: The Hijras of India and the Cultural Politics of Sexuality" (1999) 61 *Social Text* 119 and Takeshi Ishikawa, "Hijras" (2011) 55(6) *Indian Literature* 213.

176 See Thomas Krama, "Yin und Yang, Glamour und Gleichgültigkeit beim Songcontest", *Die Presse (Austria)* (6 May 2014); available at: http://diepresse.com/home/meinung/marginalien/3801339/Yin-und-Yang-Glamour-und-Gleichgultigkeit-beim-Songcontest?from=suche.intern.portal (accessed 1 October 2017).

177 See also Muna Jawhary, *Women and False Choice: The Truth about Sexism: How to Fight Sexism in the Workplace* (Bloomington: Balboa Press, 2014) and Keally DeAnne McBride, *Postliberal Politics: Feminism, Communitarianism, and the Search for Community* (Berkeley: University of California, 1999) at 68.

axiom of equal protection commanding that similar things should be treated similarly, but those that are different should be treated differently. Or else, it may also be expressed by the paradox that "sometimes the grossest discrimination can lie in treating things that are different as though they were exactly alike".[178] For this reason, the term "gender equity" may be a more appropriate term than "gender equality", as the former tries to realize fairness whereas the latter may fail to do so by treating different subjects in the same way.

Other dichotomous pairs in science have also given rise to paradoxical relations, like those between the mind and the body or the sphere of rational thoughts and that of emotional feelings. The latter was aptly described by Blaise Pascal when he stated that "the heart has its reasons, which the reason knows nothing about; we know it in a thousand things".[179] Later the same insight became merged into the apparently contradictory concept of "emotional intelligence".[180] The body–mind dichotomy is perhaps the cause of one of the greatest human dilemmas, namely the life–death dichotomy. This dilemma, which so often impacts on our happiness, is expressed not only in mysterious terms as the "illusory enigma"[181] but also in the form of paradox, like that of "life after death".[182] Life and death appear to be mutually dependent, as surfaces in the short story "The Mortal Immortal" by Mary Shelley or in the paradoxical words by Herodotus that "the immortal are mortal, the mortal immortal, each living in the other's death, and dying in the other's life".[183] Put simply, these essentially oxymoronic concepts reflect both humans' lack of knowledge but also their desire to know what life after life is like.[184] Another aspect of the life–death dichotomy is known as Solon's Paradox, which is expressed through the saying that "no one ought to be pronounced happy before his death" (*dicique beatus ante obitum nemo*).[185]

Perhaps, our logic is even incompatible with our dual human nature. Metaphorically, human nature can be compared to a candle flame described as follows:

> The flame knows no rest, for it lives in perpetual conflict between two opposite tendencies. On the one hand, it cleaves to its wick, drinking thirstily of the oil that fuels its existence. At the same time, it surges upward, seeking to tear free of its material tether.[186]

178 *Jenness v. Fortson*, 403 U.S. 431, 442 (1971).

179 Blaise Pascal, *The Thoughts, Letters, and Opuscules* (New York: Hurd & Houghton, 1869) at 236.

180 See Peter Salovey and John D. Mayer, "Emotional Intelligence" (1990) 9 *Imagination, Cognition, and Personality* 185 at 185.

181 See Hubert Benoît, *Let Go: Theory and Practice of Detachment According to Zen* (New York: Weiser, 1973) at 154–163.

182 See Kenneth Jerold Comfort, *Ego Ontogenesis and Human Behavior* (Cohoes: Public Administration Institute of New York State, 2007) at 318.

183 See Charles M. Bakewell, *Source Book in Ancient Philosophy* (New York: C. Scribner's Sons, 1907) at 32.

184 See *e.g.* Raymond A. Moody, Jr., *Life after Life: The Investigation of a Phenomenon–Survival of Bodily Death* (New York: Bantam Books, 1976).

185 See Ovid, *Ovid's Metamorphoses*, 4th ed (London: Printed for B. Law, 1797) at 100; see also Plutarch, *Plutarch's Lives* (Cincinnati: H. S. & J Applegate, 1850) at 82.

186 See Yanki Tauber, *Beyond the Letter of the Law: A Chassidic Companion to the Ethics of the Fathers* (New York: Vaad Hanochos Hatmimim, 1995) at 220.

Conflicts between two opposites are dilemmas that each one of us repeatedly faces. Paradoxically, to solve such dilemmas, humans often turn to mythology, mysticism or religion for guidance and possible answers. Strangely, mythology[187] and mysticism are replete with examples of apparent contradictions or paradoxes.[188] Is it because – as the psychoanalyst Otto Rank wrote – that many mythologies are creations by the mass dreams of the people?[189] Or is it that these contradictions are rooted in the dual nature of the human being itself, as Goethe famously voiced it through the words of Faust, exclaiming "Two souls, alas! reside within my breast, and each is eager for a separation"?[190] Mircea Eliade, the great historian of comparative religion, described the same phenomenon explaining that human existence takes place simultaneously upon two parallel planes: "that of the temporal, of change and of illusion, and that of eternity, of substance and of reality".[191] Blaise Pascal also described human nature as "a nothing compared with infinity, – a universe compared with nothing, – a mean between all and nothing".[192]

Like the oxymoronic notion of "demigod", the human paradox of feeling a divine vocation while being rooted in the mundane, or the search for the *at-one-ment* through the transcendence of the dual nature appears to be a religious theme emphasized in one way or the other in all religious ideas. For example, it is reflected in the statement that "God hath spoken once; two-fold is what I heard".[193] Perhaps this is in line with the duality that even the creative act entails, as it is captured in the book of Moses where it is written that "in the beginning God created the heaven and the earth.[194]

On a more general level, according to Eliade, the transcendence of all forms of dualities, of contradictions or of paradoxes by way of the *coincidentia oppositorum* has been said to form – albeit to varying degrees – the overarching theme common to all religious ideas.[195] Moreover, in line with the *Tabula Smaragdina*'s seemingly paradoxical insight that "that which is Below corresponds to that which is Above, and that which is Above corresponds to that which is Below",[196] and

187 See Hans Jonas, "Myth and Mysticism: A Study of Objectification and Interiorization in Religious Thought" (1969) 49(4) *The Journal of Religion* 315.

188 See Eleanor McCann, "Oxymora in Spanish Mystics and English Metaphysical Writers" (1961) 13(1) *Comparative Literature* 16.

189 Otto Rank, *Der Mythos von der Geburt des Helden: Versuch einer psychologischen Mythendeutung* (Wien: Turia & Kant, 2000) mainly at 19.

190 See Johann Wolfgang von Goethe, *Faust I & II* (Princeton: Princeton University Press, 2014) at 30.

191 Mircea Eliade, *Patterns in Comparative Religion* (Lincoln/London: University of Nebraska Press, 1996) at 460.

192 Blaise Pascal, *Thoughts on Religion and Other Subjects* (Amherst: J. S. and C. Adams, 1829) at 20.

193 See Isaac Myer, *Qabbalah* (Whitefish: Kessinger, 2003) at vi; see also Psalm 62:11.

194 Genesis 1.1.

195 See John Valk, "The Concept of the Coincidentia Oppositorum in the Thought of Mircea Eliade" (1992) 28(1) *Religious Studies* 31.

196 See Julius Ruska, *Tabula smaragdina: ein Beitrag zur Geschichte der hermetischen Literatur* (Heidelberg: Carl Winter's Universitätsbuchhandlung, 1926).

following the gradual separation of science from religion in the West, the paradoxes of metaphysics have been continuing their journey into the realm of the natural sciences. Defying dualistic thinking, even the "hard" or natural sciences have produced many oxymoronic concepts, like "constant change", the "uncertainty principle" or Einstein's "space-time continuum". The uncertainty principle was summarized by the paradoxical statement that "if you measure some things precisely, you cannot measure other things as precisely".[197] Time itself, or at least our perception of its passing, is mysterious and equally prone to contradictions. Albert Einstein has successfully shown that time and space are intertwined and that the "world we live in is a four-dimensional space-time continuum".[198] The relationship between time and space may be itself captured by an oxymoron, this is to say the notion of "spacetime", which combines terms that were previously understood to be separate and unrelated.[199] In 1908, Hermann Minkowski presented his views on space and time by stating that "from now onwards space by itself and time by itself will recede completely to become mere shadows and only a type of union of the two will still stand independently on its own".[200]

More logical contradictions inherent in our understanding of time as split into the three categories of past, present and future are known by the "grandfather paradox" or "paradoxes of time travel". "Time travel" is also said to constitute an oxymoron because it may be defined as "to traverse some temporal interval in a time that differs from the duration of that interval", which was seen as contradictory.[201] Related to our understanding of time is the grandfather paradox, which states that if a person would attempt to go back in time and try to kill his own grandfather, it will meet with a logical problem, because, if the grandson were to succeed, it would mean that he would never have been born in the first place thus enabling him to go back in time, and so on.[202] This recurring dilemma has given rise to the claim that "time travel is incompatible with the laws of logic".[203] Strangely, the reverse could also be argued, namely that our logic is incompatible with the laws governing time. This, however, seems an argument that currently only few may be ready to make.[204]

197 See Bart Kosko, *Fuzzy Thinking: The New Science of Fuzzy Logic* (New York: Hyperion, 1993) at 19.

198 Albert Einstein, *Relativity: The Special and General Theory* (New York: H. Holt and Company, 1920) at 379.

199 See also Vesselin Petkov (ed), *Space, Time, and Spacetime: Physical and Philosophical Implications of Minkowski's Unification of Space and Time* (Berlin: Springer, 2010) at v–vii.

200 Hermann Minkowski, "Space and Time" in Vesselin Petkov (ed), *Minkowski's Papers on Relativity* (Montreal: Minkowski Institute Press, 2012) 37 at 37.

201 See Paul Horwich, *Asymmetries in Time: Problems in the Philosophy of Science* (Cambridge: The MIT Press, 1992) at 114.

202 See Jim Al-Khalili, *Paradox: The Nine Greatest Enigmas in Physics* (New York: Broadway, 2012) at 135.

203 See Sorensen, *supra* note 27 at 119.

204 But see David Lewis, "The Paradoxes of Time Travel" (1976) 13(2) *American Philosophical Quarterly* 145 at 150.

As a whole, the short survey seems to show that science itself is replete with oxymora, contradictions in terms (enantioses), and paradoxes. Science can thus be characterized by the contradiction between the search for truth in the eternal laws of nature and the regular changes of paradigms by way of regular intervals of structured change. In his book, *The Structure of Scientific Revolutions*, Thomas Kuhn has aptly outlined these essential tensions caused by the dialectics underlying scientific progress and summarized the process of structured revolutions by the concept of paradigm shift (*Paradigmenwechsel*).[205] Paradoxically, though, the understanding of science is itself subject to and dependent on a particular paradigm. This means that these contradictions or tensions were not always felt. For instance, it was argued that "modern science makes an assumption in its calculations that the ancients did not, namely that the natural laws have held true in all places and at all times".[206] A kind of different scientific paradigm, possibly a paradoxical one, is found in the concept of science used by Éliphas Lévi during the nineteenth century, which appears to have relied upon a greater degree of harmony between the concepts of religion, science, magic and philosophy.[207]

Over the past century, this harmony or unity appears to have gradually been lost due to the ongoing specialization and fragmentation in the sciences and their ongoing separation from, notably, the arts but also philosophy and religion. Kuhn himself confesses having been taught to regard science and art as polar opposites, and yet he went on to discover "close and persistent parallels" between the two.[208] Etymologically, science and art are connected by the Greek word *tékhnē (*or *technē)*, which means art or craft, whence English "technic", meaning "pertinent to art or an art", which refers to the "scientific study of the arts".[209] Yet, not only science and art, but also technology, mysticism and philosophy appear to be connected. Their connection lies, to a large extent, in the fact that in their essential function they represent "modes of cognition by which man receives information about the world, including himself, that may permit him to comprehend it in a systematic manner".[210]

Perhaps it is time to seek greater unity between the different senses and modes of cognition to open the door to greater coherence between art and science, which is deemed necessary to enhance and deepen our understanding about nature's many open secrets. The benefits from a combined consideration of art and science can be seen from the field of *science fiction*. Yet again, there appears to be another essentially oxymoronic concept as science and fiction appear to stand in

205 See Thomas S. Kuhn, *The Structure of Scientific Revolutions* (Chicago: The University of Chicago Press, 1996).

206 See Mark Booth, *The Secret History of the World* (New York: The Overlook Press, 2008) at 118.

207 See Éliphas Lévi, *Paradoxes of the Highest Science* (Berwick: Ibis Press, 2004).

208 See Thomas S. Kuhn, "Comment on the Relations of Science and Art" in Thomas S. Kuhn, *The Essential Tension: Selected Studies in Scientific Tradition and Change* (Chicago: The University of Chicago Press, 1977) 340 at 340.

209 See C. T. Onions (ed), *The Oxford Dictionary of English Etymology* (Oxford: Clarendon Press, 1966) at 906.

210 See Ithamar Gruenwald, "Mysticism, Science and Art" (1974) 7(2) *Leonardo* 123.

stark opposition. However, science fiction has already formulated numerous ideas about the future of humankind in the form of oxymora which have materialized in the present day. For instance, we are not far from realizing the vision of other oxymora by creating a "virtual reality"[211] and "cyberspace" (described as "placeless place")[212]. Overall, in the search for greater unity within science as well as between science and art, language and notably the rhetorical figures called "essentially oxymoronic concepts" may provide an important and unifying element.

4.3 The senses as a bridge between art and science

> *Reorganizing our concept of the sensory channels of the mind can change our view of the human mind, and possibly of the physical world.*[213]

The survey of essentially oxymoronic concepts in art has brought to light the frequency of their use. For science, on the other hand, it seems that their usage has been on the rise recently. Their comparison seems to suggest a seamless relevance across established categories of both the arts and sciences. For art, literature and music, music and architecture, music and painting, they all seem to be intrinsically linked and to inspire each other. This surfaces in various oxymoronic concepts pointing out the specific senses on which they most heavily rely, like the German word for timbre, *Klangfarbe* (tone colour), which distinguishes the quality of tone of one instrument from another.[214] *Klangfarbe* can be construed as forming yet another oxymoron, as it blends the visual with the auditory sense, or, to use Oliver Sacks' words, allows us to "see voices".[215] The same is true for the olfactory sense that is often described by virtue of the sensory oxymoron of *Geruchsbild* (odour signature or, literally, the "image of smell"). There is thus strong evidence for a causal relationship between different art forms and their appeal to different senses and to possibly converge them. This convergence becomes visible through paintings about music, such as Edouard Léon Théodore Mesens's *La partition complète complétée*,[216] or photographs of performing musicians,[217] as well as paintings in music, such as Modest Mussorgsky's *Pictures at an Exhibition*.

211 See Gabriel Weimann, *Communicating Unreality: Modern Media and the Reconstruction of Reality* (London: SAGE, 2000) at 330.

212 See Pierre Lévy, "Collective Intelligence, a Civilisation: Towards a Method of Positive Interpretation" (2005) 18(3/4) *International Journal of Politics, Culture, and Society* 189 at 197.

213 See Cretien van Campen, *The Hidden Sense: Synesthesia in Art and Science* (Cambridge: The MIT Press, 2007) at 7.

214 See Kennedy, *supra* note 55 at 890 ("timbre").

215 See Oliver W. Sacks, *Seeing Voices: A Journey into the World of the Deaf* (London: Picador, 1989).

216 See *e.g.* Karin von Maur, *Vom Klang der Bilder: Die Musik in der Kunst des 20. Jahrhunderts* (München: Prestel, 1996).

217 See *e.g.* K. Heather Pinson, *The Jazz Image: Seeing Music Through Herman Leonard's Photography* (Jackson: University Press of Mississippi, 2010).

In their mutual relation, it seems that essentially oxymoronic concepts used in art express a desire for the single senses (or art forms) to converge to seek a higher whole to "sense together" (synaesthesia). This synaesthesia may also be called the "common sense", but not describing "beliefs held by all without need for demonstration or supportive argumentation"[218], but, taken literally, as meaning a sense combining the other remaining known and maybe still unknown senses. Such understanding also seems to have driven the Italian universal artist and scientist and genius Leonardo Da Vinci (1452–1519). Da Vinci too was fascinated by perception through the senses and used the concept of the *sensus communis* (common sense) as the centre of all senses or the mind, as the location where the information from different senses flows together and is subsequently evaluated and judged.[219]

The fact that Da Vinci was both an artist and scientist may be telling in terms of the role of the senses and oxymoronic concepts for the relation between art and science. Taking essentially oxymoronic concepts first, they have been proven more and more relevant for science too, as they were found to permeate the fields of economics and political science, biology and psychology, as well as theology and physics. More so still, these concepts seem to remind us that, paradoxically, the boundaries separating scientific fields are also connecting them to the other disciplines. The zoon politikon, crowd intelligence or glocalization to mention but a few, have all direct or indirect relevance across various scientific fields. From a scientific perspective, the rise in essentially oxymoronic concepts may be explained by the strong reliance on dualistic thinking and binary logic applied in scientific reasoning. The dominant scientific method and the reasoning applied in it, is also strongly dependent on the information received from the various sensory organs.

Already the Indian *Bhagavad Gītā* warned that "the senses are so strong and impetuous, O Arjuna, that they forcibly carry away the mind even of a man of discrimination who is endeavouring to control them".[220] Initially Aristotle can be interpreted to have observed that direct perception by an individual sense is less prone to error than the perception of different senses together.[221] But for today's increasing complexity, for the scientific method to be more reliable, a greater coherence between the different sensory channels is needed. In this regard, language in the form of essentially oxymoronic concepts provides a useful insight into how the mind works and how it relies on the senses. This is why essentially oxymoronic concepts may express a deeper desire for a greater coherence between the senses, which also provides the bridge in the converging relation between art and science.

218 See Nicholas Rescher, *Common-Sense: A New Look at an Old Philosophical Tradition* (Milwaukee: Marquette University Press, 2005) at 11.

219 See David Summers, "Three Excerpts from the Judgment of Sense" in Claire Farago (ed), *Leonardo's Writings and Theory of Art* (New York: Garland Publishing, 1999) 97 at 97–101.

220 See A. C. Bhaktivedanta Swami Prabhupāda, *Bhagavad-gītā as it is: with the Original Sanskrit Text, Roman Transliteration, English Equivalents, Translation and Elaborate Purports* (New York: Bhaktivedanta Book Trust, 1986) at 148.

221 See Irving Block, "Truth and Error in Aristotle's Theory of Sense Perception" (1961) 11(42) *The Philosophical Quarterly* 1 at 1.

The relevance of oxymoronic concepts and the senses for science also surfaces mainly in their relevance for scientific inquiries, which has been outlined as follows:

> Paradoxes are extremely important because they point out logical contradictions in assumptions. The first cousins of paradoxes are anomalies, those unexplained oddities that crop up now and again in science. Like paradoxes, anomalies are useful for revealing possible gaps in prevailing theories.[222]

Such gaps in prevailing theories also apply to the understanding of our currently known senses, i.e. seeing (visual), hearing (auditory), smelling (olfactory), tasting (gustatory), touching (somatosensory), balancing (vestibular), and sensing motion (kinaesthetic). These senses may be subject to several paradoxes, which may exist both within the perception of one single sense as well as in the combined interaction and resulting perception stemming from two or more distinct senses. Additionally, it is possible that unknown senses may interfere with the known ones. The so-called "sixth sense" used in the vernacular could be just one such example. Mythology's third eye, as well as insights by new fields of research, such as parapsychology and noetics (the study of the nature of direct inner knowing),[223] are providing further evidence for the possible existence of what could still be termed organs or senses of "parapsychological" or "extrasensory perception" (ESP). In science, the denial of such psychic experiences has created a paradox, whereby many people are said to believe in their existence but science and public opinion seem to ridicule it.[224]

In short, paradoxes should also function as a constant reminder that nothing ever appears certain, either in art or in science. The uncertainty in both areas may ultimately be linked to the senses that may at times deceive our perception and judgement. In this regard, a very interesting phenomenon is synaesthesia. Synaesthesia etymologically derives from Greek "*syn*" (together) and "*aesthesis*" (sensation).[225] It may have several meanings but most commonly denotes "a condition in which one sensory modality also gives rise to a sensation in a different modality".[226] Thus, it can be defined as the parallel sensation of two, or more, or all senses.[227] People vested with this kind of ability are called "synaesthetes" and they perceive reality in such a way that a sensation produced in one modality provides a stimulus to another modality. These phenomena range from the following variations, which may appear (especially to non-synaesthetes) as contradictions in terms, such as "colored hearing" (chromeesthesia), "colored olfaction", "colored

222 See Dean I. Radin, *The Noetic Universe: The Scientific Evidence for Psychic Phenomena* (London: Transworld Publishers, 2009) at 3.

223 *Ibid* at xi.

224 *Ibid* at 3.

225 See Philip Winn (ed), *Dictionary of Biological Psychology* (London: Routledge, 2001) at 1657.

226 See Lynn C. Robertson and Noam Sagiv (eds), *Synesthesia: Perspectives from Cognitive Neuroscience* (Oxford: Oxford University Press, 2005) at 3 and van Campen, *supra* note 213 at 1.

227 See *e.g.* Richard E. Cytowic, *Synesthesia: A Union of the Senses*, 2nd ed (Cambridge: MIT Press, 2002).

taste", "colored music" to mention but a few.[228] "Audiomotor" is another such combination of different senses which consists in the positioning of one's body in accordance with the different sounds of words.[229] It is curious to note that synaesthesia is still treated as a mental disorder rather than a gift, given the extraordinary achievements of the "colourblind painter" and the "deaf composer" so vividly and tragically exemplified in the painter Jonathan I.[230] and the composer Ludwig van Beethoven, respectively. For Beethoven, it is said that, paradoxically, "his art actually became richer as his hearing declined".[231]

Ultimately the paradoxes found both in different art forms and sources of sensory information alike are manifold and give rise to many contradictions which are also often referred to or described by essentially oxymoronic concepts.[232] The truly important question is how the senses, the different classifications in art or science are related to thoughts and logic underlying our formation of language. Related to this question is whether changes to the logic of language, e.g. through a more frequent use of oxymora, is able to change our perception through the senses and eventually the reality around us.

Evidence for a possible impact of language (and thought) on matter is provided by the work of Masaru Emoto, who visualized the impact of different music and different words or languages on water by photographing the crystals forming when being frozen.[233] Given that humans are made up of about 70 percent water, why should music and language not have a direct effect (at least in the long run). Another way of visualizing the effect of sound is captured by cymatics, i.e. study of the effects of sound waves on various forms of matter, as conducted by Ernest Chladni and Hans Jenny.[234] They "visualized sounds" by exposing matter to sound, such as scattering sand on the vibrating membrane of a loudspeaker, which results in the formation of patterns of the sand in strict geometrical figures. The resulting shapes often resemble the shapes of so-called "*mandalas*" (Sanskrit word for "circle") as used in Eastern spiritual traditions.[235] It also finds application in energy medicine and potentially in biology, geology, astrophysics, meteorology and other areas.

Perhaps there is indeed a universal or cosmic music which is responsible for the formation of the planets, galaxies and the universe in the entirety of its manifold manifestations as a whole. This question is, inter alia, the subject of the study of psychoacoustics and psychooptics in search of their common perceptual ground, which led Ronald Pellegrino to conclude that "the fundamental principles of music

228 *Ibid* at 16.

229 *Ibid.*

230 See Oliver Sacks, "The Case of the Colorblind Painter" in Oliver Sacks, *An Anthropologist on Mars: Seven Paradoxical Tales* (New York: Vintage Books, 1996) 3.

231 See William Kinderman, *Beethoven*, 2nd ed (Oxford: Oxford University Press, 2009) at 71.

232 See also Mikhail Naimy, *The Book of Mirdad* (New York: Penguin Arkana, 1962) at 19.

233 See Masaru Emoto, *Die Antwort des Wassers* (Burgrain: KOHA Verlag, 2002).

234 See Ernst Florens Friedrich Chladni, *Neue Beyträge zur Akustik* (Leipzig: Breitkopf & Härtel, 1817) and Hans Jenny, *Cymatics: A Study of Wave Phenomena & Vibration* (New Market: Macromedia, 2001).

235 See Catherine L. Albanese, "The Multi-Dimensional Mandala: A Study in the Interiorization of Sacred Space" (1977) 24(1) *Numen* 1 at 1.

are universal principles that operate at all levels of life, from particle physics to the far reaches of the cosmos, from the physical to the spiritual".[236] Or else, it can also be said that our cognitive system operates through a complex interaction between different senses. Cymatics is but one example of the combination of sensory instruments, as Pellegrino explained as follows:

> Though the ear and eye have physically evolved to respond to different types of physical waves and to different frequency spectra, they share a wealth of common time regions that speak directly to feelings.[237]

Another connection between senses that has been studied is the connection between the olfactory sense and the sense of orientation, which was also held to be paradoxical, at least for pigeons. In a paper written in the 1980s, two researchers found that homing pigeons, when deprived of their olfactory sense, had greater problems in finding their homes.[238] In humans too, olfactory substances can have a variety of impacts. As we read about interesting experiments conducted by magicians and alchemists, there may exist substances or procedures which can produce contradictory effects in relation to information from other senses and are thus capable of influencing our behaviour without our awareness or else even against our will.[239] The most popular examples are various magic love potions and aphrodisiacs, which are usually meant to arouse our mood of sexual desire. In terms of more recent scientific research, such substances have been termed "pheromones". The term derives from the Greek words "*pherein*" (to transfer) and "*hormōn*" (to excite) and defined as "substances which are secreted to the outside by an individual and received by a second individual of the same species, in which they release a specific reaction, for example, a definite behaviour or a developmental process".[240] Various experiments with pheromones suggest that we might not even perceive these odours but they are still capable of influencing our mind and subsequently of altering our behaviour.[241]

The paradoxical qualities of senses lead to another paradox of potentially much wider repercussions, namely that of "free will and determinism (or fate)"[242]

236 See Ronald A. Pellegrino, "Cymatic Music: Towards a Metatheory of Harmonic Phenomena: My Interactive Compositions and Environments" (1983) 16(2) *Leonardo* 120 at 123.

237 *Ibid.*

238 See Roswitha Wiltschko and W. Wiltschko, "Pigeon Homing: Olfactory Orientation – A Paradox" (1989) 24 *Behavioral Ecology and Sociobiology* 163.

239 See *e.g.* Lucius Parvus Albertus, *Les Secrets merveilleux de la magie naturelle et cabalistique du grand et petit Albert* (Lyon: Héritiers de Beringos, 1752).

240 See Peter Karlson and Martin Lüscher, "'Pheromones': A New Term for a Class of Biologically Active Substances" (1959) 183(4653) *Nature* 55 at 55.

241 See *e.g.* Winnifred B. Cutler, Erika Friedmann, and Norma L. McCoy, "Pheromonal Influences on Sociosexual Behavior in Men" (1998) 27(1) *Archives of Sexual Behavior* 1.

242 See *e.g.* George Foot Moore, "Fate and Free Will in the Jewish Philosophies according to Josephus" (1929) 22(4) *Harvard Theological Review* 371, Peter Van Inwagen, "The Incompatibility of Free Will and Determinism" (1975) 27 *Philosophical Studies* 185 and Shirley Matile Ogletree and Crystal D. Oberle, "The Nature, Common Usage, and Implications of Free Will and Determinism" (2008) 36 *Behavior and Philosophy* 97.

or "freedom and foreknowledge".[243] The paradox of free will and fate (or determinism) holds the mystery whether we as human beings are able to make choices and decisions based upon our own free will or whether in fact our fate is determined by deterministic forces external to our own existence, such as the universe or some kind of deity. In a different formulation, the paradox of free will is also known as "Newcomb's paradox", which relates to an experiment named after William Newcomb who conducted it.[244] The paradox arises from a card game between one player and a second player able to predict the future, which contains a contradictory assumption about the relationship between the past and the future.[245] Against the common perception that past events cannot be affected by future actions, Newcomb's paradox suggests that it is possible to affect the past event based on my ability to influence future events. This problem has also been discussed from the point of view of the brain or memory, which is summarized by the oxymoronic concept of "remembering forgetting".[246] At this point, we can state the relationship between past and future or remembering and forgetting is closely tied to the question of whether we act out of free will, or whether our decisions are ultimately made for us or at least determined by other forces. This question is as old as humanity, highly contested and yet of utmost significance. Recently it has received new attention due to research in the field of neuroscience.[247] To this date, however, we must contend with the fact that a definite answer to this paradox appears to remain remote and dependent on the discovery of new evidence or development of new faculties.

The present state of uncertainty comes as no surprise when one considers that even thoughts appear paradoxical given the paradox of "thinking without thinking". This paradox can be derived from the fact that sometimes we may gain a better insight into a situation in – what is commonly called – "the blink of an eye" or intuition rather than a long intellectual analytical process.[248] These differences could also be used to compare art and science, as they have been termed both

243 See Linda Trinkaus Zagzebski, *The Dilemma of Freedom and Foreknowledge* (Oxford: Oxford University Press, 1991).

244 See Robert Nozick, "Newcomb's Problem and Two Principles of Choice" in Nicholas Rescher, *Essays in Honor of Carl G. Hempel: A Tribute on the Occasion of His Sixty-Fifth Birthday* (Dordrecht: Springer, 1969) 114.

245 See Maya Bar-Hillel and Avishai Margalit, "Newcomb's Paradox Revisited" (1972) 23(4) *The British Journal for the Philosophy of Science* 295 at 295.

246 See Michael S. Roth, "Remembering Forgetting: Maladies de la Memoire in Nineteenth-Century France" (1989) 26 *Representations* 49.

247 See generally Gerhard Roth, *Das Gehirn und seine Wirklichkeit: Kognitive Neurobiologie und ihre philosophischen Konsequenzen*, 5th ed (Frankfurt am Main: Suhrkamp, 1996) at 303–311 and Chun Siong Soon et al., "Unconscious Determinants of Free Decisions in the Human Brain" (2008) 11(5) *Nature Neuroscience* 543.

248 See Malcolm Gladwell, *Blink: The Power of Thinking Without Thinking* (London: Penguin, 2005).

"unlike and alike".[249] In trying to answer whether art and science are one or two separate cultures, it has been suggested that they are one culture to the extent that "similar creative mental processes operate both in the formulation of hypotheses in science and in concept formation expressed through works of art".[250] The search for answers about art and science's commonalities originating in the human mind and notably the creative cognitive processes operating there was also said to be linked to a paradox. This paradox is called the paradox of prediction, which basically asks how it is possible that a theory that has been proposed is able to predict results that can be verified or refuted.[251] Put differently, it can also mean that, strangely, a "theory may predict, but the experiment that would confirm or refute that prediction may also be influenced by the prediction itself".[252] Accordingly, every theory would bear elements of a self-fulfilling prophecy. Art too has a fable for such miraculous self-fulfilling prophecy, namely Ovid's narrative of the Cypriot artist Pygmalion.[253] The story goes that Pygmalion sculpted the statue of a woman out of ivory. The statue was so realistic that he fell in love with it and asked Venus to bring the woman to life – a wish which was granted and allowed them to get married and have a daughter together. The story is akin to that of Golem.[254] Both stories explain the terminology used to describe self-fulfilling prophecies in the form of motivation being influenced in a sense that higher expectations yield higher performances (Pygmalion effect) and lower expectations lower performances (Golem effect).[255]

Underlying the paradox of prediction is the difference between explanation and prediction. Their difference lies in the understanding that an explanation "describes a phenomenon after the fact", while a prediction "characterizes a phenomenon such that its behavior can be anticipated *a priori*".[256] Hence, the key to the difference between art and science lies in our perception through the multiple senses and understanding of time as made of the dichotomy between past and future. In other words again, art first foresees the future to explain the present, whereas science first explains the present facts in order to predict the future. They appear thus united in their interest in knowledge or understanding which may both be taken for humanity's quest for light in the sense of meaning, purpose and destiny.

249 See Leo Steinberg, "Art and Science: Do They Need to be Yoked?" in Stephen R. Graubard, *Art and Science* (Lanham: University Press of America, 1986) 1 at 1.

250 See Susan P. Gill, "The Paradox of Prediction" (1986) 115(3) *Daedalus* 17 at 17.

251 *Ibid.*

252 *Ibid* at 27–28.

253 Ovid, *The Metamorphoses* (Gregory Horace, trans.) (New York: The Viking Press, 1958) at 277–279.

254 Gustav Meyrink, *The Golem* (New York: Dover Publications, 1976).

255 See Terence R. Mitchell and Denise Daniels, "Motivation" in Walter C. Borman, Daniel R. Ilgen, and Richard J. Klimoski (eds), *Handbook of Psychology*, vol 12 (Hoboken: John Wiley & Sons, 2003) 225 at 229.

256 See Gill, *supra* note 250 at 18.

4.4 Art and science: one culture?

> *This state of affairs situates us within a liminal place in-between two propositions that are separated while at the same time being gathered in a dialectical unity:* "l'art n'est rien sans la science" "la science sans art n'est rien".[257]

Essentially oxymoronic concepts have long been used in art. Now, they appear progressively to be invading the rhetoric of science as well. This trend may also indicate that art and science are but one culture and their gradual separation has lost its meaning. Cinema is an excellent example in this regard, as whether it belongs to either art or science is a matter of controversy.[258] Cinema is not the only phenomenon that calls the separation between art and science into question as there are many overlaps between them. In the present context, their separation seems problematic and artificial and the result of the process of rationalization. This rationalization Max Weber called "*Entzauberung*" (disenchantment), which denotes a process of intellectualization largely in parallel with scientific progress that drastically altered not only the perception of nature but also the expectations about the knowledge about nature.[259] Still the rationalization prevails and proceeds largely based on dualistic thinking that largely characterizes the present scientific paradigm. With time, however, the limitations of this paradigm are becoming more obvious. As for dualism, it has been said that "no dualist can leave his polar terms wholly sundered if he is going to address the problem of human knowledge or found a science of physics".[260] The same applies to the prevailing opposition between art and science.

Today their opposition seems obsolete, because even though the underlying dualism may at first help to enhance the detailed understanding of the phenomenon observed, it will eventually impede a more complete understanding needed to answer the questions that really matter in life. It is in these contexts that the use of essentially oxymoronic concepts not only critically challenges their separation but also helps to bridge their divide in the future. This can be well exemplified by the example of Mandeville's allegorical poem, "The Fable of the Bees", which was written as a literary work of art but later inspired important scientific insights.[261] The same connection between literature and science features in the comparison of Ovid's "my plentie makes me poore" with the Easterlin paradox. A similar connection was found also between science and the art of

257 See Nader El-Bizri, "Seeing Reality in Perspective: The 'Art of Optics' and the 'Science of Painting'" in R. Lupacchini and A. Angelini (eds), *The Art of Science: From Perspective Drawing to Quantum Randomness* (Cham: Springer, 2014) 25 at 26.

258 See Thomas Elsaesser and Malte Hagener, *Film Theory: An Introduction through the Senses* (New York: Routledge, 2010) at 1.

259 See Max Weber, "Science as Vocation" in John Dreijmanis (ed), *Max Weber's Complete Writings on Academic and Political Vocations* (New York: Algora Publishing, 2008) 25 at 25 and 35.

260 See Emily R. Grosholz, *Cartesian Method and the Problem of Reduction* (Oxford: Clarendon Press, 2005) at 68.

261 See Franz From, "Mandeville's Paradox" (1944) 10(3) *Theoria* 197.

magic, given that magicians were perhaps the first to experiment.[262] Numerous more instances could be enumerated but it suffices to state that the relations between art and science are manifold. In these relations, the creative cognitive processes underlying both fields appear as the common ground and are united in a desire for greater coherence beginning with the senses, which supports the frequent assertion that "*scientia sine arte nihil est*" (science without art is nothing) and vice versa.[263] Or, put differently, art and science are obsessed with the same objective but use different means. More precisely, science can be said to aim to explain the present facts to predict the future, whereas art tries to predict the future to explain the present. Where though, it is important to ask, does this finding leave the law – a question which shall be approached by a closer look at the role of oxymora in the law.

262 See Lynn Thorndike, *A History of Magic and Experimental Science*, vol 1 (New York: The MacMillan Company, 1929) at 2.

263 See Joseph Agassi, *The Very Idea of Modern Science: Francis Bacon and Robert Boyle* (Dordrecht: Springer Science+Business Media, 2013) at 108.

5 Oxymora in the law

The reconciliation of the irreconcilable, the merger of antitheses, the synthesis of opposites, these are the great problems of law.[1]

Essentially oxymoronic concepts evidently are being frequently used in art and in science. The finding of oxymoronic concepts from A(rchitecture) to Z(oology), from "atonal music" to "*zoon politikon*", necessarily invites the question about their role in law, where notably contestation and duality play such a crucial role. Law lives on contest but may equally be considered a contested concept. Law is also contested in terms of being an art or a science.[2] The question which has been famously phrased by Richard A. Posner asks: "Is law a science, a humanity, or neither?"[3]

The problem of the exact classification of law between science and art is further complicated by the different usages of the term "law" in the difference scientific disciplines or artistic fields.[4] Thus the lack of a common language of science and art not only reinforces the fragmentation of science as a whole but also obstructs the attainment of a common definition of law or an enhanced understanding of its meaning. Hence law could be a contested concept considering the endless disputes about it. Strangely, however, law also tries to order these disputes or conflicts and to minimize or completely avoid their negative effects. In this regard, we encounter a first paradox, namely that the dominant conception of law today is essentially dualistic, dichotomous or bifurcated. In short, the dualism of law is deeply rooted in our perception of justice versus injustice, legal versus illegal, or simply true versus false. Many prominent lawyers have eloquently outlined this dualistic nature of law, like Robert M. Cover, who called law a "nomos"

1 Benjamin N. Cardozo, *The Paradoxes of Legal Science* (New York: Columbia University Press, 1928) at 4.

2 See *e.g.* Joan Williams, "Is Law an Art or a Science?: Comments on Objectivity, Feminism, and Power" (1999) 7(2) *American University Journal of Gender, Social Policy & the Law* 355.

3 Richard A. Posner, *The Problems of Jurisprudence* (Cambridge: Harvard University Press, 1990) at 1.

4 See Edward Jenks, "The Function of Law in Society" (1923) 5(4) *Journal of Comparative Legislation and International Law* 169 at 169.

or normative universe, which we constantly create and maintain by "a world of right and wrong, of lawful and unlawful, of valid and void".[5] Jeremy Bentham himself is said to have been obsessed with bifurcation in nearly all his writings,[6] and described law's duality as follows:

> Nature has placed mankind under the governance of two sovereign masters, pain and pleasure. It is for them alone to point out what we ought to do, as well as to determine what we shall do. On the one hand the standard of right and wrong, on the other the chain of causes and effects, are fastened to their throne. They govern us in all we do, in all we say, in all we think.[7]

These are just a few examples of law's dualistic conception. Many more exist, like the procedural principle of hearing the other side (*audi alteram partem*). This principle is an expression of the more general adversarial conception of law – a kind of contest between opposite parties in establishing the "truth" and "justice". In terms of the application of the law, the dominant mode of reasoning is the legal syllogism, i.e. a mode of legal reasoning subsuming the facts of a case under the relevant norms or laws. In this process, classical logic as expressed through the principle that the choice of one alternative excludes another (*expressio unius est exclusio alterius*) plays an important role.[8] Applying this principle, a lawyer's mode of reasoning has been described as follows:

> For the lawyer's purpose every situation which confronts him is dealt with as falling into one or the other of two categories which are apparently supposed to be mutually exclusive and separated by a sharp boundary. Either this is a battery or not a battery, a trespass or not a trespass, etc.[9]

This characterization strongly expresses the reliance on binary logic which continues to dominate legal thought in general and Western legal thought in particular. This logic is mainly based on the methods of deduction and induction as applied in the legal syllogism as formulated by Aristotle.[10] Against the backdrop of the underlying binary modes of thought and reasoning, it can be

5 See Robert M. Cover, "The Supreme Court, 1982 Term: Foreword: Nomos and Narrative" (1983) 97(4) *Harvard Law Review* 4 at 4 [footnote omitted].

6 See Xiaobo Zhai, "Bentham's Natural Arrangement and the Collapse of the Expositor–Censor Distinction in the General Theory of Law" in Xiaobo Zhai and Michael Quinn (eds), *Bentham's Theory of Law and Public Opinion* (Cambridge: Cambridge University Press, 2014) 143 at 158.

7 See Jeremy Bentham, *Introduction to the Principles of Morals and Legislation* (London: T. Payne, 1789) at 1.

8 See generally Hermann Mosler, "General Principles of Law" in Rudolf Bernhardt (ed), *Encyclopaedia of Public International Law*, vol 7 (Amsterdam: North Holland, 1984) 89 at 92–93.

9 See Walter Wheeler Cook, "'Substance' and 'Procedure' in the Conflict of Laws" (1933) 42(3) *The Yale Law Journal* 333 at 333 [footnote omitted].

10 See Aristotle, *The Organon, or Logical Treatises of Aristotle*, vol 1 (London: Henry G. Bohn, 1853) at 80 *et seq.*

expected that the essentially contradictory nature of essentially oxymoronic concepts must be difficult to handle in the realm of law.

But before discussing in greater detail the impact of essentially oxymoronic concepts on the fundamentally dualistic conception of law,[11] it is vital to see how essentially oxymoronic concepts and especially oxymora are received in law. The ensuing analysis starts with a review of their use in case law and is followed by a brief discussion of their relevance for jurisprudence. Jurisprudence is understood here as the science of law or, as Ulpian is reported to have written, "the knowledge of things human and divine, the science of the just and unjust", to add another example of a dualistic understanding of law.[12] Paradoxically, it must be noted, law is based on a strong dualistic conception of reality but at the same time also the theory and practice concerned with the formulation of methods to transcend it. The question to be asked subsequent to the following overview is whether a dualistic conception of law is capable of transcending problems caused by a non-dualistic or fuzzier category of problems.

5.1 What is this thing called "law"?

The law is the law.[13]

An inquiry into the role of essentially oxymoronic concepts in law inevitably invites thoughts about the role and nature of law. Generally, defining the meaning, scope, or purpose of contested concepts, not to mention attempts to grasp their origin and nature, have proven to be very difficult. The same has been found about attempts to define the word "law".[14] It is telling that Frederick Pollock opens his *First Book of Jurisprudence* commenting on the nature and meaning of law by an apparent paradox, namely, that we find "in all human sciences that those ideas which seem to be most simple are really the most difficult to grasp with certainty and express with accuracy".[15] Perhaps one good exception is the definition of law given by W. H. Auden in a wonderful poem when he writes that "Law is the Law".[16] This poem also underlines that Law's nature seems thus too comprehensive and, by the same token, too contested to be defined either in a textbook or in an international treaty. It is also telling that there is no textbook which is entitled "Law" only. The closest I could find was a book on the English legal system the title of which starts with the bold statement "Law" only to be humbly narrowed down by the addition of "Or a Discourse Thereof".[17]

11 See below Chapter 7.

12 See Thomas Erskine Holland, *The Elements of Jurisprudence*, 4th ed (Oxford: Clarendon Press, 1888) at 2.

13 See also Georges Rouault, "The Law is the Law, Hard Though It Be" (1971) 16(1) *Administrative Science Quarterly* 18 and Edward Mendelson (ed), *W. H. Auden: Selected Poems* (New York: Vintage Books, 1979) at 90.

14 See J. W. Simonton, "On the Origin and Nature of Law" (1902) 11(4) *Yale Law Journal* 195 at 195.

15 Frederick Pollock, *The First Book of Jurisprudence* (London: MacMillan and Co., 1911) at 3.

16 See Mendelson, *supra* note 13 at 90.

17 See Henry Finch, *Law, or a Discourse Thereof* (London: Lintot, 1759) [first published in 1627].

So how does the understanding of law evolve over time? That law evolves with society is aptly described by the maxim "where there is a society, there is law" (*ubi homo, ibi societas. Ubi societas, ibi ius. Ergo ubi homo, ibi ius*).[18] The close relation between society and law as well as its evolving nature can be observed at different stages in history. One pertinent example of law's changing face is found in the relation between law and magic.[19] While, in early history, law and magic seem to have been aligned, they have become separated later. A case for their alignment is provided by one of the oldest known legal codes, the Code of Hammurabi. In the Code of Hammurabi law and magic are aligned in the legal treatment of claims of witchcraft where the law uses magic to render justice.[20] Later, however, law and magic (like magic and science) have become disassociated, as a result of the general process of "disenchantment" (*Entzauberung*) through intellectualization, as Max Weber called it.[21] Resulting from this process, law became considered rational, logical and scientific as opposed to magic, which was understood as irrational, illogical and pseudoscientific.[22] Their difference was well summarized as follows:

> Certainly, law conceives of itself as an ethical, conceptual, and rational endeavor devoted to abstractions such as justice, fairness, sovereignty, and interior mental states of culpability. Magic, by contrast, consists of a body of principles or rituals of practical importance, with their own internal standard of rationality, largely governed by precedent, invoked in an archaic, secret, and cryptic language, and hostile to empirical observation.[23]

In practice, their separation can be exemplified by the laws of colonial era in Africa, which outlawed magic as "witchcraft", "superstition" or "charlatanry".[24] Paradoxically, the same laws, notably, in the process of their application and enforcement through the courts, were and continue to be based on practices

18 See Giorgio del Vecchio, "Statuality of Law" (1937) 19(1) *Journal of Comparative Legislation and International Law* 1 at 19; On the origin of the maxim, see also Giorgio del Vecchio, *Justice: An Historical and Philosophical Essay* (New York: Philosophical Library, 1953) at 124 and Roger Crisp (ed), *Aristotle – Nichomachean Ethics* (Cambridge: Cambridge University Press, 2004) at 154.

19 See Rostam J. Neuwirth, "Law and Magic: A(nother) Paradox?" (2014) 37(1) *Thomas Jefferson Law Review* 139.

20 See M. E. J. Richardson, *Hammurabi's Laws: Text, Translation and Glossary* (London: TNT Clark Int'l, 2000) at 43.

21 Max Weber, "Science as Vocation" in John Dreijmanis (ed), *Max Weber's Complete Writings on Academic and Political Vocations* (New York: Algora Publishing, 2008) 25 at 35.

22 See *e.g.* Lawrence E. Jerome, "Astrology and Modern Science: A Critical Analysis" (1973) 6(2) *Leonardo* 121 at 121 and Paul R. Thagard, "Why Astrology is a Pseudoscience" (1978) 1 *Proceedings of the Biennial Meeting of the Philosophy of Science Association* 223 at 225.

23 See Suzanne Last Stone, "Rabbinic Legal Magic: A New Look at Honi's Circle as the Construction of Law's Space" (2005) 17(1) *Yale Journal of Law & Humanities* 97 at 122.

24 See *e.g.* Clyde Pharr, "The Interdiction of Magic in Roman Law" (1932) 63 *Transactions and Proceedings of the American Philological Association* 269 and C. Clifton Roberts, "Witchcraft and Colonial Legislation" (1935) 8(4) *Journal of the International African Institute* 488.

and rituals that are comparable to those of magic rites.[25] This last point has been splendidly epitomized by the relation of *abra cadabra* to due process, or by the comparison of judicial robes to magicians' costumes and law clerks to magicians' assistants.[26] A similar comparison has been made between the pleading of cases before a jury and the performance of magic tricks before an audience.[27] Yet, and again paradoxically, law, and notably its modern version, is being perceived to be entirely different from magic.[28] Jerome Frank too pointed out their similarity but stated that law frequently uses "magical phrases" to conceal the lack of certainty which is desired.[29] Or equally, that "the formal law in a jury trial consists mostly of ineffective rigmaroles, incantations, or *semi-magical rituals* which the judge utters to the jury's uncomprehending ears".[30]

The separation serves as evidence for a general trend or an increasingly dual conception of law, perhaps in line with a more dualistic conception of science. This primarily dual conception of law also surfaces in the view of Henry S. Maine, reminiscent of George Orwell's doublethink,[31] that "with respect to that great portion of our legal system which is enshrined in cases and recorded in law reports, we habitually employ a double language, and entertain, as it would appear, a double and inconsistent set of ideas".[32]

From a linguistic perspective, the duality of our conception and evolving understanding of law is also reflected in the patterns by which scholarly publications about law carry the debate forward. As the scope of law is too vast to be packed into a single book entitled "law", most publications – following a trend of scientific specialization – usually confine themselves to well-established subcategories of law, like "constitutional law", "civil law", "criminal law" or "international law". Where the scientific consensus has not yet been sufficiently established or perhaps where the nature of law has not been fully understood, authors opt for a more cautious approach in trying to link the law to various closely or remotely related subject areas. These are so-called "law and . . ." issues, of which "law and magic" provides an excellent example.[33] The "law and . . ."

25 See *e.g.* Jerome Frank, *Courts on Trial: Myth and Reality in American Justice* (Princeton: Princeton University Press, 1949), Frederick A. Brodie, "The Magic of Civil Procedure" in Christine E. Corcos (ed), *Law and Magic: A Collection of Essays* (Durham: Carolina Academic Press, 2010) 159 and Jessie Allen, "Magical Realism" in Christine E. Corcos (ed), *Law and Magic: A Collection of Essays* (Durham: Carolina Academic Press, 2010) 195.

26 See *e.g.* Loren A. Smith, "Law and Magic: An Introduction Out of a Hat" in Christine E. Corcos (ed), *Law and Magic: A Collection of Essays* (Durham: Carolina Academic Press, 2010) 3 at 3.

27 See *e.g.* Kenneth M. Trombly, "Conjuring and the Courtroom: All I Needed to Know about Trying Cases I Learned by Doing Magic Shows" in Christine E. Corcos (ed), *Law and Magic: A Collection of Essays* (Durham: Carolina Academic Press, 2010) 339 at 339.

28 See also Last Stone, *supra* note 23 at 122.

29 Jerome Frank, *Law and the Modern Mind* (New Brunswick: Transaction Publishers 2009) at 68.

30 Jerome Frank, "What Courts Do in Fact – Part One" (1930) 26(6) *Illinois Law Review* 645 at 663 [*Italics* added].

31 See George Orwell, *Nineteen Eighty-Four* (London: Penguin Books, 2000).

32 Henry Sumner Maine, *Ancient Law*, 4th ed (London: John Murray, 1870) at 31.

33 See generally Christine E. Corcos (ed), *Law and Magic: A Collection of Essays* (Durham: Carolina Academic Press, 2010).

movement itself is perhaps best captured by the global appeal of the "law and society" movement, which comprises many more pairs, such as "law and politics"[34], "law and economics"[35] (which is not supposed to be confused with law and economics in general)[36] or "law and philosophy"[37] to mention but a few.

It is interesting to note, in line with the connection between art and science, that the law and society movement and various dual pairs can be traced back to one single link, that of "law and literature", which is widely credited to have originated from an eponymous article written by Benjamin N. Cardozo.[38] This is a meaningful piece of information given that the same author has also dedicated a whole book to the study of the "paradoxes of legal science".[39] Finally, the same movement has also been aptly summarized by Richard H. Weisberg in the form of the seemingly oxymoronic term "Poethics" marrying the two – at first – seemingly unrelated terms "poetry" and "ethics", which he defined as "associating two major human enterprises: establishing justice and storytelling".[40]

The law and society movement strongly displays the dualistic conception of law. However, the growing number of such "law and . . ." pairs, like "law and death",[41] "law and emotion",[42] "law and love",[43] "law and music",[44] "law and mind"[45] or "law and the senses",[46] has also recently led to a gradual trend of their convergence into

34 See *e.g.* David Beatty, "Law and Politics" (1996) 44(1) *The American Journal of Comparative Law* 131.

35 See *e.g.* Robert Cooter and Thomas Ulen, *Law & Economics*, 6th ed (Boston: Addison-Wesley, 2012).

36 See *e.g.* John R. Commons, "Law and Economics" (1925) 34(4) *The Yale Law Journal* 371.

37 See *e.g.* Francis J. Mootz, "Law and Philosophy, Philosophy and Law" (1994–1995) 26(1) *University of Toledo Law Review* 127.

38 See Benjamin N. Cardozo, "Law and Literature" (1939) 48(3) *Yale Law Journal* 489 (first published in 1925).

39 See Benjamin N. Cardozo, *The Paradoxes of Legal Science*, *supra* note 1.

40 See Richard H. Weisberg, *Poethics, and other Strategies of Law and Literature* (New York: Columbia University Press, 1992) at ix.

41 See *e.g.* Larry D. Stephan and Margaret N. Billings, "The Law and Death – An Overview" (1975) 1(2) *Journal of Contemporary Law* 224.

42 See *e.g.* Terry A. Maroney, "Law and Emotion: A Proposed Taxonomy of an Emerging Field" (2006) 30(2) *Law and Human Behavior* 119.

43 See *e.g.* Luis Legaz y Lacambra, *El Derecho y el Amor* (Barcelona: Bosch, 1976); Linda Ross Meyer and Martha Merrill Umphrey, "On the Conjoining of Law and Love" (2010) 28(3) *Quinnipiac Law Review* 585, Linda Ross Meyer, "Law Like Love?" (2006) 18(3) *Law and Literature* 431, Benjamin Shmueli, "Love and the Law, Children Against Mothers and Fathers: Or What's Love Got to Do With It?" (2010) 17(1) *Duke Journal of Gender Law & Policy* 131.

44 See *e.g.* Hermann Weber, *Literatur, Recht und Musik* (Berlin: Berliner Wissenschafts-Verlag, 2007) and Miguel Poiares Maduro, "Contrapunctual Law: Europe's Constitutional Pluralism in Action" in Neil Walker (ed), *Sovereignty in Transition* (Oxford: Hart Publishing, 2003) 501 at 523.

45 See *e.g.* Rostam J. Neuwirth, "Law and the Mind: A New Role for Comparative Law?" in Tong Io Cheng and Salvatore Mancuso (eds), *New Frontiers of Comparative Law* (Hong Kong: LexisNexis, 2013) 11 and Jerome Frank, *Law and the Modern Mind*, *supra* note 29.

46 See Lionel Bently and Leo Flynn (eds), *Law and the Senses: Sensational Jurisprudence* (London: Pluto Press, 1996).

a more complex conception of law by means of a "law as . . ." approach,[47] like the one of "law as mnemonics"[48] or "law as process".[49] Ultimately, once the degree of understanding has reached a critical point, the dualistic conception of law makes place for a more oxymoronic one, as reflected in many legal oxymora or paradoxes. To what extent essentially oxymoronic concepts perform an important role in the evolution of law will be discussed in Chapter 7. Before their role can be assessed in detail, it is necessary to inquire into their present role in the theory and practice of law.

5.2 Essentially oxymoronic concepts in case law

THE Lawyers, of whose Art the Basis,
Was raising Feuds and splitting Cases.[50]

So far in this book, essentially oxymoronic concepts have been found to be used primarily in poetry and the arts, but they also seem gradually to have begun to pervade the realms of science and daily life. Legal science was found to be no exception in this regard. At the same time, the dominant conception of law and legal reasoning in our time was found to be dualistic in the sense that it is based on binary logic as expressed by the syllogism and many similar instruments. If this is true, then it can be expected that essentially oxymoronic concepts, and notably oxymora as concepts expressing at the same time two antagonistic meanings, must naturally cause some problems to the proper interpretation and application of laws. In short, they should also belong to the category of "hard cases". It is thus time to see if the two assumptions of essentially oxymoronic concepts being on the rise also in legal practice and causing problems in legal reasoning hold true.

As a word of clarification, it is for the sake of simplicity that the following analysis is mainly centred on the literal occurrence of oxymora alone and largely excludes paradoxes. The reason is that paradoxes or paradoxical situations seem to arise more frequently. For instance, in one case, it was opined that "the protection of private rights upon occasion involves an invasion of those rights [which] is in theory a paradox but, in the world as it happens to be, [it] is a realistic problem requiring a practical answer".[51] Moreover, paradoxes often occur more in an implicit way and are harder to detect.[52] Therefore, from the perspective of the syllogism and classical

47 See the overview in Neuwirth, "Law and Magic", *supra* note 19 at 174–175.

48 See Rostam J. Neuwirth, "Law as Mnemonics: The Mind as the Prime Source of Normativity" (2008) 2(1) *European Journal of Legal Studies* 143.

49 See *e.g.* Sally Falk Moore, *Law as Process: An Anthropological Approach* (Boston: Routledge & K. Paul 1978).

50 See Bernard Mandeville, *The Fable of the Bees: or, Private Vices and Publick Benefits*, 3rd ed (London: T. Tonson, 1724) at 4.

51 *Agnew v. Board of Governors*, 153 F.2d 785 (1946) at 171.

52 See *e.g.* the so-called "blackhole cases", which paradoxically reversed the usual roles of judges and scientists, putting judges in the role of "experts" deciding on whether the Large Hadron Collider experiments are capable of destroying the whole planet or not; see, *Sancho v. United States DOE*,

logic, oxymora are more rigid than paradoxes and, hence, pose a more serious challenge to the process of legal reasoning. For this reason, the following examples from jurisprudence will primarily focus on oxymora rather than paradoxes.

5.2.1 Soft law vs hard law – *"pure law"*

To begin with the nature and origin of law, it is interesting to look into issues related to the definition, validity and scope of law. A first important usage of the term "oxymoron" in a case is that of "pure law", which the Ontario Superior Court of Justice considered to constitute an oxymoron as law can never be pure.[53] This judicial clarification puts to end an old theoretical debate dividing protagonists of legal positivism and those of "law and society", a controversy that is also known by the dichotomy of "law in books" versus "law in action" or "law in context".[54] It is also synonymous with the debate about the relationship between law and morality, which is represented by the dichotomy of a positivist thesis of separation and its counterpart, the non-positivist thesis of connection.[55] What can be "pure", albeit only temporarily used as a method, is, as Hans Kelsen demonstrated, a "theory of law".[56] This is an example of yet another divide caused by a dual conception, like the attempt to separate theory from practice, as it continues to dominate the scientific understanding of law. Akin to the separation of theory from practice, or law from morality, is also the dichotomy of law and religion or the separation of church and state also known as secularism.[57]

Another concept in legal discourse that has been identified as an oxymoron is "soft law".[58] We have already read about the oxymora of "soft power" in political science or "tender force" in poetry. In law too, softness is used to oppose the traditional hard conception of law.[59] Generally, it can be said that "soft law" is

2010 U.S. App. LEXIS 17726 (9th Cir. Haw., 24 August 2010); German *Bundesverfassungsgericht* (Federal Constitutional Court), BVerfG, 2 BvR 2502/08 (18 February 2010); and the European Court of Human Rights (ECHR), *Goritschnig v. Austria*, Complaint No. 41028/08, ECHR-LGer11.00R(CD1) (9 December 2010) [on file with the author]; see generally Eric E. Johnson, "The Black Hole Case: The Injunction Against the End of the World" (2009) 76(4) *Tennessee Law Review* 819.

53 Ontario Superior Court of Justice, *Jackson v. Vaughan (City)*, 2010 ONSC 969, 13–14 (2010) and Ontario Superior Court of Justice, *Silveira v. Ontario (Minister of Transportation)*, 2011 ONSC 4272, 22 (2011).

54 See *e.g.* Philip Selznick, "'Law in Context' Revisited" (2003) 30(2) *Journal of Law and Society* 177 and Roscoe Pound, "Law in Books and Law in Action" (1910) 44(1) *American Law Review* 12.

55 See Robert Alexy, "On Necessary Relations Between Law and Morality" (1989) 2(2) *Ratio Juris* 167 at 167.

56 Hans Kelsen, *A Pure Theory of Law* (Berkeley: University of California Press, 1967).

57 On the origin of secularism, see also George J. Holyoake, *The Principles of Secularism*, 3rd ed (London: Austin & Co., 1871) at 8–10.

58 See also John F. Murphy, *The Evolving Dimensions of International Law: Hard Choices for the World Community* (Cambridge: Cambridge University Press, 2010) at 20 and Anthony C. Arend, *Legal Rules and International Society* (New York: Oxford University Press, 1999) at 25.

59 See also Prosper Weil, "Towards Relative Normativity in International Law" (1983) 77(3) *American Journal of International Law* 413 at 414–415 (Fn 7).

an oxymoron, because when law is soft (or non-binding) it is not law.[60] Hence, the main reason why soft law is not law is rooted in a binary conception of law expressed through the binding and non-binding divide.[61] Similarly, the term "binding policy" was called an oxymoron because the court considered that a "non-binding but valid policy statement or interpretive rule may seem a contradiction in terms".[62] It may indeed be considered an oxymoron because, as opposed to laws, policies are usually not legally binding. Similar concepts, like "mandatory guidelines" or "binding recommendations" were also termed as oxymora in other cases.[63] In further cases, the concepts of "mild persecution",[64] "forced consent",[65] "consent to an arrest"[66] and "negligent use of excessive force"[67] were qualified as oxymora. From labour law, the concept of "voluntary dismissal" – used to denote the end of a contractual relationship between employer and employee – was also qualified as an oxymoron.[68]

A final oxymoron related to the hardness or softness of the law is provided by the death penalty, as possibly the harshest sanction imposed by law. This severest form of punishment is called, in yet another essentially oxymoronic concept, "legal homicide".[69] Homicide has also been addressed in a related context, that of self-defence, where it may be termed "permissible killing".[70] Sometimes backed by a cultural defence argument, attempts to justify homicide are made by referring to "honour killings", i.e. a family member killing another for bringing dishonour to the family.[71] In a difficult case appealing the decision of custody over three

60 See also Jaye Ellis, "Shades of Grey: Soft Law and the Validity of Public International Law" (2012) 25(2) *Leiden Journal of International Law* 313 at 318–319; Andrew T. Guzman and Timothy L. Meyer, "International Soft Law" (2010) 2(1) *Journal of Legal Analysis* 171 at 172, and Malcolm N. Shaw, *International Law*, 6th ed (Cambridge: Cambridge University Press, 2008) at 117.

61 See Gregory C. Shaffer and Mark A. Pollack, "Hard vs. Soft Law: Alternatives, Complements and Antagonists in International Governance" (2010) 94(3) *Minnesota Law Review* 703 at 707 and 712–717.

62 *Vietnam Veterans of America v. Secretary of the Navy*, 269 U.S. App. D.C. 35 (D.C. Cir. 1988) at para 51–52.

63 *U.S. v. West*, 552 F. Supp. 2d 74, 75 (D. Mass. 2008) and Queens Bench Division, *R (T-Mobile (UK) Ltd and others v. Competition Commission and others*, [2003] All ER (D) 377 at para 78.

64 *Vata v. Gonzales*, 243 Fed. Appx. 930, 942 (6th Cir. 2007); see also *Shehu v. Gonzales*, 443 F.3d 435, 440–441 (5th Cir. 2006).

65 *Doe v. Prosecutor*, 566 F. Supp. 2d 862, 877 (S.D. Ind. 2008).

66 *Larez v. Holcomb*, 16 F.3d 1513, 1517 (9th Cir. 1994).

67 *Secondo v. Campbell*, 327 Fed. Appx. 126, 131 (7th Cir. 2009); see also *Rivera v. Cohen*, 2009 U.S. Dist. LEXIS 88930, 7 (M.D. Fla., 2009).

68 *Agco Ltd and another v. Kellaway*, [2007] EWHC 3354 (Ch) at para 15.

69 See *e.g.* William J. Bowers, Glenn L. Pierce, and John F. McDevitt, *Legal Homicide: Death as Punishment in America, 1864–1982* (Boston: Northeastern University Press, 1984) and Michael Petöcz, *Das unmoralische der Todesstrafe: Nachtrag zu dessen* (Leipzig: F.A. Brockhaus, 1841) at 80 ("*erlaubter Mord*" or "permitted homicide").

70 See Suzanne Uniacke, *Permissible Killing: The Self-Defence Justification of Homicide* (Cambridge: Cambridge University Press, 1994).

71 See *e.g.* John A. Cohan, "Honor Killings and the Cultural Defense" (2009–2010) 40(2) *California Western International Law Journal* 177 at 191.

children, which was taken in the wake of a series of allegations of domestic violence, the judge criticized "honour killings" as a wholly inappropriate oxymoron and, most of all, characterized them as acts of simply sordid, criminal behaviour.[72] A related term is "mercy killing", which has also been qualified as an oxymoron and said to include, for instance, "suicide" and "euthanasia", because these (and other) forms of killing are cruel and, thus, "not 'merciful' to the perpetrators, the survivors, or the human race".[73] The notion of euthanasia may well be qualified as an oxymoron, given that in its Greek origin it means "a gentle and easy death".[74] As a final point, on the softer side of the spectrum of different punishments, imposing a monetary fine of "zero penalty" also appears as an oxymoron because when the amount is zero ("0"), it stops being a penalty in the sense of a monetary fine.[75]

5.2.2 Guilt vs innocence – *"wilful negligence"*

There are also numerous occurrences of essentially oxymoronic concepts in case law, which deal with difficulties in accessing the mind of a person and establishing the precise link between the apparently intangible world of cognition and the tangible world of actions. This problem arose in a case concerning an armed robbery in which the defendant allegedly killed the owner of a petrol station and defended himself by stating that the "killing was an accident that occurred during the course of a struggle over the gun used in the robbery".[76] The court, however, found the defence argument contradictory, as "in both law and common sense, accident and malice are conceptually incompatible" and that the term "malicious accident" is an oxymoron.[77] Similar oxymora raised in other cases were "intentional negligence"[78] and "willful negligence".[79] Also "negligent aiming", in the context of the death of a person caused by the handling of a loaded firearm in an unsafe manner, was qualified as an oxymoron.[80] The opposite combination, that is to say, "deliberate indifference", was also found to constitute an oxymoron and

72 *Re B-M (Care Orders: Risk)*, [2009] EWCA Civ 205 at para 37 (United Kingdom).

73 See Saleem, *A Desire for Death* (India: Partridge Publishing, 2013) at 255 and W. Neil Gallagher, *The Money Doctor's Guide to Taking Care of Yourself When No One Else Will* (New Jersey: John Wiley & Sons, 2006) at 110.

74 See Craig Paterson, *Assisted Suicide and Euthanasia: A Natural Law Ethics Approach* (Aldershot: Ashgate, 2008) at 11.

75 Federal Court of Appeal Toronto (Ontario Canada), *(Attorney General) v. Gauley*, [2002] F.C.J. No. 815 at para 10.

76 *Houston v. Dutton*, 50 F.3d 381, 383 (6th Cir. 1995).

77 *Ibid.*

78 *Cine Forty-Second Street Theatre Corp. v. Allied Artists Pictures Corp.*, 602 F.2d 1062, 1067 (2nd Cir. 1979).

79 Alberta Court of Queen's Bench, *Wong Estate v. Liberty Mutual Insurance Co.*, [2009] A.J. No. 1073 at para 50.

80 New Brunswick Court of Appeal, *Optimum Insurance Co. v. Donovan*, [2009] N.B.J. No. 18 at para 12.

the court also went on to state, using Judge Posner's words,[81] that "like other famous oxymorons in law [deliberate indifference] evades rather than expresses precise meaning".[82]

Similarly, "conspiracy to commit second-degree murder" was defined as an oxymoron because to find intent to conspire and conclude that the defendant lacked deliberation or premeditation is contradictory and because "second degree murder is an intentional killing that is committed without deliberation and premeditation".[83] The same problem arose in a case where the court qualified the crime of attempted involuntary manslaughter as "at first blush, something of an oxymoron" as attempt is considered a specific intent crime in the law.[84] Another contradiction was detected in calling the consistent criminal behaviour aberrant, which was said to constitute not only an oxymoron (e.g. "aberrant recidivist") but – in the words of the judge – would also "make us look like oxen or morons or both".[85]

By the same token, committing a crime or a statutory violation in "good faith" was generally held to pose a classic oxymoron.[86] Indeed, it was also found that "for a Judge to find that an illegal immigrant to Canada acted in good faith, could be nothing short of an oxymoron".[87] From the US immigration laws a similar contradiction is reported in a case where the court wrote that it "may seem, at first blush an oxymoron to be 'admitted' to the United States and yet 'inadmissible' at the same time".[88] This, however, the judge explained by the "often opaque world of immigration statutes".[89] Probably, the terms "(permanent) resident alien" (or "resident immigrant") as used by immigration laws also constitute oxymora.[90] It was precisely in the context of a court determining a person's status as a resident alien that the question arose when (and where) a person "begins to usually reside" – a phrase coined by the legislature, which the court described as appearing "at first blush to be something of an oxymoron".[91] Immigration law or actually the procedures of its implementation also provided the stage for another funny but adequate oxymoron, namely that of "bureaucratic efficiency", which

81 Cf. *Duckworth v. Franzen*, 780 F.2d 645, 652 (7th Cir. 1985) see also *Simmons v. City of Philadelphia*, 947 F.2d 1042, 1060 (3rd Cir. 1991).

82 *Howard v. Adkison*, 887 F.2d 134, 139 (8th Cir. 1989).

83 *Kleve v. Hill*, 202 F.3d 1155, 1158 (9th Cir. 2000).

84 *United States v. Zabawa*, 134 Fed. Appx. 60, 64 (6th Cir. 2005).

85 *United States v. Bradstreet*, 135 F.3d 46, 56 (1st Cir. 1998).

86 *McGinty v. State of New York*, 193 F.3d 64, 69 (2nd Cir.1999).

87 Tax Court of Canada, *Haule v. M.N.R.*, 1998 Can. Tax Ct. LEXIS 3081, 21 (1998).

88 *Sum v. Holder*, 602 F.3d 1092, 1093 (9th Cir. 2010).

89 *Ibid.*

90 See *e.g.* Sections 231 and 247 Immigration and Nationality Act of 1952, 66 Stat. 163 (27 June 1952) and Section 9 Immigration and Nationality Act of 1965, 79 Stat. 911 (30 June 1968); see also Siegfried Hesse, "The Constitutional Status of the Lawfully Admitted Permanent Resident Alien: The Inherent Limits of the Power to Expel" (1959) 69(2) *The Yale Law Journal* 262.

91 Alberta Provincial Court, *Alberta (Child, Youth and Family Enhancement Act, Director) v. V.M.*, [2009] A.J. No. 1395 at para 148.

aptly described the experience of an applicant for permanent residence awaiting a decision delayed for more than a decade "after many twists and turns between federal government offices".[92]

In the beginning, the desire of the law and of lawyers for certainty realized by the establishment of sharp boundaries was presented in the form of a trespass, which is either a trespass or not.[93] It is therefore no surprise that the term "tolerated trespasser" was met with consternation in court and called an oxymoron.[94] A similar contradiction was found in a "guilty plea under the Alford doctrine", which was called a judicial oxymoron.[95] The so-called "Alford plea" originates from a case against Henry Alford, indicted with first-degree murder, who pleaded guilty to second-degree murder in view of strong evidence against him but despite himself stating that he was innocent so as to avoid the possibility of being sentenced to death.[96] In his own words, Alford said:

> I pleaded guilty on second degree murder because they said there is too much evidence, but I ain't shot no man, but I take the fault for the other man. We never had an argument in our life and I just pleaded guilty because they said if I didn't they would gas me for it, and that is all.[97]

Put briefly, the Alford plea amounts to a defendant expressing the apparent paradox of being guilty and innocent at the same time. In fact, though, as we often do, it points more to a situation where a person says one thing and believes in or means another.

Such problem was encountered in the context of the meaning of harassment. In this regard, the distinction between the concepts of "unwelcome" and "welcome sexual harassment" proved to be problematic. The latter was termed an oxymoron, because if the employee demonstrates by word or deed that the "harassment" is welcome, it no longer constitutes harassment.[98] Hypothetically, it is noteworthy that the distinction between welcome and unwelcome harassment would be more difficult to assess in the case of a sadomasochist. In another case, the notion of "negligent sexual molestation" was equally qualified as an oxymoron.[99]

92 Federal Court (Toronto, Ontario), *Tang v. Canada (Minister of Citizenship and Immigration)*, [2009] F.C.J. No. 671 at para 1.

93 See Wheeler Cook, *supra* note 9 at 333.

94 *Austin v. Southwark London Borough Council*, [2011] AC 355 at 42 (United Kingdom Supreme Court).

95 *United States v. Savage*, 542 F.3d 959, 1126 (2nd Cir. 2008).

96 See also Todd Markle, "The Misunderstood Alford Plea: A Primer" (2013) 19(1) *Georgia Bar Journal* 8.

97 *North Carolina v. Alford*, 400 U.S. 25, 28 (1970).

98 *Carr v. Allison Gas Turbine Div.*, 32 F.3d 1007 (7th Cir. 1994).

99 *Jude et al., v. City of Milwaukee*, 2007 U.S. Dist. LEXIS 82809, 17 (E.D. Wis. 2007).

Another case could have been rephrased by the question whether someone can be married and not married at the same time. Or, more precisely from a legal perspective, whether someone can be married to two persons at the same time. This question arose in an appeal case in Virginia by a person who had been convicted of bigamy in violation of the Virginia bigamy law. The appellant argued that it was "legally impossible" for him to be convicted of bigamy under Code § 18.2-362, which makes it a criminal offence for any "married" person to "marry another person". His argument was that because bigamous marriages are legally void, he could not have legally married another person, which means that "neither he nor anyone else can be prosecuted under it".[100] The court, however, disagreed and qualified his argument as constituting a "legislative oxymoron" and affirmed the conviction.[101]

Lastly, a person being dishonest by trying to "discharge just debts" was circumscribed by the antonym of an "honest bankrupt" which was characterized by the court as an oxymoron.[102] Or more generally, the oxymoronic term "just fraud" also appeared in another case. However, the judge was less impressed by literary accounts embodied in oxymora like "honourable villain"[103] to use Shakespeare's words or the legendary status given to "honest thieves" like Robin Hood.[104] Instead, he found that "a cause can hardly be 'just' when it entails helping an embezzler avoid restitution for her crimes, and when the expression of the cause involves intentional fraud", adding that "'just fraud' in this context is a perverse oxymoron that sets the modifier on its head".[105] As an epitome for the duality of thinking, or antonym to an "honest thief", the Indian Supreme Court qualified the term "dishonest judicial personage" as an oxymoron, because judges are not mere employees but are holders of public office of great trust and responsibility instead.[106]

5.2.3 Space vs time – *"spacetime"*

There is another category of "hard cases" that involve oxymora which are strongly dependent on our current framework for the perception of time and space. The oxymoron "spacetime" was mentioned above but time and space are also closely tied to law.[107] This shows that the understanding of law evolves with the dominant scientific paradigm although not always simultaneously, as Thomas Kuhn has shown. The link between the changing understanding of spacetime and the evolution of law is complex. Generally, as far as space is concerned, the conception of the

100 *Cole v. Commonwealth*, 58 Va. App. 642, 647 (Va. 2011).
101 *Ibid.*
102 *Otto v. Niles*, 106 F.3d 1456, 1464 (9th Cir. 1997).
103 See William Shakespeare, *Romeo and Juliet* (Philadelphia: J.B. Lippincott, 1871) at 172.
104 See Michael Drayton, *The Works of Michael Drayton* (London: John Hughs, 1748) at 376.
105 *Murray v. Bammer (In re Bammer)*, 131 F.3d 788, 791-92 (9th Cir. 1997).
106 Supreme Court of India, *High Court of Judicature at Bombay v. Shahikants Patil & Anor*, [2000] 1 LRI 532 at para 23.
107 See *e.g.* Irus Braverman et al. (eds), *The Expanding Spaces of Law: A Timely Legal Geography* (Stanford: Stanford Law Books, 2014).

law's validity continues to be primarily territorial. A strictly territorial conception of law, however, is increasingly becoming challenged by the notion of cyberspace and related technological and societal developments.[108] Tellingly, the link between cyberspace and law as mediator between government and the governed has been termed an "unsettled paradox".[109]

Even within the current paradigm of space, however, it may sometimes be problematic to find the right terms. In one case, it was suggested that an object is "capable of being delivered and yet incapable of being moved". This description of a fact, albeit more akin to a paradox, was described as approaching an oxymoron.[110] Similarly, in view of the strong territorial conception of international law originating from the Treaty of Westphalia,[111] it also comes as no surprise that the term "stateless corporation" was qualified as an oxymoron.[112] This, in particular, because similar to a state, and a territorial state in particular, a corporation is a legal person made from a legal fiction.[113] Put differently, a corporation is a creation purely of law, which unlike an individual, can "exist only through an exercise of sovereignty".[114] In the end, even the term "legal fiction" can be considered an oxymoron because it means that the law asserts "something which is known to be false".[115] Such was the finding of a court which called a "conclusive presumption" an oxymoron because a real presumption is usually rebuttable.[116] Finally, the question of sovereignty exercised by parliament was said to give rise to another paradox, namely "that the parliament stands above the law in the sense that it can change any law that is not to its liking" but "gains this position of being above the law only by subjecting itself to law – the law of its own internal procedure".[117]

108 See *e.g.* Henry H. Perritt, Jr., "The Internet as a Threat to Sovereignty – Thoughts on the Internet's Role in Strengthening National and Global Governance" (1998) 5(2) *Indiana Journal of Global Legal Studies* 423 at 436–437 and David R. Johnson and David Post, "Law And Borders – The Rise of Law in Cyberspace" (1996) 48(5) *Stanford Law Review* 1367 at 1367; but see Jack L. Goldsmith, "The Internet and the Abiding Significance of Territorial Sovereignty" (1998) 5(2) *Indiana Journal of Global Legal Studies* 475.

109 See David G. Post, "The "Unsettled Paradox": The Internet, the State, and the Consent of the Governed" (1998) 5(2) *Indiana Journal of Global Legal Studies* 521 at 521.

110 *Ogden Martin Sys. of Indianapolis, Inc. v. Whiting Corp.*, 179 F.3d 523, 529 (7th Cir. 1999).

111 But see Yasuaki Onuma, "When was the Law of International Society Born? – An Inquiry of the History of International Law from an Intercivilizational Perspective" (2000) 2(1) *Journal of History of international Law* 1 and Stéphane Beaulac, "The Westphalian Model in Defining International Law: Challenging the Myth" (2004) 8(2) *Australian Journal of History of Law* 181.

112 *Southern Cross Overseas Agencies, Inc. v. Wah Kwong Shipping Group Ltd.*, 181 F.3d 410, 415 (3rd Circ. 1999); see also Niron Hashaia and Tamar Almorb, "Gradually Internationalizing 'Born Global' Firms: An Oxymoron?" (2004) 13(4) *International Business Review* 465.

113 See Sanford A. Schane, "Corporation is a Person: The Language of a Legal Fiction" (1987) 61(3) *Tulane Law Review* 563 at 563.

114 *Koehler v. Bank of Bermuda*, 229 F.3d 187, 192 (2nd Cir. 2000).

115 See Lon L. Fuller, "Legal Fictions" (1930) 25(4) *Illinois Law Review* 363 at 393; see also Lon L. Fuller, *Legal Fictions* (Stanford: Stanford University Press, 1967) at 1.

116 *Ragsdale v. Turnock*, 941 F.2d 501, 508 (7th Cir. 1991).

117 See Lon L. Fuller, *The Morality of Law* (New Haven: Yale University Press, 1969) at 115.

From space back to time, the understanding of time, on the other hand, directly impinges upon the law, and notably its validity and our legal thinking.[118] Based on law, time is an abstract and yet a concretely binding, differentiated measure and a standard measure for human behaviour.[119] In its understanding and computation of time, law also relies on science. However, even the world of physics struggles with time conceived in linear terms progressing from the past into the future as expressed in Stephen Hawking's question, why do we remember the past but not the future?[120] Hence, resembling a legal version of the movie *Back to the Future*, or rather "forward to the past", the question of the interpretation of laws through inquiries into what has been termed "subsequent legislative history" was rejected on the basis of the argument that it constitutes an oxymoron because statements referring to the time after the enactment of the law cannot be taken into account in the interpretation of the legislative history.[121] The synonym "post-enactment legislative history" was also termed an oxymoron because, as it was explained, "the history of an event lies in its past, not its future".[122] By contrast to this statement, in international law, the general rule of interpretation also suggests that, together with the context, any subsequent agreement between the parties and any subsequent practice in the application of the treaty should be taken into account.[123]

Another example of a time-related oxymoron in law is the notion of "long-time, limited term positions". This concept was termed an oxymoron in a case concerning a university employee who worked for 14 years as a "limited term employee" at a university and was struggling to transform her job into a permanent position.[124] Similarly, in a case concerning a dispute over a paid retirement plan, the court defined the concept of "post-termination *contingent* 'accrued benefits'" as an oxymoron due to the inherent tension between contingent and accrued.[125] A similar linguistic problem was encountered in another case where the court encountered the concept of "substantially simultaneously", which it at first blush qualified as an oxymoron, because the "ordinary understanding of the word 'simultaneously' is binary, either something happens simultaneously or it does not".[126] As if it were dealing with a "temporary oxymoron", the court ultimately solved the dilemma by giving the term "substantially simultaneously" the construction "in substantially overlapping durations".[127]

118 See generally Günther Winkler, *Zeit und Recht: Kritische Anmerkungen zur Zeitgebundenheit des Rechts und des Rechtsdenkens* (Wien: Springer, 1995).
119 *Ibid* at 545.
120 See Stephen Hawking, *A Brief History of Time* (New York: Bantam Books, 1998) at 148.
121 *United States v. Childress*, 104 F.3d 47, 52 (4th Cir. 1996).
122 *American Hosp. Ass'n v. NLRB*, 899 F.2d 651, 657 (7th Cir. 1990); see also *United States v. Carlton*, 512 U.S. 26, 39 (1994).
123 *United Nations Convention on the Law of Treaties*, concluded at Vienna May 23, 1969, 1155 U.N.T.S. 331 (entry into force: January 27, 1980).
124 *Ashman v. Barrows*, 438 F.3d 781 (7th Cir. (Wisc.) 2006) at 782.
125 *Tilley v. Mead Corp.*, 927 F.2d 756 (4th Cir. 1991) at 763.
126 *3M v. EnvisionWare*, 2010 U.S. Dist. LEXIS 128664 (D. Minn. 2010) at 13–15.
127 *Ibid.*

Time generally matters in the pursuit of justice, as is captured by the legal maxim "justice delayed is justice denied".[128] And time also mattered greatly in a case involving an alleged injury to the freedom of the press. In the case the counsel for the newspapers argued that "even delay of the ability to report the 'news' is an injury to the Freedom of the Press", which gave rise to the characterization of "old news" as an oxymoron.[129] Finally, in times of an acceleration of perception and almost everything, it comes as no surprise that the opposite acts of buying and selling can – in certain circumstances – give rise to an oxymoron. This happened in a case where "buying with a view of reselling" was considered an oxymoron when carried out with the intention to realize a capital gain, as it were turning "the project into an adventure in the nature of trade".[130]

Another case that could also be construed as a time-related problem emerged in the context of the application of an Act aimed at guaranteeing the survival of endangered species. The Act defined "endangered species" as "any species which is in danger of extinction throughout all or a significant portion of its range".[131] In a case trying to assess the potential survival of a lizard in its public land habitat, it was the part of the phrase "extinct throughout . . . a significant portion of its range" which the court qualified as "something of an oxymoron" and led it to the conclusion that the statute is "therefore inherently ambiguous, as it appears to use language in a manner in some tension with ordinary usage".[132] The reason was that "to speak of a species that is 'in danger of extinction' throughout 'a significant portion of its range' may seem internally inconsistent, since 'extinction' suggests total rather than partial disappearance".[133] The phrase could also be understood as a hysteron proteron where the lizard will first be extinct and then fall under the protection of the Act as an "endangered species". Or, in other words, the case at issue features a problem similar to the sorites paradox. With regard to lizards, it means to assess precisely when the lizard is a species that is not endangered, is in danger of extinction, partially extinct and fully extinct.

Perhaps one of the strongest examples of a conflict between the objectives related to legal certainty and changes threatening the integrity of law over time is found in the context of reconsidering or reopening a closed case due to judicial error or the emergence of important new facts.[134] The related legal remedies are very important, especially in capital punishment cases, which have been found to be "persistently and systematically fraught with alarming amounts of error".[135]

128 See *e.g.* Nathan the Babylonian (ed), *The Ethics of the Fathers* (Edinburgh: Robert Young, 1852) at 30 [Ch. V, 9].
129 Alberta Court of Queen's Bench, *R. v. Trang (D.) et al.*, 2001 ABQB 437 at para 72.
130 Tax Court of Canada, *Frank Deluca v R.*, 2001 Can. Tax Ct. LEXIS 1704 at para 4.
131 16 U.S.C. § 1532(6); Endangered Species Act, 16 U.S.C. Sections 1531–1544.
132 *Defenders of Wildlife v. Norton*, 258 F.3d 1136, 1141 (9th Cir. 2001).
133 *Ibid.*
134 See generally Max Alsberg, *Justizirrtum und Wiederaufnahme* (Berlin: Langenscheidt, 1913).
135 See James S. Liebman et al., "Capital Attrition: Error Rates in Capital Cases, 1973-1995" (1999) 78(7) *Texas Law Review* 1839 at 1844.

From a logical perspective, however, it is not possible to reopen a dismissed case, which may be called an oxymoron because when a case is dismissed rather than closed, there is no closed case to reopen.[136]

5.2.4 Substantive vs procedural law – *"substantive due process"*

Another important element of modern law is found in the dichotomy between substantive and procedural law. Substantive law is usually understood to refer to the norms laid down in laws and statutes that define rights and duties, whereas procedural law denominates the norms that contain the rules for their implementation. Substantive law has been described as identifying the law and procedural as creating the law. Another way to differentiate them is to say that substantive law is "the rules which determine the legal relations between the parties when all the facts are known or assumed are rules of substance" and rules of procedure designate all "other rules [that] have to do with the methods by which the machinery for the administration of justice is set in motion, the methods by which the limits of the controversy are defined and the materials for decision are to be presented and handled".[137] Nonetheless, similar to the dichotomy of law and fact, the distinction between substantive and procedural norms can also be extremely difficult to draw in practically all areas of law.[138] Moreover, it is subject to variations across different contexts and notably different legal systems. At the transnational level, it gives rise to the oxymoronic term of "substantive procedural law".[139] Especially in the context of the rules of evidence, their distinction was called "artificial and illusory".[140] The fact is that the distinction is being made and their dichotomy continues to be important even if its foundation is weak or procedure is supposed to be embedded in substantive law.[141] Substantive law has been described as acting in the shadow of procedural law coupled with the statement that "procedural separateness makes little sense in the real world".[142] And it was in the "real world" of the courts where the difficult distinction gave rise to another important essentially oxymoronic concept – that of "substantive due process", which was probably coined by Judge Richard E. Posner who called it a

136 *Sole Survivor Corp. v. Buxbaum*, 2009 WL 210471, 13 (C.D.Cal 2009).

137 See *e.g.* Edmund M. Morgan, "Rules of Evidence – Substantive or Procedural?" (1957) 10(3) *Vanderbilt Law Review* 467 at 468.

138 See *e.g.* Wheeler Cook, *supra* note 9.

139 See The American Law Institute, *ALI/UNIDROIT Principles of Transnational Civil Procedure* (Cambridge: Cambridge University Press, 2006) at xxxiii.

140 See Charles Frederic Chamberlayne, *A Modern Treatise on Evidence: Administration*, vol I (Albany: Matthew Bender & Co., 1911) at 217.

141 See *e.g.* Thomas O. Main, "The Procedural Foundation of Substantive Law" (2009) 87(4) *Washington University Law Review* 1 at 3.

142 See Phyllis T. Baumann, Judith O. Brown and Stephen N. Subrin, "Substance in the Shadow of Procedure: The Integration of Substantive and Procedural Law in Title VII Cases" (1992) 33(2) *Boston College Law Review* 211 at 216.

"ubiquitous oxymoron".[143] Here the apparent contradiction arises from the view that "the due process clauses of the Constitution impose substantive restraints on governmental power".[144] In short, the emergence of several oxymora reflects not only the difficulties but perhaps also the presumptions within the dichotomous distinction between substantive and procedural law. In another case related to a tension between form and content, the notion of a "verbal invoice" was regarded as a novel form of bookkeeping and was therefore qualified as an oxymoron, albeit a not very appealing one.[145]

5.2.5 Certainty vs uncertainty – *"forensic science"*

Another crucial distinction concerns the question of the distinction between knowledge and ignorance or probability and certainty. The tensions between those antagonisms surfaced literally in one case, where a company that suspected an employee of dishonestly extending her disability leave and secretly videotaped her (instead of consulting her doctor) claimed it was guilty of an act of "knowing ignorance", which the court described as an oxymoron.[146] There are other occurrences of oxymora, especially when it comes to the distinction between laymen and experts and between experts acting diligently or not. In this regard, as opposed to witchcraft or charlatanry, the usual standard of care is that the expert did not carry out his/her duty in "accordance with the law of the art" (*de lege artis*). This is of particular relevance in negligence cases, such as medical malpractice. In proceedings of this kind, the court expressed the opinion that the term "a reasonable degree of medical probability" is a proper manner of expression for an expert physician witness in a civil negligence case whereas the term "within a reasonable degree of medical certainty" is an oxymoron in that "certainty is an absolute term, whereas reasonable degree is a relative term and connotes selection from several reasonable choices or diagnoses".[147] Following this line of distinction, the term "scientific validity" applied in the context of a "non-scientific expert testimony" was also held to form an oxymoron.[148]

In a tort liability case, which concerned the possibility of the death of a smoker having been caused by asbestos used in cigarette filters, an apparent lack of scientific authority by one expert testifying in the trial gave rise to forensic science being termed "an oxymoron".[149] Elsewhere too, forensic science has

143 *Ellis v. Hamilton*, 669 F.2d 510, 512 (7th Cir. 1982); see also *United States v. Carlton*, 512 U.S. 26, 39 (1994).

144 See James W. Ely, Jr., "The Oxymoron Reconsidered: Myth and Reality in the Origins of Substantive Due Process" (1999) 16(2) *Constitutional Commentary* 315 at 315.

145 Alberta Court of Appeal, *Calmont Leasing Ltd. v. Kredl et al.*, 165 A.R. 343, 348 (1995).

146 *Kariotis v. Navistar International Transportation Corp.*, 131 F.3d 672 (7th Cir. 1997) at 677.

147 *Bayliss v. Woodrum*, 33 Va. Cir. 338 (1994).

148 Ontario Court of Appeal, *R. v. Abbey*, [2009] O.J. No. 3534 at 108 and Ontario Superior Court of Justice, *R. v. Woodcock*, [2010] O.J. No. 1281 at para 9.

149 *Braun v. Lorillard, Inc.*, 84 F.R.D. 230 (7th Cir. 1996) at 11.

been termed an oxymoron.[150] This in spite of calls to the opposite, such as reflected in the following quote:

> To the forensic practitioner, *forensic science* is not a conundrum, an enigma, a *paradox*, or an *oxymoron*; it is a straightforward application of scientific principles to arrive at a logical, appropriate, verifiable conclusion. It is not magic, and there is no smoke and mirrors despite the insistence of a few commentators. Why then, is forensic science still shrouded in mystery?[151]

One reason for forensic science remaining mysterious may be the same as for other scientific disciplines which apparently deal with or border on subject matters which are considered to be outside the accepted scientific paradigm. It is mainly their instruments and methods of research that seem to go beyond the accepted sources of human perception and knowledge, which, like in the field of law and justice itself, means that it is essentially of human origin and thus subject to human ignorance and human errors (*errare humanum est*). As a memento of *scio nescio*,[152] or attempts to appear knowledgeable despite being ignorant, fluctuations between certainty and uncertainty may also take possession of lawyers. More concretely, the terms "purposely ignorant"[153] or "accurate estimate"[154] were found by courts to constitute oxymora. Legislators may also lay down their own uncertainty in ambiguous texts, as the next case indicates. As transparency marks an important element of legal certainty and predictability, it comes as no surprise that the notion of "implied actual notice", as laid down in a statute, was also designated as a disagreeable oxymoron.[155]

Legislators are also prone to express uncertainty through vague terms and may leave lacunae in the laws. In this regard, a court refused to dwell on the question whether in "recent years 'unambiguously expressed intent of Congress' has become an oxymoron".[156] In fact, determining the original intent of the lawmaker is not an easy task. One case saw a judge confronted with the issue of "implied rights" discussed in another case by requiring that an "implied" right of action be phrased in "clear and unambiguous terms", which was qualified as an oxymoron.[157] Obviously, it seems contradictory to require that something "implicit" be stated in "clear and unambiguous terms", which can only mean in an explicit way.

150 See Donald Kennedy, "Forensic Science: Oxymoron?" (2003) 302(5651) *Science* 1625.
151 See Kelly Pyrek, *Forensic Science Under Siege: The Challenges of Forensic Laboratories and the Medico-Legal Investigation System* (London: Elsevier, 2007) at 1 [Italics added].
152 See Gail Fine, "Does Socrates Claim to Know that He Knows Nothing?" (2008) 35 *Oxford Studies in Ancient Philosophy* 49 at 49.
153 Federal Court of Australia, *Szabo v. Dasford Holdings Pty Ltd.*, [2002] FCA 1438.
154 Ontario Court of Justice, *R. v. MacArthur*, [2002] O.J. No. 5395 at para 18.
155 *Shacket v. Philko Aviation, Inc.*, 841 F.2d 166, 170 (7th Cir. 1988).
156 *Lansing Dairy, Inc. v. Espy*, 39 F.3d 1339, 1351 (1994).
157 *McCready v. White*, 417 F.3d 700, 703 (7th Cir. 2005).

5.2.6 Mind vs matter *or* culture vs trade – *"intellectual property" and "creative economy"*

As for other dichotomies, the survey of the field of economics has proven to be a fertile ground for the coining of essentially oxymoronic concepts. The oxymoronic concept of the "creative economy", as a new paradigm for the present state of the world economy, is one of the most recent additions to this debate.[158] It marks the latest shift from the former theory of comparative advantage to one of a competitive and creative advantage as the driving force behind innovation and economic activity. Understood as comprising the economic offerings produced by the creative industries, it is no surprise that it can be considered as an oxymoron given its genealogy going back to the deliberate oxymoron of the culture industry.[159] The creative economy marks the last link in a long chain formed by dialectic processes beginning with the culture industry and passing by related notions of a knowledge-based or cultural economy.[160] For this reason it is also strongly related to other oxymora, such as creative destruction, prosumers, coopetition or glocalization. Legally, the creative economy is characterized by its strong reliance on innovation as the fruit of mental labour recognized by intellectual property laws, being itself an oxymoron and giving rise to many more. The intangible objects of intellectual property law have been called "legal fictions" because they "do not describe a reality that is external to human society or the legal system but are instead devised to create a new 'reality' that serves a legal regulatory purpose".[161] Originally, intellectual property merged the intangible with the tangible or, in other words, uses property law, i.e. the laws governing the tangible fruits of manual labour, to create ownership in the intangible fruits of mental labour.[162] It may be due to this quality that intellectual property has also been qualified as an oxymoron.[163]

Both concepts, creative economy and intellectual property, being somewhat oxymoronic, it is no surprise that they breed more such concepts. To begin with,

158 See *e.g.* United Nations Conference on Trade and Development (UNCTAD), *World Creative Economy Report 2010: Creative Economy: A Feasible Development Option* (Geneva: UNCTAD, 2010).

159 See also Nicholas Garnham, "From Cultural to Creative Industries" (2005) 11(1) *International Journal of Cultural Policy* 15.

160 See also Shalini Venturelli, *From the Information Economy to the Creative Economy: Moving Culture to the Center of International Public Policy* (Washington: Center for Arts and Culture, 2001).

161 See Alexandra George, *Constructing Intellectual Property* (Cambridge: Cambridge University Press, 2012) at 118–119.

162 See *e.g.* Brad Sherman and Lionel Bently, *The Making of Modern Intellectual Property Law: The British Experience, 1760–1911* (Cambridge: Cambridge University Press, 1999) at 9–59 and Justin Hughes, "The Philosophy of Intellectual Property" (1988) 77(2) *The Georgetown Law Journal* 287 at 300–325.

163 See Barbara Czarniawska, *A Narrative Approach to Organization Studies* (London: Sage, 1998) at 55.

a specific question on copyright concerned the common practice of "creation by committee", i.e. a number of authors contributing to a creative work, such as, for instance, software products, architectural buildings, maps, dictionaries, or encyclopaedias. The term "creation by committee" was questioned as an oxymoron, because a collective form of creation was regarded as a "dilution of the individual creative impulse".[164] Similarly, the existence of an exclusive worldwide licence for a song to be held as "co-exclusive licensees" an oxymoron.[165] In trademark law too, a mark called "Ghoulish Glamour" was qualified as an oxymoron.[166] So was the notion of a "generic mark" because "by definition, something that is generic cannot serve as a trademark because it cannot function as an indication of source".[167] A final case that is noteworthy is one of trade dress litigation concerning a scrapbook album.[168] In this case, the concept of "aesthetic functionality" was qualified as an oxymoron.[169]

Given the close connection with economics, international economic law also makes frequent use of essentially oxymoronic concepts. To begin with, good examples are provided by the area of global trade law, such as in a dispute involving the World Trade Organization (WTO), when the similarity of Korean *soju* to Western-style alcoholic beverages like whisky needed to be assessed. In the analysis, the panel qualified the argument that all alcoholic beverages are made from the "same large variety of raw materials" as oxymoronic.[170] In another case problems arose as to the customs classification of multipurpose vehicles and minivans, nowadays usually referred to by the oxymoron of SUVs, and their legality under the General Agreement on Tariffs and Trade (GATT). In this case, given that the vehicles combine the features of trucks and small passenger vehicles, it was not clear which tariff applied, the lower one applied to passenger vehicles or the higher one to trucks.[171] Interestingly, it seems that SUVs give rise to further oxymora, as can be seen from a case in which a witness gave a description of the installation in the car of what he termed "single double rear seats", on which the judge commented that "like many oxymorons" it actually gave "a more accurate description than it sounds".[172]

164 *American Dental Association v. Delta Dental Plans Association*, 1996 U.S. Dist. LEXIS 5809, 46 (1996).

165 *Nafal v. Carter*, 540 F. Supp. 2d 1128, 1138–1139 (CD Cal. 2007).

166 Federal Court (Toronto, Ontario), *Advance Magazine Publishers Inc. v. Farleyco Marketing Inc.*, [2009] F.C.J. No. 198 at para 70.

167 *Retail Services Inc. v. Freebies Publishing*, 364 F.3d 535 (4th Cir. 2004) at 549.

168 *Antioch Co. v. Western Trimming Corp.*, 347 F.3d 150 (6th Cir. 2003).

169 *Ibid*; see also J. Thomas McCarthy, *McCarthy on Trademarks and Unfair Competition*, 4th ed (St Paul: West Publishing, 2012) at § 7:80 and 7:81.

170 See WTO Panel Report, *Korea – Taxes on Alcoholic Beverages*, WT/DS75/R / WT/DS84/R (17 September 1998) at 3.45.

171 See W. Peter Cladouhos, "The Multipurpose Vehicle Reclassification and Minivan Dumping Disputes Between the United States and Japan and Their Consistency with United States Obligations under the GATT" (1995) 10(3) *The American University Journal of International Law & Policy* 1109 at 1115–1118.

172 London VAT Tribunal, *Chichester Plant Contractors Ltd v. The Commissioners of Customs and Excise*, LON/90/372Y (1991).

Frequently, oxymora also appeared in cases concerning economic and monetary terms. In a case decided in Canada, "negative income" was qualified as an oxymoron as it does not exist under the relevant statutes, the Income Tax Act and Old Age Security Act, in which income refers to a positive amount.[173] Thus, negative income can exist in fact but not in (tax) law. Not only states and natural persons may have negative income but legal persons, like companies, as well. In a merger case, the term "negative assets" was qualified as an oxymoron but later understood as meaning that the newly formed merged company had liabilities that were greater than its assets.[174] In yet another case, the court found the term "consensual underpayment" to be an oxymoron.[175] The case involved a specific provision of US tax law known as "domestic international sales corporation" (DISC), i.e. a corporation entitled to tax benefits. Arguably the term "domestic international sales corporation" marks another oxymoron which, however, was not noted by the court. The court found the argument by the government to be devoid of logic when it stated that a tax deferral can be equated with a consensual underpayment of tax. Instead, the court reasoned that it is just a synonym for "deferment".[176]

Elsewhere, the term "unpaid employee", which – as opposed to an unpaid officer – the court found to be an oxymoron.[177] Working for free or not may be a decision of one's own. Accordingly, in a case in the United Kingdom, the status of being "self-employed" was considered to constitute an oxymoron, since it means to carry on business on your own behalf by providing services to others but "you cannot in law or in common sense be employed by yourself".[178]

5.2.7 Language vs grammar – *"a dynamic status quo"*

A common thread running through all cases featuring oxymora is the difficulty for law and lawyers in drawing lines by legal reasoning between opposite terms. It is thus mainly a linguistic problem of finding the adequate language. Proof for this claim is provided, for instance, by a case in which a judge qualified a witness's testimony as "somewhat inadmissible, retroactively", which was compared to an oxymoron, like "a little bit pregnant".[179] A similar expression of the same vagueness is found in the concept of "arguable inconsistency", which was held to be fraught with ambiguity and bordering upon being an oxymoron.[180] In another

173 Federal Court of Appeal Winnipeg (Manitoba), *Mahy v. Canada*, [2004] F.C.J. No. 1677 at para. 17.

174 Supreme Court of New South Wales, *Buzzle Operations Pty Ltd (In Liquidation) v. Breirl*, [2008] NSWSC 746 at para 7.

175 *Tedori v. United States*, 211 F.3d 488, 492 (9th Cir. 2000).

176 *Ibid.*

177 *Ass'n of Am. Physicians and Surgeons, Inc. v. Clinton*, 997 F.2d. 898, 920 (D.C. Cir. 1993).

178 United Kingdom (Court of Appeal, Civil Division), *R (Tilianu) v. Secretary of State for Work and Pensions*, [2010] EWCA Civ 1397 at para 8.

179 *US v. Evans*, 27 M.J. 34, 40 (C.M.A. 1988); see also *In re FleetBoston Fin. Corp. Sec. Litig.*, 2007 U.S. Dist. LEXIS 87425, 38 (D.N.J. 2007).

180 *Pitts v. Anderson*, 122 F.3d 275, 284 (5th Cir. 1997).

case involving the dismissal of a policeman who for commercial purposes had voluntarily and freely participated with his wife in pornographic video recordings available through the Internet, the court qualified his claim for reinstitution to the police service based on privacy rights as being "virtually oxymorons".[181] Thus a "porn star's privacy" may be qualified as an oxymoron and someone participating in a porn movie may be found to have forgone all privacy rights.

In an Austrian court case, the term "matt shine" involved the alleged manipulation of a pay-and-display ticket (*Parkschein*) by an erasable pen, which may have damaged the shining surface of the original.[182] Even though the court dismissed the case due to other formal errors, it still implicitly held that the nature of oxymora should be "*amtsbekannt*", i.e. "known to the authorities".[183]

Highly interesting from the perspective of both time and space is their encounter with "change" as perhaps the sole constant in life. Likely, only the impact of change on law is more interesting. In this regard, we can note that – similar to the language of William Faulkner[184] – the term "dynamic status quo", an obvious oxymoron, was applied to describe a mandatory injunction aimed at preserving the status quo, which concerned the continued provision of different services.[185] Similarly, the terms "energized static wire" [186] and "inert reacting"[187] were qualified as oxymora.

Yet again touching upon the apparently ephemeral nature of things in a double sense, a case in the United Kingdom asked the court to rule on the legality of a cremation site under the relevant Cremation Act. Akin to a hysteron proteron, the claimant sued for his body to be cremated, after he had died, in accordance with his religious beliefs as a Hindu, which dictate that cremation should usually take place in the open air. The relevant Cremation Act and regulations, however, precluded the possibility of an open-air cremation but required that a cremation could only lawfully take place in a structure that was a "building". Thus, the court – in another manifestation of the sorites paradox – was required to rule on what constitutes a "building" and found that "a structure must be (at the risk of an oxymoron) *relatively permanent* and substantial".[188]

181 *Dible v. City of Chandler*, 515 F.3d 918, 929–930 (9th Cir. 2008).

182 Austrian Administrative Court (Verwaltungsgerichtshof (VwGh), Case 2005/17/0004 (25 April 2005) at 1.

183 *Ibid.*

184 See Susanne Frohriep, *Innovation und Tradition. Stilistische Kreativität in der Erzählkunst William Faulkners* (Würzburg: Königshausen & Neumann, 1999).

185 United Kingdom, *Jet2.com Ltd v. Blackpool Airport Ltd*, [2010] EWHC 3166 at para 35; see also Court of Appeal (Kuala Lumpur), *Sdn Bhd v Radio & General Engineering Sdn Bhd*, [2005] 2 MLJ 422 at 435.

186 *United States v. L.E. Myers Co.*, 562 F.3d 845, 848 (7th Cir. 2009).

187 Federal Court of Australia, *Aktiebolaget Hassle and another v. Alphapharm Pty Ltd.*, 44 I.P.R. 593 (1999).

188 *R (Ghai) v. Newcastle City Council and others*, [2010] EWCA Civ 59 at para 37 (United Kingdom) [*Italics* added].

5.2.8 Oxymoron vs tautology – *"voluntary consent"*

Last but not least, there are also several instances of borderline cases or cases where courts established that certain concepts are not oxymora. In fact, they may sometimes be confused with the opposite of oxymora, i.e. tautologies or the expression of the same meaning through different terms. For instance, the terms "a searching inquiry"[189] and "restitutionary compensation"[190] were rightly found not to be oxymora. On the other hand, the term "duly diligent", which reads more like a tautology, was also qualified as an oxymoron.[191]

In a different context, that of judging something to be just or unjust, a similar conclusion was made by the Canadian Supreme Court about the term "laws of war", which may appear like an oxymoron but it was actually found not to be one.[192] The reason given is that laws of war do exist and war crimes constitute a violation of them. The question of war and law, however, remains difficult, particularly considering the paradoxical aspects of war and peace from a moral perspective.[193] The overall problem remains how to govern legally a state of illegality or chaos. Or put differently, a war crime is a tautology as much as law of war is an oxymoron. Other related oxymora may be "just war" (*bellum iustum*),[194] because justice and war appear as opposed concepts. A similar problem was encountered on a smaller scale, namely in the notion of a "fair street fight", which was equally found to constitute an oxymoron as "street fights have no rules, only consequences".[195]

By contrast, confirming that torture may mean both physical and mental harm, courts in the US and in Europe held that the term "mental torture" is not an oxymoron but instead constitutes a cruel and unusual punishment.[196] Thus, the illegal practices used in various situations of detention and interrogation may answer to the affirmative the question whether "military intelligence" constitutes an oxymoron. In fact, a court may have done precisely that when it compared "rational criminal conduct", understood as the carrying out of criminal acts in an intelligent manner, to "military intelligence", calling them both oxymora.[197]

189 *Greenawalt v. Indiana Dep't of Corrections*, 397 F.3d 587, 590 (7th Cir. 2005).
190 Court of Appeal (Wellington), *Sojourner v. Robb*, [2008] 1 NZLR 751 at para 60.
191 Ontario Court of Justice, *R. v. King Paving & Materials Co.*, a division of KPM Industries Ltd., [2007] O.J. No. 5095 at para 137.
192 Supreme Court of Canada, *R. v. Finta*, [1994] 1 S.C.R. 701 at para 185.
193 See John Carl Fugel, *The Moral Paradox of Peace and War* (London: Watts & Co., 1941) at 33–34.
194 See *e.g.* Lloyd Steffen, *Ethics and Experience: Moral Theory from Just War to Abortion* (Lanham: Rowman and Littlefield, 2012) at 24.
195 Alberta Provincial Court, *Abbott v. Jarocki*, 208 A.R. 133, 136 (1997).
196 See *Dobbey v. Illinois Department of Corrections*, 574 F.3d 443 (7th Cir. 2009) and the European Court of Human Rights (ECHR), *Jalloh v. Germany*, (54810/00) July 11, 2006, [2006] ECHR 721, (2007) 44 E.H.R.R. 667 citing *Thomas v. Farley*, 31 F.3d 557, 559 (7th Cir. 1994).
197 *United States v. Dunigan*, 884 F.2d 1010, 1014 (7th Cir. 1989).

Finally, it is interesting to state that a concept's qualification as a tautology or as an oxymoron may be difficult and, most of all, depend on the wider circumstances. This can be exemplified by the notion of "voluntary consent". At first blush, voluntary consent appears to be a tautology because consent also implies an element of free will or the absence of coercion. In a specific case, however, the accused found himself in the presence of several policemen, or what were referred to as "peace officers" searching his premises. In such situation, the court cited from a research paper, which stated that "the reality of state authority-citizen interaction is inherently antithetical to the concept of 'consent'" and that "some would go so far as to suggest that voluntary consent is an oxymoron in this context".[198]

5.2.9 Life vs death – *"wrongful life"*

To conclude the overview of cases invoking and involving essentially oxymora, it is interesting to note the category of so-called "wrongful life" cases. Wrongful life cases are numerous and usually refer to negligence claims asserted by children who suffer from birth defects.[199] More narrowly, "wrongful life" refers to a case "brought by a genetically impaired child against a physician or other health care provider for preconception negligence in rendering medical counseling or testing".[200] These actions also touch upon the problem that was mentioned in the context of the moral paradox of future individuals, namely to decide whether or what obligation the present generation has towards future generations.[201] In essence, the dilemma and nature of the claims of "injury" in wrongful life cases was broken down into the essential question of assessing whether defendants through their negligence have forced upon the child the worse of two alternatives, namely, first, that of nonexistence or of never being born or, second, existence in a diseased state.[202] One court, in fact, termed this dilemma as a "metaphysical paradox", consisting in the question whether it is "better to live with a handicap than not to have lived at all".[203] Cases of this kind may also give rise to the difficult question if a person has the right not to be born.[204] In the end, these questions are similar to those raised by the grandfather paradox, namely when the person born with a hereditary disease would in fact prefer to go back in time and prevent the parents from conceiving the baby in the first place. Thus, in these cases the term paradox is occasionally used but the qualification

198 New Brunswick Provincial Court, *R. v. Harrison (G.M.)*, 342 A.P.R. 160 (1993) at para 18.

199 See Deana A. Pollard, "Wrongful Analysis in Wrongful Life Jurisprudence" (2004) 55(2) *Alabama Law Review* 327 at 327.

200 *Hegyes v. Unjian Enterprises, Inc.*, 234 Cal. App. 3d 1103, 1112 (2nd Dist. 1991).

201 See Gregory Kavka, "The Paradox of Future Individuals" (1982) 11(2) *Philosophy and Public Affairs* 93.

202 *Turpin v. Sortini*, 31 Cal.3d 220, 232 (1982).

203 *Hegyes v. Unjian Enterprises, Inc.*, 234 Cal. App. 3d 1103, 1112 (2nd Dist. 1991).

204 See *e.g.* Thomas Keasler Foutz, ""Wrongful Life": The Right Not To Be Born" (1980) 54(2) *Tulane Law Review* 480.

of "wrongful life" as an oxymoron, so far, has only occurred in legal literature as follows: "'Wrongful life' is an oxymoron itself since 'life' which has an intrinsic value and sanctity is attributed a negative aspect and is regarded as damage."[205] The article continues and states for the other categories of wrongful birth and wrongful pregnancy that their claims share the oxymoronic character, because generally "life and birth, which according to ethics, religion and law, are protected and convey a positive meaning, are attributed an element of wrong".[206]

5.2.10 Pain vs pleasure – *"anaesthesia dolorosa"*

From a symbolical perspective, a very interesting oxymoron has emerged in a case of alleged medical negligence. The great interest of this last example derives from the fact that it literally hits the nerve of probably all essentially oxymoronic concepts, that is to say their clash with the dominant essentially dualistic, dichotomous or bifurcated perception of the world, as exemplified by Jeremy Bentham calling pain and pleasure the principal two sovereign masters.[207] To be precise, the case involved a patient who had undergone surgery and after the successful operation began to encounter the complication of neurectomy known as "anaesthesia dolorosa" (or differentiation pain) which refers to the sensation of pain from an area not in fact sensitive to pain.[208] In the proceedings, the expert witness explained that "anaesthesia dolorosa" sounds like an oxymoron as it medically means the two opposites of "no sensation and pain sitting together".[209] The concept's underlying dichotomy of pain and pleasure or suffering and joy can be understood metaphorically to describe the cognitive modes or perception in general, which connects each of us to the world around us. Similar to phantom pain, i.e. pain felt in a limb which has been amputated and therefore is no longer there, it takes us to the greater depths of the human brain.[210] Symbolically, the concept mirrors the most fundamental questions of life as they are usually addressed through the different lenses of science, philosophy, or religion. Figuratively, because of its vital nature, anaesthesia dolorosa also unifies these questions, as reflected in the term "coenaesthesia", which is defined as "the blend of numerous bodily sensations that produces an implicit awareness of being alive and of being in a particular physical condition, for example, well or ill, energetic or tired".[211] Overall, it is reminiscent of the paradox laid down in the biblical statement, "The light shineth in darkness; and the darkness comprehended it not". This phrase may also be taken to refer to the great enigma of life and death, namely that life

205 Evgenia Smyrnaki, "Wrongful Life and Birth" (2012) 31(1) *Medicine and Law* 97 at 97.
206 *Ibid* at 98.
207 See Bentham, *Introduction*, *supra* note 7 at 1.
208 Supreme Court of New South Wales, *Johnson v. Biggs*, [2000] NSWCA 338 at 2.
209 *Ibid* at 11.
210 See V. S. Ramachandran and Sandra Blakeslee, *Phantoms in the Brain: Probing the Mysteries of the Human Mind* (New York: Harper, 1998).
211 See Gary R. VandenBos (ed), *APA Dictionary of Psychology*, 2nd ed (Washington: American Psychological Association, 2015) at 167.

and death do not form a dual pair and that death is not darkness. Perhaps, it means that the absence of light or else that the pain we feel in life is a mere phantom due to the present limitations of our awareness?

5.3 Essentially oxymoronic concepts in jurisprudence

> *The expression "pure law" is an oxymoron since the law always needs a context within which it is to be considered.*[212]

Evidence from numerous cases from around the world shows that oxymora are in frequent use in the courts. Even though the present survey mainly focused on oxymora and generally excluded paradoxes, it still shows their relevance for especially hard or borderline cases, where dichotomous thinking fails to provide clear answers. The presented cases were from many different, but primarily English-speaking or common law, jurisdictions. This finding suggests that the term "oxymoron" is better known in Anglophone countries than in other countries. Still it is fair to assume that all other non-Anglophone jurisdictions may also use analogous rhetorical figures or concepts to accommodate contradictions or logical conflicts as part of an emerging common language. This presumption seems to be supported by a recent study which analysed word lists covering nearly two-thirds of the world's languages and managed to demonstrate that "a considerable proportion of 100 basic vocabulary items carry strong associations with specific kinds of human speech sounds, occurring persistently across continents and linguistic lineages (linguistic families or isolates)".[213]

By the same token, the cases featuring oxymora seem to reveal a greater connection or even continuity between law and, notably, case law and other fields, such as different artistic and scientific fields. As a possible strength of the common law system, this can be seen from "The Fable of the Bees" and the many economic paradoxes the poem contains and which it gave rise to in scientific discourse, and which are also matched in similar oxymora being invoked before the courts. What remains to be seen is whether there exists a similar constructive dialogue between case law and legal scholarship. It is also to confirm the strange quality of oxymora and paradoxes that they usually come by the dozen, meaning that they seem to be intrinsically linked with each other by some invisible or inexplicable bond.

5.3.1 Global law – *"glocalization"*

A quick search of any library catalogue usually confirms that legal scholarship produces many essentially oxymoronic concepts. This may be taken as evidence

212 Ontario Superior Court of Justice, *Silveira v. Ontario (Minister of Transportation)*, [2011] O.J. No. 3157 at 22.

213 See Damián E. Blasi et al., "Sound–Meaning Association Biases Evidenced Across Thousands of Languages" (2016) 113(39) *Proceedings of the National Academy of Sciences of the United States of America (PNAS)* 10818.

that these concepts seem on the rise in scholarship too. To verify this trend, it is useful to start from a glance at the global governance debate, which in law can be expressed by the notion of "global law". At present, "global law", however, must still be qualified as an oxymoron because the conditions it portrays do not exist in reality.[214] Still, to render the oxymoronic nature explicit, it should be called "glocal law", recalling the oxymoron "glocalization" and its advantages over the concept of globalization.[215] Particularly in the legal realm, where the surface of this planet is territorially divided into numerous jurisdictions, with often great local differences, the term glocal law would be preferable, both descriptively and also normatively.[216]

Instead of glocal law, the prevalent concept in use for that purpose is still that of "international law", which has remained unchanged since the 1648 Treaty of Westphalia. But then what is international law, or the law of nations as it is also called? It is supposed to describe the law governing the relations "*inter nationes*", i.e. between states only (and more recently also including international organizations) at the exclusion of (most) private entities, like natural and legal persons. However, the notion of international law in general and the exclusion of private individuals from international law in particular have been criticized and certainly no longer correspond to the present reality and practice at the global level.[217]

The dilemma encountered at the global level can itself be traced back to a paradox, namely the so-called "global governance paradox", which, put briefly, consists in a problem similar to the chicken-and-egg paradox, namely that in order to create a global legal order, the world community needs a global governance platform which is absent so far. This is why global governance has been aptly described as a "mystery".[218] Based on the insufficient knowledge we have of these processes, "global governance" is currently more a debate than a concept vested with a precise meaning or descriptive of a reality. Consequently, "global governance" can also be deemed to form an oxymoron because of the underlying contradiction in terms created between the suggestion of the existence of a global legal and institutional framework and the present reality. Thus, the term creates a tension between what exists and the desire for what it is felt should exist.

214 See also Rafael Domingo, *The New Global Law* (Cambridge: Cambridge University Press, 2010) at 121, Andrew Halpin and Volker Roeben (eds), *Theorising the Global Legal Order* (Oxford: Hart, 2009), Harold J. Berman, "World Law" (1995) 18 *Fordham International Law Journal* 1617 and M. Cherif Bassiouni, "Challenges Facing a Rule-of-Law-Oriented World Order" (2010) 8(1) *Santa Clara Journal of International Law* 1.

215 See Habibul H. Khondker, "Globalisation to Glocalisation: A Conceptual Exploration" (2005) 13(2) *Intellectual Discourse* 181 at 187–188.

216 See also Brian Z. Tamanaha, "Understanding Legal Pluralism: Past to Present, Local to Global" (2008) 30(3) *Sydney law Review* 375.

217 See *e.g.* Beaulac *supra* note 111 and Onuma, *supra* note 111; see also Mark W. Janis, "Individuals as Subjects of International Law" (1984) 17(1) *Cornell International Law Journal* 61 at 61 and Saskia Sassen, "The Participation of States and Citizens in Global Governance" (2003) 10(1) *Indiana Journal of Global Legal Studies* 5.

218 David Kennedy, "The Mystery of Global Governance" (2008) 34(3) *Ohio Northern University Law Review* 827 at 827.

In the absence of a coherent system of global law, global affairs are governed by a great many perplexing paradoxes, as James Rosenau aptly stated.[219] These perplexing paradoxes or numerous oxymora may, in fact, be reduced and traced back to the many dichotomies as well as intradisciplinary categories used and erected by scholars and diplomats, such as those of public versus private law or national versus international law.[220] Generally paradoxes are said to emerge where dichotomies reign and where knowledge and understanding are insufficient. Indeed, the understanding of the relation between public and private international law is insufficient and therefore gives rise to a paradox, which was described as follows:

> The separation, as maintained by the public/private distinction, is reproduced by academic and practical lawyers and by governmental and private elites, obscuring the paradoxical result of private actors legitimately exercising public functions.[221]

As another oxymoron, "particular universalism" was said to point to the problem of universality versus particularity (or diversity) and related risks due to their incoherence.[222] The same problem was also characterized as follows:

> Human Rights are paradoxical. On the one hand, human rights are transcendent. Human rights gain power and purchase because they are said to belong to all people no matter who they are or where they are. On the other hand, the idea of human rights conferred on us all by virtue of being human is a convenient fiction. Humans realize their rights only in particular places with particular instruments and with particular protections.[223]

A second paradox encountered in international human rights law is "the division of the indivisible".[224] This contradiction refers to the fact that, despite the principle

219 See James N. Rosenau, "Governance in the 21st Century" (1995) 1(1) *Global Governance* 13 at 13.

220 See also Philip Allott, "The Concept of International Law" (1999) 10(1) *European Journal of International Law* 31 at 37, Rostam J. Neuwirth, "International Law and the Public/Private Law Distinction" (2000) 55(4) *Zeitschrift für öffentliches Recht* 393 and Friedrich K. Juenger, "Private International Law or International Private Law?" (1994–1995) 5 *King's College Law Journal* 45 at 46.

221 See A. Claire Cutler, *Private Power and Global Authority: Transnational Merchant Law in the Global Political Economy* (Cambridge: Cambridge University Press, 2003) at 54 [footnote omitted].

222 See Sergio Dellavalle, "Partikularistischer Universalismus – Ein Oxymoron ohne Alternative?" (2013) 24(2) *EWE – Erwägen, Wissen, Ethik* 199.

223 See Steve J. Stern and Scott Straus, "Embracing Paradox: Human Rights in the Global Age" in Steve J. Stern and Scott Straus (eds), *The Human Rights Paradox: Universality and its Discontents* (Madison: The University of Wisconsin Press, 2014) 3 at 3.

224 See Daniel J. Whelan, *Indivisible Human Rights: A History* (Philadelphia: University of Pennsylvania Press, 2010) at 76.

of the indivisibility of human rights, i.e. that human rights are indivisible, interdependent and interrelated,[225] the international human rights bill following the 1948 Universal Declaration of Human Rights[226] was divided in two separate documents, the International Covenant on Civil and Political Rights (ICCPR), on the one hand, and the International Covenant on Economic, Social and Cultural Rights (ICESCR) on the other.[227] This division also highlights the long lasting and continuing separation between politics and economics in the governance of global affairs.[228] This is also reflected in the separation of the WTO from the United Nations system and its specialized agencies[229] as in separate regulation of international intellectual property rights in the 1883 Paris Convention for the Protection of Industrial Property and the 1886 Berne Convention for the Protection of Literary and Artistic Works.[230]

Another paradox is known by the question "*sed quis custodiet ipsos custodes?*" or "but who will guard the guards themselves?".[231] Applied to human rights law, it means that the role of the state may be qualified as paradoxical, because the state is "both the guardian of basic rights and as the behemoth against which one's rights need to be defended".[232] This is closely related to "the paradox of the international accountability for the domestic practice of sovereign states", which lies in the fact that the same states that control the processes of determining human rights at the international level also apply them within their national jurisdictions.[233]

Finally, there are further paradoxes related to human rights, which are rooted in the present conception of the international legal order as well as the disciplinary divisions in legal science.[234] Arguably, a great many essentially oxymoronic concepts are the combined results of, on the one hand, the deep trenches separating

225 Vienna Declaration and Programme of Action, Section 1, para. 5, 1993.

226 Universal Declaration of Human Rights (UDHR), GA Res 217 A (III) (adopted 10 December 1948).

227 See International Covenant on Civil and Political Rights, 16 December 1966, 999 U.N.T.S. 171; International Covenant on Economic, Social and Cultural Rights, 16 December 1966, 993 U.N.T.S. 3.

228 See *e.g.* Allyn A. Young, "Economics and War: A Presidential Address" (1926) 16(1) *The American Economic Review* 1 at 7.

229 See John H. Jackson, *World Trade and the Law of GATT* (Indianapolis: The Bobbs Merril Company, 1969) at 51; see also Rostam J. Neuwirth, "Global Market Integration and the Creative Economy: The Paradox of Industry Convergence and Regulatory Divergence" (2015) 18(1) *Journal of International Economic Law* 21 at 21–24.

230 Paris Convention for the Protection of Industrial Property of March 20, 1883, 828 U.N.T.S. 306 and Berne Convention for the Protection of Literary and Artistic Works of September 9, 1886, 828 U.N.T.S. 221.

231 See Hiram Corson (ed), *The Satires of Decimus Junius Juvenalis* (Philadelphia: David McKay, 1868) at 94.

232 See Micheline Ishay, "What Are Human Rights? Six Historical Controversies" (2004) 3(3) *Journal of Human Rights* 359 at 363.

233 See Abdullah A. An-Na'im, "Human Rights" in Judith R. Blau (ed), *The Blackwell Companion to Sociology* (Malden: Blackwell, 2004) 86 at 86–87.

234 See *e.g.* Costas Douzinas, "The Paradoxes of Human Rights" (2013) 20(1) *Constellations* 51.

disciplines both from an intra- and interdisciplinary perspective and, on the other, growing efforts to overcome them. One field which contributes a lot of effort to the global debate is international economic law or international trade law. This debate is widely known as the so-called "trade linkage debate", which tries to reconcile trade issues with so-called "non-trade issues".[235] The trade linkage debate is also made up of several microdebates of so-called "trade and . . ." problems, like "trade and human rights" or "trade and culture".[236] To support this claim, the paradoxical relation between trade and human rights emerges in the context of the enforcement of human rights instruments through trade sanctions. In this context, paradoxically, even though trade sanctions have been called "the most effective mechanism for the international enforcement of human rights", they are hardly ever used to this end, or, if they are, they usually fail.[237] This has, by the way, also been generally noted as "the sanctions paradox", which was explained by the effect of economic sanctions imposed by a state on another being paradoxical or contradictory in the sense that the anticipation of a future dispute may lead the imposing state to prefer a coercive strategy but at the same time may reduce its ability to obtain concessions from the target state in order to settle the conflict successfully.[238] Even where disputes between states are solved by use of the WTO dispute settlement system, power paradoxes have been found to exist.[239]

Like human rights, the trade and culture debate has also produced several essentially oxymoronic concepts, as reflected in the related concepts of "creative economy" and "intellectual property rights" discussed above. This comes as no surprise as the recent version of the "culture and trade debate" was born out of an oxymoron coined during the Uruguay Round negotiations, namely by the trade representatives of the US (Mickey Kantor) and of the EU (Sir Leon Brittan) in a press conference "settling" their antagonistic views about the treatment of cultural products under international trade law by an "agreement to disagree".[240]

235 See *e.g.* Frank J. Garcia, "Trade and Justice: Linking the Trade Linkage Debates" (1998) 19(2) *University of Pennsylvania Journal of International Economic Law* 391.

236 See *e.g.* Frederick M. Abbott, Christine Breining-Kaufmann and Thomas Cottier (eds), *International Trade and Human Rights: Foundations and Conceptual Issues* (Ann Arbor: University of Michigan Press, 2006) and Mary E. Footer and Christian B. Graber, "Trade Liberalization and Cultural Policy" (2000) 3(1) *Journal of International Economics Law* 115.

237 See Patricia Stirling, "The Use of Trade Sanctions as an Enforcement Mechanism for Basic Human Rights: A Proposal for Addition to the World Trade Organization" (1996) 11(1) *The American University Journal of International Law and Policy* 1 at 2–3; see also Philip Alston, "International Trade as an Instrument of Positive Human Rights Policy" (1982) 4(2) *Human Rights Quarterly* 155 at 155.

238 See Daniel W. Drezner, *The Sanctions Paradox: Economic Statecraft and International Relations* (Cambridge: Cambridge University Press, 1999) at 4 and 307.

239 See Naboth Van Den Broek, "Power Paradoxes in Enforcement and Implementation" (2003) 37(1) *Journal of World Trade* 127 at 134.

240 See Larry Elliott and Edward Luce, "US and Europe Clear Obstacles to GATT Deal", *The Guardian (London)* at 1 (15 December 1993); see generally Rostam J. Neuwirth, "The "Culture and Trade Debate" Continues: The UNESCO Convention in Light of the WTO Reports in China – Publications and Audiovisual Products: Between Amnesia or Déjà Vu?" (2010) 44(6) *Journal of World Trade* 1333 at 1337–1340.

Similarly, the separate regulation of trade (or the economy) and culture (or the arts) gives rise to many essentially oxymoronic concepts, which is why it is no surprise that they proliferate in their combinations. To begin, the regulation of international trade, or national markets for that matter, can already be regarded as a contradiction because the market, it is argued, should be free from intervention and left to its own forces to perform best.[241] Thus, not only is the concept of market widely contested,[242] but also the idea of a "free market", like "free jazz", constitutes an oxymoron.[243]

If not *laissez-faire* economics[244] then, at the most, state regulation should restrict itself to the role of an "invisible hand", to use Adam Smith's metaphor.[245] Regulatory economics thus sounds as much like an oxymoron as do "competition law" and its American synonym "antitrust law".[246] Moreover, a paradox may be detected in the mainstream economic theories, which discourage the public regulation of industrial policy but support the public regulation of antitrust policy.[247] Another paradox is mentioned in the context of US antitrust laws, which appear to have been designed to protect consumers from harmful business practices but instead protect less efficient business organizations from competition.[248] Similarly, it has been said that the "future is inevitable; as an oxymoron, antitrust is obsolete".[249] In the case of either term, there seems to be some inherent contradiction as competition appears to be opposed to legal constraints of any form. As for "antitrust law", it seems like a contradiction considering that "in law we trust", or that law and trust are closely intertwined. Equally, Niklas Luhmann wrote that law and trust cannot be separated and both serve as mechanisms to reduce complexity and risk.[250] If antitrust is not considered an oxymoron,

241 See generally Richard A. Posner, "Theories of Economic Regulation" (1974) 5(2) *The Bell Journal of Economics and Management Science* 335.

242 See Eckehard F. Rosenbaum, "What is a Market? On the Methodology of a Contested Concept" (2000) 58(4) *Review of Social Economy* 455.

243 See Richard Hyman, "The Role of Government in Industrial Relations" in Jason Heyes and Ludek Rychly (eds), *Labour Administration in Uncertain Times: Policy, Practice and Institutions* (Cheltenham: Edward Elgar, 2013) 95 at 96.

244 But see John M. Keynes, "The End of Laissez-faire" in John M. Keynes, *Essays in Persuasion* (New York: W.W. Norton, 1963) 312.

245 Adam Smith, *An Inquiry into the Nature and Causes of the Wealth of Nations* (Edinburgh: Thomas Nelson, 1843) at 184; see also Gavin Kennedy, "Adam Smith and the Invisible Hand: From Metaphor to Myth" (2009) 6(2) *Econ Journal Watch* 239 at 263.

246 See Dominick T. Armentano, "Is Antitrust Law an Oxymoron?", *The Asian Wall Street Journal* (3 March 1988) at 17 and Lannon Stafford, "Letters to the Editor", *The Wall Street Journal* (12 December 1988) at 15.

247 See Maher M. Dabbah, *The Internationalisation of Antitrust Policy* (Cambridge: Cambridge University Press, 2003) at 27.

248 See Dominick T. Armentano, *Antitrust: The Case for Repeal*, 2nd ed (Auburn: Ludwig von Mises Institute, 1999) at xi.

249 See Arthur D. Austin, "Issues After a Century of Federal Competition Policy" (1988) 33(2) *Antitrust Bulletin* 417 at 427 [footnotes omitted].

250 See Niklas Luhmann, *Trust and Power* (New York: John Wiley and Sons, 1979) at 5 and Niklas Luhmann, "Familiarity, Confidence, Trust: Problems and Alternatives'" in Diego Gambetta (ed), *Trust: Making and Breaking Cooperative Relations* (Oxford: Basil Blackwell, 1988) 94 at 96 and 100.

however, it may yet be a paradox of a "policy at war with itself".[251] This is because antitrust law's "basic premises were flatly inconsistent with one another, some of them leading to the preservation of competition and others to its suppression".[252]

Nonetheless, not only does law regulate competition but law and legal regulation are – perhaps paradoxically – also in competition (or at war) with each other. This phenomenon is discussed within the framework of the dichotomy of regulatory competition versus regulatory harmonization or unification.[253] In this context, Daniel C. Esty and Damien Geradin use the oxymoron "regulatory coopetition" to solve the paradox of competition and cooperation as follows:

> Regulatory theory must reflect the diversity and complexity of the world. Optimal governance thus requires a flexible mix of competition and cooperation between government actors as well as between governmental and non-governmental actors, along both horizontal and vertical dimensions.[254]

Another paradox is that of culture and trade or cultural variety and trade liberalization, the goals of which are usually understood to be mutually incompatible. Yet, "variety" was found to be their common denominator.[255] This has been clearly laid out by Thomas G. Williams in his book, *The History of Commerce*, where he wrote that "as variety is the spice of life, so is it the spring of commerce", which explains that "differences in material wants supply the motives for exchange which we call commerce".[256] Put briefly, the rich cultural and other variety of the world poses not an obstacle but instead the prime reason for trade and commerce as it is captured by the trade theory of comparative advantage.[257] This connection between international trade and cultural variety can also be seen in trade in fashion products.[258] As often in scientific discourse, it means that economists and cultural policy makers mean the same thing but – without applying a common language – speak past each other.

251 See Robert H. Bork, *The Antitrust Paradox: A Policy at War With Itself* (New York: The Free Press, 1978).

252 *Ibid* at ix.

253 See *e.g.* Joel P. Trachtman, "International Regulatory Competition, Externalization, and Jurisdiction" (1993) 34(1) *Harvard International Law Journal* 47, Alan O. Sykes, "Regulatory Competition or Regulatory Harmonization? A Silly Question?" (2000) 3(2) *Journal of International Economic Law* 257 and Daniel C. Esty, "Regulatory Competition in Focus" (2000) 3(2) *Journal of International Economic Law* 215.

254 Daniel C. Esty and Damien Geradin, "Regulatory Co-opetition" (2000) 3(2) *Journal of International Economic Law* 235 at 235.

255 See also Rostam J. Neuwirth, "The 'Culture and Trade' Paradox Reloaded" in Christiaan De Beukelaer, Miikka Pyykkönen and J. P. Singh (eds), *Globalization, Culture and Development: The UNESCO Convention on Cultural Diversity* (Basingstoke: Palgrave MacMillan, 2015) 91 at 93–95.

256 See T. G. Williams, *The History of Commerce* (London: Sir Isaac Pitman & Sons Ltd., 1926) at 1.

257 See Neuwirth, "The 'Culture and Trade' Paradox Reloaded", *supra* note 255 at 100.

258 See Rostam J. Neuwirth, "A "Uniform Dress Code" or Cultural Variety in the Global Fashion Industry?" in Lilian Richieri Hanania, *Effectiveness and Normativity of the 2005 UNESCO Convention on the Diversity of Cultural Expressions* (London: Routledge, 2014) 136 at 137.

Shifting from trade to the cultural sphere, regulation is also problematic in the field of culture. Theodor W. Adorno, one of the fathers of the oxymoron "culture industry", wrote that culture defies regulation especially due to its spontaneous nature.[259] Therefore, subjecting the cultural industries to a regime of public policy making may also be referred to as an oxymoron.[260] Similar to the term "intellectual property", the tension between regulation and culture also surfaces in the concept of cultural property, which has been described as paradoxical because it tends "to fix culture, which if anything is unfixed, dynamic, and unstable".[261]

Essentially oxymoronic concepts also surface in (failed) attempts to legally separate culture from the economy or trade. The common way of regulating a difficult relationship, like the one between culture and trade, has been by way of exceptions enshrined in trade agreements. This is best exemplified by the special exception for cinematograph films introduced in the GATT 1947.[262] However, the regulation of particular non-trade issues, like culture, health or the environment, by way of an exception meets with a possible paradox in the phrase that "the exception confirms the rule" (*exceptio probat regulam*).[263] This paradox has also been expressed by explaining that "the most proper characteristic of the exception is that what is excluded in it is not, on account of being excluded, absolutely without relation to the rule".[264] In legal terms, the logical dilemma inherent to exceptions has been confirmed a shift in the regulatory approach to the relationship between culture and trade. The regulation of their relationship has seen a shift from the use of "general (or special) exceptions" to so-called "integration (or cross-section) clauses", i.e. from a negative towards a positive approach.[265]

259 Theodor W. Adorno, "Culture and Administration" in Theodor W. Adorno, *The Culture Industry: Selected Essays on Mass Culture* (London: Routledge, 1991) 107 at 123.

260 See Andy C. Pratt, "Cultural Industries and Public Policy: An Oxymoron?" (2005) 11(1) *International Journal* 31 at 31–32.

261 See Naomi Mezey, "The Paradoxes of Cultural Property" (2007) 107(8) *Columbia Law Review* 204 at 2005.

262 See Rostam J. Neuwirth, "*The Cultural Industries and the Role of Article IV GATT: Reflections on Policy Options for Canada and the EU in the new WTO* Round" (2002); available at: https://papers.ssrn.com/sol3/papers.cfm?abstract_id=1352171 (accessed 1 October 2017).

263 See T. K. Abbott, "Logical Notes" (1882) 4(8) *Hermathena* 344 at 344 and Pierre-Yves Quiviger, "Derrida: de la philosophie au droit" (2007) 30 *Cités* 41 at 49; see also Marcus T. Cicero, *M.T. Ciceronis Pro L. Cornelio Balbo Oratio ad Iudices* (Cambridge: Cambridge University Press, 1890) at 32 (Ch. 14, s. 32); see Marcus T. Cicero, *The Orations of Marcus Tullius Cicero*, vol 3 (London: George Bell & Sons, 1875) at 325; but see the discussion of the translation of "*exceptio probat regulam*" as the exception "tests" ("*met à l'épreuve*") the rule in Pierre-Yves Quiviger, "Derrida: de la philosophie au droit" (2007) 30 *Cités* 41 at 49.

264 See Giorgio Agamben, *Homo Sacer: Sovereign Power and Bare Life* (Stanford: Stanford University Press, 1998) at 16–17.

265 This shift from a negative to a positive approach in regulation was paraphrased by the following contradictions in terms indicating a change from a method of "exclusive inclusion" (*e.g.* Art. XX(a) and (f) GATT) to one of "inclusive exclusion" (*e.g.* Art. 164 Treaty on European Union (TEU), in Consolidated versions of the Treaty on European Union and the Treaty on the Functioning of the European Union, O.J. C 83/1 (30 March 2010); Art. 20 UNESCO Convention on the Protection and Promotion of the Diversity of Cultural Expressions (CDCE), 2440 UNTS; see Rostam J. Neuwirth, "The Future of the Culture and Trade Debate: A Legal Outlook" (2013) 47(2) *Journal of World Trade* 391 at 401 and 407.

5.3.2 Comparative law – "same, same but different?"

In law, the discipline known as comparative law is devoted to the study of the differences between international legal systems. The concept of comparative law may not precisely be an oxymoron itself but rather the attempt to overcome the contradiction in the application between different legal systems, which sometimes become oxymoronic in a sense that cross-border cases may end up in a direct conflict. However, if following the dichotomy of descriptive and normative analysis, even comparative law has been qualified as an oxymoron, because comparison may be said to be a purely descriptive process whereas law is a normative process.[266] Additionally, an inquiry into the etymology of comparative law reveals further support for its qualification as an oxymoron. This H. Patrick Glenn has shown by critically challenging the common understanding of "comparison" as the process of determining whether two things or concepts or laws are similar or different.[267] Etymologically, he writes, comparison "comes from Latin, and is a composite of two words: 'com', a version of 'cum' or 'with'; and 'pare' or peer".[268] This would normally mean the bringing together, and keeping together, of equals. But this is not necessarily so and, similar to the nature of oxymora, may also, according to Glenn, mean: "Com-paring thus involves an enduring *process* of peaceful coexistence (in spite of difference, in spite of potential conflict), in a way which ensures not uniformity but ongoing diversity".[269]

For the qualification of comparative law as an oxymoron also speaks Glenn's repeated criticism of legal thinking that relies exclusively on binary logic (as opposed to multivalent logic), the law of non-contradiction or the rule of the excluded middle.[270] It is also supported by the fact that comparative law is really at the heart of the dichotomous problem of regulatory diversity versus regulatory harmonization or total unification in the form of the adoption of uniform laws. In this sense, "comparative international law" appears at first sight to be an oxymoron because "international law" is presumed to be uniform and comparing the identical may not make much sense. Therefore, "comparative international law" can be considered more as a tautology. By way of the *argumentum e contrario*, this view is supported by Martti Koskenniemi in an article on comparative international law, in which he writes that "the title of a 'Finnish Yearbook of International Law' might seem to have something oxymoronic about it".[271]

266 See George A. Bermann et al., "Comparative Law: Problems and Prospects" (2011) 26(4) *American University International Law Review* 935 at 943.

267 H. Patrick Glenn, "Com-paring" in Esin Örücü and David Nelken (eds), *Comparative Law: A Handbook* (Oxford: Hart, 2007) 91 at 91.

268 *Ibid* at 92.

269 *Ibid.*

270 *Ibid*; see also H. Patrick Glenn, "Mixing It Up" (2003) 78(1&2) *Tulane Law Review* 79 at 80, H. Patrick Glenn, "A Concept of Legal Tradition" (2008) 34(1) *Queen's Law Journal* 427 at 439 and 443–445, H. Patrick Glenn, "Cosmopolitan Legal Orders" in Halpin and Roeben (eds), *supra* note 214 at 35 and H. Patrick Glenn, *The Cosmopolitan State* (Oxford: Oxford University Press, 2013) mainly at 260–265.

271 Martti Koskenniemi, "The Case for Comparative International Law" (2009) 20 *Finnish Yearbook of International Law* 1 at 1.

In brief, the present structure of the international legal order, with its numerous different states and jurisdictions, does make comparative law appear to be an oxymoron. Practical examples of direct and real legal conflicts between these different national legal systems are provided by what is called a "limping marriage" (*matrimonium claudicans*), which means a marriage that is valid only within a limited territory, because it was formed by a marriage concluded under the formal requirements of one country that are not recognized within a second country.[272] The same exists in its negative form of a limping divorce, which refers to "marriages in which a spouse is presumed to be divorced according to the law of one country but retains the status of a married person according to the law of another country".[273] In the end, both limping cases amount to serious conflicts of laws, which the law does not conclusively resolve and instead end in a logical deadlock similar to those of oxymora in the application of the syllogism. Thus, it is no surprise that these problems have been called the "ultimate shame of private international law".[274] Generally, situations of this kind have been referred to as "limping legal acts (or relations)", which are acts that are treated differently in different countries and, thus, give rise to international disharmony.[275]

In spite of their general separation, similar problems occur not only in the realm of private or civil law but also of criminal law and criminal justice. Criminal justice, like military justice,[276] has itself been qualified as a "nice sounding oxymoron", unless a new way of conceiving the nature of criminal justice is being explored.[277] It is certain that the pursuit of justice through criminal law gives rise to many essentially oxymoronic concepts. For instance, a criminal justice paradox was identified in the trend of modern nations to generate high rates in crime and deviance while at the same time their criminal justice systems are lacking the capacity to counter the social problems that lie behind these figures.[278] In a legal thriller titled *Blood-Stained Justice*, one of the characters says that the problem with laws is that they protect criminals, which is why criminal justice is an oxymoron and should read instead "victim justice".[279] Further paradoxes deal

272 See Adolf F. Schnitzer, *Handbuch des internationalen Privatrechts*, vol 1, 4th ed (Basel: Recht und Gesellschaft, 1957) at 355.

273 See William Latey, "Jurisdiction in Divorce and Nullity: Proposed British Code of International Private Law" (1956) 5(4) *International and Comparative Law Quarterly* 499 at 499.

274 See Otto Kahn-Freund, *General Problems of Private International Law* (Leyden: Sijthoff, 1976) at 14.

275 See e.g. Christian von Bar, *Internationales Privatrecht*, vol 1 (München: C.H. Beck, 1987) at 163–164 and Mads Andenaes and Robert Wintemute, *The Legal Recognition of Same-Sex Partnerships: A Study of National, European and International Law* (Oxford: Hart, 2001) at 459.

276 See *e.g.* Janet Walker, "Military Justice: From Oxymoron to Aspiration" (1994) 32(1) *Osgoode Hall Law Journal* 1 at 32.

277 See *e.g.* Robert H. Craig, "The Search for Justice in an Unjust World" (1997) 9(1) *Journal for Peace and Justice Studies* 53 at 54 and Donald R. Dixon, "Understanding the Criminal Justice System" in Christopher W. Bruce, Steven R. Hick and Julie P. Cooper (eds), *Exploring Crime Analysis: Readings on Essential Skills* (North Charleston: BookSurge, 2004) 37 at 37.

278 See Hans Boutellier, "Beyond the Criminal Justice Paradox: Alternatives between Law and Morality" (1996) 4(4) *European Journal on Criminal Policy and Research* 7 at 7–8.

279 See Rick Ward, *Blood-Stained Justice* (New York: Spring Morning Publishing, 2009) at 195.

with the dichotomy of retributive and restorative justice. To begin with the latter, "restorative justice" has also been related to paradoxes.[280] Put simply, restorative justice is concerned with the problem of the reversibility of the irreversible. Restorative justice has also been expressed in terms of other oxymora,[281] such as it being a form of "compulsory compassion".[282] Another paradox related to restorative justice is provided by the story of Michael Kohlhaas, the eponymous central character of a novel written by Heinrich Kleist.[283] The moral of this story perhaps tells us of the paradox that, after suffering injustice and a denial of fundamental rights, pursuing justice through unjust means itself leads not to justice but to calamity and more suffering. This is an important lesson, especially in the context of what has been misnamed a "war on terror",[284] possibly another oxymoron but more likely a serious assault on the rule of law.

As for retributive justice and its relation to restorative justice, a paradox can be found in the law of talion (*ius talionis*), or the right of retaliation.[285] The right of retaliation is usually expressed by the adage "an eye for an eye, a tooth for a tooth" drawn from the Old Testament.[286] Commonly it is understood to mean that someone having lost an eye or tooth due to the action by another person, is now legally entitled to take an eye or tooth from that person. However, it has been explained that "paradoxically, this provision of Jewish law relates not to a measure of punishment, but rather a principle of just compensation in the civil law".[287] In other words, it is meant to function as a standard for the determination of the correct amount of compensation to be paid rather than an automatic right to retaliate.

280 See *e.g.* George Pavlich, *Governing Paradoxes of Restorative Justice* (London: GlassHouse Press, 2005).

281 But see Patty LaTaille, "Restorative Justice – Not an Oxymoron" (2014) 2 *Full Circle Restorative Justice Newsletter* 1; available at: http://www.fullcirclerj.net/wp/wp-content/uploads/FCRJ-Spring-2014-Newsletter1.pdf (accessed 1 October 2017).

282 See Annalise Acorn, *Compulsory Compassion: A Critique of Restorative Justice* (Vancouver: UBC Press, 2004) at 137.

283 Heinrich Kleist, *Michael Kohlhaas*, reprinted in Kurt Francke (ed), *The German Classics: Masterpieces of German Literature*, vol 4 (New York: The German Publications Society, 1913) 308.

284 See *e.g.* Russell Hogg, "Criminology Beyond the Nation State: Global Conflicts, Human Rights and the 'New World Disorder'" in Russell Hogg and Kerry Carrington (eds), *Critical Criminology* (Cullompton: Wilan Publishing, 2002) 185 at 190, Katrina Lee-Koo, "'War on Terror'/'War on Women': Critical Feminist Perspectives" in Alex J. Bellamy et al. (eds), *Security and the War on Terror* (London: Routledge, 2008) 42 at 53, Hew Strachan, "The Idea of War" in Kate McLoughlin (ed), *The Cambridge Companion to War Writing* (Cambridge: Cambridge University Press, 2009) 7 at 11 and Laura Westra, *Faces of State Terrorism* (Boston: Brill, 2012) at 27.

285 See also Aaron X. Fellmeth and Maurice Horwitz, *Guide to Latin in International Law* (Oxford: Oxford University Press, 2009) at 160.

286 *Exodus* 21:24.

287 See Myer S. Lew, *The Humanity of Jewish Law* (New York: Soncino Press, 1985) ch 1, cited in Simon Bronitt, "Visions of a Multicultural Criminal Law: an Australian Perspective" in Marie-Claire Foblets and Alison Dundes Renteln (eds), *Multicultural Jurisprudence: Comparative Perspectives on the Cultural Defense* (Oxford: Hart, 2009) 121 at 137.

Generally, the emphasis of criminal justice systems on either restorative or retributive justice was subject to cyclical changes.[288] Generally, global criminal justice may also be understood as an oxymoron given the present fragmentation of the international legal system. At the global level, despite assurances in the International Human Rights Bill that all humans are guaranteed equality before the law, or courts and tribunals for that matter,[289] the term "equal justice" is also frequently considered an oxymoron.[290] Equal justice at the global level seems especially oxymoronic, or else utopian, in view of the many different national legal systems and their divergent standards. Additionally, cultural differences, under the term "cultural relativity", are often invoked as a reason for a deviation from universal standards of justice or human rights. The legal and cultural aspects involved in the debate about global justice have given rise to frequent considerations of "global justice" as an oxymoron, as the following example shows:

> If what counts as justice is always culturally defined, any effort to discern cross-cultural principles of justice is doomed, rendering the term "global justice" an oxymoron, and the Universal Declaration of Human Rights indefensible insofar as it asserts a moral standard of universal applicability.[291]

In the meantime, the search for global justice must continue and it does, often along the lines of the idea of global legal pluralism.[292] However, even the universal acceptance of a concept of legal pluralism seems like a paradox.[293] It has equally been denominated an oxymoron,[294] equally also available in different forms, such as "'universal' legal pluralism".[295] Both concepts share the tension created within the dichotomy of unity versus diversity, a dichotomy that is often confused with uniformity and diversity, which is also the subject of the area of law called "constitutional law".

5.3.3 Constitutional law – "pouvoir constituant constitué"

Strangely, the area of constitutional law also produces essentially oxymoronic concepts, even though its role in the legal field is supposed to take a hierarchically

288 See also John Braithwaite, *Restorative Justice and Responsive Regulation* (Oxford: Oxford University Press, 2002) at 3–12.

289 See Article 7 UDHR, *supra* note 226; and Article 14(1) ICCPR, *supra* note 227.

290 See *e.g.* Oxymoronlist; available at: http://www.oxymoronlist.com/ (accessed 1 October 2017).

291 See Eric Blumenson, "Cultural Relativism" in Deen K. Chatterjee (ed), *Encyclopedia of Global Justice* (Dordrecht: Springer, 2011) 223 at 224.

292 See generally Ralf Michaels, "Global Legal Pluralism" (2009) 5 *Annual Review of Law & Social Science* 243.

293 See Gordon R. Woodman, "Social and Religious Diversity, Legal Pluralism: Can State Law Survive?" (2007) 15(2) *IIUM Law Journal* 154 at 162.

294 See *e.g.* William Twining, "Normative and Legal Pluralism: A Global Perspective" (2010) 20(3) *Duke Journal of Comparative & International Law* 473 at 475.

295 See Richard Nobles and David Schiff (eds), *Law, Society and Community: Socio-Legal Essays in Honour of Roger Cotterrell* (Surrey: Ashgate Publishing, 2014) at 257.

superior, unitary and, hence, reconciliatory position. A constitutional order, as Hans Kelsen wrote, "is a system of norms whose unity is constituted by the fact that they all have the same reason for their validity; and the reason for the validity of a normative order is a basic norm".[296] But then what about contradictory or conflicting norms? Does the unity provided by the basic norm also allow for these norms' equal validity?[297] In this regard, the US Supreme Court in the highly controversial case of *Roe v. Wade* stated that "the Constitution is made for people of fundamentally differing views".[298] Hence, should constitutional law not stand above contradictions as locked into an oxymoron? Apparently, not at all. Constitutional law is still widely subject to a dichotomous understanding. First, constitutional law is still held to be a matter of purely domestic and, to a lesser extent, regional, international or global nature. There are several debates that try to elevate a constitutionalist debate to the global level, such as establishing the UN Charter as the constitution of the international community, or the WTO Agreement as the constitution for international trade or for an emerging "global market".[299] These debates, however, must – alas and in spite of urgent practical needs – still be regarded as wishful thinking for the time being. Even below the global level, at the regional but supranational level of European integration, constitutionalism, as will be seen below, still meets with fierce practical and theoretical resistance.

Generally, the debate about global constitutionalism is – like that of global governance – replete with paradoxes, which have been outlined as follows:

> Thus, international relations in the 21st century reveals the *paradoxical* increase of things constitutional such as constitutionalisation, quasi-constitutional settings and practices, as opposed to contested compliance with international law, rules and procedures by powerful actors in the international system. The *paradox* rests on an imbalanced parallel development of a quantitative change on the terms of engagement, negotiation, bargaining and arbitration among a multiplicity of groups, organisations and actors, on the one hand, and the lack of qualitative constitutional means to bind decisions and ground them in normative roots demonstrating their universal validity, on the other.[300]

Many more paradoxes of the world community against the backdrop of an emerging global constitution have been identified that involve the dichotomy of law and

296 Kelsen, *supra* note 56 at 31.

297 *Ibid* at 195.

298 US Supreme Court, *Roe v. Wade* [1973] 410 US 113, 116.

299 See *e.g.* Bardo Fassbender, *The United Nations Charter as the Constitution of the International Community* (Leiden: Martinus Nijhoff Publishers, 2009) and John H. Jackson, *The World Trade Organization: Constitution and Jurisprudence* (London: The Royal Institute of Foreign Affairs, 1998).

300 See Antje Wiener et al., "Editorial: Global constitutionalism: Human Rights, Democracy and the Rule of Law" (2012) 1(1) *Global Constitutionalism* 1 at 2–3 [*Italics* added].

politics.[301] For instance, the "paradox of constitutional democracy" is made of the two clashing commitments of, on the one hand, following the ideal of a government constrained by law ("constitutionalism") and the ideal of government by act of the people ("democracy") on the other.[302] The same tensions arising from this antagonism have also been denominated as the paradox of constitutionalism per se, which was fleshed out as follows:

> Modern constitutionalism is underpinned by two fundamental though antagonistic imperatives: that governmental power ultimately is generated from the "consent of the people" and that, to be sustained and effective, such power must be divided, constrained, and exercised through distinctive institutional forms.[303]

It was also expressed by Gunther Teubner as a self-referential and paradoxical process "in which any creating of law always already presupposes rudimentary elements of its own constitution, and at the same time constitutes these only through their implementation".[304] And Giorgio Agamben explained it as a paradox of sovereignty, which "consists in the fact the sovereign is, at the same time, outside and inside the juridical order" or that "the law is outside itself" or "I, the sovereign, who am outside the law, declare that there is nothing outside the law [*che non c'è un fuori legge*]".[305] He continues to explain that "nowhere else does the paradox of sovereignty show itself so fully as in the problem of constituting power and its relation to constituted power", in the sense that the "*constitution presupposes itself as constituting power*".[306] This thought has also been expressed in terms of the paradoxical relationship between *pouvoir constituant* (constituting power or power to make a constitution) and *pouvoir constitué* (constituted power or power originating from the constitution).[307] Expressed as the ultimate paradox of the constituent sovereign, it has also been written that "the constituent power is the potentiality of law, while the constitution is law in its actuality".[308]

301 See *e.g.* Andreas Fischer-Lescano, "Die Emergenz der Globalverfassung" (2003) 63 *Zeitschrift für ausländisches und öffentliches Recht* 717 at 722–723 and Christine E. J. Schwöbel, *Global Constitutionalism in International Legal Perspective* (Leiden: Martinus Nijhoff Publishers, 2011) at 18.

302 See Frank I. Michelman, *Brennan and Democracy* (Princeton: Princeton University Press, 1999) at 4–6; see also Jürgen Habermas, "Constitutional Democracy: A Paradoxical Union of Contradictory Principles?" (2001) 29(6) *Political Theory* 766.

303 See Martin Loughlin and Neil Walker, "Introduction" in Martin Loughlin and Neil Walker (eds), *The Paradox of Constitutionalism: Constituent Power and Constitutional Form* (Oxford: Oxford University Press, 2008) 1 at 1.

304 Gunther Teubner, "Societal Constitutionalism: Alternatives to State-Centered Constitutional Theory?" in Christian Joerges, Inger-Johanne Sand and Gunther Teubner, *Transnational Governance and Constitutionalism* (Oxford: Hart, 2004) 3 at 16.

305 See Agamben, *supra* note 264 at 15.

306 *Ibid* at 39–40.

307 See Gunther Teubner, *Constitutional Fragments: Societal Constitutionalism and Globalization* (Oxford: Oxford University Press, 2012) at 61.

308 See Andreas Kalyvas, "Popular Sovereignty, Democracy, and the Constituent Power" (2005) 12(2) *Constellations* 223 at 234.

Overall, these paradoxes are akin to the classic conundrum of medieval philosophy, termed the divine omnipotence paradox, which was phrased as follows:

> For if God cannot do so, then how can one say that he is omnipotent, seeing that there is something he cannot do? But if he can do so, then how can he qualify as omnipotent, seeing that there is, or could be, another no less powerful being who can check his actions?[309]

Returning to constitutional law, there are more expressions of constitutional essentially oxymoronic concepts. To give but a few examples, a first similar dilemma was also expressed in the question of whether the Supreme Court's current doctrine of stare decisis requires adherence to the Supreme Court's current doctrine of stare decisis.[310] This is just another manifestation of the self-referential nature of constitutional power, as, in this case, vested in the Supreme Court. Another expression is found in the term "legislative intent", which was also held to be an oxymoron. The reason given was that "legislative intent is an internally inconsistent, self-contradictory expression", which has no meaning and provides a very insecure foundation for statutory interpretation.[311]

As another example from America's most fundamental constitutional document,[312] even the pursuit of happiness, referred to as an inalienable right in the preamble of the American Declaration of Independence adopted in 1776,[313] may be construed to form a paradox. This is because the Declaration of Independence was itself said to contain "audacious novelties and paradoxes".[314] Although not binding, by virtue of listing the pursuit of happiness the declaration gives expression to the idea that the happiness of society is the first law of every government.[315] But how to secure society's happiness in practice? Is it a right or duty, and what if the pursuit of happiness collides with other obligations?[316] Why was not happiness but merely the "pursuit" of it recognized as a right?[317] An answer may be found

309 See Nicholas Rescher, *Paradoxes: Their Roots, Range and Resolution* (Chicago: Open Court, 2001) at 130.

310 See Michael S. Paulsen, "Does the Supreme Court's Current Doctrine of Stare Decisis Require Adherence to the Supreme Court's Current Doctrine of Stare Decisis?" (2007–2008) 86(5) *North Carolina Law Review* 1165.

311 See Kenneth A. Shepsle, "Congress is a 'They', Not an 'It': Legislative Intent as Oxymoron" (1992) 12(2) *International Review of Law and Economics* 239 at 239.

312 See Dennis J. Mahoney, "Declaration of Independence" (1986) 24(1) *Society* 46 at 46.

313 See James Brown Scott (ed), *The Declaration of Independence; the Articles of Confederation; the American Constitution* (New York: Oxford University Press, 1917) at 3.

314 See Moses Coit Tyler, *The Literary History of the American Revolution 1763–1783* (New York: G.P. Putnam's Sons, 1897) at 499.

315 See Carl Becker, *The Declaration of Independence: A Study in the History of Political Ideas* (New York: Harcourt, Brace and Company, 1922) at 108–109.

316 See also Herbert W. Schneider, "Obligations and the Pursuit of Happiness" (1952) 61(3) *The Philosophical Review* 312 at 313–316.

317 See Arthur M. Schlesinger, "The Lost Meaning of "The Pursuit of Happiness"" (1964) 21(3) *The William and Mary Quarterly* 326 at 326.

in the paradox of happiness, according to which focusing solely on happiness would result in frustration and unhappiness, whereas practising different meaningful activities would indirectly but eventually lead to happiness. Paradoxically, it has also been stated that the active pursuit of the ideal may also lead to the neglect of the actual possibilities of the present.[318] The very same advice, quite useful in times of an acceleration of everything, was given by Bertold Brecht in the *Threepenny Opera*: "Go running after luck but don't you run too fast: We are all running after luck and luck is running last".[319]

The paradox of the pursuit of happiness invites thoughts about its role in a quest for a global constitutional framework. In this context, the term "comparative constitutionalism" gains particular relevance. But comparative constitutionalism may and must therefore be considered an oxymoron as much as comparative international law, even though for different reasons. While in the case of comparative international law a comparison seemed superfluous, because comparing the identical (i.e. uniform laws) seems like a waste of time, in the case of comparative constitutional law, it may be the claim for a unitary and hierarchically higher position that is at the heart of the apparent contradiction.[320] This last point is supported by the critical question of whether "constitutional pluralism" (like dogmatic scepticism) amounts to an oxymoron.[321]

In this sense, even at the purely national level, a "cosmopolitan state", as H. Patrick Glenn discussed in his book of that title, is still widely considered to be an oxymoron.[322] Glenn himself confirmed to me in an email that he had been told it is an oxymoron.[323] This is most likely because statehood is – unlike the strong evidence to the contrary presented by Glenn – widely held to be synonymous with national interest. The same can most likely be said about the "globalization of nationality".[324]

In the end, comparative law and constitutional law are closely intertwined with all the subcategories comprised in the distinction between public and private international law or even international public and international private law. These brief instances show that today's reality is often difficult to reconcile with a traditional classification of legal disciplines and subdisciplines. Strong evidence for the process of the blurring of former categories is provided by another area of law, that of the European Union.[325]

318 See John Moffitt, Jr, "The Pursuit of Human Happiness" (1938) 49(1) *Ethics* 1 at 5.

319 Bertolt Brecht, *The Threepenny Opera* (Eric Bentley, trans.) (New York: Grove Press, 1964) at 76.

320 See also Yaniv Roznai, "The Theory and Practice of 'Supra-Constitutional' Limits on Constitutional Amendments" (2013) 62(3) *International and Comparative Law Quarterly* 557.

321 See Martin Loughlin, "Constitutional Pluralism: An Oxymoron?" (2014) 3(1) *Global Constitutionalism* 9 at 9 and 30.

322 H. Patrick Glenn, *The Cosmopolitan State* (Oxford: Oxford University Press, 2013).

323 Email from Prof. H. Patrick Glenn, (6 February 2014; 8:41 PM) [on file with author].

324 See generally Francisco Orrego Vicuña, "The Globalization of Nationality" (2005) 38(150) *Estudios Internacionales* 119.

325 See also Bruno de Witte, "The Crumbling Public/Private Divide: Horizontality in European Antidiscrimination Law" (2009) 13(5) *Citizenship Studies* 515.

5.3.4 *European Union law* – discordia concors *or united in diversity*

The EU and its law is not only one of the foremost and most dynamic laboratories for the development of supranational law and trends in international law,[326] it is also a fertile ground for essentially oxymoronic concepts. This is no surprise given that the term "European Union" can itself be regarded as an oxymoron, because a union between nation states that have developed as such over centuries appears impossible. As a euphemism, perhaps, the apparent impossibility due to its inherent contradiction is being circumscribed by virtue of the oxymoronic terms "*discordia concors*" (harmonious discord) [327] or its unofficially official motto "united in diversity".[328] More so, the term may even have evolved in line with the broader trend from an essentially contested to an oxymoronic concept but the contestation of the project itself remains the same.[329] The supranationalism advocated by the EU and its predecessor, the European Community, was also described as dualistic and, therefore, giving rise to several contradictions.[330] As a "European Polity", the EU has also been characterized as a paradox, which consists in various "features of the process of European integration which suggest that the European Union is simultaneously both 'near-state' and antithetical to stateness" and "a parallel development of two dimensions: one institutional, the other theoretical".[331] From a legal perspective, the law of the EU (EU law) has changed its structure by moving (slowly) from a dual to a more complex but cooperative form of federalism.[332]

Progressively, EU law has even advanced to a paradox related to its own law, due to the fact that "European legal integration provides an enduring challenge to social scientists and lawyers, who have not yet been able to establish the integration processes as a coherent scientific object".[333] This means that, despite being multidisciplinary and cross-sectional in its scope and application, EU law

326 See also Rostam J. Neuwirth, "Global Governance and the Reform of the Global Legal Order: Insights from the European Union's Legal System" in Pascaline Winand, Andrea Benvenuti, Max Guderzo (eds), *The External Relations of the European Union* (Brussels: P.I.E. Peter Lang, 2015) 331.

327 See Werner Kaegi, "Discordia Concors: Vom Mythos Basels und von der Europa-idee Jacob Burckhardts" in Marc Sieber (ed), *Discordia Concors – Festgabe fur Egar Bonjour zu seinem siebzigsten Geburtstag am 21. August 1968*, vol 1 (Basel: Helbing & Lichtenhahn, 1968) 131.

328 See the Declaration No. 52 on the Symbols of the European Union, O.J. C 83 (30 March 2010) at 355.

329 See also Zenon Bańkowski and Emilios Christodoulidis, "The European Union as an Essentially Contested Project" (1998) 4(4) *European Law Journal* 341.

330 See Joseph Weiler, "The Community System: The Dual Character of Supranationalism" (1981) 1(1) *Yearbook of European Law* 267 at 267.

331 See Jo Shaw and Antje Wiener, "The Paradox of the 'European Polity'" in Maria Green Cowles and Michael Smith (eds), *The State of the European Union: Risks, Reform, Resistance, and Revival*, vol 5 (Oxford: Oxford University Press, 2000) 64 at 64.

332 See Robert Schütze, *From Dual to Cooperative Federalism: The Changing Structure of European Law* (Oxford: Oxford University Press, 2009).

333 See Mikael Rask Madsen et al., "General Introduction: Paradoxes of European Legal Integration" in Hanne Petersen et al. (ed), *Paradoxes of European Legal Integration* (Aldershot: Ashgate, 2008) 1 at 1.

is still largely divided along the traditional lines of various dichotomies, such as national versus international law, public versus private or civil versus criminal law, to mention but a few. Only slowly does even the overall legal framework of the EU overcome the fragmentations deriving from these dichotomies and its resulting fragmentation.[334] It suffices to mention here, first, the institutional split or "separation of twins at birth" between a political and economic process of integration, manifest in the original bifurcation of competences between the European Economic Community, on the one hand, and the Council of Europe on the other;[335] or else, the birth as an ordinary organization of international law and its gradual transformation into a sui generis supranational organization by having "limited their sovereign rights and hav[ing] thus created a body of law which binds both their nationals and themselves".[336]

More paradoxes have been identified in what has been termed "in practice a set of relative oppositions which are important drivers in the continuous making of Europe".[337] In other words, the EU, in its present "dynamic status quo", is driven by a great number of dichotomies, or apparently antagonistic forces, such as widening and deepening or negative and positive forms of integration.[338] Also the method is controversial and combines elements of a constitutionalist and a functionalist method of integration.[339] Further dividing dichotomies in Europe are those of cooperation versus competition or of centralization versus decentralization, which are perhaps not expressed in essentially oxymoronic but at least essentially contested concepts or disguised in a plethora of technical terms or "Eurospeak" (a kind of EU version of Orwell's "doublethink"), like the open method of coordination or the principle of subsidiarity. The open method of coordination is a kind of oxymoronic soft law mechanism of decision making notably in areas where the EU has no competence and is said to organize "a learning process in order to promote the exchange of experiences and best practices" as a departure from the traditional forms of legislative procedures.[340] Interestingly, the open method of coordination was itself born out of a paradox, namely that this "'new' mode of governance was not originally recognised as such by the summit which launched it".[341] Subsidiarity is defined to require a

334 See also Marise Cremona, "Coherence through Law: What Difference Will the Treaty of Lisbon Make?" (2008) 3(1) *Hamburg Review of Social Sciences* 11.

335 See also Gerard Guinn, "The European Union and the Council of Europe on the Issue of Human Rights: Twins Separated at Birth?" (2001) 46(4) *McGill Law Journal* 849.

336 See Case 6/64, *Costa v E.N.E.L.*, (1964) E.C.R. 585 at pt. 3.

337 See Madsen et al., *supra* note 333 at 1.

338 See *e.g.* Markus Jachtenfuchs, "Deepening and Widening Integration Theory" (2002) 9(4) *Journal of European Public Policy* 650 and Fritz W. Scharpf, *Balancing Positive and Negative Integration: The Regulatory Options for Europe*, EUI Policy Paper 97/4 (1997).

339 See *e.g.* Léontin-Jean Constantinesco, *Das Recht der Europäischen Gemeinschaften: Das institutionelle Recht* (Baden-Baden: Nomos, 1977) at 113–122.

340 See *e.g.* Sabrina Regent, "The Open Method of Coordination: A New Supranational Form of Governance?" (2003) 9(2) *European Law Journal* 190 at 190–191.

341 See Claudio M. Radaelli, *The Open Method of Coordination: A New Governance Architecture for the European Union?* (Stockholm: Swedish Institute for European Policy Studies, 2003) at 14.

justification for proposed actions in areas which do not fall within the EU's exclusive competence so that the objectives of the proposed actions can be better achieved at the Union level.[342] It too has been referred to as a paradox, namely in a sense that its function and aim are antithetical because "subsidiarity seeks to integrate nations and individuals while simultaneously sustaining the diversity of the EU's Member States and their regions by preserving their autonomy in certain fields of governance such as 'culture'".[343] Subsidiarity has also been found to be in a paradoxical relation to democracy, because when subsidiarity is fully applied, the decision-making process becomes more complex and less transparent, which is the opposite of what democratic decision making implies.[344]

Together, the problems tackled by the open method of coordination and subsidiarity have also been discussed in the context of the oxymoron "flexicurity", a portmanteau of flexibility and security, which are usually seen as diametric opposites.[345] Gradually, the opposition has given way to a gradual approach where flexibility and security are no longer contradictory to one another, but in many situations can be mutually supportive.[346] Latterly flexicurity has been defined as a policy strategy that

> attempts, synchronically and in a deliberate way, to enhance the flexibility of labour markets, work organization and labour relations on the one hand, and to enhance security – employment and social security – notably for weaker groups in and outside the labour market, on the other hand.[347]

Even at a broader level, social policies in the context of the EU's new growth strategy for the next decade, termed "Europe 2020", have been described as a potential oxymoron.[348] This means that economic and social policies are still widely regarded as mutually incompatible or their goals contradictory. The whole

342 Article 5(3) Treaty on European Union (TEU), in Consolidated versions of the Treaty on European Union and the Treaty on the Functioning of the European Union, O.J. C 83/1 (30 March 2010).

343 See Jeff Edmund Katcherian, "Unraveling the Paradox: Competence and the Failure of Subsidiarity in the European Union" (2012) 35(2) *Political and Legal Anthropology Review* 271 at 271 (citing Chantal Millon-Delsol, *Le Principe de Subsidiarité* (Paris: Presses Universitaires de France, 1992).

344 See Steven van Hecke, "The Principle of Subsidiarity: Ten Years of Application in the European Union" (2003) 13(1) *Regional & Federal Studies* 55 at 67.

345 See Pascale Vielle and Jean-Michel Bonvin, "Putting Security at the Heart of the European Social Pact – Proposals to Make Flexicurity More Balanced" (2008) 14(3) *Transfer: European Review of Labour and Research* 419 at 421.

346 See Per Kongshøj Madsen, "Flexicurity" A New Perspective on Labour Markets and Welfare States in Europe" (2007) 14(1) *Tilburg Law Review* 57 at 75.

347 See Luigi Burroni and Maarten Keune, "Flexicurity: A Conceptual Critique" (2011) 17(1) *European Journal of Industrial Relations* 75 at 77 [references omitted].

348 See Bart Vanhercke, "Is the 'Social Dimension of Europe 2020' an Oxymoron?" in Christophe Degryse and David Natali (eds), *Social developments in the European Union* (Brussels: ETUI and Observatoire Social Européen, 2010) 141.

process is in fact also referred to by the paradox of the EU just running to stand still.[349] This widely characteristic phenomenon may also be captured by the term "dynamic status quo" or the Lampedusa paradox, in the sense that the EU keeps changing (and amending the treaties as well as reforming the institutions) only to keep things the same. In 2011, Giuliano Amato and Yves Mény also referred to some of the institutional changes in the EU as paradoxes, or else even serious problems, which bring the EU back into a state of paralysis and inefficiency, as the United Nations has been over the past half a century.[350] Among these problems, they mention the difficulty in taking decisions, the defence of national interests, and the supremacy of the larger countries, which also characterize the UN, the management of which has also been termed an oxymoron.[351]

Clearly, there are many more apparent contradictions found along the lines of various dichotomies, such as between old and new Europe in different contexts, from security questions to the global banking system.[352] These various dichotomies can be summarized by the European integration process often proceeding in the form of "agreements to disagree" or, stated in more euphemistic terms, "compromises". The ongoing Brexit talks are not only another example of an agreement to disagree but, in the form of a "soft Brexit" was also termed an oxymoron.[353] To cut a long and complex story short, the process of European integration as governed by EU law is both explicitly and implicitly replete with oxymora, contradictions and paradoxes. This is caused by many dichotomies, which, paradoxically, signify both its strength and weakness, blessing and curse, challenge and chance. In general, among such forces, EU law scholars and EU lawmakers oscillate nervously between the extreme poles of antagonistic concepts as much as EU citizens struggle to understand the dual nature of "state citizenship" and "union membership" as printed on the passports of each of the

349 See David Natali and Bart Vanhercke, "Foreword: European Paradox: Is the EU Running to Stand Still?" in David Natali and Bart Vanhercke (eds), *Social Developments in the European Union* (Brussels: ETUI and Observatoire Social Européen, 2011) 11.

350 See Giuliano Amato and Yves Mény (with Cécile Barbier and David Natali), "Is the EU Becoming More Like the UN? Paradoxes Around EU Institutional Developments in 2011 and Risks for Future Integration" in David Natali and Bart Vanhercke (eds), *Social Developments in the European Union* (Brussels: ETUI and Observatoire Social Européen, 2011) 25; see also Neuwirth, "Global Governance and the Reform of the Global Legal Order", *supra* note 326.

351 See *e.g.* United Nations High Level Panel on Coherence, *Delivering as One: Report of the High-level Panel on United Nations System-wide Coherence in the Areas of Development, Humanitarian Assistance and the Environment*, G.A. A/61/583 (9 November 2006); see Franz Baumann, "United Nations Management—An Oxymoron?" (2016) 22(4) *Global Governance* 461.

352 See *e.g.* Jiri Sedivy and Marcin Zaborowski, "Old Europe, New Europe and Transatlantic Relations" (2004) 13(3) *European Security* 187 and Allen N. Berger, "Obstacles to a Global Banking System: 'Old Europe' versus 'New Europe'" (2007) 31(7) *Journal of Banking & Finance* 1955.

353 See "Theresa May's Brexit moves from tautology to oxymoron but makes the best of a bad job" (20 January 2017); available at: http://thinkingliberal.co.uk/theresa-mays-brexit-moves-from-tautology-to-oxymoron-but-makes-the-best-of-a-bad-job/ (accessed 1 October 2017).

EU member states.[354] European citizens must thus feel schizophrenic, like Dr Jekyll and Mr Hyde,[355] wondering which is the "evil personality", the national or the supranational (i.e. European) identity? Related to this issue is the question of whether European citizens feel alienated from the EU or, put simply, whether Europe is a democracy without a *demos*?[356] It also invites the question of whether the EU's dual federalism is cooperative, which at times appears as oxymoronic and at other times as tautological.[357] In all cases the answers appear clear as European scepticism or "Euroscepticism" have been on the rise, while support for European integration is waning as was also confirmed recently by the Brexit vote in the United Kingdom.[358] Therefore, it is debatable whether "mainstream Eurosepticism" is a trend or an oxymoron.[359]

In either case, the answer to this question is complex, as both the causes of the problems of Euroscepticism and their possible solutions may be found in paradoxes, as Joseph Weiler explained in the following paragraph:

> We come to understand here one of the *profound paradoxes* of European Integration. These very values, which find their legal and practical expression in, e.g., enhanced mobility, breakdown of local markets, and insertion of universal norms into domestic culture are also part of the deep modern and postmodern anxiety of European belongingness and part of the roots of European angst and alienation. A meaningful, legitimate and legitimating concept of Constitutionalism would have to face and mediate this *paradox*.[360]

Thus constitutionalism, or more concretely the adoption of a European Constitution, was seen as a possible way out of the dilemma. Adopting a European Constitution was seen as a chance finally to put an end to the uncertainty and indeterminacy about the EU's legal status, which was thus far merely approached by vague and contested concepts or paradoxical phrases like being "less than a federation but more than a regime" or "an international agreement

354 See also Joseph H. H. Weiler, "Does Europe Need a Constitution? Demos, Telos and the German Maastricht Decision" (1995) 3(1) *European Law Journal* 219 at 250–256.

355 See Robert L. Stevenson, *The Strange Case of Dr. Jekyll and Mr. Hyde* (London: Longmans & Green, 1886).

356 See *e.g.* Mette Jolly, "A Demos for the European Union?" (2005) 25(1) *Politics* 12.

357 See Schütze, *supra* note 332.

358 See *e.g.* Eurobarometer, *Public Opinion on the European Union* (Brussels: European Commission, 2007) and Sara B. Hobolt, "The Brexit Vote: A Divided Nation, a Divided Continent" (2016) 23(9) *Journal of European Public Policy* 1259.

359 See Leonard Ray, "Mainstream Euroskepticism: Trend or Oxymoron?" (2007) 42(2–3) *Acta Politica* 153.

360 See Joseph H. H. Weiler, "Epilogue: The European Courts of Justice: Beyond 'Beyond Doctrine' or the Legitimacy Crisis of European Constitutionalism" in Anne-Marie Slaughter, Alex Stone Sweet and Joseph H. H. Weiler (eds), *The European Court and National Courts—Doctrine and Jurisprudence: Legal Change in Its Social Context* (Oxford: Hart, 1998) 365 at 371 [*Italics* added].

but none the less constituting the constitutional charter of a Community based on the rule of law".[361]

In fact, it was the way chosen following the speech by Joschka Fischer on 12 May 2000, which turned a "constitutional conversation"[362] or the EU's "constitutional *Sonderweg*"[363] into concrete action.[364] To this end, the Laeken Declaration on the Future of the European Union was intended to pave the way towards a constitution for European citizens.[365] However, what ensued from the work of the European Convention on the Future of Europe was not a European Constitution but the birth of an oxymoron. The reason for treating it as an oxymoron is given by Giuliano Amato, as retold by Jacques Ziller, as follows:

> "È un maschio!", exclaimed Giuliano Amato (former Prime Minister of Italy and Vice-President of the Convention), referring to the text which the Convention had just ushered into the world in June 2003: "It's a boy!" And this remark plays on the fact that, in Italian, the word for "treaty" (*tratatto*) is masculine, whereas Amato would have preferred a "girl", since the word *Costituzione* is feminine. The remark was thus a kind of gentle indictment of the Convention for its lack of boldness, i.e., for its failure to go beyond the existing Treaties and transform them into a true Constitution. Amato also made reference to Neil Jordan's film *The Crying Game*, in which a militant of the IRA holding a British soldier captive falls in love with his prisoner's girlfriend, only to find in due course that this "girlfriend" is in fact a transvestite.[366]

So the final result of the convention, the 2004 Treaty Establishing a Constitution for Europe, was, factually and legally speaking, an oxymoron, or, put differently, a legal "transvestite".[367] Technically speaking, it was considered "a hybrid text

361 See William Wallace, "Less than a Federation. More than a Regime: The Community as a Political System" in Helen Wallace and William Wallace (eds), *Policy-Making in the European Community* (Oxford: Oxford University Press, 1983) 403 and Opinion 1/91, Draft agreement between the Community, on the one hand, and the countries of the European Free Trade Association, on the other, relating to the creation of the European Economic Area, [1991] E.C.R. I-6079 at para. 1.

362 See Bruno de Witte, "The Closest Thing to a Constitutional Conversation in Europe: The Semi-Permanent Treaty Revision Process" in Paul Beaumont, Carole Lyons and Neil Walker (eds), *Convergence and Divergence in European Public Law* (Oxford: Hart, 2002) 39.

363 See Joseph H. H. Weiler, "In Defence of the Status Quo: Europe's Constitutional Sonderweg" in Joseph H. H. Weiler and Marlene Wind (eds), *European Constitutionalism Beyond the State* (Cambridge: Cambridge University Press, 2003) 7.

364 See Joschka Fischer, "From Confederacy to Federation: Thoughts on the Finality of European Integration" in Christian Joerges, Yves Mény and Joseph H. H. Weiler (eds), *What Kind of Constitution for What Kind of Polity? – Responses to Joschka Fischer* (San Domenico: European University Institute, 2000) 19.

365 See Laeken Declaration on the future of the European Union, (December 15, 2001), EC Bulletin 12-2001.

366 See Jacques Ziller, *The European Constitution* (The Hague: Kluwer, 2005) at 29.

367 See Treaty Establishing a Constitution for Europe, [2004] O.J. C 310/1 (16 December 2004); see also Draft Treaty Establishing a Constitution for Europe, [2003] O.J. C 169/7 (18 July 2003).

reflecting hard-won compromises between opposing visions of the purpose and direction of European integration".[368] The rest of the story is well known and the Constitutional Treaty failed to be ratified after negative referenda in France and the Netherlands.[369] The final result was also explained by essentially oxymoronic concepts, such as a "successful failure" or the paradox of "No" meaning "Yes".[370] In concrete terms, the "successful failure" of the Constitutional Treaty led to the adoption of the so-called Lisbon Treaty in 2007 instead. Thus, ever since, the EU has continued its present practices and search for a future *finalité* through various essentially oxymoronic concepts, such as a quest for a constitution without a constitutional treaty"[371], a shift from "dual to cooperative federalism",[372] and strong ambivalence towards the process of European integration altogether.[373]

5.4 Is law "essentially oxymoronic"?

> *The claim is that a legal system necessarily yields a significant range of "borderline cases"—cases in which the application of the standards of the law is subject to doubt and disagreement.*[374]

At the outset of this chapter the question was put whether essentially oxymoronic concepts also play a fundamental or – similar to art and science – even an increasingly significant role in law. Quantitatively speaking, it can be stated that their role in law is important and still growing. Generally, the numerous examples from case law and jurisprudence seem to support this proposition, precisely because of the largely dualistic conception of the law. With notable exceptions, a non-exhaustive review of case law mainly in the English language from around the world shows that oxymora are frequently invoked, discussed or used for a variety of reasons in courts. Due to an excessive number of search results, paradoxes and other linguistic constructions that point out conflicts or contradictions of thoughts and concepts were not even included; these would have drastically increased the number of cases. The same confirmation came from a selective

368 See Ziller, *supra* note 366 at 29.

369 See Giuliano Amato and Jacques Ziller, *The European Constitution Cases and Materials in EU and Member States' Law* (Cheltenham: Edward Elgar, 2007) at 1–67.

370 See Andreas Philippopoulos-Mihalopoulos, "Moment of Stasis: The Successful Failure of a Constitution for Europe" (2009) 15(3) *European Law Journal* 309 and Andreas Philippopoulos-Mihalopoulos, "When 'No' Means 'Yes': A Constitution for Europe and the Limits of Ignorance" in Maria Green Cowles and Michael Smith (eds), *The State of the European Union: Risks, Reform, Resistance, and Revival*, vol 5 (Oxford: Oxford University Press, 2000) 29.

371 See the Treaty on European Union (TEU) and the Treaty on the Functioning of the European Union (TFEU) (consolidated version), (2010) O.J. C 83/01 (30 March 2010); see also Stefan Griller and Jacques Ziller (eds), *The Lisbon Treaty: EU Constitutionalism without a Constitutional Treaty?* (Wien: Springer, 2009).

372 See Schütze, *supra* note 332.

373 See Rostam J. Neuwirth, "The European Union and the Ambivalence towards the Process of European Integration" (2008) 1(1) *NUJS Law Review* 33.

374 Timothy Endicott, "Law Is Necessarily Vague" (2001) 7(4) *Legal Theory* 379 at 379.

analysis of scholarly writings in different legal disciplines. A critical reader can easily verify this assertion by browsing the terms "oxymoron" or "paradox" in an Internet browser or the catalogue of any university library.

In view of these statistics in general and the cases and legal literature presented in particular, it is fair to say that essentially oxymoronic terms are of great and rising significance in law. This is surprising, given that their essentially contradictory nature is opposed to the black-and-white thinking or binary logic strongly established in law in general and by the syllogism in particular. What may be regarded as surprising too is that there is a widespread trend for an almost seamless communication or actual overlap between case law and scholarship, or legal theory and practice. This is manifest, for instance, in the many paradoxes formulated in the context of intellectual property law, such as the copyright, trademark and patent paradoxes.[375] At the same time, several court cases were confronted with the blurring of several lines of distinctions in this field, which they expressed through IP-related oxymora such as "aesthetic functionality",[376] copyright held as "co-exclusive licensees"[377] or a registered trademark called "Ghoulish Glamour".[378] This came as no surprise given that the term "intellectual property" itself bears strong traits of an oxymoron, trying to govern intangible assets based on the laws of tangible property or balancing individual reward with collective welfare. The conclusion to be drawn is that a strict separation of legal theory from legal practice may be artificial and counterproductive.

The same finding about theory and practice may apply to the relation of law to science and art, in a sense that law is both a science and an art. The seamless connection between law, art and science can be exemplified by the oxymoronic concept of *Kulturindustrie* (culture industry), which evolved from the context of a philosophical, aesthetic and social critique of the commodification of culture through mass production through the fields of sociology, economics and political economy finally to reach the sphere of law.[379] Today it has become transformed into the equally oxymoronic notion of the "creative economy", where it continues to breed more essentially oxymoronic concepts, from "glocalization" via "real fakes" to "coopetition" and "multilateralizing regionalism".

Another paradoxical example is provided by the concept of "happiness". Happiness has been mentioned through essentially oxymoronic terms in literature more than a dozen times, Brecht's phrase of "luck running last" to mention

375 See *e.g.* Tim Wu, "The Copyright Paradox" (2005) 2005 *The Supreme Court Review* 229, Catherine M. Manley, *The Trademark Paradox: Trademarks and Their Conflicting Legal and Commercial Boundaries* (Brussels: Peter Lang, 2015) and Bronwyn H. Hall and Rosemarie Ham Ziedonis, "The Patent Paradox Revisited: An Empirical Study of Patenting in the U.S. Semiconductor Industry, 1979–1995" (2001) 32(1) *The Rand Journal of Economics* 101.

376 See *Antioch Co. v. Western Trimming Corp.*, 347 F.3d 150 (6th Cir. 2003) at 156.

377 See *Nafal v. Carter*, *supra* note 165 at 1138–1139.

378 Federal Court (Toronto, Ontario), *Advance Magazine Publishers Inc. v. Farleyco Marketing Inc.*, [2009] F.C.J. No. 198 at para 70.

379 See also Rostam J. Neuwirth, *The Cultural Industries in International Trade Law: Insights from the NAFTA, the WTO, and the EU* (Hamburg: Dr. Kovač, 2006) at 30–67.

just one.[380] Psychology and economics give rise to several paradoxes of happiness, or the Easterlin paradox,[381] which may be translated into the realm of (constitutional) law by virtue of the "right to the pursuit of happiness". In a few words, law and society, as epitomized by Cardozo in the "law and literature" link, is more closely related than some legal scholars or lawyers are ready to admit. This was also well put by the Ontario Supreme Court stating that "pure law" is an oxymoron.[382]

The need for greater scientific unity, including art, is also justified by the finding that oxymora and paradoxes often "come by the dozen" in the sense that they seem to be intrinsically linked by some invisible or inexplicable bond.[383] This also proves that interdisciplinary as well as even intradisciplinary classifications obstruct the possibility of painting a more complete picture of the field researched. A look at specific legal problems shows with great clarity that the various classifications, taxonomies and categories obstruct a comprehensive presentation and, with it, a broader understanding of the complexities underlying the problem due to the linkages that exist between the different fields. Any concrete legal problem, which perhaps contains some transnational elements to be legally analysed and solved today in either theory or practice, will testify to this. Again, their separation may be a useful means but not a recommended end in itself. By contrast, essentially oxymoronic concepts seem to eschew – like cats shun water – such static classifications and disciplinary boundaries. Instead, they seem to support the proposition that interdisciplinarity is reality and not a mere buzzword of scientific endeavour.

As a consequence of the quantitative evidence, the real interest is in trying to determine the qualitative role of essentially oxymoronic concepts in law. What are the main causes for their increasing appeal in law? This may relate to the problem of overregulation and the increasing proliferation of both legal instruments and legal institutions, nationally, regionally and globally. This trend has led to more and longer legal documents, ironically captured by the oxymoronic term "lengthy briefs":

> As things stand today, however, the greatest paradox in jurisprudence is the use of the term "brief" to characterize the over-burdened, voluminous masses of complexity which are too often presented to our already over-burdened Bench.[384]

380 See Brecht, *Threepenny Opera*, *supra* note 319.

381 See Mike W. Martin, "Paradoxes of Happiness" (2008) 9(2) *Journal of Happiness Studies* 171 at 177 and Richard A. Easterlin, "Does Economic Growth Improve the Human Lot? Some Empirical Evidence" in Paul A. David and Melvin W. Reder (eds), *Nations and Households in Economic Growth: Essays in Honor of Moses Abramovitz* (New York: Academic Press, 1974) 89.

382 Ontario Superior Court of Justice, *Jackson v. Vaughan (City)*, 2010 ONSC 969, 13–14 (2010) and Ontario Superior Court of Justice, *Silveira v. Ontario (Minister of Transportation)*, 2011 ONSC 4272, 22 (2011).

383 See *e.g.* the combination of the "patent paradox" and the "antitrust paradox" in Michael A. Carrier, "Unraveling the Patent-Antitrust Paradox" (2002) 150(3) *University of Pennsylvania Law Review* 761 at 826–827.

384 See I. Maurice Wormser, "A Legal Paradox: Lengthy Briefs" (1934) 6 *N.Y.S. Bar Association Bulletin* 385 at 386.

The trend of an increased production of legal sources has already been observed for a long time under different concepts, including "plethora of law",[385] a "legal explosion"[386] or "a gigantic legislative and regulatory magma",[387] and a "deluge of norms".[388] It may also be caused by an increasing complexity of the legal issues, created inter alia by progress in science and technology. Globalization and the intensification of legal relations that increasingly connect the diversity of national (and subnational), supranational and international regimes may also be a reason for their increase. Similarly, the accelerating perception of change, caused by all these and more factors, may equally play a crucial role in the rise of essentially oxymoronic concepts. As law is closely tied to language, it is useful to look at various linguistic aspects of the perception of change before trying to evaluate the impact of essentially oxymoronic concepts on law. To summarize, law is more likely dualistic and not oxymoronic but it is the human mind that – in light of an acceleration of change and greater complexity – thinks in oxymoronic ways and therefore begins to construe and formulate laws accordingly.

385 See *e.g.* H. Patrick Glenn, "Persuasive Authority" (1987) 32(2) *McGill Law Journal* 261 at 286.
386 See *e.g.* John H. Barton, "Behind the Legal Explosion" (1974–1975) 27(3) *Stanford Law Review* 567.
387 See Bruno Oppetit, "Les tendances régressives dans l'évolution du droit contemporain" in Jean-François Pillebout (ed), *Mélanges dédiés à Dominique Holleaux* (Paris: Litec, 1990) 317 at 317.
388 See *e.g.* Andreas Heldrich, "The Deluge of Norms" (1983) 6(2) *Boston College International and Comparative Law Review* 377.

6 Change of language or language of change?

Classification must be provisional, for forms run into one another.[1]

Generally, the present epoch is not only described as the age of paradox or the Anthropocene but is also characterized by the emergence of a "global information society", i.e. an era in which information assumes an increasing importance for a wide range of human activities.[2] It is the age of mind or, as Teilhard de Chardin also called it, the "noosphere", i.e. the "sphere of reflexion, of conscious invention, of the conscious unity of souls".[3] The various terms seem related and their relevance fuelled by the rise of information and communication technologies which were said to generate a new industrial revolution.[4] To quantify the trend, it has been said that "a weekday edition of The New York Times contains more information than the average person was likely to come across in a lifetime in 17th-century England".[5] In sum, the rise of the global information society appears to occur in parallel to the growing technological capacity, first of all, to communicate, but also to store and compute information.[6] As language is an important source of information, it comes as no surprise that the vocabulary of humanity as a whole is growing. For the English language alone, it has been reported that each month about 150 million words are added to the Oxford Dictionary corpus database to track and verify new and emerging words, which leads to approximately 1,000 new entries to Oxford Dictionaries Online every year.[7] This confirms a wider historical trend but with an increased quantity, since

1 Benjamin N. Cardozo, "Law and Literature" (1939) 48(3) *Yale Law Journal* 489 (first published in 1925) at 493.

2 See generally Frank Webster, *Theories of the Information Society*, 2nd ed (London: Routledge, 2002) at 8–29.

3 See Pierre Teilhard de Chardin, *The Vision of the Past* (New Work: Harper and Row, 1966) at 63.

4 See European Commission, "Report on Europe and the Global Information Society", Bulletin of the European Union Supplement 2/94 at 10.

5 See Richard S. Wurman, *Information Anxiety 2* (Indianapolis: Que, 2001) at 5.

6 See generally Martin Hilbert and Priscila López, "The World's Technological Capacity to Store, Communicate, and Compute Information" (2011) 332(6025) *Science* 60.

7 See Oxford Dictionaries, "Oxford Dictionaries Online quarterly update: new words added to oxforddictionaries.com today" (28 August 2013); available at: http://blog.oxforddictionaries.com/august-2013-update/ (accessed 1 October 2017).

it has been found that "the number of new words added to English in the last thousand years has greatly exceeded the number of old words that have become obsolete".[8] Additionally, it was said that the "ratio of words gained to words lost has been greatly accelerated during the last five hundred years".[9]

This trend may be particular to the English language because of its status as a global language and the world's *lingua franca*, but it is in no way limited to it.[10] Generally, the number of words in all languages appears to increase over time, adding to the overall human vocabulary. Yet, it is also noteworthy that roughly half of the estimated 6,912 languages spoken today are facing extinction by the end of the twenty-first century.[11] Thus the acceleration of perception assisted by digital technologies and the Internet seems to also have increased the pace of the process of the "creative destruction" of languages. This comes as no surprise given the rise of electronic communication media which largely contribute to the current trend of information overload. But fears for the survival and integrity of languages have repeatedly been expressed in the wake of new communication technologies.[12] Changes in the means of communication have certainly left their traces in languages. As a recent trend, the ongoing screening of the language used on the Internet has revealed that "portmanteau words, or blends of words, such as phablet [phone and tablet] and jorts [(jeans) denim shorts], remain popular, as do abbreviations".[13] Unfortunately, the same source does not specify whether this particularly applies to oxymora but it suffices to show two parallel and apparently contradictory trends of blending and abbreviating words, which means making words longer and shorter at the same time. This fact, however, raises the question for the future whether it is possible that, by the year 2100, the dominant languages will be made largely of essentially oxymoronic concepts? Such a prediction seems fairly plausible given the existing rise in essentially oxymoronic concepts for which there are numerous causes.

6.1 The evolution of language: neologisms and semantic change

It is possible for any man, any woman, or any child to make new words.[14]

Why "*scio nescio*", or why, paradoxically, does it seem that the more knowledge we accumulate, the less we know or the more uncertainty we seem to face?

8 Edward L. Thorndike, "Semantic Changes" (1947) 60(4) *The American Journal of Psychology* 588 at 588.

9 *Ibid.*

10 See *e.g.* "Die deutsche Sprache wächst um 10.000 Wörter", *Die Welt* (18 July 2011); available at: http://www.welt.de/13493509 (accessed 1 October 2017).

11 See K. David Harrison, *When Languages Die: The Extinction of the World's Languages and the Erosion of Human Knowledge* (Oxford: Oxford University Press, 2007) at 3.

12 See David Crystal, *Language and the Internet* (Cambridge: Cambridge University Press, 2003) at 2.

13 See Oxford Dictionaries, *supra* note 7.

14 See John Algeo, "Where Do All the New Words Come From" (1980) 55(4) *American Speech* 264 at 272.

Alternatively, having established that essentially oxymoronic concepts are increasingly used in law and in the arts and other sciences, it means to ask what are the wider implications of this trend or their more frequent occurrence? Casting light on this trend means to understand what causes underlie this drastic change in language and the more frequent use of these rhetorical figures. In other words, why do oxymora or paradoxes seem to appear everywhere and what is it that we can derive from them? Hence, this endeavour is not only crucial for the preparation of future laws and policies but also to understand the wider trends in our globalizing societies or perhaps the evolution and eventual destiny of humanity as a whole. Thus, understanding essentially oxymoronic concepts can contribute to the urgent need "to find ways to make sense of the paradoxes, to use them to shape a better destiny".[15]

First, we can state that language usually reflects our acquired knowledge based on important changes in our environment or the discovery of new phenomena. In simplified terms, language can be said to have two principal means of accounting for change, one explicit and another more implicit. A first and more explicit means by which language reacts to change is to create a new word, a so-called "neologism".[16] A neologism is simply "any new word, morpheme or locution and any new meaning for a pre-existent word, morpheme or locution that appears in a language".[17] Examples of neologisms include the terms "catch-22" derived from Joseph Heller's novel,[18] or "black hole" for a region of space-time with a strong gravitational field,[19] or the verb "to google" meaning to browse the Internet using search engines.[20]

A second and more implicit means to embrace change in language is to use an existing term but try to expand and adapt its meaning. This is known as "semantic change" or "semantic shift", which means to keep old words but to fundamentally change the meaning attached to them.[21] Semantic changes happen in different ways, such as widening or narrowing, or metaphor.[22] It has also been stated that semantic change often goes through a stage of polysemy, where a word has more than one meaning (like the French verb "*baiser*").[23] An example

15 Charles Handy, *The Age of Paradox* (Boston: Harvard Business School Press, 1995) at xi.

16 See generally Alain Rey, "The Concept of Neologism and the Evolution of Terminologies in Individual Languages" (2005) 11(2) *Terminology* 3.

17 See Michael D. Picone, *Anglicisms, Neologisms and Dynamic French* (Amsterdam: John Benjamins Publishing, 1996) at 3.

18 Joseph Heller, *Catch-22* (New York, Simon and Schuster, 1961).

19 See Stephen A. Hawking, *Black Holes and Baby Universes and Other Essays* (Toronto: Bantam Books, 1993) at 55 and 105.

20 See *e.g.* Scott Brown, ""I Tweeted on Facebook Today:" Re-Evaluating Trademark Genericide of Internet-Based Trademarks" (2012) 7(2) *I/S: A Journal of Law and Policy for the Information Society* 457 at 471.

21 See also Leonard Bloomfield, *Introduction to the Study of Language* (New York: Henry Holt, 1914) at 237.

22 See Lyle Campbell, *Historical Linguistics: An Introduction* (Cambridge: MIT Press, 1999) at 254–267.

23 *Ibid* at 254 and 268.

of semantic change, which answers the question raised in the heading above is provided by the continued use of the terms "sunset" or "sunrise". The reason is that, following the replacement of a geocentric by a heliocentric world view, the phenomenon observed should actually mean and, therefore, be replaced by the terms "earthrise" or "earthset".

Generally, the explicit change of language as reflected in the creation of neologisms is more relevant to the emergence of essentially oxymoronic concepts. Nonetheless, even semantic change in its different forms may be relevant in both oxymora and paradoxes. This is also reflected in the distinction between paradoxes of language (semantic paradoxes) and paradoxes of mathematics (logical paradoxes).[24]

Returning to change, an interesting aspect of its nature, at least within the confines of the current framework of perception made of time and space, the opposite trend can also be possible. This is when language or literature creates new words before they have become reality or are even found to exist. A first example of this kind includes "quark", as coined by James Joyce in *Finnegans Wake*, which was later used in theoretical physics to denote a hypothetical particle, the fundamental building block of all matter.[25] This possibility is not only interesting in terms of human ingenuity and the ability to predict future events but also closely related to the normativity of law. The normativity of law can be understood as the ability to influence human behaviour or, on a wider scale, developments and possibly "fate".[26] Put differently, the principal challenge is to find out how law can both deal with change and produce the desired changes by using language.

In law, examples of an active introduction of change by neologisms include, for instance, the concept of "transnational law", which was coined to describe a new understanding of the formerly separated disciplines of public and private international law as well as criminal and civil law.[27] By contrast, an example of the second case would be the concept of "international law", which – despite its evident terminological and legal limitations – continues to be used today for numerous kinds of problems of a more complex global nature. In this regard, it is noteworthy that the concept "international law" itself constitutes a neologism that was most likely first used by Jeremy Bentham in 1780.[28] Later it replaced the

24 See Hans G. Herzberger, "Paradoxes of Grounding in Semantics" (1970) 67(6) *The Journal of Philosophy* 145 at 145.

25 John Algeo, *The Origins and Development of the English Language* (Boston: Wadsworth, 2010) at 245.

26 On normativity, see generally Chaim Gans, "The Normativity of Law and Its Co-Ordinative Function" (1981) 6(3) *Israel Law Review* 333 and Jonathan Yovel, "In the Beginning was the Word: Paradigms of Language and Normativity in Law, Philosophy, and Theology" (2001) 5 *Mountbatten Journal of Legal Studies* 5.

27 See Philip C. Jessup, *Transnational Law* (New Haven: Yale University Press, 1956) at 106.

28 See Jeremy Bentham, *Introduction to the Principles of Morals and Legislation* (London: T. Payne, 1789) at 324.

older terminology of "law of nations".[29] The term is also widely associated with the Treaty of Westphalia concluded in 1648, which is considered the starting point of the present international legal system.[30] As mirrored in another ironic neologism, namely "Westfailure",[31] however, both "Westphalia", denoting an "international political system of states claiming exclusive authority", as well as the concept "international law", applied to describe a global legal framework today, are clearly outdated and inadequate to describe successfully and to address legally the complexity and diversity of global affairs today.[32]

Interestingly, it can also happen that a term is coined before the phenomenon described by it has been discovered or created by human ingenuity, which confirms Wittgenstein's insight that "what is thinkable is also possible".[33] This is the case, for instance, with the so-called "Higgs boson" or the "memristor", which were formulated long before they were actually scientifically discovered or created.[34] The same could also be said of the term "Euro" (€) which was officially adopted in 1995, several years before it was introduced as the official currency of the Eurozone in a non-physical form on 1 January 1999.[35] Advertisements or brand names, such as Aspirin, Hoover, or Xerox also often become used in generic language afterwards, which is why they have been referred to as "generonyms", which in itself constitutes a neologism to describe genericized trademarks.[36]

Finally, neologisms also very often appear in the form of oxymora, such as "culture industry" (*Kulturindustrie*), "Brangelina" (for Brad Pitt and Angelina Jolie), or "working holidays" (for temporary visas for young people who want to holiday and work). These are further examples to show that essentially oxymoronic concepts were for a long time used primarily in the arts and notably poetry and have now more recently advanced to penetrate widely, or even "dominate", scientific discourses (including law) as well as daily colloquial speech. To understand why essentially oxymoronic concepts are on the rise, it seems that a perceived acceleration of change due to a number of factors is among its principal causes. Another cause of change in language is related to the global information society and the information overload it produces. For these two reasons, it is

29 See Peter Malanczuk, *Akehurst's Introduction to Modern International Law*, 7th ed (London: Routledge, 1997) at 5.

30 See Dionisio Anzilotti, *Cours de droit international*, vol I (Paris: Recueil Sirey, 1929) at 5.

31 See Susan Strange, "The Westfailure System" (1999) 25(3) *Review of International Studies* 345 at 345.

32 See also Yasuaki Onuma, "When was the Law of International Society Born? – An Inquiry of the History of International Law from an Intercivilizational Perspective" (2000) 2(1) *Journal of History of International Law* 1 and Stéphane Beaulac, "The Westphalian Model in Defining International Law: Challenging the Myth" (2004) 8(2) *Australian Journal of History of Law* 181.

33 Ludwig Wittgenstein, *Tractatus Logico-Philosophicus* (London: Routledge, 1960) at 43 (3.02).

34 See John Alison, *The Road to Discovery: Detector Alignment, Electron Identification, Particle Misidentification, WW Physics, and the Discovery of the Higgs Boson* (Cham: Springer, 2015) at 285 and Dmitri B. Strukov et al., "The Missing Memristor Found" (2008) 453 (7191) *Nature* 80.

35 See the Madrid European Council Presidency Conclusions, 15 and 16 December 1995.

36 See John Dwight Ingram, "The Genericide of Trademarks" (2004) 2(2) *Buffalo Intellectual Property Law Journal* 154.

important to inquire how language deals with change. More concretely, before assessing the role of paradoxes and oxymora in language change, it is helpful to look at the creation of neologism as the dominant but not exclusive tool for the adaptation of language to changes.

First, several reasons have been mentioned for the creation of neologisms. For instance, analogical creations, puns, language play, figures of speech and rhetorical devices and verbal art are named as the main reasons for the crafting of new words.[37] For the creation of neologisms, it nonetheless remains questionable whether a new word has ever been coined from scratch. Most of the time, a neologism is created from existing terms or parts thereof.[38] For instance, even "quark", coined by James Joyce, existed as a form of fresh dairy product or a kind of curd cheese in the German language.[39] Similarly, many oxymora can be considered new coinages but from existing or at least partially existing concepts.

Second, many new words or oxymora are so-called "derived words", like "coopetition" which is derived from cooperation and competition. Interestingly, even abbreviations and acronyms are listed as sources for neologisms. It is not clear why they are listed separately, as acronyms are a subcategory of abbreviations. An abbreviation denotes a shortened form of a word or phrase, whereas an acronym is an abbreviation that is formed from the initial letter or letters of each of the successive or major parts of a compound term.[40] The far more common usage of abbreviations is in acronyms, however. For an acronym, one could for instance think of the term BRIC(S) coined in 2001,[41] which now refers to Brazil, Russia, India, China and South Africa. Similarly, the abbreviation "CHINDIA" (for China and India) could also be considered as an oxymoron of not just two but multiple contradictions.[42]

Another source for new words is so-called "collocation", which includes noun compounds or adjective plus noun. This category is most relevant to the coinage of oxymora, like "*Kulturindustrie*" in German being later translated into English as both "culture industry" (noun-noun) and "cultural industry" (adjective-noun). A fifth are eponyms, which are words derived from proper names of persons, places or things. Examples of eponyms related to persons are "Freudian slip" or "Alford plea". For a place (or toponym), an example is the "bikini", which was named by its inventor after a nuclear testing site in the Pacific, namely the Bikini Atoll in

37 See D. Gary Miller, *English Lexicogenesis* (Oxford: Oxford University Press, 2014) at 88–96.

38 *Ibid* at 84.

39 See Peter Newmark, *A Textbook of Translation* (New York: Prentice-Hall International, 1988) at 142.

40 See Thomas D. Oakland, Stephen C. Lansdowne and Christopher J. Baker, "Acronyms and Abbreviations: Convention or Confusion?" (1981) 62(10) *The Phi Delta Kappan* 764 at 764.

41 See Rostam J. Neuwirth, "The Enantiosis of BRICS: BRICS La[w]yers and the Difference That They Can Make", in Rostam J. Neuwirth, Alexandr Svetlicinii and Denis De Castro Halis (eds), *The BRICS-Lawyers' Guide to Global Cooperation* (Cambridge: Cambridge University Press, 2017) 8.

42 See Pete Engardio, *Chindia: How China and India are Revolutionizing Global Business* (New York: McGraw-Hill, 2007).

the Marshall Islands, anticipating its "explosive impact" on fashion.[43] Equally, an eponym can be modified by use of a collocation to become an oxymoron, like, for instance, "burqini".[44] The burqini is a combination of bikini and a burqa, two obviously quite different fashion items when it comes to their respective coverage of bare skin. The burqini has recently created a legal controversy in France where its use on the beach has been banned by several towns. Later the highest administrative court suspended the ban in at least one town.[45]

A final category of interest is "transferred words", which may also be related to an increasing globalization of language. Transferred words are words from a foreign language, which may have kept just one or part of their sense in their original language. An oxymoronic version of this could be the gourmet pizza, a combination of originally French and Italian words but now also an English term.

These are thus different expressions by which neologisms and also oxymora are being created. The principal reason underlying their creation is change as apparently the only constant. Related to change is the instability of language, which is due to the fact that – because of change – experience is always new. Because of that, language also constantly changes,[46] and an easy way for language to change is through new words. New words are reported to "have been entering English at an ever increasing rate" given that in the last decades "blends have become even more common, and nowadays, one encounters new blends almost every day".[47]

The phenomenon of change and the need to adapt to it can, therefore, be named the principal common ground between neologism and oxymora (and paradoxes).[48] They are related because neologisms are coined to follow change and a large part of them are oxymora, because they are better equipped to describe change perceived by the contrasting effects between antagonistic references. Moreover, it was found that frequently used forms tend to become shorter, which is also known as Zipf's law of the principle of least effort.[49] According to Zipf's law "every language is demonstrably undergoing formal and semantic changes which act on the whole in the direction of shortening the sizes of longer words, or of increasing the frequencies of shorter words".[50] The shortening effect can also occur in oxymora when they combine in one word contradictions that used to be expressed in lengthy paradoxes before.

Neologisms, especially in the form of blends, and oxymora also bear important similarities when it comes to their impact on the reader's or listener's mind. The

43 See *e.g.* Jennifer Craik, *The Face of Fashion: Cultural Studies in Fashion* (London: Routledge, 1993) at 144.
44 See Heather Marie Akou, "A Brief History of the Burqini" (2013) 39(1) *Dress* 25.
45 See Conseil d'État, Ordonnance du 26 août 2016, Nos 402742 at 402777.
46 See also Bloomfield, *supra* note 21 at 195.
47 See Adrienne Lehrer, "Understanding Trendy Neologisms" (2003) 15(2) *Rivista di Linguistica* 371 at 371.
48 As for neologisms, *ibid* at 371.
49 See John Algeo, "Where Do All the New Words Come From", *supra* note 14 at 271.
50 See George Kingsley Zipf, *Human Behavior and the Principle of Least Effort* (Boston: Addison-Wesley, 1949) at 66.

meaning of different forms of neologisms based on blends have been found to be harder to grasp.[51] Equally, neologisms are easier to grasp in context than without context.[52] It is their touch of novelty that brings a desirable effect, particularly in a world of constant stimuli in the age of information overload. Particularly in politics and advertising, neologistic blends, and likely also oxymora, are useful tools to avoid automatic responses and to catch the addressee's attention.[53] Another principal function of neologisms is said to lie in the "facilitation of communication".[54]

By comparison, as for oxymora, the relevant criteria are mainly their more or less poetic nature and the degree of the difficulty of grasping them. For this purpose, oxymora are categorized as direct and indirect oxymora. Direct oxymora are constituted by two antonyms like "feminine man", whereas indirect oxymora are made of one term and one hyponym of the antonym of the first term, like "sweet sorrow" (sorrow being a hyponym or subordinate of the term "bitterness").[55] First, it has been established statistically that indirect oxymora are more frequent than direct ones.[56] In this regard, the experiments conducted showed that people regard indirect oxymora to be more poetic than direct ones.[57] Second, readers took considerably longer time to process and understand direct oxymora than indirect oxymora.[58] Third, and finally, it was found that the process of understanding oxymora creates "emergent" features not associated with either of the oxymoron's constituent parts, which is why it is necessary to "access world knowledge to constrain their creative interpretations of seemingly contradictory concepts".[59] In other words, this finding confirms that oxymora (like paradoxes) are valuable for teaching audiences to foster independent critical, paradoxical or creative thinking.[60] More still, oxymora have been named as the archetypical metaphors, which play an important role for understanding novelty and creativity.[61] Lastly, it also confirms the finding from neologisms, whereby grasping oxymora is easier in context than without context. The importance of context and the

51 See Lehrer, *supra* note 47 at 376.
52 *Ibid* at 372.
53 *Ibid* at 380.
54 See Miller, *English Lexicogenesis, supra* note 37 at 87.
55 See Yeshayahu Shen, "On the Structure and Understanding of Poetic Oxymoron" (1987) 8(1) *Poetics Today* 105 at 108–110 and Raymond W. Gibbs Jr. and Lydia R. Kearney, "When Parting is Such Sweet Sorrow: The Comprehension and Appreciation of Oxymora" (1994) 23(1) *Journal of Psycholinguistic Research* 75 at 76.
56 See Shen, *supra* note 55 at 112.
57 See Gibbs Jr. and Kearney, *supra* note 55 at 86.
58 *Ibid.*
59 *Ibid.*
60 Cf. James L. Eliason, "Using Paradoxes to Teach Critical Thinking in Science" (1996) 25(5) *Journal of College Science Teaching* 341 at 344, Marianne W. Lewis and Gordon E. Dehler, "Learning through Paradox: A Pedagogical Strategy for Exploring Contradictions and Complexity" (2000) 24(6) *Journal of Management Education* 708 and Matthew Bryant, *Oxymoron? A Practical Guide to Fun and Effective Teaching* (New York: iUniverse, 2006).
61 See Carl R. Hausman, *A Discourse on Novelty and Creation* (The Hague: Martinus Nijhoff, 1975) at 85 and 108.

difference between new words (neologisms) and semantic change in terms of the difficulty of grasping the meaning has been described as follows:

> The comprehension of a new word puts a burden on knowledge and memory, but the comprehension of a new meaning requires also a watchful and intelligent evaluation of the context.[62]

Finally, these insights into the subtle differences of new words and new meanings give rise to important questions about the nature, function and evolution of language in general. In this regard, it was suggested in the context of neologisms that the effect of suddenly understanding the meaning of new words, like getting the punchline of a joke releases sudden laughter, creates a connection between the speaker and listener. Laughter, too, was defined as a form of "buoyant immersion", which was described as paradoxical in a sense that "it refers to plunging-down-rising-up all at once".[63] In this respect, essentially oxymoronic concepts and jokes are very similar. They share the same tensions, coming from logical contradictions in the case of the former, and from apparent incongruities in the case of the latter.[64] Moreover, they also share the fact that they rely on concepts or phrases which allow for two different interpretations or "double entendres" (double meanings), such as the following example of a headline:

> Man struck by lightning faces battery charge.[65]

In the case of oxymora and paradoxes, double entendres are also possible. Actually, the different nature of essentially oxymoronic concepts (e.g. oxymora (direct or indirect), or contradictions *in adiecto*, or paradoxes) also allow for multiple meanings of the two opposite concepts they combine. In the case of an oxymoron, a multiple meaning given to each constituent can translate into it being qualified as either an oxymoron or a tautology. For instance, the term "culture industry" can be read as either, depending on the quality of their mutual relation.

The analogy between new words and oxymora is also supported by both their reliance on and close relevance to creativity. This commonality also surfaces in humour, whereby the meaning is suddenly understood by the recognition that the dissimilarity between words can be equated (new words or metaphors) or that the apparently unfuseable, the fusion of a thesis with its antithesis, is possible (oxymora).[66]

62 See Thorndike, *supra* note 8 at 597.

63 See Rosemarie Rizzo Parse, "The Experience of Laughter: A Phenomenological Study" (1993) 6(1) *Nursing Science Quarterly* 39 at 42.

64 See Zhihui Wu, "The Laughter-Eliciting Mechanism of Humor" (2013) 2(1) *English Linguistics Research* 52 at 55–57.

65 See Robert Ornstein, *The Right Mind: Making Sense of the Hemispheres* (San Diego: Harcourt Brace, 1997) at 108.

66 See also Frank W. Wicker, "A Rhetorical Look at Humor as Creativity" (1985) 19(3) *The Journal of Creative Behavior* 175 at 179 and Alison Ross, *The Language of Humour* (London: Routledge, 1998) at 31–37.

The effect of getting the meaning of new words has been compared to the concept of "phatic communion" used by Bronislaw Malinowski. Such phatic communion, Malinowski wrote, "serves to establish bonds of personal union between people brought together by the mere need of companionship and does not serve any purpose of communicating ideas".[67] This also corresponds to the presumed effect of essentially oxymoronic concepts as opposed to contested concepts, which assumes different effects on the mind. The difference to essentially contested concepts is that "essentially oxymoronic concepts elevate conflicts from the external and interpersonal to the internal and intrapersonal level of the mind".[68] Externally, this may also mean that forms of oxymoronic thinking may help to overcome conflicts between two arguing interlocutors.

For example, in a dominant political culture of left and right or right and wrong, one can assume a debate about the true causes of climate change, namely whether it is of local or global origin. Assuming that two speakers in a parliament argue in support of these two apparently antagonistic explanations, it would be interesting to what extent the ferocity of their arguments would change if the third and oxymoronic concept of "glocal" were introduced into the debate.[69] Would then the argument still be strongly characterized by the usual fierce opposition (often between government and, literally, the "opposition")? This question has far wider implications, as experiments have been conducted in the context of intractable politico-military conflicts, where paradoxical thinking may bring positive results for the promotion of peace and, perhaps eventually, the settlement of the dispute.[70] The issue of oxymoronic or paradoxical thinking is also of utmost importance in a number of serious present-day problems. Taking the challenge of global terrorism, it is a problem that follows neither state boundaries nor binary lines of distinction and two opposed countries, military blocks or armies. This is why the call for a "war on terror" by French President Hollande in the wake of the terrorist attacks on Paris in 2015, apparently copying earlier language used by former US President George W. Bush, was considered doomed to fail as "calling for war on terror means to have already lost the war".[71]

67 See Bronislaw Malinowski, "The Problem of Meaning in Primitive Languages" in C. K. Ogden and I. A. Richards, *The Meaning of Meaning: A Study of the Influence of Language upon Thought and of the Science of Symbolism*, 5th ed (New York: Harcourt, Brace & World, 1946) 296 at 315–316.

68 See Rostam J. Neuwirth, "Essentially Oxymoronic Concepts" (2013) 2(2) *Global Journal of Comparative Law* 147 at 147 and 159.

69 See *e.g.* Joyeeta Gupta, Kim van der Leeuw and Hans de Moel, "Climate Change: A 'Glocal' Problem Requiring 'Glocal' Action" (2007) 4(3) *Environmental Sciences* 139.

70 See Boaz Hameiria et al., "Paradoxical Thinking as a New Avenue of Intervention to Promote Peace" (2014) 111(30) *Proceedings of the National Academy of Sciences* 10996.

71 See *e.g.* Jakob Augstein, "S.P.O.N. - Im Zweifel links: Wir sind der Gegner", *Der Spiegel* (16 November 2015); available at: http://www.spiegel.de/politik/deutschland/krieg-gegen-terror-wir-sind-der-gegner-kolumne-a-1062979.html (accessed 1 October 2017) and Nat Perry, "The 'War on Terror' Has Been Lost", *Consortium News* (20 November 2015); available at: https://consortiumnews.com/2015/11/20/the-war-on-terror-has-been-lost/ (accessed 1 October 2017).

This approach is likely to fail again as it did before. It is unlikely to succeed as it fails to inquire deeper into the causal relation between a problem and its solution. Most of the time, a problem cannot be fixed by using the same means as the problem, because then the problem would not even have occurred in the first place. A problem always includes an unknown element rooted in the realm of its causes, which must be discovered before the problem can be effectively solved. Nonetheless, experience or even oxymora seem to remind us that every problem always bears within it elements, at least partial, for its later solution. This also applies to the issue of global terrorism, elements of which were also described as forming paradoxes. For instance, the terror exercised by the group called "Islamic State" (IS) (or Daesh) has been called a paradox because it seems that the more it is fought, the more its appeal and the resulting danger grows.[72] It is also widely unnoticed that generally the term "Islamic state", as it is also (ab)used by terrorist groups, may – more as a postcolonial invention[73] – constitute an oxymoron.[74] This is because the principal conception of a collective polity in Islamic law is not the "state" but the "*umma*", which denotes "a 'global' or translocal community of believers in which racial, ethnic or national differences are irrelevant".[75] Given the paradoxes related to terrorism, these are more reasons why novel methods for the prevention and solution of the issue of global terrorism must be sought.[76] These novel methods require us to look first in the cognitive sphere and to formulate the most suitable language before strategies can be successfully applied.

Not surprisingly for this book, the principal question underlying the many dichotomies surrounding language also find their expression in a possible oxymoron, namely that of "cognitive neuroscience". Cognition and neuroscience, as was written by Dan Lloyd, may cohere only to the extent that "the entities identified as 'cognitive' can be coordinated with entities identified as neural".[77] This also resonates with the scientific characterization of the brain as "paradoxical".[78]

72 See *e.g.* Jessica Stern, "The Islamic State Paradox: The More We Fight It, the More Its Appeal Grows", *Politico Magazine* (17 November 2015); available at: http://www.politico.com/magazine/story/2015/11/the-islamic-state-paradox-213368 (accessed 1 October 2017).

73 See Abdullahi Ahmed An-Na'im, *Islam and the Secular State: Negotiating the Future of Shari'a* (Cambridge: Harvard University Press, 2008) at 7.

74 See also Wael B. Hallaq, *The Impossible State: Islam, Politics, and Modernity's Moral Predicament* (New York: Columbia University Press, 2013) at ix and Mojtaba Mahdavi, "Islam and the Secular State: Negotiating the Future of Shari'a, by Abdullahi Ahmed An-Na'im (Book Review)" (2013) 32(1) *Religious Studies and Theology* 133 at 133.

75 See Peter Mandaville, *Transnational Muslim Politics: Reimagining the Umma* (London: Routledge, 2001) at 18.

76 See *e.g.* David W. Orme-Johnson et al., "International Peace Project in the Middle East: The Effects of the Maharishi Technology of the Unified Field" (1988) 32(4) *The Journal of Conflict Resolution* 776, John L. Davies and Charles N. Alexander, "Alleviating Political Violence through Reducing Collective Tension: Impact Assessment Analyses of the Lebanon War" (2005) 17(1) *Journal of Social Behavior & Personality* 285 and David W. Orme-Johnson, "Applications of Maharishi Vedic Science to Public Policy" (2005) 17(1) *Journal of Social Behavior & Personality* 377.

77 See Dan Lloyd, "Is 'Cognitive Neuroscience' an Oxymoron?" (2011) 18(4) *Philosophy, Psychiatry, & Psychology* 283 at 283.

78 See *e.g.* Narinder Kapur (ed), *The Paradoxical Brain* (Cambridge: Cambridge University Press, 2011).

The scientific paradox and oxymoron of the relation between cognition and neuroscience confirms the findings of the preceding inquiry. More concretely, it revealed that the rise of essentially oxymoronic concepts and notably oxymora (and similar related rhetorical figures) can be related to the study of change in both perception and in language, manifest in neologisms and semantic changes. Put simply, the change of language and the language of change seem to function primarily through conceptual shifts or semantic drifts.[79] Considering oxymora as part of the trend of neologisms, their rise has been confirmed both in quantitative terms as well as qualitative terms. Put briefly, the main factors for the rising appeal of essentially oxymoronic concepts in the present age are the following.

A first notable factor for the rise of oxymoronic concepts is an acceleration of the perception of change. This trend can be paired with and compared to the invention of cinematography. Cinematography has achieved the paradoxical effect of creating a sense of motion through the projection of successive "still photographs". Cinematography is therefore as much of an oxymoron as is the Latin adage "*festina lente*" (make haste slowly). Oxymora and paradoxes thus assist language in better adapting to the increasing pace of (the perception of) change. This has also been confirmed by the study of the organization of change or change management by the finding that "our current terminology and conceptual language for organizational change make it difficult to address the range of changes confronting contemporary organizations".[80] Thus by condensing the ever faster oscillating extremes or contrasts between two different poles of our perception into one, essentially oxymoronic concepts drastically facilitate the communication of dynamic processes. In a seemingly contradictory way, they provide a static tool for the definition and communication of dynamic processes.

A second factor is the exponential increase in the communication of information, a kind of information overload,[81] produced and aided by new information and communication technologies. Symbolically, these technologies advanced rapidly, developing further from, first, the invention of cinematography, followed by the computer and related developments. This phenomenon is also reflected in oxymora like "raw data" or "global village". This is also a process largely driven by the invention of new and especially digital technologies. Interestingly, digital technologies are fuelled by a system known as binary arithmetic, using numeric values using two different symbols: typically 0 (zero) and 1 (one). However, recently, the binary codes seem to have been replaced by more fuzzy or oxymoronic ones, as in the case of soft or quantum computing.[82]

79 See generally Elisabeth Davenport and Blaise Cronin, "Knowledge Management: Semantic Drift or Conceptual Shift?" (2000) 41(4) *Journal of Education for Library and Information Science* 294.

80 See Robert J. Marshak, "Changing the Language of Change: How New Contexts and Concepts are Challenging the Ways We Think and Talk about Organizational Change" (2002) 11(5) *Strategic Change* 279 at 279.

81 See Alvin Toffler, *Future Shock* (London: Pan Books, 1971) at 318.

82 See *e.g.* Rudolf Seising (ed), *Views on Fuzzy Sets and Systems from Different Perspectives: Philosophy and Logic, Criticisms and Applications* (Berlin: Springer, 2009).

Convergence is the third factor, as, paradoxically, the dualistic system itself leads to a process whereby numerous lines of distinction between antagonistic concepts or antonyms are coming under pressure. The distinctions seem to come under pressure from both an acceleration of perception (of change) and from oxymoronic concepts, as both have the tendency to blur our perception by pulling antonyms closer together by an invisible force. In the visible world, the tendency can be observed as convergence between many distinct and often opposite fields or concepts, such as "nutriceutics" which merges products of the food and health industries.

Fourth comes uncertainty, as the acceleration of change, information overload and the blurring of formerly established lines of distinction through convergence together contribute to a greater sense of uncertainty. The uncertainty is coupled with the unknown, the scientifically inexplicable, and the verbally ineffable. In cognitive terms, these combined factors interfere with our ability to think and contribute to a reduction of the quality of decision making.[83] In short, various mysteries are also a strong factor for the crafting of essentially oxymoronic concepts.[84] The reason is that they have the power to highlight inadequate knowledge and also fuel scientific progress.[85]

In sum, these four interrelated factors underpin the recent rise of essentially oxymoronic concepts. With regard to language, it was first noted that, from a synchronic perspective, language change is a paradox itself and an "evolving language", a *contradictio in adiecto*.[86] Yet, languages appear to change constantly for several reasons.[87] Most of all, they seem to change in accordance with a pattern similar to the change of the physical conditions between solids, fluids and gases. Thus, with regard to language, it seems that sounds (phonetics) change faster than meanings (semantics), ideas faster than words, but the spoken word faster than the written word, and all words change faster than grammar.[88] Grammar does change, but the changes usually proceed "slowly and [are] invisible at close range".[89] By comparison, grammar seems to change faster than language as a whole and, possibly, language faster than logic. If indeed words

83 See also Toffler, *supra* note 81 at 318 and Cheri Speier, Joseph Valacich and Iris Vessey, "The Influence of Task Interruption on Individual Decision Making: An Information Overload Perspective" (1999) 30(2) *Decision Sciences* 337 at 338.

84 See also Alois M. Haas, *Sermo mysticus: Studien zu Theologie und Sprache der deutschen Mystik* (Freiburg: Universitätsverlag, 1989) at 27–28.

85 See Narinder Kapur et al., "The Paradoxical Nature of Nature" in Narinder Kapur (ed), *The Paradoxical Brain* (Cambridge: Cambridge University Press, 2011) 1 at 1 and Margaret Cuonzo, *Paradox* (Cambridge: The MIT Press, 2014) at 209–210.

86 See Eugenio Coseriu, *Sincronía, diacronía e historia: el problema del cambio lingüístico*, 3rd ed (Madrid: Biblioteca Románica Hispánica, 1978) at 11–12.

87 See Ulrich Detges and Richard Wallereit, "Introduction" in Ulrich Detges and Richard Waltereit (eds), *The Paradox of Grammatical Change: Perspectives from Romance* (Amsterdam: John Benjamins Publishing Company, 2008) 1.

88 See Algeo, "Where Do All the New Words Come From", *supra* note 14 at 264.

89 See Geoffrey Leech et al. (eds), *Change in Contemporary English: A Grammatical Study* (Cambridge: Cambridge University Press, 2009) at xix.

can change our brains,[90] then essentially oxymoronic concepts are able to influence and change the way we think, feel, reason, speak, and perceive.

In sum, these issues raise important questions about human cognition, and the existence and nature of humans. In particular, they raise serious concerns about the present state of science and notably the inadequacy of the present scientific paradigm, which seems to rely on a strongly dualistic conception but then only seems to produce contradictory or paradoxical results.[91] This point was also aptly expressed in the question of whether it is "a paradox or have we entered a world order in which Western dualistic thinking has somewhat lost its validity?".[92]

As yet another paradox, it seems that the "hard" natural sciences, which used to deliver hard and concrete scientific insights, have abandoned the dualistic paradigm (and binary logic) to embrace a more paradoxical thinking based on polyvalent or fuzzy logic. For instance, it was argued that "the world has a logic and that the logic of the world is quantum logic and not classical logic".[93] The support for quantum logic through paradoxes has been aptly summarized as follows:

> But early in the twentieth century, mathematicians began to discover paradoxes that cannot be ignored. These paradoxes occur in the very foundation of mathematics, on which natural science rests. One can even build machines, or computers, that embody these paradoxes. These paradoxes are thus far from mere games, and they reach much further than human language. The paradoxical tensions at which I have just hinted occupy much the same place: they are built into the foundation of the world. *They are everywhere.*[94]

Based on this paragraph, we currently encounter a paradoxical contradiction between the hard and the soft sciences. The paradox is that while in the past the hard sciences were considered to be more reliable than the soft sciences, it is now where the hard sciences "soften" their stance on binary logic that the soft (social) sciences insist stubbornly on the prevalence and sole relevance of dualistic thinking and binary logic. In view of this contradiction, it is perhaps time to rethink the validity of the question instead of pondering the different answers further. A change in the question is always a good idea when numerous different questions

90 See also Andrew Newberg and Mark Robert Waldman, *Words Can Change Your Brain: 12 Conversation Strategies to Build Trust, Resolve Conflict, and Increase Intimacy* (New York: Plume, 2013).

91 See Kapur et al., *supra* note 85 at 1.

92 See Dorothea Steiner, "Globalization and Its Challenge to Higher Education: Some Reflections of a European Americanist Educator and Life-Long Learner" in Valeria Gennaro Lerda (ed), *Which "Global Village"?: Societies, Cultures, and Political-Economic Systems* in *A Euro-Atlantic Perspective* (Westport: Praeger, 2002) 213 at 216.

93 See Peter Gibbins, *Particles and Paradoxes: The Limits of Quantum Logic* (Cambridge: Cambridge University Press, 1987) at 3.

94 See Andreas Wagner, *Paradoxical Life: Meaning, Matter, and the Power of Human Choice* (New Haven: Yale University Press, 2009) at 3 [*Italics* added].

result in the same set of unsatisfactory answers. This applies to logic in general and to change in particular. For logic it may be time to expand classical logic by more fuzzy forms of logic. For change it may be time to express doubts about the existence of change, at least as measured in terms of a three-dimensional framework of space and time. For both questions, essentially oxymoronic concepts provide useful insights as incorporated into oxymora like constant change and spacetime. Ultimately, they may hold the key to a better understanding of the mind and its underlying cognitive framework, and even human nature.

6.2 Two minds or one? Dual process

At forty I was never in two minds.[95]

Apparently the world of science produces more and more contradictory results and language follows suit by coining more and more new words, including notably oxymora or paradoxes. Is it then possible that even our brains, our cognitive framework, our tools of sense perception are dualistic? Is it coincidence that the dominant logic is binary and most of our sense organs, like the eyes, ears and nostrils, are organized in pairs or perceive by contrasts between opposites? Similar to gender, even the biological brain has been classified dually as having a left and a right hemisphere, one being more artistic and intuitive, the other more analytical and logical. Is it then that duality is the principal origin of the troubles with the logical apprehension of paradoxes and oxymora? This last question obviously raises other more complex and interrelated questions, such as whether the duality is innate or learned, as is addressed by the so-called "nature vs nurture" or "nativism vs empiricism" debate. One may also consider that there are individual, cultural or geographic differences, whereby some individuals are born with either a dualistic or a holistic mindset. Equally, the question whether some languages are more prone to dualistic or holistic thinking than others is of great relevance for the role of oxymora, which again leads back to the initial question of whether language is acquired or innate. Across various cultural and linguistic differences, we are also ignorant whether the brain functions individually or collectively, separately or jointly, consciously or unconsciously, to mention but a few more dichotomies unable to explain the underlying phenomena.

All these possible answers can be summarized by two apparently opposite statements. The first is that "God hath spoken once but twofold is what I heard" featured in the Book of Psalms.[96] This adage would suggest that humans are designed in a dualistic way, or else perceive reality in dualistic terms while it really is one. The second is from the *Analects* of the Chinese philosopher Confucius where it is written that, "At forty I was never in two minds".[97] This sentence would suggest that being in one or two minds is a matter of learning, of

95 Confucius, *The Analects* (Beijing: Zhonghua Book Company, 2008) at 15.

96 See Isaac Myer, *Qabbalah* (Whitefish: Kessinger, 2003) at vi; see also Psalm 62:11.

97 Confucius, *supra* note 95 at 15.

enhancing the understanding, which usually but not necessarily comes with age. But perhaps this is only true for people born in the East or taught in Chinese or Eastern philosophy. By contrast, someone taught or born in the Western hemisphere would have seen her/his brain develop differently and, perhaps, still insist on a largely dualistic conception of law or reality like Jeremy Bentham or Robert M. Cover.[98] As a contrary example, the writer H. G. Wells expressed a more holistic attitude in a lecture given in 1936 by stating that he disliked isolated events and disconnected details and preferred the world as "coherent and consistent as possible".[99]

Perhaps the difference from Confucius is that Wells was already beyond his forties at the time of uttering these words. Or else, they were born or educated differently and the scientific paradigm may have changed since then as well. But has it? Even from the study of change come dualistic statements, as in the following:

> Wherever we look in Nature, animate or inanimate, we see widespread evidence of periodic systems. These systems show a continuously repeated change from one set of conditions to another, opposite set.[100]

Unfortunately, clear scientific answers to these questions are scarce. Or else, they may themselves lead first to dichotomies and later to contradictions and oxymoronic concepts, like that of the "paradoxical brain" or "cognitive neuroscience". What is striking is that most approaches seem to favour an analytical and fragmented method, which is euphemistically called "scientific specialization". According to specialized views in science, we are really in two minds, in a duality of hemisphere asymmetries, where one mind is attributed to the left and the other to the right brain hemisphere.[101] The brain difference may also have some roots in genetics.[102] Moreover, there seem to be major differences in the hemispheres (or the weight given to them) between women and men.[103] Yet, the division between the two hemispheres was maintained in spite of a small isthmus of nerve tissue called the "corpus callosum" connecting the two hemispheres.[104] According to this asymmetry, the brain is split into two

98 See Bentham, *supra* note 28 at 1 and Robert M. Cover, "The Supreme Court, 1982 Term: Foreword: Nomos and Narrative" (1983) 97(4) *Harvard Law Review* 4.

99 See Herbert G. Wells, *World Encyclopaedia* (Lecture delivered at the weekly evening meeting of the Royal Institution of Great Britain, 20 November 1936); see Herbert G. Wells, *World Brain* (San Bernardino: Read Books Ltd, 2016) at 17.

100 See Hans Jenny, *Cymatics: A Study of Wave Phenomena & Vibration* (New Market: Macromedia, 2001) at 17.

101 See also Hughlings Jackson, "On the Nature of the Duality of the Brain" (1874) 68 *Medical Press and Circular* 19, 41and 63.

102 See Tao Sun, "Differential Gene Transcription in the Left and Right Cerebral Cortex" in Kenneth Hugdahl and René Westerhausen (eds), *The Two Halves of the Brain: Information Processing in the Cerebral Hemispheres* (Cambridge: MIT Press, 2010) 21.

103 See also Larry Cahill, "Why Sex Matters for Neuroscience" (2006) 7(6) *Nature Reviews. Neuroscience* 477.

104 See Michael S. Gazzaniga, "The Split Brain in Man" (1967) 217(2) *Scientific American* 24 at 24.

hemispheres, which serve different functions.[105] For the movement of muscles, it can be said that "your right brain makes your left arm wave and your left brain allows your right leg to kick a ball".[106] In terms of thinking, the left brain is said to be "the seat of rational thinking, intellectual thinking, analysis, and speech" and it "also processes numerical information deductively or logically".[107] By contrast, the right brain has been identified as "the seat of intuition, emotion, non-verbal thinking, synthetic thinking, which allows representations in space, creation, and emotions".[108] Many of these theories were derived from the study of brain injuries as a means to locate specific functions in specific parts of the brain. The theories on a left–right brain dichotomy, however were criticized and later quieted down but did not vanish.[109] They have stayed with us at least as so-called "neuromyths".[110] In an article of 1986, the criticism of two-brain theories was formulated as follows:

> Since one of the most complicated things in a very strange universe is the human brain, it may well be that we will never find out how the two brains function together. As things stand at the moment, though, it appears that the two brains act in concert, and that their actions, ways of perception, and cognitive strategies are complex, subtle, and not capable of being discovered by direct experimentation.[111]

Another commentator also criticized it as a myth and equated the dichotomy to the mind-body distinction, calling both conceptions erroneous.[112] Still the dichotomy was retained even though the emphasis seems to have shifted to the right side of the brain.[113]

Later, and again displaying a scientific preference for dichotomies and dual thinking, the horizontal distinction was replaced by a vertical one. Not being sure about a possible correlation (yet), it almost seems that the shift in neuroscience coincided with the shift in international relations, where the East–West dichotomy of the Cold War era was gradually replaced by a North–South divide. In neuroscience, the new approach is known as the "top brain–bottom brain

105 *Ibid.*

106 See V. S. Ramachandran and Sandra Blakeslee, *Phantoms in the Brain: Probing the Mysteries of the Human Mind* (New York: Harper, 1998) at 14.

107 *Ibid.*

108 See *e.g.* Organization for Economic Co-operation and Development (OECD), *Understanding the Brain: The Birth of a Learning Science* (Paris: OECD, 2007) at 114.

109 See Ronald Shook, "The Two-Brain Theory: A Critique" (1986) 18(3) *English Education* 173 at 173.

110 See OECD, *Understanding the Brain*, *supra* note 107 at 107–126.

111 See Shook, *supra* note 108 at 180.

112 See Charles G. Wieder, "The Left-Brain/Right-Brain Model of Mind: Ancient Myth in Modern Garb" (1984) 10(2) *Visual Arts Research* 66 at 72.

113 See *e.g.* Ornstein, *supra* note 65 and Daniel H. Pink, *A Whole New Mind: Why Right-Brainers Will Rule the Future* (New York: Riverhead, 2005).

dichotomy"; now the top and the bottom of the brain are assigned different functions. The origins of this theory go back to trials on rhesus monkeys conducted in 1982.[114] In a book published in 2013, however, the authors insisted that they did not understand the top–bottom brain theory as a dichotomy but as different "systems" and called it "the theory of cognitive modes".[115] Still one may wonder why then they chose the dichotomy for their book title. By cognitive mode, they understand the "general way of thinking that underlies how a person approaches the world and interacts with other people", which at least appears to be more nuanced than a mere dichotomy.[116]

Considering the shortcomings of both dichotomous approaches to the brain, perhaps a more integrated and holistic approach through the so-called "whole brain" view is more promising. The whole brain approach proposes that "integrative brain function is based on the coexistence and cooperative action of many interwoven and interacting submechanisms".[117] In other words, to understand fully the brain and its connection with the body and the mind may require a more holistic approach. Even this is difficult to establish as we are not sure where the whole brain ends or begins. It has been, for instance, illustrated that we may avail ourselves of four brains: the Cerebrum, the Cerebellum, the Medulla Oblongata (continuation of the spinal cord) and the Solar Plexus as the "abdominal brain".[118] As strange as it may sound, it seems to make perfect sense when considering the speculations about the seat of the mind in the head, heart or abdomen as described in intuition or "gut feeling".

At this point, regardless of the interpretation of the biological shape of the brain, it is interesting to see that even the cognitive processes taking place in the brain (or its different parts or neurons) functioning as the mind are being moulded – not surprisingly – into another dichotomy, namely two modes of cognitive functioning, or two modes of thought. According to the cognitive psychologist Jerome Bruner, these two modes of cognitive functioning provide "distinctive ways of ordering experience" and even "of constructing reality".[119] These two modes differ in the operating principles, the kind of logic, as well as the types of causality applied by them. Roughly corresponding to the overall distinction between logic and artistic thinking rooted in the two brain hemispheres,

114 See Leslie G. Ungerleider and Mortimer Mishkin, "Two Cortical Visual Systems" in David J. Ingle, Melvyn A. Goodale, and Richard J. W. Mansfield (eds), *Analysis of Visual Behavior* (Cambridge: MIT Press, 1982) 549.

115 See Stephen M. Kosslyn and G. Wayne Miller, *Top Brain, Bottom Brain: Surprising Insights Into How You Think* (New York: Simon Schuster, 2013) at 1–15.

116 *Ibid* at 1.

117 See Erol Başar, *Brain-Body-Mind in the Nebulous Cartesian System: A Holistic Approach by Oscillations* (New York: Springer, 2011) at 179.

118 See Theron Q. Dumont, *The Solar Plexus: The Abdominal Brain* (Chicago: Advanced Thought Publishing, 1920) at 1–9.

119 See Jerome Bruner, *Actual Minds, Possible Worlds* (Cambridge: Harvard University Press, 1986) at 11.

these two modes Bruner called the "paradigmatic" and the "narrative mode", which he described as follows:

> One mode, the paradigmatic or logico-scientific one, attempts to fulfill the ideal of a formal, mathematical system of description and explanation. It employs categorization or conceptualization and the operations by which categories are established, instantiated, idealized, and related one to the other to form a system. [. . .]
>
> The imaginative application of the narrative mode leads instead to good stories, gripping drama, believable (though not necessarily "true") historical accounts. It deals in human or human-like intention and action and the vicissitudes and consequences that mark their course. It strives to put its timeless miracles into the particulars of experience, and to locate the experience in time and place.[120]

More generally, the different theories about two cognitive modes of thought or of mind are known as "dual process theories", which have emerged from the belief in a fundamental duality in the brain. Thus, in line with the duality of the brain, the mind also functions by way of two processes, which have been outlined as follows:

> Dual-process theories hold that human thought processes are subserved by two distinct mechanisms, one fast, automatic, and nonconscious, the other slow, controlled, and conscious, which operate largely independently and compete for behavioral control. In their boldest form, they claim that humans have, in effect, *two separate minds.*[121]

This means that we actually use two systems (System I and System II) to process a great variety of tasks. The differences between the two systems may lead to very different outcomes in the process and quality of decision making. Moreover, System I seems to be more influential than is believed and seems to influence the choices and judgements we make more than expected.[122] These differences have also been outlined for a number of cases, where intuition within the "blink of an eye" may lead to more accurate results than, for instance, the rational analysis of a large number of data. In other words, paradoxically, less information can be more. This is true for all decisions we take but was shown experimentally in the assessment of an antique sculpture's authenticity or the diagnosis of people complaining of chest pain before attending an Accident & Emergency unit.[123]

120 *Ibid* at 12 and 13.

121 See Jonathan S. B. T. Evans and Keith Frankish, *In Two Minds: Dual Processes and Beyond* (Oxford: Oxford University Press, 2009) at v [*Italics* added].

122 See Daniel Kahnemann, *Thinking, Fast and Slow* (New York: Farrar, Straus and Giroux, 2011) at 13.

123 See Malcolm Gladwell, *Blink: The Power of Thinking Without Thinking* (London: Penguin, 2005) at 1–17 and 125–145.

Thus the relation between the two systems, between thinking slow and fast, and which one leads to better results, is not clear. What also remains unclear is whether these two systems coincide also with the classification of modes of thinking into more analytical versus holistic thinking as undertaken by cultural psychologists.[124] Cultural psychologists have argued that analytic and holistic thinking may be unevenly distributed across the globe and its many cultures, notably simplifying the argument by stating that the "former is more prevalent in Western cultures, whereas the latter is more prevalent in East Asian cultures".[125] This directly relates to the important question of the connection between nature and nurture or nativism and empiricism, which means to understand what part of cognition is learned and what is inherited.

Before addressing this question, the issue of the cultural difference in cognition is of great relevance for the assessment of the role of essentially oxymoronic concepts in other languages and cultures and, with a view to the quest for a common language and paradigm underlying the future global legal order, it is useful briefly to address the issue of the culture and geography of mind.

6.3 Culture and geography of mind

> *One must see then that the daunting double task of translation of cultures and their comparative study raises not only the question of the mentality of us and other peoples, but also ultimately the issue of "rationality" itself and the limits of western "scientism" as a paradigm.*[126]

Similar to the left–right brain dichotomy, the most common cultural difference in thinking is attributed to the West–East dichotomy. It is to a lesser extent applied to the North–South dichotomy but it exists, both globally and locally.[127] The former dichotomy is usually paired with the stereotype that Westerners rely on analytical thinking while their Eastern counterparts favour holistic thinking. In terms of logic, this is often expressed by the difference between classical (or binary) Aristotelian logic versus fuzzy (or polyvalent) Confucian logic.[128] This

124 See Jonathan S. B. T. Evans, "How Many Dual-Process Theories Do We Need? One, Two, or Many?" in Jonathan S. B. T. Evans and Keith Frankish, *In Two Minds: Dual Processes and Beyond* (Oxford: Oxford University Press, 2009) 33 at 35.

125 See Emma E. Buchtel and Ara Norenzayan, "Thinking Across Cultures: Implications for Dual Processes" in Jonathan S. B. T. Evans and Keith Frankish, *In Two Minds: Dual Processes and Beyond* (Oxford: Oxford University Press, 2009) 217 at 218.

126 See Stanley J. Tambiah, *Magic, Science and the Scope of Rationality* (Cambridge: Cambridge University Press 1990) at 3.

127 See *e.g.* Joseph A. Vandello, Dov Cohen, and Sean Ransom, "U.S. Southern and Northern Differences in Perceptions of Norms about Aggression: Mechanisms for the Perpetuation of a Culture of Honor" (2008) 39(2) *Journal of Cross-Cultural Psychology* 162, Katie Wales, "North and South: An English Linguistic Divide?" (2000) 16(1) *English Today* 4 and Timothy Brennan, "The Cuts of Language: The East/West of North/South" (2001) 13(1) *Public Culture* 39.

128 See Richard E. Nisbett, *The Geography of Thought: How Asians and Westerners Think Differently . . . and Why* (New York: Free Press, 2003) at 29–30.

seemingly merely philosophical difference has been found to give rise to major differences in warfare, politics and diplomacy but also how we experience life and "nourish" it.[129] The difference is also frequently outlined in the different approaches to health and medicine. More precisely, Western medical science is said to divide body (essence) and mind (spirit) into two separate domains ignoring the role of energy.[130] By contrast, Eastern medical science follows "a holistic approach to health that attempts to bring the body, mind and spirit into harmony".[131] In practice, this results in a division of labour in Western medicine where "the medical physician treats the body of patients, the social worker attends to their emotions and social relations, while the pastoral counselor provides spiritual guidance".[132] The same division of labour is also dominant at the global level, where a coherent global health governance framework is currently nonexistent.[133]

The same cognitive differences may have much further reaching implications. In particular, when considering the contrast between two opposites as the principal framework for perception of change or for the measurement of different phenomena, the difference in the applied logic (e.g. "either/or" as opposed to "both/and" or "classical formal logic" as opposed to "dialectical thinking")[134] may affect the cognition of the lines of distinction and with it the precise relation existing between the phenomena. This is because if the nature of the contrast were to differ, it would then mean a different understanding of the phenomenon under observation. This hypothesis has been tested by experiments using eye-tracking technology in the context of the recognition of emotions.[135] Despite several limitations to the experiment, the test results seemed to confirm that the contextual information for the attribution of emotions was used differently by Chinese and American participants.[136]

The same differences should then also affect the way that essentially oxymoronic concepts are received and processed and what meaning and implications will be attached to them. A different outcome would have equally far-reaching

129 See François Jullien, *A Treatise on Efficacy: Between Western and Chinese Thinking* (Honolulu: Hawaii University of Hawai'i Press, 2004) and François Jullien, *Vital Nourishment: Departing from Happiness* (New York: Zone Books, 2007).

130 See Daniel P. Reid, *The Tao of Health, Sex, and Longevity: A Modern Practical Guide to the Ancient Way* (New York: Touchstone, 1989) at lvi.

131 See Elena Chan et al., "Interactions Between Traditional Chinese Medicines and Western Therapeutics" (2010) 13(1) *Current Opinion in Drug Discovery & Development* 50 at 50.

132 See Cecilia Chan, Petula Sik Ying Ho and Esther Chow, "A Body-Mind-Spirit Model in Health: An Eastern Approach" (2002) 34 (3–4) *Social Work in Health Care* 261 at 261.

133 See Rostam J. Neuwirth and Alexandr Svetlicinii, "Law as a Social Medicine: Enhancing International Inter-Regime Regulatory Coopetition as a Means for the Establishment of a Global Health Governance Framework" (2015) 36 (3–4) *The Journal of Legal Medicine* 330 and Lawrence O. Gostin, *Global Health Law* (Boston: Harvard University Press, 2014).

134 See also Kaiping Peng and Richard E. Nisbett, "Culture, Dialectics, and Reasoning About Contradiction" (1999) 54(9) *American Psychologist* 741 at 741.

135 See Jennifer Tehan Stanley et al., "Cultural Differences in Gaze and Emotion Recognition: Americans Contrast More Than Chinese" (2013) 13(1) *Emotion* 36 at 34.

136 *Ibid* at 46.

implications for decision making and the entire organization of life. Evidently, it has also utmost relevance for decision making in the legal sphere, particularly in "judging" the guilt or innocence of a person, the validity or voidness of a contract or the severity of a crime to name but a few. With regard to culturally different ways of receiving oxymora, an interesting related experiment involving not oxymora but proverbs was conducted. In the experiment, Chinese and American students were given two different sets of proverbs, the first set containing contradictions and the second set none.[137] Initially it was found that Chinese proverbs usually contained more contradictions than their American counterparts. For this reason (and to avoid familiarity with a proverb as an influencing factor) the experiment was also conducted with Yiddish proverbs, i.e. proverbs from a third cultural setting. The experiment yielded similar results whereby the Chinese students seemed to prefer the contradictory proverbs over those without contradictions.

By analogy, this would mean that Chinese or Eastern people would prefer or be less disturbed by essentially oxymoronic concepts than their Western counterparts. Richard E. Nisbett attributes the difference between Eastern and Western people to the following main three reasons.[138] First, "change" and notably the constantly changing nature of reality has received greater attention in Eastern traditions of thought. Second, "contradictions" equally have higher significance, which was explained by the fact that when "the world is constantly changing, oppositions, paradoxes, and anomalies are continuously being created".[139] Third, and resulting from change and contradiction, is a holistic principle, i.e. a view that focuses on the relations more than the individual subject.

If we assume these cultural differences in cognition to be true, they could explain the recent rise of oxymora in the West and in the English language in particular. It would mean that the production of an increasing amount of essentially oxymoronic concepts in the West in scientific, political, advertising and daily discourses is a reaction to a vacuum created by a stronger emphasis on analytical rather than holistic thinking in the past. This would be supported by the observation that traditional Eastern proverbs contain more contradictory statements than Western proverbs. By the same token, it is – as part of the law of attraction between opposites – that the West is becoming more fascinated with Eastern thought or values (e.g. meditation, yoga, spirituality), while the East is becoming attracted to Western thought and values (e.g. materialism, entertainment, lifestyle). Perhaps even something new, a third and entirely new way of thinking, will be born from their convergence – a way, which could be described as a kind of "rational mysticism", to use yet another apparent oxymoron.[140] If the birth of a new and global cognitive mindset also included the convergence between the

137 See Nisbett, *supra* note 127 at 173–174.

138 *Ibid.*

139 *Ibid* at 175.

140 See John Horgan, *Rational Mysticism: Dispatches from the Border between Science and Spirituality* (Boston: Houghton Mifflin Company, 2003) at 8.

North and South, it would largely reflect the evolution of brain theories from left–right to top–bottom and thence to a whole brain approach.

Finally, it is also interesting to note that, despite the apparent cultural differences in cognition, it is still not possible "to make a sharp distinction between cognitive process and cognitive content".[141] This finding allows for an analogy with similar difficulties in distinguishing between substantive law and procedural law as captured by the oxymoron of "substantive due process". Applying another principle of law, it is the potential paradox of the exception proving the rule (*exceptio probat regulam*) mentioned before[142] that on every place on the planet, there exist people fitting more in one than the other category.

It is fairly obvious that cultural, linguistic or geographic differences have an impact. One may just think of trying to translate a joke into another language and presenting it to someone in a different place. In addition to culture, place has also been said to have a special power. The power of the place is said to lie in the "the accumulated geography whose formative imprint still dominates the planet".[143] Yet, the principal question is how and with what speed these diverse factors may influence and change the cognition of a person. Possible answers depend on other open questions, namely whether we are determined exclusively by either genes or experiences (and not a combination of both). The impact of culture and geography gives rise to puzzling questions of the greatest significance for many pressing problems. It is, for instance, significant for global peace and stability, the universality of human rights, and international trade regulation. All these objectives have in common that they have been challenged by different forms of cultural arguments, namely a clash (and argued incompatibility) of civilizations or cultures,[144] cultural relativism as an obstacle to the universality of human rights,[145] and cultural diversity being threatened by international trade liberalization.[146] This is why the question whether cognitive processes or differences in brain tissue are innate or rooted in cultural or geographic factors is of such great importance, particularly in a shrinking global village with the need for a "global brain" to awaken.[147]

141 See Richard E. Nisbett et al., "Culture and Systems of Thought: Holistic Versus Analytic Cognition" (2001) 108(2) *Psychological Review* 291 at 306.

142 See Chapter 5, note 263.

143 See Harm de Blij, *The Power of Place: Geography, Destiny, and Globalization's Rough Landscape* (Oxford: Oxford University Press, 2009) at 3; see also Winifred Gallagher, *The Power of Place: How Our Surroundings Shape Our Thoughts, Emotions, and Actions* (New York: Harper Perennial, 2007).

144 See *e.g.* Samuel P. Huntington, *The Clash of Civilizations and the Remaking of the World Order* (New York: Touchstone, 1996) at 22.

145 See *e.g.* John J. Tilley, "Cultural Relativism" (2000) 22(2) *Human Rights Quarterly* 501 at 502–506.

146 See *e.g.* Rostam J. Neuwirth, "The 'Culture and Trade' Paradox Reloaded" in Christiaan De Beukelaer, Miikka Pyykkönen and J.P. Singh (eds), *Globalization, Culture and Development: The UNESCO Convention on Cultural Diversity* (Basingstoke: Palgrave MacMillan, 2015) 91 at 93–95.

147 See also Peter Russell, *The Global Brain Awakens: Our Next Evolutionary Leap* (Palo Alto: Global Brain, 1995) at 127–133.

This question has been puzzling me personally for years, as every time I take a long trip to another place by plane, it feels like my whole personality has undergone an instant change once I have landed at the place of destiny. The same can be observed with people instantly changing their body language and facial expressions by simply shifting from one language to another. Put simply, it almost seems that changing the place or language has an immediate and visible impact on a person. The main problem lies in measuring change with great accuracy. It appears common sense that different places, climates, foods,[148] and even people have different impacts on all of us. As a result of external factors, internal cognitive processes are likely to have an impact on external expressions of our thoughts, for instance, in actions and even in genes. The existence of a possible link between cognition and genes was expressed in the following sentence:

> Cultural variation is socially acquired and can bring about changes in cognition and behavior in a much shorter time than genetic or individually learned change.[149]

This may also mean that geography and culture may have a mysterious impact not only on the mind and cognition, but also on genes, albeit more slowly. To understand the causes of the impact on the mind is relevant for an assessment of the wider role of oxymora in changes in cognition as well as in the context of biological aspects of evolution. For these reasons it is necessary to undertake a brief inquiry into human nature as a possible origin of the many dualities and dichotomies encountered in the field of brain and cognition.

6.4 Duality of human nature: "nature vs nurture" or cognitive genetics

> *Two souls, alas! reside within my breast,*
> *And each withdraws from, and repels, its brother.*[150]

So far, the inquiry into the origins and causes of essentially oxymoronic concepts has advanced through numerous dichotomies related to the brain and cognition. These range from two minds, apparently opposite brain hemispheres, to differences in female and male brains, or cultural and geographic differences between Eastern and Western as well as Northern and Southern modes of cognition, to mention but a few. These dichotomies seem largely to simplify the complex phenomena underlying the mind. Most of all, they seem to follow and depend on the primary dichotomy of nature versus nurture or nativism versus empiricism. Thus

148 See Jean Anthelme Brillat-Savarin, *Physiologie du goût, ou Méditations de gastronomie transcendante* (Paris: Librairie Garnier Frères, 1825) at 1.

149 See Elizabeth E. Price, Christine A. Caldwell, and Andrew Whiten, "Comparative Cultural Cognition" (2010) 1(1) *Cognitive Science* 23 at 21.

150 See Johann Wolfgang von Goethe, *Faust: A Tragedy* (London: Strahan & Co., 1871) at 54.

whether the human being or human perception is essentially dualistic is related to deeper problems. In this regard, we have also formulated important dichotomies, such as a divine or mundane origin of humans, or whether God created humans or humans created God. These questions relate to the essence of human existence, namely whether it is predetermined by fate and genetics or decided by free will and choice. In this conflict also fits the saying that "we do not see things as they are; we see things as we are".[151] Perhaps, then, the rising number of essentially oxymoronic concepts in science, for instance, may be an indicator of the fact that we are essentially dualistic but would like to break free from the limitations that come with dualism. Not only scientists but numerous writers would make us believe so too, as Goethe outlined in the quote from *Faust*. Another writer, Robert Louis Stevenson, described the possible duality of humans in his book *The Strange Case of Dr Jekyll and Mr Hyde*, which lets Dr Jekyll state:

> With every day, and from both sides of my intelligence, the moral and the intellectual, I thus drew steadily nearer to that truth, by whose partial discovery I have been doomed to such a dreadful shipwreck: that man is not truly one, *but truly two*.[152]

In this passage, Stevenson combines dual-process theory with the duality of human personality. We also seem to make the same assumption about humans by classifying them in two different categories, namely by way of the dichotomous distinction between women and men. In law, paradoxically, it seems that we follow more a single category, which is why "gender equality" seems to be an oxymoron that should perhaps be replaced by the more adequate term "gender equity". Leaving the law aside, in a recent BBC news report, the gender difference in cognition was outlined as follows:

> Men and women do not think in the same ways. Few would disagree with that. And science has quantified some of those differences. Men, it is pretty well established, have better motor and spatial abilities than women, and more monomaniacal patterns of thought. Women have better memories, are more socially adept, and are better at dealing with several things at once. There is a lot of overlap, obviously. But on average these observations are true.[153]

Yet another scientific study seems to confirm the opposite, namely that "although there are sex/gender differences in the brain, human brains do not belong to one

151 See Jonathan Kadane Crane and Joseph Born Kadane, "Seeing Things: The Internet, the Talmud and Anais Nin" (2008) 9(2) *The Review of Rabbinic Judaism* 342.

152 Robert L. Stevenson, *The Strange Case of Dr. Jekyll and Mr. Hyde* (London: Longmans & Green, 1886) at 108 [*Italics* added].

153 See "Sex and Brains – Vive la différence!" *The Economist* (7 December 2013); available at: http://www.economist.com/news/science-and-technology/21591157-new-technique-has-drawn-wiring-diagrams-brains-two-sexes/ (accessed 1 October 2017).

of two distinct categories: male brain/female brain".[154] This renders the question of what elements in our gender classification derive from either experiences or genes. Thus, are we either women or men because of the external sex features, or because from the day of our birth we were treated (and dressed) differently in accordance with our genitals? But even to use the genitals as a criterion for the distinction of gender seems to provide no clear answer in both law and biology. As for law, an interesting paradox is that most laws that attach a different legal qualification or different rights or duties to a specific gender, do not define the gender. They merely use a legal fiction based on what has been written in the birth certificate. Due to several cases and advances in science, the mere distinction of gender based on external genitals has been rendered inadequate. In sum, the legal inadequacy of a binary sex paradigm was already outlined,[155] but it is gaining greater significance given that gender differences seem to become increasingly blurred based on new discoveries, which suggest that the differentiation between sexes depends not only on the genitals but at least seven more criteria.[156] It also seems to confirm the "one sex became two" theory, as "during the first seven weeks after conception, all human embryos are sexually undifferentiated".[157]

Thus even the primordial dichotomy of female–male seems not to be as certain as one would want to think. As for the nativism versus empiricism debate, it is therefore not clear what is causal for the other, the sexual identity or the features of the sex organs. This lack of clarity poses a serious challenge for the law, which has presumed the gender difference to be stable and static as well as exclusively dichotomous or dimorphic.

The question about links between nature and nurture was first addressed by a direct opposition but was recently more expressed in dynamic as well as oxymoronic ways. Experiences of all kinds seem to have a direct relevance for genes. This would mean that everything, including gender, is in a constant state of flux and change but perhaps at different speeds. Some changes may take so long that we cannot measure them during a lifetime, or even in millennia, or else we have not developed the technologies that allow us to observe them. This may apply to climate change as much as to biological change.

Perhaps one reason why we are held back is the strictly dualistic conception of reality and nature. In this regard, it has been stated that "the idea that we are born dualists is also supported by the stubbornness of dualism".[158] This "stubborn dualism" persists for the simple reason that "we cannot shake off our dualistic way of thinking because it is innate and modular, and innate modular beliefs are

154 See Daphna Joel et al., "Sex Beyond the Genitalia: The Human Brain Mosaic" (2015) 112(5) *Proceedings of the National Academy of Sciences*, 15468 at 15468.

155 See Julie A. Greenberg, "Defining Male and Female: Intersexuality and the Collision between Law and Biology" (1999) 41(2) *Arizona Law Review* 265 at 275.

156 See Julie A. Greenberg, *Intersexuality and the Law: Why Sex Matters* (New York: New York University Press, 2012) at 11–12.

157 *Ibid* at 12.

158 See Gabriel Segal, "Poverty of Stimulus Arguments Concerning Language and Folk Psychology" in Peter Carruthers, Stephen Laurence and Stephen Stich, *The Innate Mind: Foundations and the Future*, vol 3 (Oxford: Oxford University Press, 2008) 90 at 101.

extremely hard to shift".[159] In other words, "old habits die hard" and "old logic dies even harder"; but perhaps it is precisely the role of oxymora to speed up the process of ending the dualistic stubbornness. Already, criticism of dualism is mounting in all scientific fields. In the area of health, for instance, the dualistic division of body and mind associated with Western thought has been criticized as being not only "highly irrational and unscientific" but also being based more on "religious dogma than on scientific fact".[160]

Another critique of dualism is directed at the dilemma it produces, namely that "once such dichotomies are assumed, they create absolute unbridgeable gaps that cannot capture the continuous and multi-dimensional character of our experience and understanding".[161] Despite the mounting awareness of the shortcomings of dichotomous or dualistic thinking, dichotomies stubbornly persist and new ones are being created. One dichotomy of particular interest here is that between "soft inheritance" and "hard inheritance". The latter refers to largely invariant effects and is also known as the "inheritance of acquired characters", while the former points to traits that are less stable between successive generations.[162] In other words, soft inheritance is concerned with the possible impact of the environment on genes. Ultimately, this dichotomy leads to the heart of the problem of the division between body and mind or fate and free choice or scientifically uncertain concepts, like the soul.[163] The scientific relevance of the soul is emphasized in the context of the topics of the mind, brain, and spirit, which are said to "cohere in surprising yet unified ways".[164]

Soft inheritance may provide further insights to unify the views on these topics. In this regard, it is "Lamarckanism", named after the French biologist Jean-Baptiste Lamarck (1744–1829), that contends that "soft inheritance", i.e. the heritability of certain acquired characteristics, is possible. Among his findings, first published in 1809 and 1815, is the law he formulated as follows:

> All the acquisitions or losses wrought by nature on individuals, through the influence of the environment in which their race has long been placed, and hence through the influence of the predominant use or permanent disuse of any organ; all these are preserved by reproduction to the new individuals which arise, provided that the acquired modifications are common to both sexes, or at least to the individuals which produce the young.[165]

159 *Ibid.*

160 See Reid, *supra* note 129 at lvi.

161 See Mark Johnson, "The Philosophical Significance of Image Schema" in Beate Hampe (ed), *From Perception to Meaning: Image Schemas in Cognitive Linguistics* (The Hague: Mouton de Guyter, 2005) 15 at 17.

162 See Root Gorelick and Manfred D. Laubichler, "Genetic = Heritable (Genetic ≠ DNA)" (2008) 3(1) *Biological Theory* 79 at 79.

163 See generally Ken Wilber, *The Marriage of Sense and Soul: Integrating Science and Religion* (New York: Random House, 1998).

164 See Mark Graves, *Mind, Brain and the Elusive Soul: Human Systems of Cognitive Science and Religion* (Aldershot: Ashgate, 2008) at 1.

165 See Jean-Baptiste Lamarck, *Zoological Philosophy: An Exposition with Regard to the Natural History of Animals* (London: MacMillan, 1914) at 113; see also Jean-Baptiste P. A. De Lamarck, *Histoire naturelle des animaux sans vertèbres*, vol I, 2nd ed (Paris: J.B. Baillere, 1835) at 151–152.

Thus, elements of use or disuse would be crucial for the evolutionary changes in organisms, even allowing for the creation of new organs. Charles Darwin referred to Lamarck's ideas in his book *The Origin of Species* and also formulated similar thoughts under the term "pangenesis", which etymologically points to a more holistic conception of inheritance.[166] Darwin formulated his idea as a provisional hypothesis to await a more advanced understanding of inheritance but, at the time, attempted to bring together "a multitude of facts which are at present left disconnected by any efficient cause".[167] Even today, this multitude of facts is still subject to scientific inquiries and the controversy between soft and hard inheritance continues. Even if the weight of soft inheritance may have declined, it has been said that hard inheritance means that evolution is nearly constant and not subject to changes but that "complete constancy" would preclude evolution itself.[168]

It is telling that some theories of soft inheritance, which had been discredited in the past, are now seen in a different light. This is best exemplified by the case of the Austrian biologist Paul Kammerer (1880–1926), who published a book called *The Inheritance of Acquired Characteristics*.[169] In the book he presented a theory of soft inheritance based on experiments with midwife toads (alytes). His research was later discredited as forgery but it remains unclear whether the experiments were forged or deliberately tampered with by a jealous colleague in the person of a hostile Nazi sympathizer.[170] This question remains unsolved as does the cause of Kammerer's mysterious death, which was either explained as suicide or murder.[171] This example serves to underscore how fierce the scientific battle based on apparently opposite views and hypotheses can become, especially in an environment of "academic venom".[172] Thus, the case of Kammerer shows that – alas – people do die perhaps not from, but due to, contradictions.

Tragically, recent scientific comments appear to confirm Kammerer's ideas under the term "epigenetics".[173] Generally, the trend in the understanding of inheritance or the opposite views between soft and hard inheritance or nature and nurture seem to be in a process of a critical reconsideration.[174] The present

166 Charles Darwin, *On the Origin of Species*, 5th ed (London: John Murray, 1869) at xv, 145, 296 and 505.

167 Charles Darwin, *The Variation of Animals and Plants under Domestication*, vol II (London: John Murray, 1868) at 357.

168 See Ernst Mayr, *The Growth of Biological Thought: Diversity, Evolution, and Inheritance* (Massachusetts: Belknap Press, 1982) at 669, 681, 687–698.

169 Paul Kammerer, *The Inheritance of Acquired Characteristics* (New York: Boni and Liveright, 1924).

170 See Arthur Koestler, *The Case of the Midwife Toad* (New York: Randomhouse, 1971) at 115.

171 *Ibid* at 15.

172 *Ibid* at 124.

173 See *e.g.* Alexander O. Vargas, "Did Paul Kammerer Discover Epigenetic Inheritance? A Modern Look at the Controversial Midwife Toad Experiments" (2009) 312B(7) *Journal of Experimental Zoology* 667 and Elizabeth Pennisi, "The Case of the Midwife Toad: Fraud or Epigenetics?" (2009) 325(5945) *Science* 1194.

174 See *e.g.* Maria E. Kronfeldner, "Is Cultural Evolution Lamarckian?" (2007) 22(4) *Biology and Philosophy* 493, Eva Jablonka and Marion J. Lamb, "Soft Inheritance: Challenging the Modern Synthesis" (2008) 31(2) *Genetics and Molecular Biology* 389 and R. Bonduriansky, "Rethinking Heredity, Again" (2012) 27(6) *Trends in Ecology and Evolution* 330.

trend seems to lead to more complex scientific theories in line with the trend ascribed to essentially oxymoronic concepts. Such theories are of a more holistic character and are often discussed under interdisciplinary portmanteau words or oxymoronic concepts, like sociobiology,[175] behavioural genetics[176] or "psychogenetics",[177] cognitive genetics,[178] or even the notion of "human nature".[179]

To cut a long story short, it seems that the relation between dichotomies and the duality of human nature is a mystery. It is a *mysterium coniunctionis*, to use the words of Carl Gustav Jung.[180] Or actually, it is a *quaternio* (quaternity) of relations constituted by two dichotomies: nature versus nurture and left versus right brain. The key to the mysterium is thus to find the right procedure which would allow, after separating and analysing the findings, to synthesize and consolidate them with a view of bringing them back to unity again.[181]

At the moment, this challenge constitutes a self-referential problem, like asking which came first: the chicken or the egg?[182] For the chicken–egg problem it was said that "Charles Darwin demonstrated that the chicken was preceded by borderline chickens and so it is simply indeterminate as to where the pre-chickens end and the chickens begin". [183] It is thus a question of where to draw the line. Or else, we may not have the necessary understanding, knowledge or perceptive tools to explain scientifically the mutual relation between nature and nurture and all related dichotomies. Science, hence, does not know how the opposite terms in dichotomous pairs relate to each other and let alone all these different dichotomies among each other. Science only seems to know for certain now that there are too many dichotomies and all of them fail to deliver a more accurate explanation of the phenomena they aim to explain. This failure can be exemplified by one of the many neuromyths, namely that we arguably

175 See Edward O. Wilson, *Sociobiology: A New Synthesis* (Cambridge: Belknap Press, 1975); see also Daniel G. Freedman, *Human Sociobiology: A Holistic Approach* (New York: The Free Press, 1979) at 1.

176 See *e.g.* Wim E. Crusio, "Key Issues in Contemporary Behavioral Genetics" (2015) 2 *Current Opinion in Behavioral Sciences* 89.

177 See *e.g.* Arthur Ernest Davies, "Suggestions Toward a Psychogenetic Theory of Mind" (1907) 4(13) *The Journal of Philosophy, Psychology and Scientific Methods* 342 and John Wilcock, "Comparative Psychology Lives on under an Assumed Name Psychogenetics" (1972) 27(6) *American Psychologist* 531.

178 See *e.g.* Gaia Scerif and Annette Karmiloff-Smith, "The Dawn of Cognitive Genetics? Crucial Developmental Caveats" (2005) 9(3) *TRENDS in Cognitive Sciences* 126, Dorothy V. M. Bishop, "Developmental Cognitive Genetics: How Psychology Can Inform Genetics and Vice Versa" (2006) 59(7) *The Quarterly Journal of Experimental Psychology* 1153 and Michèle Carlier and Pierre Roubertoux, "Genetics and Cognition: The Impact for Psychologists in Applied Settings" (2010) 15(1) *European Psychologist* 49.

179 See David Heyd, "Human Nature: An Oxymoron?" (2003) 28(2) *Journal of Medicine and Philosophy* 151 at 155.

180 See Carl G. Jung, *Mysterium Coniunctionis: An Inquiry into the Separation and Synthesis of Psychic Opposites in Alchemy* (Princeton: Princeton University Press, 1963).

181 *Ibid* at xiv.

182 See Roger Teichmann, "The Chicken and the Egg" (1991) 100(3) *Mind* 371.

183 See Roy A. Sorensen, "The Egg Came Before the Chicken" (1992) 101(403) *Mind* 541.

only use 10 per cent of our brain.[184] This myth has been found to be incorrect and we seem to use 100 per cent of the brain. Thus it seems that science is still in the dark about the brain and merely understands about 10 per cent of how and what we use the brain for. This can be taken as a metaphor for many other fields and unsolved scientific conundrums.

More generally, the current state of scientific theories seems to reflect the consensus that human life does not evolve by genes in a strictly biological sense alone.[185] Instead, culture, language and even thoughts also play crucial and possibly causal roles.[186] The logical dilemma inherent in a dichotomous approach was ironically rephrased by the paradox that "we are 100% innate, 100% acquired" or else "100% biological, 100% cultural".[187] The inadequate understanding can be exemplified by the notion of "information", which we usually understand in terms of data or facts. However, from the perspective of the duality of human nature, it may also have a double role, which not only refers to what a person knows but also a process that "forms" the recipient of "in-formation".[188]

This understanding suggests rather that "information" combines elements of nature and nurture. Their increasingly combined consideration also resonates with pronounced revolutionary changes in biological thinking about heredity and evolution taking place. These changes in thinking entail the observations that "there is more to heredity than genes", that "some hereditary variations are nonrandom in origin", that "some acquired information is inherited", and that "evolutionary change can result from instruction as well as selection".[189] In line with this view, evolution thus relies on a four-dimensional process, including a genetic, an epigenetic, a behavioural, and, fourth, a symbolic dimension.[190] The fourth dimension is especially relevant to the question to what extent and how language can change genes.[191] It is interesting to note that there are interesting similarities between language and genetics. For instance, DNA has been called the "language of life", and our characteristics were said to be "written in our genes".[192] And, similar to words changing faster than grammar, cultural evolution is said to move faster than

184 See OECD, *Understanding the Brain*, *supra* note 107 at 113–114.

185 See also Peter J. Richerson and R. Boyd, *Not by Genes Alone: How Culture Transformed Human Evolution* (Chicago: University of Chicago Press, 2005).

186 See *e.g.* Bradd Shore, *Culture in Mind: Cognition, Culture, and the Problem of Meaning* (Oxford: Oxford University Press, 1996), Charles J. Lumsden and Edward O. Wilson, *Genes, Mind, and Culture: The Coevolutionary Process* (Cambridge: Harvard University Press, 2005) and Michael Rutter, *Genes and Behavior: Nature-Nurture Interplay Explained* (London: Blackwell, 2006) at 221.

187 See Freedman, *supra* note 174 at 141; see also D. O. Hebb, "Heredity and Environment in Mammalian Behaviour" (1953) 1(2) *The British Journal of Animal Behaviour* 43.

188 See Ervin Laszlo, *Science and the Akashic Field: An Integral Theory of Everything*, 2nd ed (Rochester: Inner Traditions, 2007) at 13.

189 See Eva Jablonka and Marion J. Lamb, *Evolution in Four Dimensions: Genetic, Epigenetic, Behavioral, and Symbolic Variation in the History of Life* (Cambridge: The MIT Press, 2005) at 1.

190 *Ibid.*

191 *Ibid* at 306–317.

192 *Ibid* at 201.

genetic evolution.[193] Not only are the two spheres similar but they also seem to be mysteriously intertwined. The mutual influence between language and genetics widely corresponds to the observation that words can change the brain or that "a single word has the power to influence the expression of genes that regulate physical and emotional stress".[194] In another account, the latest scientific findings on nature vs nurture have been summarized as follows:

> Human development occurs through a process of dynamic relations involving variables from biological through sociocultural and historical levels of organization. Influences from all levels – genes, individual behavior, parental rearing practices, or social policies, for instance – contribute integratively, and *only* integratively, to the structure and function of human behavior and development. No one level of organization, no one set of influences – be it genes or environmental/cultural – can be factually construed as an exclusive, or even prime, impetus to the full development. Neither system functions without the other.[195]

It is thus a process, often experienced through change, which marks the duality of life. The process of influence has also been transmitted by way of the following chain of causal effects between nativism and empiricism or a thought and fate:

> Sow a thought, and reap an action. Sow an action, and reap a habit. Sow a habit, and reap a character. Sow a character, and reap destiny.[196]

This saying establishes a link between nurture and nature but in a unilinear direction of influence and thus fails to explain the origin of duality. However, applied to the inquiry about the impact and role of essentially oxymoronic concepts for the evolution of humanity, it may help to point out the limitations of our current scientific paradigm and, equally, the predominant form of binary logic and possibly our framework of sense perception altogether. It confirms that there is a causal link between mind and reality. This link has also been described in the following two principal observations:

> *First*, that all higher levels of thinking are dependent on language.
> *Second*, that the structure of the language one habitually uses influences the manner in which one understands his environment. The picture of the universe shifts from tongue to tongue.[197]

193 *Ibid* at 390.

194 See also Newberg and Waldman, *supra* note 90 at 3.

195 See Cynthia García Coll, Elaine L. Bearer, and Richard M. Lerner, "Conclusions: Beyond Nature Versus Nurture to More Complex, Relational, and Dynamic Developmental Systems" in Cynthia García Coll, Elaine L. Bearer, and Richard M. Lerner (eds), *Nature and Nurture: The Complex Interplay of Genetic and Environmental Influences on Human Behaviour and Development* (New York: Psychology Press, 2004) 225 at 226.

196 See James Strachan, *Hebrew Ideals from the Story of the Patriarchs: A Study of Old Testament Faith and Life* (Edinburgh: T. & T. Clark, 1906) at 50 and Alice A. Bailey, *The Labours of Hercules: An Astrological Interpretation* (New York: Lucis, 2000) at 38.

197 See John B. Carroll (ed), *Language, Thought, and Reality: Selected Writings of Benjamin Lee Whorf* (Cambridge: MIT Press, 1956) at 6.

Thus, as an important linguistic tool to analyse and describe reality, essentially oxymoronic concepts play an important role in the way we perceive the environment, the universe we inhabit. They must have a considerable impact at the level of thoughts, considering the law of associations in psychology. As formulated by Ernst Mach, the law means that whenever one concept (or content of consciousness) is invoked simultaneously with a second one (which is directly the case in oxymora), "one of them, when it arises, will evoke the other".[198] This means that oxymora do gradually change our thinking. However, this leaves the essence of the question of how they will impact human evolution in the future unanswered for the time being. Eventually, we need to ask if oxymora and paradoxes will, after affecting first our language, then our thinking, and possibly our perception, at some point also alter our biological appearance, our organs and eventually our fate? In this regard, it was said that as humans have evolved both in terms of consciousness and biology, they also developed new organs of cognition.[199]

With this possibility in mind, it is important to ask whether, and if so how, we can actively influence the process of evolution. Is it that we see duality everywhere because we are dual and we are dual because we think in dualities? Do we have the power to break free from this vicious circle and change how we are by changing the way we think and speak? Ultimately, these are not only fundamental questions about life but also for law, especially in a normative sense that would allow us to have a say in the direction that the evolution of humanity takes. Would, for instance, a prohibition on the use of essentially oxymoronic concepts in legal discourse change the way law evolves and justice is done? Inversely, one may ask if law in the time of oxymora must change to tackle the global challenges faced today.

198 See Ernst Mach, *The Analysis of Sensations and the Relation of the Physical to the Psychical* (New York: Dover Publications, 1959) at 239 [first published in 1885].
199 See Arthur Zajonc, *Catching the Light: The Entwined History of Light and Mind* (Oxford: Oxford University Press, 1993) at 184 and 185.

7 Law in the time of oxymora

Just injustice?

Is the law law because it is just, or is the law just because it is the law?[1]

Law, following art and science, also appears to feature an increasing amount of essentially oxymoronic concepts. The main cause for art, science and law to share this trend may be rooted in them actually sharing similar goals in evolution but pursuing them through different means. Linguistically, they are also bound by the same constant necessity for language to adapt to changes in (the perception of) reality based primarily on the creation of neologisms and semantic change. More specifically, in an age of acceleration of the perception of change, changes in language are also found to be accelerating. Together these factors favour the creation of neologisms, notably in the form of portmanteau words, which are often oxymora. As a result of oxymora, the lines of distinctions between concepts or disciplines are also increasingly becoming blurred, both in science and in law. For science, this phenomenon has been expressed in the following statement:

> One by one we have seen how categories, which at first seem sharply defined, merge one into another, and how every classification when analyzed shows that some imaginary line has been arbitrarily taken as a boundary.[2]

The same trend has also seized the law, where the classifications are becoming subject to change, as reflected in the following account:

> But such is the complexity of the universe as it presents itself to us that continually new combinations of elements appear; new, that is, in the sense that when we made our classification we did not have them in mind, and now that they present themselves we are in doubt into which class to put them.[3]

As language is the prime but not the sole medium through which law acts,[4] the great relevance of these rhetorical figures for law is obvious. Language, however,

1 Costas Douzinas and Ronnie Warrington, "'A Well-Founded Fear of Justice': Law and Ethics in Postmodernity" (1991) 2(2) *Law and Critique* 115 at 117.

2 See Gilbert N. Lewis, *The Anatomy of Science* (New Haven: Yale University Press, 1926) at 178.

3 See Walter Wheeler Cook, "'Substance' and 'Procedure' in the Conflict of Laws" (1933) 42(3) *The Yale Law Journal* 333 at 333–334.

4 See also Brian Bix, "Conceptual Questions and Jurisprudence" (1995) 1(4) *Legal Theory* 465 at 1.

is not the end of the story. Language merely points only to a deeper layer of cognition from where this trend ultimately emerges, which is rooted somewhere between genes and cognition or nature and nurture.

In the search for the origin of this trend, we need next to investigate the impact that essentially oxymoronic concepts have on law and legal reasoning as well as the sense of justice. In this regard, the overview of oxymora in the law in Chapter 5 produced a significant amount of evidence that essentially oxymoronic concepts appear notably in so-called "hard cases". They are considered "hard cases" not in the sense of those cases "in which the result is not clearly dictated by statute or precedent" as defined by Dworkin.[5] Instead they are considered "hard cases" in the sense of "borderline cases". Akin to the paradox of boundary, "borderline cases" are those where it is hard to draw the borderline between various antagonisms, like just or unjust, legal or illegal, and right and wrong. As a result, they denominate "cases in which the application of the standards of the law is subject to doubt and disagreement".[6] The reason for the difficulty in drawing the line is either because of changes occurring faster, which makes it difficult to draw a line, in the same way it was said to be difficult to step into the same river once (or twice). Similarly and possibly related to the first cause, the difficulty may also be due to the facts being contradictory, which makes the application of the law more difficult. How the application of the law becomes more difficult in light of essentially oxymoronic concepts will be shown by an overview of law in action and law in books.

7.1 Essentially oxymoronic concepts "in action"

> *Indeed, like other famous oxymorons in law – "all deliberate speed" for example or "substantive due process" – it evades rather than expresses precise meaning.*[7]

In line with perception in general and perhaps based on the dual nature of humans, dichotomous thinking and binary logic in line with a general culture of contestation was found to have dominated the legal nomos for a long time. The link between the mind and a dualistic conception of law has been confirmed by the claim that resolving adversarial disputes "engenders an adversarial mindset, a win/lose attitude in legal life".[8] The opposite may also be true, namely that it was the adversarial or dualistic mindset that engendered a dualistic conception of law and justice as well as of science. The frequency of the use of oxymoronic language, however, revealed a general trend of the transcendence of the dualistic conception towards a more open but possibly also confusing or complex conception of law. Perhaps an effective way of presenting the different impact of oxymoronic as opposed to contested or vague concepts is by way of the process of legal reasoning known as the legal syllogism. This is because the legal syllogism

5 See the editorial comment in Ronald Dworkin, "Hard Cases" (1975) 88(6) *Harvard Law Review* 1057 at 1057.

6 But see Timothy Endicott, "Law Is Necessarily Vague" (2001) 7(4) *Legal Theory* 379 at 379.

7 *Duckworth v. Franzen*, 780 F.2d 645, 652 (7th Cir. 1985).

8 See William van Caenegem, "Adversarial Systems and Adversarial Mindsets: Do We Need Either?" (2003) 15(2) *Bond Law Review* 111 at 113.

is a common (but not undisputed) method for the interpretation and formulation of laws.[9] The syllogism describes the different reasoning schemes of logical arguments in which the conclusion is inferred from a major and one or more minor premises.[10] Aristotle (384–322 BCE), who contributed to the development of the syllogism, is often cited in the prime example, which reads as follows:

Major premise:	All humans are mortal.
Minor premise:	Aristotle is human.
Conclusion:	**Aristotle is mortal.**

This seems a fairly easy problem of legal reasoning and shows the dual world of right and wrong is still intact. To underscore further the duality in the process of legal reasoning and establishing justice, the following example will be formulated in both the position and the negation (A and -A).

Major premise:	Everyone guilty of a crime will be punished (implying that everyone not guilty or innocent will not be punished or acquitted).
Minor premise:	Aristotle is guilty (Aristotle is not innocent and will not be acquitted).
Conclusion:	**Aristotle will be punished (and not be acquitted).**

In this example too, provided that the facts and the law in the case were clear, legal reasoning based on dual logic seems to have yielded the correct result and justice was done. What then about cases where the facts underlying the case contain an oxymoron or paradox?

A famous case that best exemplifies the problem of legal reasoning that oxymora or paradoxes may cause is found in the so-called "Gallows paradox" found in *Don Quixote*, a Spanish novel written by Miguel de Cervantes Saavedra (1547–1616).[11] The said paradox is explained in the following paragraph:

> **The Gallows Paradox**
>
> "Anyone who crosses this river shall first take oath as to whither he is bound and why. If he swears to the truth, he shall be permitted to pass; but if he tells a falsehood, he shall die without hope of pardon on the gallows that has been set up there." Once this law and the rigorous conditions it laid down had been promulgated, there were many who told the truth and whom

9 See also Neil MacCormick, *Rhetoric and the Rule of Law: A Theory of Legal Reasoning* (Oxford: Oxford University Press, 2005) 32–48.

10 See *e.g.* Giovanni Sartor, *Legal Reasoning: A Cognitive Approach to the Law* (Dordrecht: Springer, 2005) at 50–85.

11 Miguel de Cervantes Saavedra, *Don Quixote de la Mancha* (New York: Modern Library, 1998).

> the judges permitted to pass freely enough. And then it happened that one day, when they came to administer the oath to a certain man, he swore and affirmed that his destination was to die upon the gallows which they had erected and that he had no other purpose in view.[12]

This case highlights well the logical dilemma faced by the presiding judge, who is confronted with a true legal paradox. The dilemma consists in the problem that if the "certain man", whom we call "Cervantes" here, is allowed to pass, then he was telling a lie and should have been hanged instead. If, however, he was hanged, he would have been telling the truth and should have been allowed to pass. The dilemma can also be expressed by an oxymoron, namely that, in order to survive,[13] he was telling a "true lie". Expressed in a syllogism, the problem presents itself as follows:

Major premise:	Everyone telling the truth shall pass – everyone telling a lie shall die.
Minor premise:	Cervantes is telling a "true lie".
Conclusion:	**Cervantes shall . . . ?**

In view of the oxymoron "true lie", the conclusion is far from clear but the "logical" solution to the problem is given in the book by Sancho, in the following way:

> "Well, then," said Sancho, "my opinion is this: that part of the man that swore to the truth should be permitted to pass and that part of him that lied should be hanged, and thus the letter of the law will be carried out."[14]

A judgment of this kind, however, poses a serious problem in reality, as is also mentioned in the following reply given:

> "But, my Lord Governor," replied the one who had put the question, "it would be necessary to divide the man into two halves, the lying half and the truthful half, and if he were so divided it would kill him and the law would in no wise be fulfilled, whereas it is essential that its express provisions be carried out."[15]

This kind of solution would fulfil the requirements of dualistic thinking but certainly not the expectations of justice. However, before these expectations can be addressed, it is first necessary to provide not a historical but a contemporary problem of international legal practice.

12 *Ibid* at 997.
13 See Pamela Meyer, *Liespotting* (New York: St. Martin's Griffin, 2010) at 9 ("Paradoxically, we have to lie to survive as well").
14 De Cervantes Saavedra, *supra* note 11 at 998.
15 *Ibid.*

Such a case can be presented by referring to a series of concrete problems encountered at the international level. Exemplified by the strict division of competences between the WTO for international trade matters and the United Nations Organization for Education, Science and Culture (UNESCO) for culture in a broad sense, the following problem with the interpretation of laws in the form of international agreements and notably the decision about the competent international organization can occur when they concern an oxymoron, like that of the culture industry. In line with the present architecture (and fragmentation) of the present international legal order, the syllogism would apply in the following manner:

Major premise:	International trade matters fall within the competence of the World Trade Organization (WTO) (Art. II and III WTO Agreement); international cultural matters fall within the competence of the United Nations Educational, Scientific and Cultural Organization (UNESCO) (Art. 1 Constitution UNESCO).
Major premise 1:	The regulation of goods (GATT) and services (GATS) are international trade matters.
Minor premise 2:	The cultural industries cover both goods and services and are both economic and cultural in nature (cf. Recital 18 of the Preamble of the Convention on the Protection and Promotion of the Diversity of Cultural Expressions (CDCE) "that cultural activities, goods and services have both an economic and a cultural nature, because they convey identities, values and meanings, and must therefore not be treated as solely having commercial value").
Minor premise 3	Products produced by the culture industries have both a trade and a cultural nature.
Conclusion:	**The regulation of the cultural industries falls within the competence of . . . ?**

In this scenario finding the correct conclusion appears less clear than in the previous examples. Obviously, the right answer that comes to mind is that the cultural industries should be regulated by both international organizations, which they actually are. The real problem, however, is that the two organizations are not linked and, most of all, do not offer the same treatment for them. Worse still, as an expression of another "trade and . . ." paradox, both organizations are considered to be opposed in their proposed treatment of the cultural industries, namely that the WTO aims to liberalize all trade in the goods and services covered by the notion whereas the UNESCO advocates restrictions aimed at the preservation and promotion of the diversity of all cultural expressions. In a predominantly dualistic conception of things, the two aims are considered to be incompatible.

Thus, it is realistic for many more constitutional and notably federal and quasi-federal systems to encounter similar problems of competence conflicts. This case thus means a real conflict, beyond mere policy divergences, which may amount to differing approaches to the same subject matter. A real conflict in the strict sense was defined as involving a direct incompatibility between legal obligations that parties to two treaties entered into, meaning that they cannot simultaneously comply with their obligations under both treaties.[16] But such real conflicts are not only possible in competence conflicts or between two different international treaties but in many more contexts too.

In addition, this case reflects not a theoretical problem but also a practical one. Or else, it is further evidence for the distinction between theory and practice to be untenable and unreasonable particularly in law. A good argument showing the mutual relevance and inseparability of the theory and practice of law is an ancient paradox, known also as the "lawyer paradox" resulting in a logical dilemma for the considering court.[17] The paradox arose from a contract between Protagoras, a teacher of rhetoric, and his student Euathlus. The contract foresaw that Euathlus pay Protagoras a large sum of money for his teaching, of which one half was to be paid on his first day of study and the remaining half on the day when he should successfully plead a cause before the judges. But Euathlus, although he made progress in learning the art of pleading, refused to take up any case to be pleaded before a court. Hence Protagoras lost patience, demanded the payment of the remaining sum and decided to sue Euathlus in court. Appearing before the judges, Protagoras made the following statement:

> Be assured, thou most absurd young man, thou must in either case pay what I demand, whether the decision be for or against you. If the decision be against you, the sentence will compel you to fulfil your agreement, because I shall conquer. If the decision be for you, the terms of the bargain will be due to me, because you conquer.[18]

When Euathlus was called to testify, he – displaying good skills of rhetoric he had obviously learned – replied the following:

> I might meet this your captious subtlety if I did not reply a word, but apply to another advocate; but I have a much greater delight in this victory, beating you not only in the cause, but the argument. Learn, therefore, you most wise master, that in either case I will not pay what you demand, whether it be determined for or against me. If the judges shall determine for me, according to their sentence nothing will be due to you: if they decide against me, according to the agreement, nothing will be due to you, because I shall not overcome.[19]

16 See C. Wilfred Jenks, "The Conflict of Law-Making Treaties" (1953) *British Yearbook of International Law* 401 at 425–426.

17 See Aulus Gellius, *The Attic Nights*, vol 1 (London: J. Johnson, 1795) at 305–307, Diogenes Laertius, *The Lives and Opinions of Eminent Philosophers* (London: Henry G. Bohn, 1853) at 399 and R. M. Sainsbury, *Paradoxes*, 3rd ed (Cambridge: Cambridge University Press, 2009) at 160.

18 See Gellius, *supra* note 17 at 306.

19 *Ibid.*

The judges were reported to have been puzzled by the fact that whatever their determination might be, it might be turned against itself. Aulus Gellius, reporting this case, called this instance of imperfections of arguments "*reciproca*", meaning that "an argument proposed can be turned back and inverted against him by whom it is used, and on both sides appear like valid".[20] Consequently, as there seemed no rational way to solve the paradox and to find a way out of this logical dilemma, the judges "left the question undecided, and deferred the cause to a very distant day".[21]

While it is unclear whether this case of *Protagoras vs. Euathlus* is anecdotal or was actually decided, it is certain that, in a distant day thereafter, it was cited in a real case decided before a US court in 1946, which was confronted with a similar dilemma, namely a jury verdict implying its own negation. It was in *State vs. Jones* that a court had to rule on the legality of a ruling convicting a doctor on charges of (illegally performing) abortions on a total of six counts.[22] In this case the logical dilemma consisted in the problem that, at least in one count, the conviction was based on the uncorroborated testimony of an accomplice, i.e. one of the women on whom the abortion was performed.[23] To understand the problem, the law at issue considered anyone an accomplice "who aids, abets, procures, conspires or participates with another in the commission of an offense against the law".[24] Equally, the law also required, as the jury in the case was informed, that testimonies of accomplices should be approached with great care and caution and therefore a conviction should not be based on the testimony alone but be supported by other evidence.[25] The dilemma consisted in the fact that the jury must, like following the oxymoron of a hysteron proteron, first convict the accused before he could be found guilty. More concretely, the judge wrote that "the jury must assume or presuppose the guilt of the accused before it can find the witness to be an accomplice", adding that this means a violation of the rule of the "presumption of innocence and the rule that there can be no accomplice without a guilty principal".[26] In this case, the judge did not defer the case to a distant day but still confirmed the conviction of the accused by relying on a previous case, which left the decision of determining whether a witness is an accomplice or not to the jury.[27] Thus, it could be said that the ruling was confirmed but the solution to the logical dilemma was avoided by the court and the problem merely passed to the members of the jury, who, however, did not provide a detailed reasoning of their "mental gymnastics".[28]

20 *Ibid* at 305.
21 *Ibid* at 307.
22 *State v. Jones*, 80 Ohio App. 269 (1946).
23 *Ibid* at 275.
24 *Ibid* at 271.
25 *Ibid* at 271.
26 *Ibid* at 275–276.
27 *Ibid* at 277 and *Curtis v. The State of Ohio*, 113 Ohio St. 187 (1925) at 187, and 209–210.
28 *State v. Jones*, 80 Ohio App. 269 (1946) at 277.

This example merely serves as a reminder of the difficult and perhaps artificial distinction between theory and practice, or mental gymnastics and law enforcement, which are inextricably linked. More so, it reminds us of the dominant underlying dual conception of law, by which "circular arguments have been viewed as *petitio principii* forbidden by the iron law of legal logic".[29] Nonetheless, cases of this sort also underline that real conflicts moulded in oxymoronic language are not hypothetical but do occur in practice.

This problem of real conflicts based on the direct opposition between one law or legal rule has also been described by the term "antinomy", which was explained as follows:

> As a result, the antinomies, as far as they concern the law, do not consist in the discovery of a contradiction caused by the simultaneous affirmation of the truth and falsehood of a proposition, but in the existence of an incompatibility between the relevant laws applicable to the same subject matter.[30]

Similar to Wilfred Jenks before,[31] Chaïm Perelman and others thus define "antinomy" as a real conflict between laws or legal norms.[32] In addition, Perelman also elaborates, like Dworkin did in hard cases, on the role of lacunae, namely that antinomies are usually accompanied by lacunae, that is to say, when there exists no conflict of law norm that allows the judge to solve the antinomy.[33] But for all that, there exist several types of "hard cases" that a judge or interpreter of laws may face, especially in view of essentially contested concepts. Such hard cases include, first, cases where the judge has no relevant law, statute or precedent at her/his disposal – a so-called "lacuna". Second, the judge can use one or more relevant laws, treaties, statutes, or even precedents but their legal content is conflicting, i.e. the case of a "real conflict" or "antinomy". In this case, the judge may have access or not to a conflict or law rule, which helps to solve the case. Nevertheless, in all these instances the judge's task of legal reasoning based on the syllogism may be aggravated by problems of fact related to the implication of vague or essentially contested concepts. In this case, and still assuming that each case has a "legally best and therefore uniquely correct decision",[34] the judge is called upon to render her/his best solution to the case by presenting the best arguments and maybe scientific support provided by experts. But what then, when the facts are presented in the form of essentially oxymoronic concepts (e.g. "cultural industries")? Then, automatically,

29 See Gunther Teubner, "Introduction to Autopoietic Law" in Gunther Teubner (ed), *Autopoietic Law: A New Approach to Law and Society* (New York: de Gruyter, 1988) 1 at 1.

30 See Chaïm Perelman, "Les antinomies en droit" (1964) 18 *Dialectica* 392 at 393 [translation from French by author].

31 See C. Wildfred Jenks, *supra* note 16.

32 See also Paul Foriers, "Les antinomies en droit" (1964) 18 *Dialectica* 20–38.

33 See Perelman, *supra* note 30 at 400.

34 See Thomas D. Perry, "Contested Concepts and Hard Cases" (1977) 88(1) *Ethics* 20 at 23.

it appears that none of the conflicting opinions can be supported because both extreme positions are equal. Last but not least, it may also be possible that the facts are clear and not oxymoronic but the law itself uses "legislative oxymora". Then how, one may ask, can the syllogism be applied in a consistent way? Is the impracticability of the syllogism in dealing with paradoxes and oxymora the reason why the syllogism's repute itself is low these days?[35] These questions explain why, in the end, essentially oxymoronic concepts can be said to form another category of so-called "hard" or "borderline cases", i.e. cases where it is hard to draw a boundary between opposites or antonyms. Before trying to find ways to solve these legal riddles, it is deemed useful to inquire into the impact of essentially oxymoronic concepts on jurisprudence and the progressive development of legal scholarship.

7.2 Essentially oxymoronic concepts "in books"

The one Law has become two laws.[36]

Following the assessment of practical problems caused by essentially oxymoronic concepts in law, it is time to look at how jurisprudence and scholarship have reacted to the rise of essentially oxymoronic concepts. In this regard it is interesting to continue the story from the time when legal scholarship moved from a more comprehensive conception of law, or at least a more comprehensive discourse thereof, to a debate of "law and . . ." issues, as perhaps initiated by the "law and literature" movement. This movement gradually expanded from literature to law and society and even further to a dialectical process by which law became contrasted and eventually linked with other scientific branches (like law and economics) or other areas of legal relevance (like law and sexuality). This trend was matched by an increasing specialization in the field of law (like that experienced by science in general but art as well). Law, like the many faculties teaching it, became divided into numerous subdisciplines, like public and private, or national and international law, to mention but a few.[37] What followed from this trend is that the complexity increased, as well as the amount of new legislation or laws, and, most of all, the confusion as to the meaning, scope and mutual relation between all the norms, laws or legal regimes.

This self-reinforcing vicious cycle of the evolution of law was met by scholarship in a gradual transition from publications on numerous dichotomous pairs of "law and . . ." issues (e.g. "law and magic") or ". . . and the law" (e.g. "art and

35 See Nathan Isaacs, "The Law and the Facts" (1922) 22(1) *Columbia Law Review* 1 at 1.

36 Babylonian Talmud, *Sanhedrin* 88b.

37 See *e.g.* Franz Bydlinski, "Kriterien und Sinn der Unterscheidung von Privatrecht und öffentlichem Recht" (1994) 194(4) *Archiv für die civilistische Praxis* 319, Friedrich K. Juenger, "Private International Law or International Private Law?" (1994–1995) 5 *King's College Law Journal* 45, and Rostam J. Neuwirth, "International Law and the Public/Private Law Distinction" (2000) 55(4) *Zeitschrift für öffentliches Recht* 393.

the law") to constructions including three or more "contested concepts". This happens when the dualistic line of reasoning has been exhausted or has met with its own limitations. In this scenario, the respective dual links are often replaced by triple pairs, such as "law, love, and language",[38] "law, biology, and culture",[39] "law, courts, and policy",[40] "law, sex, and society",[41] or "law, economics, and evolutionary theory".[42] Finally, when the possibilities for triple combinations have been exhausted or the research field conclusively been explored, then it may face an even greater degree of inter- or multidisciplinary complexity.

In view of such complexity, authors consciously or subconsciously then may have recourse to the rhetorical construct of "law as . . .".[43] Examples of this construct include "law as a social system",[44] "law as a means to an end",[45] "law as institution",[46] "law as a social science",[47] "law as fact",[48] "law as process",[49] or "law as a means to change".[50] Other examples may read even more strangely, such as "law as mnemonics"[51] or "law as ouroborous".[52] Additionally, as in "law and . . ." issues before, in this context too, the dual construction becomes complemented by a triple one, such as "law as logic and experience"[53] and "law as rule and principle".[54] More complex still are dialectic pairs like "law as rhetoric, rhetoric as law"[55] or "the rule of law as a law of rules".[56] Overall, the "law

38 See *e.g.* Herbert McCabe, *Law, Love and Language* (London: Sheed & Ward, 1968).
39 See *e.g.* Margaret Gruter and Paul Bohannan (eds), *Law, Biology and Culture: The Evolution of Law* (Santa Barbara: Ross Erikson 1983).
40 See *e.g.* Mitchell S. G. Klein, *Law, Courts, and Policy* (Englewood Cliffs: Prentice-Hall, 1984).
41 See *e.g.* James A. Brundage, *Law, Sex, and Christian Society in Medieval Europe* (Chicago: University of Chicago Press, 1987).
42 See *e.g.* Peer Zumbansen and Gralf-Peter Calliess (eds), *Law, Economics and Evolutionary Theory* (Cheltenham: Edward Elgar 2011).
43 See the overview in Rostam J. Neuwirth, "Law and Magic: A(nother) Paradox?" (2014) 37(1) *Thomas Jefferson Law Review* 139 at 174–175.
44 See *e.g.* Niklas Luhmann, *Law as a Social System* (Oxford: Oxford University Press, 2004).
45 See *e.g.* Brian Z. Tamanaha, *Law as a Means to an End* (Cambridge: Cambridge University Press, 2006).
46 See *e.g.* Massimo La Torre, *Law as Institution* (Dordrecht: Springer, 2010).
47 See *e.g.* Huntington Cairns, "Law as a Social Science" (1935) 2(4) *Philosophy of Science* 484.
48 See *e.g.* Karl Olivecrona, *Law as Fact* (London: Stevens & Sons, 1971).
49 Sally Falk Moore, *Law as Process: An Anthropological Approach* (Boston: Routledge & K. Paul, 1978).
50 See *e.g.* John F. Goins, "Law as a Means to Change" (1961) 3(2) *Journal of Inter-American Studies* 53.
51 See *e.g.* Rostam J. Neuwirth, "Law as Mnemonics: The Mind as the Prime Source of Normativity" (2008) 2(1) *European Journal of Legal Studies* 143 at 145–146.
52 See *e.g.* Guilherme Vasconcelos Vilaça, *Law as Ouroboros* (unpublished Ph.D. thesis) (Florence: European University Institute, 2012).
53 See *e.g.* Max Radin, *Law as Logic and Experience* (New Haven: Yale University Press, 1940).
54 See Theodore M. Benditt, *Law as Rule and Principle: Problems of Legal Philosophy* (Stanford: Stanford University Press, 1978).
55 See James Boyd White, "Law as Rhetoric, Rhetoric as Law: The Arts of Cultural and Communal Life" (1985) 52(3) *University of Chicago Law Review* 684.
56 Antonin Scalia, "The Rule of Law as a Law of Rules" (1989) 56(4) *University of Chicago Law Review* 1175.

as . . ." debate has been defined as an attempt to move away from the "law and society" approach and to establish a new framework, namely one that "does not depend on a binary, or a conjunction of two distinct fields imagined as outside of each other".[57]

Consequently, when the "law as . . ." approach seems to be exhausted, it is gradually replaced by the use of oxymoronic language. This means that, as a last phase, publications are more likely to be titled with or to introduce oxymoronic concepts. This shift from a dialectical process via "law as . . ." to oxymoronic concepts can also be exemplified by the scholarly debate in the field of intellectual property law. It was Herbert L.A. Hart who pointed out the dual structure of the idea of justice by the example of a "fake diamond" that may still be a "genuine antique".[58] At present, the global debate about adequate levels of intellectual property rights protection is largely bifurcated. This can be seen in the fact that the debate evolves by, first, the identification of the problems in negative terms, i.e. focusing on the problem of piracy and counterfeiting of products protected by intellectual property laws. The bifurcation of the debate is also reflected in its evolution based on antonyms, like copyright being contrasted with "copyleft" or "copywrong",[59] just as the term "creative economy"[60] was soon thereafter mirrored in the "knockoff economy".[61] On the one hand, there are arguments emphasizing the financial losses and other negative consequences attributed to piracy and counterfeiting,[62] and on the other hand, those supporting stricter laws protecting intellectual property and those fearing for the "future of ideas" and arguing for their adjustment or relaxation instead, such as the creative commons movement.[63]

More recently the shortcomings and misconceptions in the debate using black-and-white thinking have become more obvious. These shortcomings concern, for instance, the accuracy of the statistical methods applied to the calculation of losses caused by piracy or counterfeiting.[64] The criticism mirrors the gradual emergence of a more differentiated approach, which is formulated to

57 See Catherine L. Fisk and Robert W. Gordon, "'Law As ...': Theory and Method in Legal History" (2011) 1(3) *U.C. Irvine Law Review* 519 at 519.

58 Herbert L. A. Hart, *The Concept of Law*, 2nd ed (Oxford: Clarendon Press, 1994) at 160.

59 See Paul B. de Laat, "Copyright or Copyleft? An Analysis of Property Regimes for Software Development" (2005) 34(10) *Research Policy* 1511 and Siva Vaidhyanathan, *Copyrights and Copywrongs: The Rise of Intellectual Property and How It Threatens Creativity* (New York: New York University Press, 2011).

60 See *e.g.* John Howkins, *The Creative Economy: How People Make Money From Ideas* (London: Penguin, 2002).

61 See *e.g.* Kal Raustiala and Christopher Sprigman, *The Knockoff Economy: How Imitation Sparks Innovation* (Oxford: Oxford University Press, 2012).

62 See *e.g.* Organization for Economic Co-operation and Development (OECD), *The Economic Impact of Counterfeiting and Piracy* (Paris: OECD, 2010) and Alan Zimmerman, *The Economics of Counterfeit Trade: Governments, Consumers, Pirates and Intellectual Property Rights* (Berlin: Springer, 2009).

63 See *e.g.* Lawrence Lessig, *The Future of Ideas: The Fate of the Commons in a Connected World* (New York: Random House, 2001).

64 See *e.g.* Daniel Chow, "Counterfeiting as an Externality Imposed by Multinational Companies on Developing Countries" (2011) 51(4) *Virginia Journal of International Law* 785.

some extent by "IP law as . . ." approaches[65] but more by means of essentially oxymoronic concepts. There now exist critical writings using oxymoronic language for almost all branches of intellectual property law. Formulated in positive terms, these publications are entitled, for example, the "copyright paradox",[66] the "trademark paradox",[67] the "patent paradox"[68] or the "paradox of geographical indications".[69] The same phenomenon exists in negative terms, like the "piracy paradox" and "counterfeit paradox".[70] These paradoxes consist in empirical data supporting the somewhat counterintuitive assumption that piracy or lower levels of intellectual property protection may paradoxically serve the creative authors better than comparatively higher levels of protection. Similar problems of a precise legal classification are also captured by the oxymoron of "real fakes", which may refer to products protected by either trademarks or copyright, which are sold as fakes on the "grey market" but may actually, knowingly or unknowingly, originate from the same factory where the "real" or "genuine" merchandise is produced.[71]

In sum, there are many other regulatory fields where oxymora and paradoxes or other contradictory elements play an increasingly important role. They may also be used to respond to the challenges caused by them. For instance, in Austrian law, there is the so-called "Janus-headed administrative act" (*Januskopfiger Verwaltungsakt*), which combines in one several legal acts which are substantively connected but formally belong to separate and even contradicting categories and which therefore causes interpretational problems.[72] Oxymora have also been used to denominate the difficulties of connecting different legal cultures or systems to legal concepts originating from other places, like Chinese culture to law, or

65 See *e.g.* Elizabeth F. Judge, "Intellectual Property Law as an Internal Limit on Intellectual Property Rights and Autonomous Source of Liability for Intellectual Property Owners" (2007) 27(4) *Bulletin of Science, Technology & Society* 301.

66 See *e.g.* Tim Wu, "The Copyright Paradox" (2005) 2005 *The Supreme Court Review* 229.

67 See *e.g.* Catherine M. Manley, *The Trademark Paradox: Trademarks and Their Conflicting Legal and Commercial Boundaries* (Brussels: Peter Lang, 2015).

68 See *e.g.* Bronwyn H. Hall and Rosemarie Ham Ziedonis, "The Patent Paradox Revisited: An Empirical Study of Patenting in the U.S. Semiconductor Industry, 1979-1995" (2001) 32(1) *The Rand Journal of Economics* 101.

69 See *e.g.* Michelle Agdomar, "Removing the Greek from Feta and Adding Korbel to Champagne: The Paradox of Geographical Indications in International Law" (2008) 18(2) *Fordham Intellectual Property, Media & Entertainment Law Journal* 541.

70 See *e.g.* Peggy E. Chaudhry and Michael G. Walsh, "An Assessment of the Impact of Counterfeiting in International Markets: The Piracy Paradox Persists" (1996) 31(3) *The Columbia Journal of World Business* 34 and Kal Raustiala and Christopher Sprigman, "The Piracy Paradox: Innovation and Intellectual Property in Fashion Design" (2006) 92(8) *Virginia Law Review* 1687.

71 See Rostam J. Neuwirth, "Counterfeiting and Piracy in International Trade: The Good, the Bad and the . . . Oxymoron of 'Real Fakes'" (2017) 7(4) *Queen Mary Journal of Intellectual Property Law* 444.

72 See Elisabeth Dujmovits, "Januskopfige Verwaltungsakte und alles was es gibt" in Iris Eisenberger, et al. (eds), *Norm und Normvorstellung: Festschrift für Bernd-Christian Funk zum 60. Geburtstag* (Wien: Springer, 2003) 111 at 118–119.

Indian culture to the rule of law.[73] Two other examples are the terms "regulatory coopetition" (combining the opposites of "cooperation" and "competition"),[74] and "multilateralizing regionalism"[75] or "regionalizing multilateralism" (combining "multilateralism" with "regionalism"). In parallel, these publications make prolific use of paradoxes to denote and highlight the increasing complexity of the legal world today, such as, for instance, the "paradox of constitutionalism".[76] In sum and to deal with the growing complexity better, thus, legal scholarship gradually moves from one law via two laws to many laws, or, put briefly, from a world of contestation (contested concepts) to a world of contradiction (oxymoronic concepts).

7.3 "Just injustice": changes of the law and the law of changes

Law changes as language changes – perhaps because language changes.[77]

The discussion of the impact of essentially oxymoronic concepts on the theory and practice of law made evident several deficiencies of the present conception of law. To begin with, it is a strong dualistic conception of law expressed in many dichotomies that can be named the root cause for law's inability to effectively deal with change and complexity. The weakness of dichotomies can be shown by the separation of legal theory and practice, which is actually flawed and in contrast to the old Latin proverb "*Teoria sine praxis, sicut rota sine axis*" ("Theory without practice is like a wheel without an axle"). The fact that their lines of distinction are actually blurry or that they need to be seen in closer relation to each other is also being recognized in the field of legal education.[78] Another distinction, that of law and of fact, is just another good example of difficulties in drawing a clear line.[79] Overall, the conception of law is far too static and needs more dynamic instruments to tackle the challenges arising from an acceleration of change. The problems of law (or the rule of law) in embracing "change" seem to be tied to conceptual problems related to our understanding of space and time.

73 See Teemu Ruskola, "Law Without Law, or Is 'Chinese Law" an Oxymoron?" (2007) 11(2) *William & Mary Bill of Rights Journal* 655 and J. Eckert, "Indisches Oxymoron: Rechtsstaat ohne Rule of Law" in R. Kappel (ed), *Rechtsstaatlichkeit im Zeitalter der Globalisierung* (Freiburg i. B.: Rombach, 2005) 341.

74 See Daniel C. Esty and Damien Geradin, "Regulatory Co-opetition" (2000) 3(2) *Journal of International Economic Law* 235 at 235.

75 See Richard Baldwin and Patrick Low (eds), *Multilateralizing Regionalism* (Cambridge: Cambridge University Press, 2008).

76 See Martin Loughlin and Neil Walker (eds), *The Paradox of Constitutionalism: Constituent Power and Constitutional Form* (Oxford: Oxford University Press, 2008).

77 See the Foreword by Adolph S. Oko in Nathan S. Isaacs, *The Law and the Change of Law* (Miami: Hardpress, 2012) at 6.

78 See also Gerald E. LeDain, "The Theory and Practice of Legal Education" (1961) 7(3) *McGill Law Journal* 192.

79 See Isaacs, "The Law and the Facts", *supra* note 35 and Clarence Morris, "Law and Fact" (1942) 55(8) *Harvard Law Review* 1303.

In general, the many problems raise the issue of the limitation of a dominantly dualistic conception of law based on binary logic. In this regard, it is noteworthy that – throughout history – the understanding of law seems to have shifted from the perception of law as a singularity to one of duality. Such a shift was already recorded in the Talmudic legal tradition by the adage that "the Torah became as two Toroth", or "The one Law has become two laws".[80] The introduction of the two schools (or houses) of Hillel and Shammai carried that shift further. The two schools not only followed a dualistic or dialectical method of interpretation of law but also resulted in disputes multiplying.

Even millennia later, the same problem that duality – as well described by Robert M. Cover – poses to the idea of justice was noted by Herbert L.A. Hart in his book *The Concept of Law*:

> There is therefore a certain complexity in the structure of the idea of justice. We may say that it consists of two parts: a uniform or constant feature, summarized in the precept "Treat like cases alike" and a shifting or varying criterion used in determining when, for any given purpose, cases are alike or different.[81]

Here is the duality of the constant and the changing, the static and the dynamic, similar to the two planes, the temporal and the eternal, found by Eliade in comparing religions.[82] Since then, law has been divided and further subdivided into numerous opposites, like international law in international treaty and international customary law,[83] the legal debate in one on the "law as it is" (*de lege lata*) and another on the "law as it should be" (*de lege ferenda*). The shift from singularity to duality can also be found in the evolution of procedural law, namely the change from a non-adversarial (or inquisitorial) to an adversarial system. Here the dualism lies largely in the method of finding the truth.[84] In a non-adversarial system, the judge combines in one the role of judge, prosecutor and defence counsel, whereas in the adversarial system, the judge merely presides over the two central opponents in the trial, the prosecutor and the defendant, and the judge (or jury) eventually decides the case based on the pro and contra arguments presented before the court. Symbolically, this *procedere* is depicted in numerous sculptures or paintings depicting the goddess of justice (*Iustitia*) blindfold and carrying a set of scales and a sword. The blindfold represents "blind justice" meaning neutrality or objectivity, while the scales represent the dual process of weighing of claims and counterclaims, with the sword literally finding a "clear-cut" separation between the right and the wrong before a judgment is made.

80 Babylonian Talmud, *Sanhedrin* 88b.

81 Hart, *supra* note 58 at 160.

82 Cf. Mircea Eliade, *Patterns in Comparative Religion* (Lincoln/London: University of Nebraska Press, 1996) at 460.

83 See *e.g.* Gary L. Scott and Craig L. Carr, "The International Court of Justice and the Treaty/Custom Dichotomy" (1981) 16(3) *Texas International Law Journal* 347.

84 See also Ellen E. Sward, "Values, Ideology, and the Evolution of the Adversary System" (1989) 64(2) *Indiana Law Journal* 301 at 302.

In this regard, it is noteworthy that the adversarial, as compared to an inquisitorial, presentation of evidence not only makes a substantial difference as to the outcome of the case but it also has the following advantage:

> As a case is presented, the adversary mode apparently counteracts judge or juror bias in favor of a given outcome and thus indeed seems to combat, in Fuller's words, a "tendency to judge too swiftly in terms of the familiar that which is not yet fully known."[85]

The "tendency to judge too swiftly that which is not yet fully known" is still a key problem even within an adversarial system. While dualism or bifurcation may have its advantages in trying to understand a complex reality, it also has its limitations. In fact, do the limitations mean that, from a certain angle taking into account the spatial and temporal features of perception, there is no justice?

Justice is closely related to perception; divergent views of justice are often based on "disagreement about what are the appropriate fixed points for analysis".[86] In this regard, it is important to consider whether essentially oxymoronic concepts will also alter the way we perceive and think of law and reality. Put differently, does the rise of essentially oxymoronic concepts mean that the role of law as a tool for seeking and establishing justice, in our dominant perception today as a tool to distinguish right from wrong or lawful from unlawful, is led ad absurdum? This could mean that in all our striving for justice, there is "just injustice" in the double sense of the term. The double sense means that, there is both "'just' (or only) injustice" or the oxymora of "just injustice" or "unjust justice" for that matter. Both cases do not suggest the degree of certainty that we may expect from law in rendering just decisions. Yet, every just decision seems to bear unjust elements, which is reflected in the fact that almost every final legal decision or judgment rendered remains controversial, or in part or as a whole disputed. In short, there remain doubts *when* justice has been done.[87]

Legally, these "doubts" are even built into legal systems, for instance, by allowing appeals or the reopening of closed cases.[88] But usually, these remedies can be invoked after the judgment has been rendered. Another way is found in an instrument where the "doubt" is already built into the verdict at the time of the judgment, namely by the practice of some jurisdictions to allow for dissenting opinions. This is, for instance, the case for the International Court of Justice, where the question of allowing dissenting opinions itself is met by opposite views.[89] Similar concerns have been raised in the US legal system, where allowing

85 See John Thibaut, Laurens Walker, and E. Allan Lind, "Adversary Presentation and Bias in Legal Decisionmaking" (1973) 86(2) *Harvard Law Review* 386 at 401.

86 See Cass R. Sunstein, "On Analogical Reasoning" (1993) 106(3) *Harvard Law Review* 741 at 753.

87 See also Paul M. Bator, "Finality in Criminal Law and Federal Habeas Corpus for State Prisoners" (1963) 76(3) *Harvard Law Review* 441 at 443.

88 See Max Alsberg, *Justizirrtum und Wiederaufnahme* (Berlin: Langenscheidt, 1913).

89 See R. P. Anand, "The Role of Individual and Dissenting Opinions in International Adjudication" (1965) 14(3) *The International and Comparative Law Quarterly* 788 at 790.

dissenting opinions is discussed as damaging to the authority of law itself, or else helping a legal system to lay the foundations for correcting an erroneous legal understanding over time.[90] Paradoxically, some dissenting opinions have even become "canonized", in the sense that they later come to be considered as established legal doctrine.[91] Moreover, dissent has been named the "basis of freedom in modern society".[92] It has also been held to help avoid mistakes, if only by sharing with others "what we actually know and believe".[93] Yet, the controversy over dissenting opinions only further confirms the dialectical or dualistic conception of law, where consenting or dissenting, and majority or minority, views are opposed. In the end, after time has passed allowing changes to take place, the opposing views culminate again in the question of which decision was right and which one was wrong.

To cut a long story short, it seems that the history of justice is frequently or, depending on the criteria, perhaps regularly one written by injustice. Many infamously famous cases, from the past to the present, seem to confirm such a proposition.[94] Consequently, justice truly seems "transitional" in a sense that the understanding of just or unjust oscillates and thus changes over time. How time may affect the perception of justice as opposed to injustice can easily be exemplified by a few selected examples. An ancient trial, or possibly two trials (one Hebrew (Sanhedrin), one Roman) against the same person, which was called one of the "greatest and most memorable acts of injustice", was the trial of Jesus.[95] Even if the historical accounts are fragmented and unreliable, the vast literature on the subject shows not only the interest in the trial's role for the course of world events ensuing from it until today, but also the many different views on justice and legality.[96] Despite the continuing debate about the historicity of Jesus,[97] the trials of Jesus shed important light on the

90 See also Mark Tushnet, "Why Dissent?" in Mark Tushnet (ed), *I Dissent: Great Opposing Opinions in Landmark Supreme Court Cases* (Boston: Beacon Press, 2008) XI.

91 See Anita S. Krishnakumar, "On the Evolution of the Canonical Dissent" (2000) 52(3) *Rutgers Law Review* 781 at 781–782.

92 See Øjvind Larsen, *The Right to Dissent: The Critical Principle in Discourse Ethics and Deliberative Democracy* (Copenhagen: Museum Tusculanum Press, 2009) at 9.

93 See Cass R. Sunstein, *Why Societies Need Dissent* (Cambridge: Harvard University Press, 2003) at 5.

94 See also Brian Harris, *Injustice: State Trials from Socrates to Nuremberg* (Stroud: The History Press, 2006); see also Adam Benforado, *Unfair: The New Science of Criminal Injustice* (New York: Crown, 2015).

95 See Giovanni Rosadi, *The Trial of Jesus* (New York: Dodd, Mead and Company, 1905) at 1.

96 See *e.g.* J. Salvador, "Jugement et Condamnation de Jésus" in J. Salvador, *Histoire des institutions de Moïse et du peuple hébreu*, vol II (Paris: Ponthieu, 1828) at 80–90, M. B. Rodrick, *The Trial and Crucifixion of Jesus Christ of Nazareth* (London: John Murray, 1908), S. Srinivasa Aiyar, *The Legality of the Trial of Jesus* (New York: Platt & Peck, 1915) and Richard Wellington Husband, *The Prosecutions of Jesus, Its Date, History and Legality* (Princeton: Princeton University Press, 1916) at 281–282.

97 See *e.g.* John M. Robertson, *The Historical Jesus: A Survey of Positions* (London: Watts & Co., 1916), Amy-Jill Levine, "Introduction" in Amy-Jill Levine, Dale C. Allison, Jr., and John Dominic Crossan (eds), *The Historical Jesus in Context* (Princeton: Princeton University Press, 2006) 1 and Bart D. Ehrman, *Did Jesus Exist? The Historical Argument for Jesus of Nazareth* (New York: HarperOne, 2012).

sense of justice or injustice. They reflect how the sense of justice or injustice depends notably on perception at large, its context, the interpretation of facts or fictions, the use of sources and laws. The contemporary significance of the trials show the sense of justice's changing nature over time and how the practical relevance of that sense is rarely congruent with questions of legality.

Other cases of changing perceptions of justice from the more recent past include the past practice of burning of alleged "witches" or heretics. This practice was previously considered just but is now considered unjust. The time frame for changing perceptions of justice may vary. In the case of Joan of Arc, who was first tried and put to death by fire in 1431, her trial was nullified a mere 25 years later and she was canonized in 1920, i.e. 489 years later.[98] This also indicates that important changes in perception had taken place within 25 years after her death and again in the 489 years leading to her canonization.

The importance of perception also played a crucial role in the case of the "Salem witch trials" in which several people were accused of witchcraft and prosecuted in Massachusetts between February 1692 and May 1693. Most striking in these cases was the admission of spectral evidence before the courts.[99] Spectral evidence was defined as "the common belief that, when a person had made covenant with the devil, he was given permission to assume that person's appearance in spectral form in order to recruit others, and to otherwise carry out his nefarious deeds".[100] In these cases too, the perception of injustice developed over the years and only led to the convicts' partial rehabilitation in 1957.[101] Yet, the use of spectral evidence generally raises the issue of the invisible world in the courtroom or how to deal with the unknown in general. The problem of the "invisible world" is still relevant today as it generally points to the impossibility to grasp and verify objectively the truthfulness of the evidence. This is exemplified by spectral evidence, because it is "invisible to everyone except those who were supposedly afflicted by the specters—the out-of-body manifestations of the witches".[102] The separation of the invisible from the visible is just one more dichotomy underlying the wider fragmentation of perception in relation to justice. Other legal forms of fragmentation, such as the divide between criminal and civil justice or procedure, is another expression of the same problem.[103]

98 See Joseph Fabre, *Procès de réhabilitation de Jeanne d'Arc raconté et traduit d'après les textes latins officiels*, vol I and II (Paris: Delagrave, 1888) and Ruth Schirmer-Imhoff (ed), *Der Prozeß Jeanne d'Arc: Akten und Protokolle 1431–1456* (Munich: DTV, 1961).

99 See Jane Campbell Moriarty, "Wonders of the Invisible World: Prosecutorial Syndrome and Profile Evidence in the Salem Witchcraft Trials" (2001) 26(1) *Vermont Law Review* 43 at 66.

100 See Wendel D. Craker, "Spectral Evidence, Non-Spectral Acts of Witchcraft, and Confession at Salem in 1692" (1997) 40(2) *The Historical Journal* 331 at 332.

101 See Bernard Rosenthal, *Salem Story: Reading the Witch Trials of 1692* (Cambridge: Cambridge University Press, 1993) at 85.

102 See Peter Charles Hoffer, "Invisible Worlds and Criminal Trials – The Cases of John Proctor and O.J. Simpson" (1997) 41(3) *American Journal of Legal History* 287 at 295.

103 See also Mary M. Cheh, "Constitutional Limits on Using Civil Remedies to Achieve Criminal Law Objectives: Understanding and Transcending the Criminal-Civil Law Distinction" (1991) 42(5) *Hastings Law Journal* 1325, Kenneth Mann, "Punitive Civil Sanctions: The Middleground

A positive example of speaking justice in a courtroom when being confronted with the invisible or "unknown" world comes from a 1920 copyright case. In the case, the judge was asked to rule about the ownership of a literary work written by a female journalist in the course of "psychic" séances. This left the judge with the option of granting the copyright to the woman, the spirit or the man who had published and allegedly infringed the copyright. Judicially constraining himself to the known and visible world, the judge ruled as follows:

> The conclusion which the defendant invites me to come to in this submission involves the expression of an opinion I am not prepared to make, that the authorship rest with someone already domiciled on *the other side of the inevitable river*. That is a matter I must leave for solution by others more competent to decide than I am. I can only look upon the matter as a terrestrial one, of the earth earthy, and I propose to deal with it on that footing.[104]

Thus the visible–invisible or known–unknown dichotomies are often expressed through fundamental paradoxes, like that of life and death. These fundamental paradoxes describe conditions where the scientific knowledge is incomplete or which cannot be analysed by the accepted standards of science. Beyond these accepted standards we speak of paranormal activities or phenomena which are not taken into account in the courtroom. However, these questions play an important role in the perception of justice and perception in general. The importance of perception stems from the role of the senses as a reliable source for judging reality, which in turn raises important questions about the number of senses, their hierarchy and their role in jurisprudence.[105] Just as paradoxes are understood as a contradiction bearing a possible truth, so should paranormal phenomena not be merely dismissed by considerations of justice as irrational or unscientific. Great caution should be displayed by justice systems around the world in how they deal with "paranormal" things, i.e. things which are not fully understood. For instance, the death penalty, aptly called "legal homicide", should not be applied but rather dismissed as injustice. Apart from the possibility of legal or factual error, the chance is high that future scientific insights into the life and death paradox may produce scientific evidence that will prove it to be a harmful and unjust practice, as was burning for the reasons of heresy in earlier times.

But again, more trivial and recent cases seem to support a conclusion of the problem of change of perception in time or space. For instance, in terms of space, a more trivial example may be when today an employee is fined for

Between Criminal and Civil Law" (1992) 101(8) *Yale Law Journal* 1795, and Carol S. Steiker, "Punishment and Procedure: Punishment Theory and the Criminal-Civil Procedural Divide" (1997) 85(4) *Georgetown Law Journal* 775.

104 High Court (Chancery), *Cummins v. Bond*, 1927, L.R. 1 Ch. 167 [*Italics* added].

105 See Lionel Bently, "Introduction" in Lionel Bently and Leo Flynn (eds), *Law and the Senses: Sensational Jurisprudence* (London: Pluto Press, 1996) 1.

"moonlighting" (clandestine employment) under the tax code. Such punishment, albeit legally consistent within the national legal system, still appears as injustice, particularly against the backdrop of a highly fragmented global tax system, in which multinational corporations or politicians may freely evade taxes due to legal loopholes in a globally fragmented tax system.[106]

Likewise, the WTO is often criticized for its panel and appellate body reports. Criticism is mainly directed at its preference for trade matters over other so-called "non-trade concerns", such as the environment, health, human rights, labour rights and culture, to mention but a few "trade and . . ." problems.[107] In these cases too, the sense of injustice attached to its decisions is rooted more in the fragmentation or institutional division of labour between the different competent international organizations rather than in a failure by the WTO dispute settlement system to apply the law justly and correctly. Underlying the overall problem of the division of labour and the fragmented international legal order seems again the continuing dominance of dichotomies and dual thinking based on a binary logic or the "law of the excluded middle".

But it is precisely this kind of reasoning, which the previous chapters traced back to the brain, mind, culture, geography and human nature, which is coming under attack from the rise of essentially oxymoronic concepts. Most of all, these essentially oxymoronic concepts, as both the cause and result of an acceleration of the perception of change by an ever faster oscillation between opposites functioning as contrasts, seem to question the general understanding of reality as created by space and time (or, at least, our present understanding of them). Especially in a globalizing context based on new information technologies, the differences in time and space are becoming, paradoxically, both more obvious and less significant or less obvious but more significant. In metaphorical terms, these differences in time and space have been translated into differences in culture and geography, i.e. the power of tradition and the power of place, which both have a determinant influence on each one of us. Ultimately, they are also communicated via language and words. In this regard, the principal problem of law remains change, change of reality, change of perception and change of experiences, eventually reflected in changes of language. Inevitably and eventually, with changing images of reality, carried by changing concepts, come changing views of law as well. The key concepts for this process are semantics and neologisms, as outlined above.

106 See generally Usman W. Chohan, "The Panama Papers and Tax Morality" (6 April 2016); available at: http://papers.ssrn.com/sol3/Papers.cfm?abstract_id=2759418 (accessed 1 October 2017).

107 See *e.g.* Oren Perez, *Ecological Sensitivity and Global Legal Pluralism: Rethinking the Trade and Environment Conflict* (Oxford: Hart, 2004), Benn McGrady, *Trade and Public Health: The WTO, Tobacco, Alcohol, and Diet* (Cambridge: Cambridge University Press, 2011) at 1–14, Frank J. Garcia, "Trading Away the Human Rights Principle" (1999) 25(1) *Brooklyn Journal of International Law* 51, William A. Dymond, "Core Labour Standards and the World Trade Organization: Labour's Love Lost" (2001) 8(3) *Canadian Foreign Policy* 99, and Rostam J. Neuwirth, "The "Culture and Trade Debate" Continues: The UNESCO Convention in Light of the WTO Reports in China – Publications and Audiovisual Products: Between Amnesia or Déjà Vu?" (2010) 44(6) *Journal of World Trade* 1333.

Thus, new meanings given to old words or the creation of new words altogether function as the principal cognitive response to change. The significance of semantics or language as a whole for law, as a tool to influence reality, is outlined in the following paragraph:

> Semantics is about the relation of words to thoughts, but it is also about the relation of words to other human concerns. Semantics is about the relation of words to reality—the way that speakers commit themselves to a shared understanding of the truth, and the way their thoughts are anchored to things and situations in the world. It is about the relation of words to a community—how a new word, which arises in an act of creation by a single speaker, comes to evoke the same idea in the rest of a population, so people can understand one another when they use it.[108]

As law deals with human concerns and mainly functions through words and is implemented by their interpretation, there seem to exist paradoxical linkages between law, language and reality. Yet, the paradoxicality of these linkages obscures the actual role that law may have in influencing changes. This question ultimately conceals the mystery of human destiny and our individual and collective role in shaping it. In this regard, it seems that law really proceeds by jurisgenesis, i.e. the multiplicity of meaning.[109] Law thus proceeds closely with human evolution, as outlined in *ubi societas, ibi ius*, and is a projection of the mind.

In addition to badly designed laws, the problem of justice and injustice in the history of law also appears to be rooted in change in time (and space) as well as a flawed understanding of human nature. This in particular, as the human nature is causal for the formulation of the laws. But it can also be argued that the understanding of human nature is inadequate because we apply an inadequate cognitive mode in our scientific quest of it. Thus, essentially oxymoronic concepts may both be the harbingers of a change or provide the opportunity for a new scientific paradigm based on new modes of perception to come into being. This is why they are everywhere and increasingly so. The same was confirmed by the following paragraph:

> These paradoxes are thus far from mere games, and they reach much further than human language. The paradoxical tensions at which I have just hinted occupy much the same place: they are built into the foundation of the world. *They are everywhere.*[110]

108 See Steven Pinker, *The Stuff of Thought: Language as a Window into Human Nature* (New York: Penguin, 2007) at 3.

109 See Robert M. Cover, "The Supreme Court, 1982 Term: Foreword: Nomos and Narrative" (1983) 97(4) *Harvard Law Review* 4 at 16.

110 See Andreas Wagner, *Paradoxical Life: Meaning, Matter, and the Power of Human Choice* (New Haven: Yale University Press, 2009) at 3 [*Italics* added].

If they are thus built into the foundations of the world, they may even be built into human beings, at least their modes of perception. Thus to confront the challenge of the history of justice written by unjust legal acts, it is perhaps time to search for the deeper causes of the problem. It is to search for the divine light to do away with the darkness representing the unknown. But how to proceed in this respect? How can law contribute and adapt to the process of evolution in the near and medium-term future?

7.4 Law and justice: from "dual process" to "due process"

God hath spoken once; two-fold is what I heard.[111]

As the law, like language, seems to shift from a culture of contestation to one of contradiction, a general perception of "just injustice" gains momentum. Such sense of injustice increases, particularly from the perspective of "global law" and "global justice", because both of these terms can be regarded as oxymora and utopian. In view of the divergences or conflicts between many different national and subnational, regional and even international legal regimes, a coherent body and consistent institutional framework of "global law" is absent and the realization of "global justice" seems impossible. One may merely think of different legal approaches to marriage (e.g. monogamy versus polygamy) or same-sex marriages, but also seemingly more trivial issues, like the right to vote, to reside or work abroad, the right to drive a car, to smoke a cigarette or marihuana or drink alcohol.

So how to counter this trend and how to assist the law in finding its noble role as a means to establish justice? To recap briefly, in line with the close links between law and language, essentially oxymoronic concepts were found to penetrate the law, both the theory and practice associated with it. They were also found to cause serious problems in the process of adjudication, which are closely reflected in legal scholarship. The close links with language also tie law to science and art, as language is merely a single aspect of the mysterious processes governing the mind and brain that sometimes surface in language. In all these issues, the dominance of a dualistic mindset, including its advantages and disadvantages, surface. The advantages of bifurcation lie in the possibility of an exhaustive analysis and understanding of a complex reality; the disadvantages, on the other hand, are that this possibility is illusory, given that the validity is merely for a short time or within a limited space. In short, it was aptly stated that bivalence (as opposed to multivalence) "trades accuracy for simplicity".[112]

Herein lies the principal problem but also the major benefit of essentially oxymoronic concepts, which is their quality to question explicitly existing assumptions about reality, about human nature, and about law and justice. In positive

111 See Isaac Myer, *Qabbalah* (Whitefish: Kessinger, 2003) at vii; see also Psalm 62:11.

112 See Bart Kosko, *Fuzzy Thinking: The New Science of Fuzzy Logic* (New York: Hyperion, 1993) at 21.

terms, they point out situations where the knowledge is insufficient or incomplete, where even science has no answer. Incomplete knowledge is ignorance, which "shows up as uncertainty in predictions, whether at Las Vegas gaming tables or weather predictions" and in turn, "ignorance leads to chance".[113] In law, incomplete knowledge leads not only to chance in the sense of uncertainty but mainly to injustice. This is related to the deeper problem of coincidence versus fate, whereby events that cannot be explained appear as coincidental or "bad luck". Strictly speaking, however, "bad luck" is also an oxymoron, which invites a more serious inquiry into laws of evolution.

At the same time, essentially oxymoronic concepts were also found to provide powerful opportunities at the level of scientific methodology in order "to test models and conceptual frameworks, and to enable true 'paradigm shifts' in certain areas of scientific inquiry".[114] This should also apply to the field of law, where oxymora and paradoxes give expression to antinomies, which pose fundamental problems to law in the form of "the reconciliation of the irreconcilable, the merger of antitheses, the synthesis of opposites".[115] By confirming a close connection between law, language, the mind and all related phenomena, essentially oxymoronic concepts provide a great opportunity to reformulate both the laws governing global affairs as well as those processes governing perception and the mind.

The important role of oxymoronic language in the reform of the global legal system derives from the cognitive challenge that renders the legal decision-making process more difficult, as distinctions between right and wrong, legal or illegal, and valid and void are becoming ever more difficult to draw. This is very much in line with the role of the mind, where it was said that, from the "perspective of the brain, there's a thin line between a good decision and a bad decision".[116] This is also true for most of our language, the dualistic conception of which has its limitations, as can be seen from the "paradox of boundary". The paradox of boundary has many formulations, as the following "simple" questions show:

What day is midnight?
Is noon A.M. or P.M.?
Is dawn day or night? Is dusk?
Which hemisphere is the equator on?
Which longitude are the poles at?
Which country owns the border?
Is zero plus or minus?[117]

113 See Arthur Zajonc, *Catching the Light: The Entwined History of Light and Mind* (Oxford: Oxford University Press, 1993) at 307.

114 See Narinder Kapur et al., "The Paradoxical Nature of Nature" in Narinder Kapur (ed), *The Paradoxical Brain* (Cambridge: Cambridge University Press, 2011) 1 at 1.

115 Benjamin N. Cardozo, *The Paradoxes of Legal Science* (New York: Columbia University Press, 1928) at 4–5.

116 See Jonah Lehrer, *How We Decide* (Boston: Houghton Mifflin Harcourt, 2009) at xiv.

117 See Nathaniel S. Hellerstein, *Diamond: A Paradox Logic*, 2nd ed (River Edge: World Scientific Publishing Co., 2010) at 27.

The paradox of boundary reflects the limitations of the dualism and binary thinking, as outlined by the following observation:

> If a statement is true at point A and false at point B, then somewhere in-between lies a boundary. At any point on the boundary, is the statement true, or is it false?[118]

The same is true for law and justice, but then the question arises where, on the thin line separating guilt from innocence, a person is guilty or innocent in the eyes of the law.

Representative for many more contradictions or antinomies in law, it may be wise to follow the advice by George P. Fletcher that, to avoid disabling contradictions, it is necessary to search for the deeper causes of the legal premises that guide our thinking.[119] This is to evaluate whether it is not the law that is inadequate but instead the human understanding of law. And here the underlying problem is that, paradoxically, even the human understanding of humans, their nature, their cognitive modes of perception and logic, is incomplete.

In sum, the present scientific paradigm, the understanding of the relation between science and art as well as the law, is governed by some fixed but possibly obsolete assumptions. The problem with assumptions is that they distort perception, as is well analysed in the following paragraph:

> To be emphasized is that the assumptions with which the observer approaches a given situation, assumptions which are derived from previous interpretations of selected data made by himself and others, will determine even more than his eyesight "what" he sees, i.e., what aspects he selects as his "data" and what interpretation he gives to them after they have been selected.[120]

For the present scientific paradigm, it may be time to give up the assumption that even the natural laws are immutable and "have held true in all places and at all times".[121] The same should apply to the mind, and notably dual processes or binary logic as the base of legal reasoning and legal decision making. Therefore, "logic", as the science of thought, as the ancient Greeks called it, should not be perceived as an immutable constraint on cognitive processes in general and legal reasoning in particular. The opinion of logic as an area immune to change was critically outlined by Karl Menger in 1930:

> That the exact sciences are subject to crises and reconstruction and that even geometry has undergone changes is widely known. Moreover, as far as experience and intuition are concerned, anyone, even though he be unfamiliar

118 *Ibid.*

119 George P. Fletcher, "Paradoxes in Legal Thought" (1985) 85(6) *Columbia Law Review* 1263 at 1292.

120 See Walter W. Cook, "'Facts' and 'Statements of Fact'" (1937) 4(2) *University of Chicago Law Review* 233 at 240.

121 See Mark Booth, *The Secret History of the World* (New York: The Overlook Press, 2008) at 118.

> with the details, can well understand that new empirical discoveries may overthrow the most venerable of ancient theories, and that intuition, if it ventures too far afield, may be forced to retire from positions erroneously occupied. One subject, however, is generally supposed to be unchanging and unshakable. *That subject is logic.*[122]

Against the view of classical logic being unchanging and unshakable, Menger stated that the old logic became "inadequate for the demands of modern mathematics in both precision and completeness".[123] Denying the significance of logic for law, US Supreme Court Justice Oliver Wendell Holmes wrote that logic has not been the life of law, but rather "it has been experience".[124] Gunther Teubner too confirmed that among other concepts notably "paradoxes are the new core concepts utilized in the contemporary controversies on law and society".[125] It should also not be forgotten that logic appears manmade and that even genes are susceptible to changes from words. So why not change logic, as suggested by oxymoronic language?

Even laws or the sense of justice are never fixed as the changing and more rapidly changing legal qualifications of trials have shown. Change being perhaps the only constant requires that we "recognize that general legal rules and principles are working hypotheses, needing to be constantly tested by the way in which they work out in application to concrete situations".[126] In other words, law and justice form a continuous process entangled with the changing perception of society and each of the individual members which constitute it. Furthermore, this finding may equally mean the necessity for an "infiltration into law of a more experimental and flexible logic" being a social as well as an intellectual need, as John Dewey phrased it.[127] It may also mean a critical reconsideration of the legal syllogism and other instruments in law. These are some of the opportunities for law that derive from the confusing effects that essentially oxymoronic concepts seem to have on law and legal reasoning today. It is their complex entwinement with the sense of an acceleration of the perception of change, whereby former dualistic distinctions between opposites are becoming blurred, which seems to invite new thoughts about the future of law. Already, the legal community has addressed the faster changing environment by replacing various static terms by more dynamic ones, like replacing or complementing legislation with regulation, litigation with arbitration, and government with governance. In this regard, it is interesting to note that as cinematography complemented (still) photography, governance complementing government also shares the same element of motion.

122 See Karl Menger, "The New Logic" in Henk L. Mulder (ed), *Karl Menger: Selected Papers in Logic and Foundations, Didactics, Economics* (Dordrecht: D. Reidel, 1979) 17 at 18 [*Italics* added].

123 *Ibid* at 20.

124 See Oliver W. Holmes, *The Common Law* (Boston: Little, Brown and Company, 1923) at 1.

125 Gunther Teubner, "Global Bukowina: Legal Pluralism in the World Society" in Gunther Teubner (ed), *Global Law Without a State* (Dartmouth: Brookfield, 1997) 3 at 12.

126 John Dewey, "Logical Method and Law" (1924) 10(1) *Cornell Law Quarterly* 17 at 26.

127 *Ibid* at 27.

In the future, law and legal problem solving is not likely to disappear but its nature may change drastically. For the future of law, it was predicted that the "emphasis will shift towards legal risk management supported by proactive facilities, which will be available in the form of legal information services and procedures".[128] But in view of the increasing number of global threats in the era of the Anthropocene or challenges for law in the time of oxymora, perhaps more revolutionary proposals for change have to be made. Perhaps, time is too short to let scientific paradigm changes "proceed by funerals".[129] Nonetheless, these are some preliminary conclusions drawn from the previous observations related to the analysis of essentially oxymoronic concepts in science, art and the law, which shall now be developed further in the realm of the impact of change, and change in language on the mind and logic in particular.

128 Richard E. Susskind, *The Future of Law: Facing the Challenges of Information Technology* (Oxford: Clarendon Press, 1996) at 290.

129 See Dean Radin, *The Noetic Universe* (London: Corgi Books, 2009) at xxi.

8 Cognition

Mind the change or change the mind?

Conflict is a category of man's mind, not in itself an element of reality.[1]

So far, the evidence has confirmed that essentially oxymoronic concepts, which have been the language of art and mysticism for a long time, have begun creepingly to penetrate the language of science and, more recently, even law. Together these fields were called the "modes of cognition which allow man to receive information about the world permitting him to comprehend it in a systematic manner".[2] Oxymoron and paradox have been named the special *modi loquendi* for the mystical experience.[3] The same can be applied to art in general, where paradox was said to be reserved for special, often aesthetic concerns, such as those of poetry, visual art or music.[4] But there is more to it considering that art is also termed the "language of the future", because "art anticipates a psychic evolution and divines its future forms".[5] Gradually, as the future has continuously unfolded, the increasing role of oxymoronic concepts has been confirmed in science and in other areas of human endeavour, ranging through political, literary and social activities.[6] As a last step, numerous law reports on cases from jurisdictions worldwide were screened for oxymoronic concepts and they confirmed that they are being used too and more frequently so.

Again, representative of these rhetorical figures, paradoxes have been named "the new core concepts utilized in the contemporary controversies on law and

1 Constantin Virgil Negoita, "Cybernetics and Society" (1982) 11(2) *Kybernetes* 97 at 98.

2 See Ithamar Gruenwald, "Mysticism, Science and Art" (1974) 7(2) *Leonardo* 123 at 123.

3 See Alois M. Haas, *Sermo mysticus: Studien zu Theologie und Sprache der deutschen Mystik* (Freiburg: Universitätsverlag, 1989) at 27–28.

4 See George Kalamaras, *Reclaiming the Tacit Dimension: Symbolic Form in the Rhetoric of Silence* (Albany: State University of New York Press, 1994) at 6.

5 See Peter D. Ouspensky, *Tertium Organum: The Third Canon of Thought – A Key to the Enigmas of the World*, 2nd ed (New York: Alfred A. Knopf, 1922) at 80 and 83.

6 See Raymond W. Gibbs, *The Poetics of Mind: Figurative Thought, Language, and Understanding* (New York: Cambridge University Press, 1994) at 395 and Narinder Kapur et al., "The Paradoxical Nature of Nature" in Narinder Kapur (ed), *The Paradoxical Brain* (Cambridge: Cambridge University Press, 2011) 1 at 1.

society".[7] In the area of law, they have revealed their seemingly contradictory character, which causes friction and inconsistencies in legal theory and practice.[8] At the same time, they also proved useful as messengers of change and possibly also harbingers of the future. This is where art and mysticism, science and law, including every individual, share an interest, namely an interest in using knowledge to forecast and plan the future.[9] The problem with the future already begins with our understanding of time, as divided between past, present and future. Here we encounter another "paradox of boundary", namely when we ask: Is "*now*" past or present?

This problem exemplifies especially the wider problem with a dualistic tradition of thinking or binary logic, which is often attributed to Western European origins, being widely based on a divide and rule (*divide et impera*) approach. The Indian poet Rabindranath Tagore eloquently outlined both the origins of this tradition of thought and the problems in one single paragraph:

> The civilization of ancient Greece was nurtured within city walls. In fact, all the modern civilisations have their cradles of brick and mortar. These walls leave their mark deep in the minds of men. They set up a principle of "divide and rule" in our mental outlook, which begets in us a habit of securing all our conquests by fortifying them and separating them from one another. We divide nation and nation, knowledge and knowledge, man and nature. It breeds in us a strong suspicion of whatever is beyond the barriers we have built, and everything has to fight hard for its entrance into our recognition.[10]

This quote reflects not only the power of the mind, but also the limitations of a dualistic mode of thinking. In fact, wherever you look in life, in scientific, political, economic or legal discourses, fragmentation or a lack of coherence caused by such a mindset seem to have become the central problem.

The multiple divisions and the lack of understanding of their interactions due to complexity are the breeding place for contradictions. These contradictions accompanied by an accelerating pace of change of perception, in turn, help to explain the rise in essentially oxymoronic concepts. The reason is that they represent the latest rhetorical devices that seem to make sense, or at least, provide the basis for the communication of a constructive criticism, of the world we have created. Yet, this information still leaves room for doubt about their precise role in human evolution. These doubts can be framed by questions as to whether they merely provide a mirror of the reality we have created or will allow us to reach a

7 See Gunther Teubner, "Global Bukowina: Legal Pluralism in the World Society" in Gunther Teubner (ed), *Global Law Without a State* (Dartmouth: Brookfield, 1997) 3 at 12.

8 See also Oren Perez and Gunther Teubner (eds), *Paradoxes and Inconsistencies in the Law* (Oxford: Hart, 2006).

9 See also Lee Blewett, "The Fortune-Teller" (1923) 9(4) *Virginia Law Review* 249 at 249.

10 Rabindranath Tagore, *Sadhana: The Realisation of Life* (New York: The MacMillan Company, 1925) at 3.

deeper understanding of the processes governing life and nature. Ultimately, the question is if essentially oxymoronic concepts will even allow for the solution of some of the greatest enigmas of life usually formulated in opposite pairs, such as the nature of life and death, mundane and divine, or free will and fate.

In this regard too, Rabindranath Tagore, as a visionary poet writing in the language of the future, not only identified the major cause of the problem as quoted above but he also managed to tie the problems to the objectives for the future:

> The conflict between the individual and the state, labour and capital, the man and the woman; the conflict between the greed of material gain and the spiritual life of man, the selfishness of nations and the higher ideals of humanity; the conflict between all the ugly complexities inseparable from giant organisations of commerce and state and the natural instincts of man crying for simplicity and beauty and fullness of leisure – all these have to be brought to a *harmony in a manner not yet dreamt of.*[11]

Thus the search for harmony in disharmony, simplicity in complexity, or order in chaos, poses the main challenge for the future as also expressed by James N. Rosenau for the future of global governance.[12] It is no coincidence that these (and many other) pairs are now all discussed as essentially oxymoronic concepts, like "*discordia concors*", "simplexity" and "systemic chaos".

To contribute to a better comprehension of these issues, it is useful to look at different aspects of essentially oxymoronic concepts in their impact on cognition. Or conversely, whether changes in traditional modes of cognition characterized by an extension from analytical to holistic and perhaps "paradoxical" or "oxymoronic" thinking is capable of dissolving the contradictions inherent in oxymora and paradoxes.

8.1 Oxymoronic reasoning or other contradiction-solving mechanisms

> *Most generally, the psychological evidence shows that people can make immediate sense out of novel oxymoronic statements.*[13]

In line with the increasing emergence and relevance of essentially oxymoronic concepts in art, science and law as well as daily life, the interest in how to deal with their intrinsic contradictions is growing. This comes as little surprise given that the confusion caused by the linguistic supply of oxymora also creates the demand for possible ways towards their solution. Given the confusion, it is evident that

11 Rabinandrath Tagore, "Nationalism" in Rabinandrath Tagore, *Omnibus III* (New Delhi: Rupa & Co., 2005) 1 at 7 [*Italics* added].

12 James N. Rosenau, "Governance in the 21st Century" (1995) 1(1) *Global Governance* 13 at 13.

13 See Gibbs, *supra* note 6 at 397.

a dualistic mode of thinking or worldview alone appears inapt for successfully tackling problems caused by fuzzy or paradoxical factors. As the origins of the contradictions lie in the mind, it is obvious that solutions to the problem must be sought there as well. Therefore, education, as the formation of the mind, is one of the prime target areas for such efforts. In this context, the educational challenge to be tackled by future generations was described as follows:

> The educated person of the next century will be required to adapt to constant change and apply the basic skills of language, mathematics, and problem solving in a variety of situations that cannot be predicted today.[14]

The solution for this challenge proposed by the author was to use paradoxes in education to teach critical thinking in science. As constant change is already an oxymoron and given that even multiple scientific discourses about many urgent global problems have coined oxymora and produced paradoxes in large numbers, the challenge of the future is to decipher successfully their inherent contradictions. In this regard, the proposed contradiction- and problem-solving mechanisms also seem to reflect a gradual shift as symbolized in language by the shift from essentially contested to oxymoronic concepts outlined in the beginning.

This can, for instance, be seen by a comparison of the attempts to draw up taxonomies of educational goals in 1956 and 2002, including inter alia the different cognitive categories of knowledge, comprehension, application, analysis, synthesis and evaluation.[15] In this regard, it is interesting to note a shift from one-dimensional to two-dimensional learning objectives,[16] similar to "one sex became two sexes" or "one law became two laws". Moreover, various categories of modes of thinking also shifted from a lateral to a vertical model, with the theories of the brain hemispheres following suit.[17] Perhaps as a result of the shift to dualism and various methodologies applied by it, like the thesis–antithesis dichotomy, the taxonomy of different cognitive modes has become more contradictory itself.

14 See James L. Eliason, "Using Paradoxes to Teach Critical Thinking in Science" (1996) 25(5) *Journal of College Science Teaching* 341 at 341, Marianne W. Lewis and Gordon E. Dehler, "Learning through Paradox: A Pedagogical Strategy for Exploring Contradictions and Complexity" (2000) 24(6) *Journal of Management Education* 708, Matthew Bryant, *Oxymoron? A Practical Guide to Fun and Effective Teaching* (New York: iUniverse, 2006) and Douglas Thomas and John Seely Brown, *A New Culture of Learning: Cultivating the Imagination for a World of Constant Change* (Lexington: CreateSpace Independent Publishing Platform, 2011).

15 Cf. Benjamin S. Bloom, *Taxonomy of Educational Objectives: The Classification of Educational Goals* (London: Longmans, 1956) and D. Krathwohl, "A Revision of Bloom's Taxonomy: An Overview" (2002) 41(4) *Theory Into Practice* 212.

16 See Krathwohl, *ibid* at 213.

17 Cf. Edward de Bono, *Lateral Thinking: Creativity Step by Step* (New York: Harper and Row, 1970) and Stephen M. Kosslyn and G. Wayne Miller, *Top Brain, Bottom Brain: Surprising Insights How You Think* (New York: Simon Schuster, 2013).

This includes different taxonomies of thinking, ranging from "atomistic", "analytical",[18] "critical",[19] "lateral" and "vertical",[20] "complex",[21] "strategic"[22] and "holistic"[23] thinking to newer forms, such as "intuitive",[24] "systemic",[25] "fuzzy",[26] "creative",[27] or "paradoxical"[28] thinking. In line with the dualistic tradition of thought, these various notions are also often presented by means of opposite pairs.[29] As for the underlying distinctions in terms of logic, different classifications oppose classical or binary logic to concepts like "fuzzy logic",[30] "multi- or polyvalent"[31] as well as "paraconsistent logic",[32] to mention but a few.

Generally, the many proposals for altering the dominant modes of thinking and logic indicate that changes in the environment are being recognized and also start to transform the way we think before we act. The overall trend of changes noticed in science has also been connected with language, as was restated as follows:

18 See *e.g.* Robert D. Behn and James W. Vaupel, "Teaching Analytical Thinking" (1976) 2(4) *Policy Analysis* 663 at 668–681.

19 See *e.g.* Linda Elder and Richard Paul, "Critical Thinking: A Stage Theory of Critical Thinking: Part I" (1996) 20(1) *Journal of Developmental Education* 34 at 34.

20 See *e.g.* de Bono, *supra* note 17 at 7, 9, 12 and 39–46.

21 See *e.g.* Robert Chia, "From Complexity Science to Complex Thinking: Organization as Simple Location" (1998) 5(3) *Organization* 341 at 363.

22 See *e.g.* Jeanne Liedtka, "Strategic Thinking; Can It Be Taught?" (1998) 31(1) *Long Range Planning* 120 at 121.

23 See *e.g.* Janet McIntyre, "Consideration of Categories and Tools for Holistic Thinking" (1998) 11(2) *Systemic Practice and Action Research* 105 at 105.

24 See *e.g.* William J. Stewart, "Stimulating Intuitive Thinking through Problem Solving" (1988) 62(4) *The Clearing House* 175 at 175.

25 See *e.g.* Raul Espejo, "What Is Systemic Thinking?" (1994) 10(2–3) *System Dynamics Review* 199 at 210.

26 See Bart Kosko, *Fuzzy Thinking: The New Science of Fuzzy Logic* (New York: Hyperion, 1993) at 176.

27 See *e.g.* John Adair, *The Art of Creative Thinking: How to Be Innovative and Develop Great Ideas* (London: Kogan Page, 2007) at 109.

28 See *e.g.* Jerry L. Fletcher, *Paradoxical Thinking: How to Profit from Your Contradictions* (San Francisco: Berrett-Koehler Publishers, 1997) at 2.

29 See *e.g.* Sharon B. Berlin, "Dichotomous and Complex Thinking" (1990) 64(1) *Social Service Review* 46, Julia Tao and Andrew Brennan, "Confucian and Liberal Ethics for Public Policy: Holistic or Atomistic?" (2003) 34(4) *Journal of Social Philosophy* 572, Julie C. Forrester, "Thinking Creatively; Thinking Critically" (2008) 4(5) *Asian Social Science* 100, Uri Leron and Orit Hazzan, "Intuitive vs Analytical Thinking: Four Perspectives" (2009) 71(3) *Educational Studies in Mathematics* (2009) 263, and Incheol Choi, Minkyung Koo and Jong An Choi, "Individual Differences in Analytic Versus Holistic Thinking" (2007) 33(5) *Personality and Social Psychology Bulletin* 691.

30 See *e.g.* Kosko, *supra* note 26.

31 See *e.g.* Louis Rougier, "The Relativity of Logic" (1941) 2(2) *Philosophy and Phenomenological Research* 137 at 145.

32 See *e.g.* Anna Pietryga, "Paraconsistent Logics, Conventionalism and Ontology" (1999) 7 *Logic and Logical Philosophy* 119 at 124–125.

> Generally speaking, by 1930 mathematicians had questioned Euclidean geometry and started playing substitution at its axioms; physicists rejected some most well-established dichotomies and expressed their epistemological doubts; linguists claimed that our view of the world depends upon the grammar of our language; philosophers of mathematics attacked basic logical principles and expressed their distrust towards language.[33]

In short, the changes predicted by the arts as the language of the future were also noticed by science in a mounting criticism of "well-established dichotomies" and also reflected in changing patterns in language, which the rise of essentially oxymoronic concepts largely confirms. As a result it is time to ponder on how contradictions arising from dichotomies or dual thinking may be transcended, dissolved or, eventually, lifted to a higher level of cognition.

8.1.1 Ockham's razor and Chatton's anti-razor

An accelerating pace of change, globalization in the information society against the backdrop of the world's diversity, as well as the blurring of lines of distinction between well-established concepts and dichotomies as expressed in oxymora or paradoxes, are all factors that characterize the growing complexity of society today. This complexity underlines the necessity to find novel problem-solving methods for dealing with its implications in general and contradictions in particular. It is a search for new modes of thinking and reasoning that are both induced and inspired by art, philosophy, literature, science and the humanities, as well as by law.[34]

At this stage, there are four possible psychological responses to apparent contradictions, identified by Peng and Nisbett, which may be useful: (1) denial; (2) discounting; (3) differentiation; and (4) dialectical thinking and which they characterize as follows.[35] Denial, as the first approach, simply means to pretend that there is no contradiction between two apparently opposed concepts or problems and to proceed on the ordinary basis of dual thinking. The second approach, discounting, consists in disregarding both pieces of information contradicting each other. Third, differentiation involves a comparison of both items of information, including the decision that one prevails over the other in terms of right or wrong. In this sense, it is akin to methods trying to solve paradoxes by prioritizing different inconsistent propositions against each other, either eliminating or retaining them.[36] Finally, the fourth approach is labelled "dialectical thinking" and reflects the beginning of a tendency to accept contradictions in a sense that both items of information can be regarded as true.

33 *Ibid.*
34 See also Chia, *supra* note 21 at 341.
35 See Kaiping Peng and Richard E. Nisbett, "Culture, Dialectics, and Reasoning About Contradiction" (1999) 54(9) *American Psychologist* 741 at 741.
36 See *e.g.* Nicholas Rescher, *Paradoxes: Their Roots, Range and Resolution* (Chicago: Open Court, 2001) at 25–31.

In sum these four approaches really consist of a gradual range between the dual opposites of rejecting or tolerating contradictions as they are intrinsic to oxymoronic concepts. A similar problem-solving approach is already known by the principle of "Ockham's (or Occam's) Razor",[37] named after William of Ockham (1287–1347 CE) although he himself never explicitly mentioned the principle.[38] Ockham is reported to have written "plurality is not to be posited without necessity" (*pluralitas non est ponenda sine necessitate*) and also, less frequently quoted, that "what can be explained by the assumption of fewer things is vainly explained by the assumption of more things" (*frustra fit per plura quod potest fieri per pauciora*).[39] Generally, Ockham's razor or the *lex parsimonae* (law of parsimony) is also known by the sentence that "[E]ntities must not be multiplied without necessity" (*Entia non sunt multiplicanda sine necessitate*).[40] Thus, Ockham's razor really advocates "economy" in the process of reasoning. This is similar to the concept of "judicial economy" in legal proceedings, which "requires the judge to obtain the best result in the management of a controversy with the most rational and efficient use possible of his or her powers".[41] In other scientific fields it has found many different applications as well, such as in evolutionary biology (cladistics)[42] or in physics.[43]

Generally, in the process of reasoning and also in the context of facing contradictions, the principle of Ockham's razor means that unnecessary elements will be "shaved" off, or that it "is vain to postulate more causes when fewer suffice to explain".[44] Put differently, it may also be characterized by the proposition that "similarities are better explained as stemming from a single (common) cause than as the result of multiple (separate) causes".[45] In essence, it restates the paradox that "less is more". As for the solution of paradoxical problems, the main deficiency of Ockham's razor is that it is only as good as the applicant's mode of reasoning. In other words, it proposes to apply a dualistic mode of reasoning to a phenomenon of paraconsistent or paradoxical reasoning. The fact that Ockham's razor is caught in the cage of dual reasoning can be observed in the argument of

37 See Paul Vincent Spade, "Ockham's Nominalist Metaphysics: Some Main Themes" in Paul Vincent Spade (ed), *The Cambridge Companion to Ockham* (Cambridge: Cambridge University Press, 2006) 100 at 101–102.

38 See W. M. Thorburn, "The Myth of Occam's Razor" (1918) 27(107) *Mind* 345.

39 See William of Ockham, *Philosophical Writings – A Selection* (Indianapolis: The Bobbs-Merrill Company, 1984) at xxi.

40 *Ibid* at xxi; see also Elliott Sober, "The Principle of Parsimony" (1981) 32(2) *The British Journal for the Philosophy of Science* 145 at 145.

41 See Fulvio Maria Palombino, "Judicial Economy and Limitation of the Scope of the Decision in International Adjudication" (2010) 23(4) *Leiden Journal of International Law* 909 at 909 [footnote omitted].

42 See Ian J. Kitching et al., *Cladistics: The Theory and Practice of Parsimony Analysis* (Oxford: Oxford University Press, 1998).

43 See Andrei N. Soklakov, "Occam's Razor as a Formal Basis for a Physical Theory" (2002) 15(2) *Foundations of Physics Letters* 107.

44 See Elliott Sober, *Reconstructing the Past: Parsimony, Evolution, and Inference* (Cambridge: The MIT Press, 1988) at 71.

45 *Ibid* at 53.

its negative impact on the unity of science. In this regard, Ockham's razor was criticized for contributing to an increasing disintegration of the unity of science, i.e. its division into multiple subdisciplines to the detriment of a more complete understanding of complex phenomena.[46] The criticism targets reductionism that claims "that some object, state, process, event, or property 'is just' or 'is nothing more than' the physical ingredients that compose it".[47] Combined with dualistic theories of the mind (or dualistic thinking), the reductionist view of science has not only caused its greater fragmentation but is also said to have eliminated "vitalistic accounts of life".[48] The ensuing fragmentation of science through specialization may also be an undesired result of the "shaving off" of all seemingly unnecessary elements from a phenomenon observed. This reductionism results in a large number of single and isolated constituents that may no longer provide reliable information about the entity as a whole, like a jigsaw puzzle before it has been assembled to form a coherent picture.

Similar to Ockham, Nicholas Rescher also proposes as a solution to paradoxes "to appraise the comparative plausibility of what we accept and restore consistency by making what is less plausible give way to what is more so".[49] In a subsequent book he elaborates further on aporetics as the theory of rational deliberation in the face of inconsistencies, which also proposes a kind of reductionism in the form of abandoning superfluous elements inherent in a contradiction.[50] In other words, reducing some of the irrelevant aspects related to paradoxes can be useful to highlight the core of the problem, for instance, by trying to reduce a paradox and squeeze it into an oxymoron. On the other hand, it can mean oversimplification by taking away important elements of the contradiction. In this regard, the key to the solution of paradoxes and contradictions lies in the cognitive realm. Rescher rightly states that paradoxes are the "product of cognitive overcommitment" in the sense that they are rooted in an "information overload, a literal embarrassment of riches".[51] The quantitative problem related to paradoxes raises a great flaw of reductionism, namely, that it fails to see the paradox between quantity and quality and confuses explanation with understanding.[52] Thus, the core problem of contradictions is not the quantity or quality of the raw data, but the inadequacy of the cognitive tools to restore consistency from inconsistency. From this perspective, a rational theory of paradox management leaves the mindset unaltered, which may pose an obstacle to the solution of the problem. In the

46 See J. J. C. Smart, "Sensations and Brain Processes" (1959) 68(2) *The Philosophical Review* 141 at 142.
47 See J. D. Trout, "Reductionism and the Unity of Science" in Richard Boyd, Philip Gasper, and J. D. Trout (eds), *The Philosophy of Science* (Cambridge: The MIT Press, 1999) 387 at 387.
48 *Ibid.*
49 See Rescher, *Paradoxes, supra* note 36 at 10.
50 See Nicholas Rescher, *Aporetics: Rational Deliberation in the Face of Inconsistency* (Pittsburgh: University of Pittsburgh Press, 2009) at ix.
51 *Ibid* at 86.
52 See Erwin Chargaff, "In Dispraise of Reductionism" (1997) 47(11) *BioScience* 795 at 796.

end, it means that no coherent solution to a true contradiction has been found but merely one element was found to prevail over the other.

In principle, a purely rational approach, when applied in a dualistic mindset, can contribute either positively or negatively to the unity of science. This can be seen from the case of criticism voiced against Ockham's razor, namely by the formulation of a so-called "anti-razor".[53] The anti-razor was formulated by Ockham's contemporary, Walter Chatton, as follows:

> Whenever an affirmative proposition is verified of things, if one thing does not suffice to verify the proposition two things must be posited, and if two things are insufficient then three, and so on to infinity.[54]

Thus the razor and the anti-razor are a strong expression of a dualistic reasoning itself, by advocating either the subtraction or addition of contextual elements of a given phenomenon. Both paths are certainly useful and are best applied together, as is laid down in the medieval maxim of *solve et coagula*. The anti-razor also resembles the thirteenth rule of interpretation by Rabbi Ishmael whereby practically two contradictory texts are reconciled by finding a third text reconciling the two.[55] In practice, this could mean that when we encounter two opposite terms, like culture and industry, we proceed with the term "culture industry" reconciling the two. But the oxymoron "culture industry" does not reconcile them but merely yokes them together by force. This is why Ockham's razor and Chatton's anti-razor appear helpless in view of the solution of problems of contradictions as enshrined in oxymora and paradoxes. The main reason is that often the solution of a paradoxical problem by dualistic reasoning risks ending up in another dual pair of opposites, just like the razor and the anti-razor. Or else, applying the razor can mean that the contradiction inherent in a paradox or oxymoron is "denied, discounted and differentiated" and, thereby, reduced to the preference for one of the two apparently contradicting elements. Proof for this outcome exists in the case of the "obesity paradox", which describes seemingly contrary relationships between body fat and health/ill-health.[56] When the paradox is solved by the razor, the principal cause for obesity is reduced to just one cause even though there may be either multiple causes or a single cause but resulting from the complex interplay of multiple distinct elements. Applied to the cultural industries in international trade law, the solution to the culture and trade paradox would thus lie in the answer that the WTO regime is inadequate to deal with cultural products, whereby it is the

53 See generally Armand A. Maurer, *Being and Knowing: Studies in Thomas Aquinas and Later Medieval Philosophers* (Toronto: Pontifical Institute of Mediaeval Studies, 1990) at 431–443.

54 *Ibid* at 433.

55 See David Instone Brewer, *Techniques and Assumptions in Jewish Exegesis before 70 CE* (Tübingen: J. C. B. Mohr, 1992) at 228.

56 See Harold Bays, "Adiposopathy, 'Sick Fat,' Ockham's Razor, and Resolution of the Obesity Paradox" (2014) 16(5) *Current Atherosclerosis Reports* 409 at 409.

complexity of the nature of these goods (their dual, i.e. economic and cultural value) that constitutes the paradox in the first place. This is why "denial", for instance by way of the exclusion of one element of a paradox as a way to solve it, was said to constitute a misuse of the principle of Ockham's razor.[57]

In general, it means that either a complex phenomenon is reduced to a more simplistic understanding or, in the case of a paradoxical or self-referential problem, like the liar paradox, the outcome is a new loop of competing or contradictory propositions about their solution. This paradox of paradox was aptly observed by the following words:

> Paradox. Paradox lost. Paradox regained. A transition from paradox to paradox through the negation of paradox, the entire cycle itself being a paradox![58]

For these reasons, it is likely that a satisfactory solution to contradictions by their mutual reconciliation must proceed by ways of reasoning and problem solving other than those based on "dualistic reasoning" or "binary logic" alone. The reason is that usually a problem is truly solved by transcending the current level of understanding and replacing it with a higher level of understanding.

8.1.2 Oxymoronic and other novel modes of thinking

The essential quality of paradoxes and oxymora is said to lie in their capacity to express the ineffability of the experienced.[59] In more scientific terms, they are said "to represent instances where current knowledge may be deficient" and, furthermore, to serve as drivers of paradigm shifts.[60] In art, they are the means to express the so far unknown or invisible but – through imagination and creativity – speak the language of the future, indicating the possibility of the existence of a higher dimension of perception and understanding. By contrast, at the level of cognition, they also carry a silent criticism of the limitations imposed by dualistic reasoning and binary logic. Hence, trying to solve their contradiction may be the key to finding a new mode of reasoning in order to tackle the complex challenges of the present better. With regard to the solution of paradoxical problems, the following has been proposed:

> So three different reactions to the paradoxes are possible: to show that the reasoning is fallacious; or that the premisses are not all true after all; or that the conclusion can in fact be accepted.[61]

57 See Catarina Dutilh Novaes, "Tarski's Hidden Theory of Meaning: Sentences Say Exactly One Thing" in Shahid Rahman, Tero Tulenheimo and Emmanuel Genot (eds), *Unity, Truth and the Liar: The Modern Relevance of Medieval Solutions to the Liar Paradox* (New York: Springer Science + Business Media B.V., 2008) 41 at 44.

58 See Michael Kosok, "The Dynamics of Paradox: Phenomenological Dialectics of Science" (1970) 5 *Telos* 31 at 31.

59 See Haas, *supra* note 3 at 27–28.

60 See Kapur et al., *supra* note 6 at 1.

61 See Stephen Read, *Thinking about Logic* (Oxford: Oxford University Press, 1994) at 150.

These three reactions are, however, mysteriously tied together by the possibility of a fourth reaction combining them all, as a fourth dimension of reality would include all the other three dimensions. Therefore, the three reactions deserve a closer look, as they may not only influence the judgement of the correctness of the underlying premises, but can possibly achieve much more. They can perhaps influence cognition in a deeper way, as even words may change the brain. They may restructure the modes of cognition and reorganize the senses perhaps even to create a "super-sense" in terms of a sense combining all individual senses to a higher one, similar to a "melody" in music, which is not just the sum of the individual tones but also constitutes in their entirety something new in terms of sensations.[62]

For these reasons, oxymora and paradoxes provide a strong incentive to "think outside the box", i.e. to liberate the mind from the chains imposed by old habits and usual assumptions. Paradoxically, some hints for ways out of the "box" are usually found in existing problems. Thus, there already exist several books dedicated to stimulating the emergence of a new cognitive mode of thinking under the many different terms possibly addressing the same challenge, such as "intuitive", "creative" or "paradoxical" thinking, which will be combined here in the term "oxymoronic thinking".

A first possible step towards the solution of contradictions inherent in paradoxes or oxymora may lie in the scientific rating of the degree of "paradoxicality" enshrined in a paradox.[63] Such a paradoxicality rating is based on an intuitive understanding of the subjective probability of the paradox. It aims to classify different paradoxes in terms of the difficulty in solving them. Yet, even this approach leads to the finding that paradoxes engender more paradoxes, inviting the final conclusion that "the paradox is itself paradoxical".[64] Therefore, the only plausible way out of the paradox appears to lie in a "re-education of intuition" or sending our "intuitions back to school".[65] In essence, the various paradox-solving methods are similar to denial, discount or differentiation mentioned above but are given different names.[66] "Intuition" seems to be the wrong notion to apply, however, because intuition can also mean the perception of a higher reality, or one which is apparently paradoxical but turns out to be true and not erroneous. For the context of the present book, the notion of "assumption" is more appropriate in the sense that we need to unlearn the learned as far as it forms the basis of assumptions or "ready-made formulae" which we no longer critically question. Yet, the essential finding is that paradoxes need some kind of novel way of thinking and logic, especially because they are essential for progress in understanding.[67]

Another important question is whether there is a one-size-fits-all solution for paradoxes.[68] Again, in this context, a classification of different paradoxes is

62 See Christian von Ehrenfels, "On 'Gestalt Qualities'" in Barry Smith (ed), *Foundations of Gestalt Theory* (Wien: Philosophia Verlag, 1988) 121 at 121.

63 Margaret Cuonzo, *Paradox* (Cambridge: The MIT Press, 2014) at 26–37.

64 *Ibid* at 41.

65 *Ibid* at 43–47.

66 *Ibid* at 48–49.

67 *Ibid* at 209–210.

68 See Roy T. Cook, *Paradoxes* (Cambridge: Polity Press, 2013) at 186–196.

useful in order to extract a possible single solution for many distinct paradoxes or paradoxes expressed through oxymora. Here, Ockham's razor can be useful when understood to mean that there may be one single underlying cause for the "swoon" that oxymoronic concepts cause in the mind of humans.

As for the swoon that oxymoronic concepts may cause to the mind, another way to dissolve their contradiction is simply to accept the contradiction.[69] Known by the neologism of "dialetheism", this means that there can be contradictions which are true (while there may be others which are false).[70] Applied to oxymora and paradoxes it means that some of them can make sense or turn out to be true while others do not. The approach of dialetheism that there are true contradictions that can make sense is still seen as abhorrent and even threatening to many contemporary philosophers.[71] Yet, accepting the initial proposition that not all contradictions are false may have an important indirect effect on reasoning and thinking in terms of a re-education of basic assumptions and traditional modes of thinking. In this regard, dialetheism and the rejection of the claims to universality of classical logic may be an important preliminary step to the gradual emergence and use of new modes of thinking and logic.[72] Dialetheism may thus pave the way to transcend classical binary logic, by extending it to bivalent, trivalent and even polyvalent logic.[73] In this sense, dialetheism is both a transconsistent and paraconsistent logic. Not only that, but it may also be a necessity to bring logic, as the science of thought, in line with progress in the understanding of "reality".[74] In this regard, it is the "new reality", as unearthed by quantum physics and new understandings of energy, that provides a greater need to transcend the boundaries imposed by classical logic.[75] This means not to end classical logic altogether but to complement classical logic by new forms of logic better suiting the needs of the present understanding of reality. This adaptation of logic to reality has been exemplified by the shift from the law of an excluded middle to the law of an included middle. In contrast to the laws of classical logic,[76] their amended version in the form of the laws of "logic in reality" (LIR) would thus read as follows:

> LIR1: *(Physical) Non-Identity*: There is no A at a given time that is identical to A at another time. This formulation is essentially that of Leibniz.

69 See R. M. Sainsbury, *Paradoxes*, 3rd ed (Cambridge: Cambridge University Press, 2009) at 150–157.

70 See Graham Priest, "Dialectic and Dialetheic" (1990) 53(4) *Science and Society* 388.

71 See Graham Priest, *Beyond the Limits of Thought* (Cambridge: Cambridge University Press, 1995) at 4.

72 See Stéphane Lupasco, "Valeurs logiques et contradiction" (1945) 135(1/3) *Revue Philosophique de la France et de l'Étranger* 1 at 25; see also Graham Priest, *In Contradiction: A Study of the Transconsistent* (Oxford: Clarendon Press, 2006) at 207.

73 See also Lupasco, *supra* note 72 at 1.

74 See also Joseph E. Brenner, *Logic in Reality* (New York: Springer Science + Business Media, 2008).

75 See Stéphane Lupasco, *Le Principe d'antagonisme et la logique de l'énergie. Prolégomènes à une science de la contradiction*, 1st ed (Paris: Hermann & Cie, 1951) at 3, cited in Basarab Nicolescu, "Stéphane Lupasco et le tiers inclus: De la physique quantique à l'ontologie" (2005) 5(2) *Revue de synthèse* 431 at 434.

76 See Bertrand Russell, *The Problems of Philosophy* (London: Williams & Norgate, 1912).

LIR2: *Conditional Contradiction*: A and non-A both exist at the same time, but only in the sense that when A is primarily actual, non-A is primarily potential, and *vice versa*, to a reciprocal extent.

LIR3: *Included (Emergent) Middle*: An included or additional third element or T-state emerges from the point of maximum contradiction at which A and non-A are equally actualized and potentialized, but at a higher level of reality or complexity, at which the contradiction is resolved.[77]

The present reformulation of the laws of logic basically consists in an extension from binary to fuzzy thinking and logic. In other words, it marks an evolutionary extension from contestation to contradiction as covered by the shift from contested to oxymoronic concepts.

Most importantly, this shift in logic may be useful not only for enlarging the ability to explain rationally a wide set of phenomena but also, by allowing simultaneously several different dimensions of reality, to understand art.[78] This last point also supports the observed mutual approach between art and science and their need for a combined consideration when trying to enter new dimensions of reality. The most important aspect to this new logic adapted to reality lies in the fact that it is based on a dynamic approach, which is summarized in the following terms:

> Contradiction can never be considered as absolute, because it never takes place between rigorously actual terms, between absolutely contradictory elements, such as those of classical logic and mathematics. Contradiction never occurs except between antagonistic dynamisms.[79]

Accepting a more dynamic approach to contradiction also has repercussions for the understanding of truth vis-à-vis falsity. The reason is that, from the view of dynamic antagonisms, "a truth cannot be absolute, because it can never be rigorously (totally) actualized" whereas "a contradictory truth (falsity) can be potentialized as much as one wants theoretically without ever completely disappearing in reality".[80] Through the importance of truth for perception and of perception for law, the same can be applied *mutatis mutandis* to law and justice.

Thus matching thoughts, logic and language with perceptions of reality poses the central problem. It is a problem that both essentially contested and oxymoronic concepts aim to realize but through different means. While the former pursues a dialectical method based on classical logic and the excluded middle, the latter adopts a dialetheic method based on paraconsistent logic and the included middle, meaning that the first rejects and the second both accepts and rejects

77 See Brenner, *supra* note 74 at 4.

78 See Basarab Nicolescu, "Stéphane Lupasco: Du monde quantique au monde de l'art" in Basarab Nicolescu and Magda Stavinschi (eds), *Transdisciplinarity in Science and Religion*, vol I (Bucharest: Curtea Veche Publishing, 2007) 203 at 209.

79 See Brenner, *supra* note 74 at 5–6.

80 *Ibid.*

contradictions. This is itself consistent when accepting that dialectics takes a static and dialetheism a dynamic view of reality. This largely corresponds to the difference between state descriptions (e.g. this is a cake) and process descriptions (e.g. this is a recipe to make a cake). Both descriptions are useful and possibly even complementary, even though the latter have been held to provide "clue[s] for the simple description of the complex".[81] This is also the advantage of paraconsistent logic because it does not nullify or replace classical logic but, by both embracing and extending classical logic, it may provide a possible solution to paradoxes, possibly by means of an extension of the logic to higher dimensions of reality.[82] In this sense, the advantage of dialethism over dialectics is that the former includes the latter but not vice versa. Yet, the problem of the relation between the two methods is of a cognitive nature rooted in the current mode of perception, which seems to favour a dialectic over a dialetheic approach. Hence, when perception confirms a dialetheic approach, contradictions will no longer be seen as a problem. Paradoxically, as part of the apparently insoluble problem of paradoxes of self-reference,[83] such cognitive changes can only be expected to materialize when contradictions are accepted by our thinking in the first place.

The way to the acceptance of contradictions thus appears a slow and thorny one. It is a way that essentially oxymoronic concepts pave but perhaps more indirectly rather than through a direct or active effort on behalf of the person undertaking it. This explains why the numerous proposals for solutions to contradictions inherent in paradoxes or oxymora in the form of novel modes of thinking fail. The reason is that our cognitive apparatus is not yet adapted to the needs of dialetheism or oxymoronic thinking. In other words, problems cannot be solved at the same level at which they have arisen. Put differently, the problems caused by dualistic thinking and classical logic cannot be solved by themselves – they need to be transcended and solved at a higher mode of thinking or through a novel logic. In the same way, an emotional problem cannot be solved by rational means and vice versa; it needs their combination into something new, something created out of the convergence of intellect and emotion. At best, the present language allows for an indication of the traits of a higher dimension but does not hold the key for the entrance to it. This is why most manuals list or describe paradoxes but provide little guidance as to how their inherent contradictions can be overcome in a meaningful way.[84] Advice

81 See also Herbert A. Simon, "The Architecture of Complexity" 106(6) *Proceedings of the American Philosophical Society* 467 at 479 and 481.

82 See also Michael Clark, *Paradoxes from A to Z*, 3rd ed (London: Routledge, 2012) at 119–120, Harty Field, *Saving Truth from Paradox* (Oxford: Oxford University Press, 2008) at 15 and Doris Olin, *Paradox* (Bucks: Acumen, 2003) at 21–36.

83 See also Roy Sorensen, *A Brief History of the Paradox: Philosophy and the Labyrinths of the Mind* (Oxford: Oxford University Press, 2003) at 194–196.

84 See *e.g.* Barry Schwartz, *Paradox of Choice: Why More is Less* (New York: HarperCollins, 2007) at 25 and Andreas Wagner, *Paradoxical Life: Meaning, Matter, and the Power of Human Choice* (New Haven: Yale University Press, 2009) at 200.

given often includes phrases like "practice serendipity",[85] "think in opposites";[86] or else "find your core personal paradox" and "choose a High Performance Oxymoron".[87] In view of the limitations of language, some authors complement their advice by trying gradually to induce paradoxical thinking through paradoxical images, like the Necker cube.[88] Often the proposed problem-solving methods for paradoxes or oxymora seem to be caught in a loop by creating more paradoxes. This means that the boundaries and limitations in the current mode of reasoning or thinking need to be rethought and perhaps even unlearned. This may be necessary to make way for new modes of reasoning and possibly, in the longer run, even the emergence of a new organ of sense perception used for cognition. It seems that forging that key is the purpose that essentially oxymoronic concepts have been serving for a long time and more intensively so in the recent decades. Once the key turns the lock, it will be interesting to see what is waiting behind the door. Perhaps, ironically, something of a sneak preview may be given by some ancient "precedents" which will be discussed next.

8.2 West-Eastern considerations of oxymora: *analysis vs synthesis*

God's very own the Orient!
God's very own the Occident!
The North land and the Southern land
Rest in the quiet of His hand.[89]

Often obstacles for the creation of a truly global legal order are said to lie in the complexity of global affairs and the diversity of cultures characterizing this world. Yet, diversity in law, on a large scale, has been found not only "compatible with all major legal traditions" but also a means to guarantee the efficiency, legitimacy and sustainability of law itself.[90] It seems therefore that the real conflict or incompatibility lies less in differing laws but in the minds of the lawyers.[91] This means that the solution to legal conflicts must be sought at the cognitive level.

85 See Adair, *supra* note 27 at 25–28.

86 See *e.g.* Derm Barrett, *The Paradox Process: Creative Business Solutions...Where You Least Expect to Find Them* (New York: AMACOM, 1998) at 20.

87 See *e.g.* Jerry L. Fletcher, *Paradoxical Thinking, supra* note 28 at 3 and 22–34.

88 See *e.g.* Barrett, *supra* note 86 at 18–51 and Thomas B. Ward, Ronald A. Finke and Steven M. Smith, *Creativity and the Mind: Discovering the Genius Within* (New York: Springer Science + Business Media B. V., 1995) at 59–88.

89 Johann Wolfgang von Goethe, *West-Eastern Divan* (London: J. M. Dent & Sons, 1914) at 5.

90 See H. Patrick Glenn, *Legal Traditions of the World: Sustainable Diversity in Law*, 3rd ed (Oxford: Oxford University Press, 2007) at 358.

91 See H. Patrick Glenn, "Choice of Logic and Choice of Law" in H. Patrick Glenn and Lionel D. Smith (eds), *Law and the New Logics* (Cambridge: Cambridge University Press, 2017) 162 at 162 (citing L. Collins (ed), *Dicey and Morris on the Conflict of Laws*, vol 1, 12th ed (London: Stevens, 1993) at 33 as follows: " ...laws may differ but they do not conflict: the only possible conflict is in the mind of the judge...").

Thus, diversity poses more a challenge to the modes underlying thought and logic rather than laws. Diversity is even said to pose a greater challenge as important differences in the minds of Eastern and Western as well as Southern and Northern people are said to exist and operate. This geographic distinction along longitudes and latitudes is matched by shifts in brain theories from left and right hemispheres to the bottom and top parts of the brain. Maybe, these shifts merely indicate the acceleration of perception which, imagined as a horizontal line being set in motion, first shifts to a vertical position before it actually forms a circle. This process is, in fact, depicted by the Eastern symbol of *Yin Yang* (or *Taijitu*), another primordial oxymoron postulating a "dualistic universe based on negative and positive principles",[92] which literally combines "dark" and "bright" or "female and male", albeit in dynamics terms indicating their mutual complementarity. In cognitive terms, it can also be used as a symbol for black and white, or "zebra thinking", which is another way to express a dualistic conception of reality. Even the chessboard in its alternating colours is said to symbolize many aspects of duality.[93]

Duality is certainly a defining but also a universal feature of humanity and possibly nature. Perhaps the approaches to interpreting and handling it vary. This is where East and West are said to differ in their philosophies of thought or modes of cognition.[94] Broadly speaking, the main difference in cognition is found in the holistic thinking attributed to the East and the analytical thinking of the West. The difference between the two modes as contrasted between Eastern and Western people has been outlined as follows:

> Holistic approaches rely on experience-based knowledge rather than on abstract logic and are dialectical, meaning that there is an emphasis on change, a recognition of contradiction and of the need for multiple perspectives, and a search for the "Middle Way" between opposing propositions.
>
> We define analytic thought as involving detachment of the object from its context, a tendency to focus on attributes of the object to assign it to categories, and a preference for using rules about the categories to explain and predict the object's behavior. Inferences rest in part on the practice of decontextualizing structure from content, the use of formal logic, and avoidance of contradiction.[95]

Thus an important difference between the two cognitive approaches lies in the distinct treatment of "contradictions" as they characterize oxymora and paradoxes.

92 See James Hall, *Illustrated Dictionary of Symbols in Eastern and Western Art* (Boulder: Westview Press, 1996) at 8.

93 *Ibid* at 62.

94 See Richard E. Nisbett, *The Geography of Thought: How Asians and Westerners Think Differently… and Why* (New York: Free Press, 2003) at 108–109.

95 See Richard E. Nisbett et al., "Culture and Systems of Thought: Holistic Versus Analytic Cognition" (2001) 108(2) *Psychological Review* 291 at 293.

But even paradoxes are said to be received differently in the East and the West, with their difference outlined in the following paragraphs:

> Paradox, in the West, is often conceived of as a condition based in conflict. Indeed, the etymology of "paradox" comes from the Greek *paradoxos*, "incredible, conflicting with expectation," suggesting opposition, particularly with regard to the temperament of the condition, "conflict." Furthermore, within Western discourse, we find a privileging of the rationally "expected," while paradox is reserved for special, often aesthetic concerns, such as those of poetry, visual art, or music.
>
> However, paradox to the Eastern mystic is neither "incredible" nor illogical. In fact, because of the ineffable quality of the mystical experience, Eastern philosophy often privileges the use of paradox over a more conceptually-oriented discourse as perhaps the only way it can attempt to communicate the dimensions of its nonconceptual awareness.[96]

Another way to express the difference in the reception of paradoxes is found in the dichotomy of atomism versus holism, which, simply put, could be characterized by a preference for the single constituent over the shape as a whole. Even if this difference is a mere stereotype, it still has severe practical repercussions as can be seen from examples in various areas. One such prominent area is health and medicine, which have both been qualified as contested concepts above. In the context of establishing a global health governance system, there is also an obstacle found in the wide distinction between Western conventional medicine and Eastern traditional medicine.[97] Similar distinctions have been applied in research in many other areas, such as ethics and public policy, the perception of brand names, or the degrees of respect for intellectual property rights.[98]

By contrast, there is also ample evidence that such geographical distinctions are absurd and poor stereotypes at best. There are many people from the West who seem to prefer more holistic approaches in art, science and philosophy. As for literature, I have already cited a poem by Johann W. Goethe from his *West-Eastern Divan*. Furthermore, the Austrian Ludwig Wittgenstein was said to have gradually shifted between, or combined aspects of, "logical atomism" and "practical holism".[99]

96 See Kalamaras, *supra* note 4 at 6.

97 See generally Rostam J. Neuwirth and Alexandr Svetlicinii, "Law as a Social Medicine: Enhancing International Inter-Regime Regulatory Coopetition as a Means for the Establishment of a Global Health Governance Framework" (2015) 36 (3–4) *The Journal of Legal Medicine* 330.

98 See *e.g.* Tao and Brennan, *supra* note 29, Alokparna Basu Monga and Deborah Roedder John, "Cultural Differences in Brand Extension Evaluation: The Influence of Analytic versus Holistic Thinking" (2007) 33(4) *Journal of Consumer Research* 529 and William P. Alford, *To Steal a Book Is an Elegant Offense: Intellectual Property Law in Chinese Civilization* (Stanford: Stanford University Press, 1995).

99 See David Stern, "The "Middle Wittgenstein": From Logical Atomism to Practical Holism" (1991) 87(2) *Synthese* 203.

As a theory of Western origin, *Gestalt* psychology also combines aspects of atomism with those of holism by trying to consider simultaneously the relation between the whole and its constituent pieces.[100] Similarly, the work of Carl Gustav Jung is known for his close reliance on Eastern thought, merging, if one permits the present-day language, Swiss and Tibetan traditions.[101]

Another example of a combined view of atomism and holism is provided by Arthur Koestler, who even coined an oxymoron, the so-called "holon" (from the Greek *holos* – whole, with the suffix *on* (cf. neutron, proton), from the two, which he defined as follows:

> The concept of the *holon* is meant to supply the missing link between atomism and holism, and to supplant the dualistic way of thinking in terms of "parts" and "wholes," which is so deeply engrained in our mental habits, by a multi-levelled, stratified approach.[102]

The whole history of Western mysticism seems to provide interesting overlaps or similarities between mystical movements from all around the world. These similarities come as no surprise if one accepts the definition of mysticism as the "art of the union with Reality" or a mystic as "a person who has attained that union in greater or less degree; or who aims at and believes in such attainment".[103] To give another concrete example, the comparison of the Christian mysticism of Meister Eckhart with Buddhism was also described as revealing the closeness of his thinking to that of Mahāyāna Buddhism, especially of Zen Buddhism.[104]

Different religions or philosophies, such as Buddhism and Christianity, also show strong elements of complementarity when it comes to matters pertaining to the so-called "hard" or natural sciences.[105] Corresponding to that, Niels Bohr's description of quantum matter was found to equal that of the Buddhist teacher Dignaga from the sixth century as much as Einstein and Buddha were said to share a common language.[106] Finally, supported by selected examples of mysticism, literature, science and technology, art too has shown similarities between different places on the planet, such as for instance with regard to the depiction in images of visual perception.[107] Certainly, the arts (like law) from

100 Max Wertheimer, "Gestalt Theory (With a Foreword by Kurt Riezler)" (1944) 11(1) *Social Research* 78 at 84.

101 See Radmila Moacanin, *The Essence of Jung's Psychology and Tibetan Buddhism: Western and Eastern Paths to the Heart* (Boston: Wisdom Publications, 2003).

102 Arthur Koestler, "Beyond Atomism and Holism – The Concept of the Holon" (1970) 13(2) *Perspectives in Biology and Medicine* 131 at 136 [*Italics* added].

103 See Evelyn Underhill, *Practical Mysticism* (New York: Dodo Press, 2007) at 2.

104 See D. T. Suzuki, *Mysticism: Christian and Buddhist* (London: Routledge, 2002) at 1.

105 See Fritjoff Capra, *The Tao of Physics*, 3rd ed (London: Flamingo, 1991) and Lai Pan-chiu, "Buddhist-Christian Complementarity in the Perspective of Quantum Physics" (2002) 22 *Buddhist-Christian Studies* 149.

106 See *e.g.* Don Foresta, "The Many Worlds of Art, Science and the New Technologies" (1991) 24(2) *Leonardo* 139 at 139 and Thomas J. McFarlane, *Einstein and Buddha: The Parallel Sayings* (Berkeley: Ulysses Press, 2002).

107 See *e.g.* Daniel J. Graham and David J. Field, "Variations in Intensity Statistics for Representational and Abstract Art, and for Art from the Eastern and Western Hemispheres" (2008) 37(9) *Perception* 1341.

East and West or elsewhere have met and frequently mutually influenced and enhanced each other.[108]

Strangely, it appears that even though systems of cognition of the East and the West as well as other parts of the world appear to differ greatly, they still feature many similarities or stand in a relation of complementarity to each other. This may be explained by the fact that in certain times at specific places one approach was adopted as the dominant approach trying to oppress the other. This can be exemplified by the Greek philosopher Protagoras, known also for the "lawyer paradox",[109] who was certainly familiar with paradoxical thinking. He is said to have been "the first person who asserted that in every question there were two sides to the argument exactly opposite to one another" but his books were burnt and he himself was banished by the Athenians.[110] Hence, today's apparent global differences in approaches to paradoxes may have been more the outcome of a local contest, which later crystallized into habits or path dependency based on educational materials, rather than in innate human differences of cognition. Being on the verge of challenging contestation as the dominant path of progress, the question is then whether essentially oxymoronic concepts are capable of creating the basis for a common language and understanding of reality. Consequently, it raises the question of what their emergence indicates for the future evolution of cognition in particular and humanity in general.

8.2.1 Towards a common language: oxymora as Western "kōans"?

As is often the case, attempts to understand the future start by remembering the past. Thus, to assess whether essentially oxymoronic concepts can change perception and even the brain or genes, there exists an interesting precedent in history, which may provide useful insights. It is literally a "precedent" we speak of, when we invoke the concept of "koan" (or kōan) derived from Zen Buddhism or, more broadly, Asian philosophy. The reason is that in its origin, koan derived from the Chinese term *kung-an* (公案), used in the field of jurisprudence, where it meant "legal precedent".[111] Later, it was understood as a "public document setting up a standard of judgment" or more generally a "public matter for thought".[112] Its principal value derives from its function as a riddle, a non-rational riddle perhaps,[113] usually in the form of a statement by

108 See *e.g.* Michael Sullivan, *The Meeting of Eastern and Western Art. From the Sixteenth Century to the Present Day* (New York: Graphic Society, 1973) and Hall, *supra* note 92.

109 See Aulus Gellius, *The Attic Nights*, vol 1 (London: J. Johnson, 1795) at 305–307, Diogenes Laertius, *The Lives and Opinions of Eminent Philosophers* (London: Henry G. Bohn, 1853) at 399 and Sainsbury, *supra* note 69 at 160.

110 See Laertius, *supra* note 109 at 397–398.

111 See M. S. Diener, "Kôan" in G. Schoeller (ed), *Dictionnaire de la sagesse orientale: bouddhisme - hindouisme - taoïsme - zen* (Paris: Robert Laffont, 1989) 291.

112 See D. T. Suzuki, *The Zen Koan as Means of Attaining Enlightenment* (Boston: Charles E. Tuttle Co., 1994) at 81; see also K. Barber (ed), *The Canadian Oxford Dictionary* (Toronto: OUP, 1998) at 787–788.

113 See also Charles G. Zug III, "The Nonrational Riddle: The Zen Koan" (1967) 80(315) *The Journal of American Folklore* 81.

a Zen master, or some answer of his given to a questioner.[114] The fundamental character of such a riddle is its paradoxical character, which implies that it cannot be answered on the basis of rational thinking (alone) and demonstrates the frequent inadequacy of logical reasoning.

A koan or its true essence perhaps, it is said, "cannot be understood by logic; it cannot be transmitted in words; it cannot be explained in writing; it cannot be measured by reason".[115] In brief, the koan exercise can be compared to reading a poem.[116] Or else, a koan may be understood as a psycholinguistic riddle "capable of generating a certain type of experience or as a literary genre with a complex history embodying centuries of religious and philosophical discourse".[117] In other words, a koan conveys an experience beyond mere knowledge which is used as a means to realize *satori* or attaining enlightenment.[118] *Satori*, as an equivalent to enlightenment, is defined as follows:

> The attainment of satori is nothing else than the becoming conscious of existing which actually is unconscious in me; becoming conscious of the Reality, unique and original, of this universal vegetative life which is the manifestation in my person of the Absolute Principle (that in which I am I and infinitely more than I; imminence and transcendence). It is that which Zen calls "seeing into one's own nature".[119]

Thus koans are used to expand awareness, to go beyond mere knowledge and especially knowledge based on duality by way of non-duality.[120] It is supposed to open the path for a higher level of awareness. However, it is difficult to describe a higher level of awareness if someone has not yet obtained it. All such attempts may sound like someone speaking a foreign language to one who has never heard it before. Or else, assuming that humans have a higher awareness than animals, trying to explain to your pet the latest amendments to the tax code. Inversely, we may also see it from the perspective of a bat flying in darkness while a man walking in the forest bangs his head on a nearby tree. To share experiences, there needs to be a common perceptory framework.

Again, the experience to which koan exercises lead cannot be rationally or logically explained. There is no single manual to follow to attain *satori* but there

114 See Suzuki, *The Zen Koan as Means of Attaining Enlightenment*, *supra* note 112 at 81.

115 See Ruth F. Sasaki, "The History of the Koan in Rinzai (Lin-Chi) Zen" in Isshū Miura and Ruth Fuller Sasaki, *The Zen Koan: Its History and Use in Rinzai Zen* (San Diego: A Harvest/HBK Book, 1965) 1 at 5.

116 See also Henry Rosemont, Jr., "The Meaning Is the Use: Kōan and mondō as Linguistic Tools of the Zen Masters" (1970) 20(2) *Philosophy East and West* 109 at 115 and 119.

117 See Barry Stephenson, "The Kōan as Ritual Performance" (2005) 73(2) *Journal of the American Academy of Religion* 475 at 476.

118 See Suzuki, *The Zen Koan as Means of Attaining Enlightenment*, *supra* note 112 at 11.

119 See Hubert Benoit, *Zen and the Psychology of Transformation: The Supreme Doctrine* (Rochester: Inner Traditions International, 1990) at 38.

120 On non-duality, see also Michel Mohr, "Emerging from Nonduality: Koan Practice in the Rinzai Tradition since Hakuin" in Steven Heine and Dale S. Wright (eds), *The Koan: Texts and Contexts in Zen Buddhism* (Oxford: Oxford University Press, 2000) 244 at 247.

are many ways. Paradoxically, the attainment of *satori* is said to happen suddenly and unpredictably. The experience of *satori* was described as follows:

> Satori is experienced in connection with any ordinary occurrence in one's daily life. It does not appear to be an extraordinary phenomenon as is recorded in Christian books of mysticism. Someone takes hold of you, or slaps you, or brings you a cup of tea, or makes some most commonplace remark, or recites some passage from a sūtra or from a book of poetry, and when your mind is ripe for its outburst, you come at once to satori.[121]

In this regard, *satori* or the experience of "seeing into one's own nature" related to koans resembles the concept of "intuition". Generally, intuition can be defined as "a perception that spontaneously occurs without conscious deliberation" and that "intuitive thoughts usually follow intensive contemplation relative to a particular problem and, inexplicably, may happen at any time".[122] For instance, famous cases include students becoming suddenly enlightened by sweeping a stone against a bamboo or by gazing at plum blossoms.[123] Most likely, some koan exercise will help in this regard. It is said that a Zen student needs to solve 1700 koans before he can be called a fully qualified master.[124] Sometimes, when even that does not work the master can help to open the mind to *satori* by slapping the student, or kicking and knocking him down.[125]

As for the exercise of koans, there exists a large collection of them in the *Mumonkan*, or "Gateless Gate", compiled by the Chinese Zen master Mumon Ekai (1183–1260 CE).[126] The *Mumonkan* features one of the most cited koans, which runs as follows:

> A monk once asked Jōshū, "Has a dog the Buddha-Nature?"
> Jōshū answered, "Mu!"[127]

Another famous koan, which was claimed to awaken a spirit of inquiry more easily than the "mu" koan, is the one from Hakuin, which reads as follows:

> The koan is, "Hear the sound of one hand." A sound issues when two hands are clapped, and there is no way of its issuing from one single hand. Hakuin now demands his pupils to hear it.[128]

121 See Suzuki, *The Zen Koan as Means of Attaining Enlightenment*, *supra* note 112 at 29.

122 See William J. Stewart, "Stimulating Intuitive Thinking through Problem Solving", *supra* note 24 at 175.

123 See R. H. Blyth, *Zen and Zen Classics: Mumonkan*, vol iv (Tokyo: The Hokuseido Press, 1974) at 134.

124 See Suzuki, *The Zen Koan as Means of Attaining Enlightenment*, *supra* note 112 at 11 (Fn 1).

125 *Ibid* at 20 and 29.

126 See Blyth, *supra* note 123 at 22; see also John F. Fisher, "An Analysis of the Kōans in the Mu Mon Kwan" (1978) 25(1) *Numen* 65.

127 See Blyth, *supra* note 123 at 22.

128 See Suzuki, *The Zen Koan as Means of Attaining Enlightenment*, *supra* note 112 at 182 (Fn 1).

Even though this appears at first absurd, or apparently nonsensical and therefore the method of finding an answer seems beyond the possibility of a rational method, it does not mean that it excludes rationality completely. In this regard, it was noted that reason in the context of koan practice "is not jettisoned in favor of the irrational but may be used as a bridge to the suprarational".[129] In other words, it does not stop short in reason but transcends it and allows the mind to reach out to other "suprarational" dimensions, similar to surrealism when understood to denote a "higher reality", a reality that is yet to materialize. Interestingly, the solution to the riddle does not come smoothly but usually occurs by a swift change in the comprehension, a sudden transcendence by way of intuition of the usual perception caused by the limitations the intellect imposes on the mind.[130]

One important element of koans related to oxymora is that they effectively question duality or dual thinking. This is manifest in another question asked by a *roshi*, or master, to a young monk, which is the following:

> If you call this a stick, you affirm; If you call it not a stick, you negate. Beyond affirmation and negation what would you call it?[131]

This question goes to the heart of dichotomies or dualistic modes of thinking as they are also challenged by oxymora. As usual, there is no definite or correct answer to the question in rational terms. This is because it is asserted that the ultimate truth cannot be expressed in words, not even in the metalanguage of the *kung-an* (koan).[132] Nonetheless, the story continues and unfolds as follows:

> Bewildered by this baffling riddle, the young monk can only stare back in confusion. Thirty seconds of profound silence pass. Abruptly the roshi leaps to his feet and commences striking the monk across the shoulders with his bamboo stick. The monk turns and rapidly flees the master's quarters, and the sanzen, or interview, is completed.[133]

The same bewilderment may also befall the reader unfamiliar with koans, particularly from the West. Yet there are more similarities between koans and paradoxes or oxymora. It is not only in mysticism where "East meets West", such as by virtue of analogies between koans and meditative prayer.[134] There are

129 See Steven Heine, "Philosophical and Rhetorical Modes in Zen Discourse: Contrasting Nishida's Logic and Koan Poetry" (1997) 17 *Buddhist-Christian Studies* 3 at 3.

130 See Diener, *supra* note 111 at 291.

131 See Zug III, *supra* note 113 at 81.

132 See Morten Schlutter, "'Before the Empty Eon' versus 'A Dog Has No Buddha-Nature': Kung-an Use in the Ts'ao-tung Tradition and Ta-hui's Kung-an Introspection Ch'an" in Steven Heine and Dale S. Wright (eds), *The Koan: Texts and Contexts in Zen Buddhism* (Oxford: Oxford University Press, 2000) 168 at 173.

133 See Zug III, *supra* note 113 at 81.

134 See *e.g.* David Loy, "A Zen Cloud? Comparing Zen 'Koan' Practice with 'The Cloud of Unknowing'" (1989) 9 *Buddhist-Christian Studies* 43.

more examples, in all art, science and law. To begin with, mathematics, usually understood as the most rational science, has also been found to coin koans, namely as follows:

> Multiplying by one-half is the same as dividing by two.[135]

For art, again literature can be used to exemplify similarities in Eastern koans and poetic expressions from the West. Even though Franz Kafka, the author of novels or short stories with a legal background, like *The Trial* or *The Judgment*, is said to have had no exposure to Zen Buddhism, it was yet found that "all of Kafka's fictions are remarkably koan-like in their style and spirit, but it is above all the short parables that show the deepest affinity to the Zen form".[136]

Finally for law, a good example of Western uses of rhetoric or language to express experiences similar to koans comes from the legal field regarding justice. It goes as follows:

> A student came to a dean asking to study equity. "First you must study law," said the dean, and sent the student away. Three years later, the student returned. "I studied law as you insisted," he said. "It was a worthless endeavor. The law is unjust, formalistic, nonsensical, and hopelessly confused. I have never been so frustrated in my life as in the last three years." "Now you are ready to study equity," said the dean.[137]

This shows that koans carry a universal value or are universally applicable. There even exists an explanation for Western people willing to approach koans or Zen.[138] This equity koan is similar to the paradox of justice, according to which giving everyone what s/he deserves can mean "a variety of contradictory things".[139] It is thus in the origins of contradictions that answers to the riddles must be sought. It is in this quest where the close analogy between essentially oxymoronic concepts and koans lies.

In sum, this brief look at koans supports the analogy of essentially oxymoronic concepts being something like "Western koans". In particular paradoxes resemble koans, even etymologically, given that paradox denotes something "beyond thought" and notably suprarational. This is why a koan, in essence, was called "a paradoxical problem that in principle cannot be solved by using our usual, rational method of analysis".[140] Koans, however, go further than paradoxes in a

135 See Theodore John Szymanski, "Zen Koans and the Art of Mathematics" (1995) 12(1) *Research and Teaching in Developmental Education* 75 at 76.

136 See Dennis McCort, "Kafka Koans" (1991) 23(1) *Religion & Literature* 51 at 52.

137 See James Grimmelmann, "Koans of Equity" (2008) 58(3) *Journal of Legal Education* 472 at 473.

138 See Christmas Humphreys, *A Western Approach to ZEN* (Madras: The Theosophical Publishing House, 1971) at 101–109.

139 See Charles Handy, *The Age of Paradox* (Boston: Harvard Business School Press, 1995) at 39–41 and 195.

140 See Loy, *supra* note 134 at 44.

sense that they suggest the existence of a "supra-reality" or "higher reality" of perception, which is not different from rational thought or binary logic but builds upon it, transforms it and finally transcends the dual worldview – given that even koans are related to law by the role of "precedent" and the difficulty of establishing justice, which from the perspective of perception would mean to have the greatest possible understanding of reality or a unity of all senses including even some which may lie dormant or are unknown to this date. As the essence of koans is difficult to transmit in words or explain in writing, just like in oxymora or paradoxes, it is difficult to try to implement it and its implications in the practice of law. In this regard, there exists another concept from Chinese thought, which may provide some useful insights. This concept is the *chung yung* (or *zhong yong*) which is translated as the "practice of the mean" or the "middle way".

8.2.2 **"Chung yung"** *or the practice of the mean or the search for the "perfect oxymoron"*

The problem of duality and the quest for its possible transcendence also lies at the heart of the principle of *chung yung* (or *zhong yong*), i.e. the doctrine (or practice) of the mean.[141] *Chung yung* is both the title of one of the four important books of Confucianism but also a doctrine. As a book it was called "a treatise on human and cosmic harmony, dealing with how equilibrium (*zhong*) and commonality (*yong*) are attained".[142] As a doctrine, the mean, when perceived as a way of life, was described as "a dynamic process rather than a static structure", which "encompasses the whole range of human experience".[143] But putting the mean into practice, as the *chung yung* restates, represents the highest degree of human attainment which few of the common run of men are capable of sustaining for any appreciable length of time.[144] In substance, it can be said to deal with the dualistic mode of perception and its limitations for cognition or the cognition of a higher level of reality. Borrowing from Confucius, it refers to a man of wisdom, who is characterized by never being "in two minds (about right and wrong)".[145]

The effort to put the mean into practice, however, is more complex than the comparison with the simple concept of the "middle way", which has more the taste of a shallow compromise between two opposites. That understanding of the mean would be better characterized by "mediocrity" as opposed to the "middle" or, in German by the subtle difference between "*Gleichgültigkeit*" (indifference) as

141 See Andrew Plaks (trans.), *Ta Hsüeh* and *Chung Yung (The Highest Order of Cultivation and On the Practice of the Mean)* (London: Penguin, 2003) and James Legge, *The Chinese Classics: With a Translation, Critical and Exegetical Notes, Prolegomena and Copious Indexes*, vol I (London: Trübner & Co., 1861) at 246–298.

142 See Karyn L. Lai, *An Introduction to Chinese Philosophy* (Cambridge: Cambridge University Press, 2008) at 45.

143 See Tu Weiming and Daisaku Ikeda, *New Horizons in Eastern Humanism: Buddhism, Confucianism and the Quest for Global Peace* (London: L.B. Tauris, 2011) at 122.

144 § 2 *Chung Yung*, in Plaks, *supra* note 141 at 26.

145 Confucius, *The Analects* (Beijing: Zhonghua Book Company, 2008) at 157 and 265.

opposed to "*gleicher Gültigkeit*" (bivalence). In this regard, it is important to note that Aristotle has also dedicated time to the mean and also extracted more subtle nuances.[146] In Greece, even the inscriptions at the temple locating the oracle of Delphi read not only "know thyself" but also "nothing too much".[147]

By contrast to *chung yung*, a compromise means merely avoiding a dilemma by not engaging in a deeper inquiry into both extremes and notably their mutual implications. This aspect of human nature was well outlined by Blaise Pascal in the following paragraph:

> For after all what is man in nature? A nothing in regard to the infinite, a whole in regard to nothing, a mean between nothing and the whole; infinitely removed from understanding either extreme.[148]

The failure to understand either of two extremes and, especially, their mutual relations may lead to failure. This problem has also been outlined for the concept of the "third way", formulated and applied in Europe and the United States as a way to transcend the opposite extremes of right and left politics:[149]

> A third or middle way must logically stand in some relation to at least two others. What the nature of the relationship is between the elements is significant and cannot be deduced: is it a compromise, a synthesis or just the third of three, for example?[150]

In this regard, the *chung yung* reports the story of a man whose "way of putting the balanced mean into practice in the world of men was simultaneously to grasp both ends of the moral spectrum".[151] Unfortunately, it fails to give advice how he managed to grasp them. Worse, it even cites the master's fear that "the Way" will never again be put in practice.[152]

Paradoxically, a proper understanding of the mutual implications of the two extremes so as to successfully take a "third way" depends on an additional element, which is change, and notably from the angle of perception. This may be what Paul Nora had in mind when he wrote about the acceleration of history (or time) that it indicates a rupture of equilibrium, namely that the path of the mean

146 See *e.g.* J. O. Urmson, "Aristotle's Doctrine of the Mean" in Amelie Oksenberg Rorty (ed), *Essays on Aristotle's Ethics* (Berkeley: University of California Press, 1980) 157.

147 See also Plato, "Charmides" in George Burges (ed), *The Works of Plato: Philebus, Charmides, Laches*, vol IV (London: Henry G. Bohn, 1985) 111 at 128.

148 See Blaise Pascal, *Thoughts on Religion and Other Subjects* (Amherst: J. S. and C. Adams, 1829) at 20.

149 See *e.g.* Flavio Romano, *Clinton and Blair: The Political Economy of the Third Way* (London: Routledge, 2006).

150 See Stephen Driver and Luke Martell, "Left, Right and the Third Way" (2000) 28(2) *Policy & Politics* 147 at 148.

151 § 6 *Chung Yung*, in Plaks, *supra* note 141 at 27.

152 See § 5 *Chung Yung*, *ibid*.

was lost.[153] In other words, as long as we perceive change, the relations between opposites constantly change, which make a definite statement impossible. The problem of judging a changing situation by the use of dual reasoning is mirrored in the Taoist "story of the horse":

> This farmer had only one horse, and one day the horse ran away. The neighbors came to condole over his terrible loss. The farmer said, "What makes you think it is so terrible?"
>
> A month later, the horse came home—this time bringing with her two beautiful wild horses. The neighbors became excited at the farmer's good fortune. Such lovely strong horses! The farmer said, "What makes you think this is good fortune?"
>
> The farmer's son was thrown from one of the wild horses and broke his leg. All the neighbors were very distressed. Such bad luck! The farmer said, "What makes you think it is bad?"
>
> A war came, and every able-bodied man was conscripted and sent into battle. Only the farmer's son, because he had a broken leg, remained. The neighbors congratulated the farmer. "What makes you think this is good?" said the farmer.[154]

As the story shows, it is only when change would no longer be perceived, which – based on contrast effects – would mean that we have transcended duality, then a definite solution to a problem could be formulated and found or a situation be judged exhaustively.

The difficulty of putting the mean into practice in mere linguistic terms can be exemplified by the varying degrees of contradiction inherent in oxymoronic concepts or what can be called the search for the "perfect oxymoron". In other words, how is it possible to combine two opposite terms and merge them into one in a fully balanced way, i.e. to dissolve their contradiction by finding their mutual equilibrium like the scales held by Justice?

For instance, the oxymoron *Kulturindustrie* (culture industry) is made of two equal nouns, which historically have been perceived as standing in a relation of opposition and mutual incompatibility. Later the term evolved and the cultural element seemingly began to weaken in their reformulation as a *contradictio in adiecto* by way of the adjectival use of culture in "cultural industry". This clearly indicates that cultural elements have started to penetrate the industrial world. It is interesting to note that the inverse order of connecting both nouns in "*Industriekultur*" (industry culture) would give a different meaning to the term altogether. "Industry culture" or "industrial culture" would refer not to

153 See Paul Nora, "Between Memory and History: Les lieux de mémoire" (1989) 26 *Representations* 7 at 15.

154 See Llewellyn Vaughan-Lee, *In the Company of Friends: Dreamwork Within a Sufi Group* (Inverness: The Golden Sufi Center, 1994) at 68–69; see also Huston Smith, *The World's Religions: Our Great Wisdom Traditions* (New York: HarperOne, 1991) at 215–216.

the tensions between the industrial production of artistic and cultural products but to considerations to cultivate or improve the practices of industrial production processes,[155] as is also captured by the alleged oxymoron of business ethics.[156] Even paradoxes when reversed change their meaning, as the "pursuit of happiness" is different from the "happiness of pursuit".

A problem with language is thus that the change in order of words can drastically change the meaning. On the other hand, changing the order can also be an effective means to account for change. This is because the order in language may indicate priority. This can be exemplified by the debate about the paradoxical relation between culture and trade by either calling it the "trade and culture"[157] or the "culture and trade" debate.[158] Finally, the same is also reflected by the oxymoronic concept of the hysteron proteron, which reverses the logical order of causality and thereby emphasizes one special aspect of an ongoing story. Thus in Goethe's "your husband's dead, and sends a greeting", the death is probably emphasized over the greetings. At the same time, it also points out insufficient knowledge about the afterworld. The insufficient knowledge about underlying facts also poses a serious problem in the process of establishing justice. We can use Shakespeare's oxymoron of "honourable villain" to show that someone may be honourable first but a villain later and vice versa. This constitutes one major problem with the interpretation of oxymora. The same can be exemplified by the German oxymoron "*Raumzeit*" (spacetime) as opposed to "*Zeitraum*" (time space), which alters the meaning from combining space and time into a single continuum to a period in time (and space). Here, the underlying problem is the inadequate knowledge about the laws of the universe, as, for instance, the question of whether the order between cause and effect can be altered or not. The possibility that effect comes before causality seems counterintuitive but may be possible in view of observations from quantum physics.[159]

Thus oxymora, even when constituted by two opposite nouns, rarely make up a perfect oxymoron where changing the order would not affect the meaning and thereby the basis for the judgement of a given situation. A rare example may be the oxymoron of pianoforte, which in Italian means "silent-loud", which in its opposite ordering of "fortepiano" (loud-silent) still refers to the

155 See *e.g.* Lauge Rasmussen and Felix Rauner (eds), *Industrial Cultures and Production: Understanding Competitiveness* (London: Springer, 1996); see also H. Frederick Willkie, "General Education for an Industrial Culture" (1947) 1(4) *The Journal of General Education* 267.

156 See Ronald Duska, "Business Ethics: Oxymoron or Good Business?" (2000) 10 *Business Ethics Quarterly* 111.

157 W. A. Dymond and Michael M. Hart, "Abundant Paradox: The Trade and Culture Debate" (2002) 9(2) *Canadian Foreign Policy Journal* 15.

158 See *e.g.* Rostam J. Neuwirth, "The 'Culture and Trade' Paradox Reloaded" in Christiaan De Beukelaer, Miikka Pyykkönen and J. P. Singh (eds), *Globalization, Culture and Development: The UNESCO Convention on Cultural Diversity* (Basingstoke: Palgrave MacMillan, 2015) 91.

159 See *e.g.* Ognyan Oreshkov, Fabio Costa and Časlav Brukner, "Quantum Correlations with No Causal Order" (2012) 3(1092) *Nature Communications* 1.

same musical instrument, the piano and is used interchangeably (even though it may refer to different conceptions and constructions in time).[160] Even in this example, subtle differences in time and context may render one concept more accurate over the other.

Generally the importance in oxymora (and paradoxes) is first to identify the opposite extremes and then try to understand the whole range of their possible mutual relations. This first marks the advantage of dual reasoning as a simplistic form of addressing the issue as a whole (holism) while at the same time taking into account its two main constituent elements. Unfortunately, analytical thinking often falls short of completing the process and merely stops at the analytical stage before having completed a holistic assessment. This process of analysing and synthesizing is also known by the medieval adage of "*solve et coagula*", which Carl G. Jung outlined as follows:

> As is indicated by the very name which he chose for it—the "spagyric" art—or by the oft-repeated saying "solve et coagula" (dissolve and coagulate), the alchemist saw the essence of his art in separation and analysis on the one hand and synthesis and consolidation on the other. For him there was first of all an initial state in which opposite tendencies or forces were in conflict; secondly there was the great question of a procedure which would be capable of bringing the hostile elements and qualities, once they were separated, back to unity again.[161]

This is where the Eastern philosophy provides an important reminder of completing the analytical process notably by emphasizing the complementarity between dual opposites. In this endeavour there exists a book of Chinese philosophy that contains perhaps better advice on how to practise the mean than the *chung yung*.[162] This book is the *Tao Te Ching* written by the ancient Chinese philosopher Lao Tzu. The so-called "*tao*" (or *dao*) that characterizes the philosophical tradition of Taoism, is often translated by terms like logos, way, path or road. The notion of *tao*, however, is also something that cannot be truly expressed in words, because "the name that can be uttered in words is not the true and eternal name".[163] The notion of *tao* emphasizes the harmony of opposites, like good and

160 See Piero Rattalino, *Storia del pianoforte*, 2nd ed (Milano: Il Saggiatore, 2003) at 40 and August E. Müller, *G. S. Löhleins Klavierschule oder Anweisung zum Klavier- und Fortepiano-Spiel nebst vielen praktischen Beispielen und einem Anhange vom Generalbasse*, 6th ed (Jena: Friedrich Frommann, 1804) at 1.

161 See Carl G. Jung, *Mysterium Coniunctionis: An Inquiry into the Separation and Synthesis of Psychic Opposites in Alchemy* (Princeton: Princeton University Press, 1963) at xiv [footnote omitted].

162 But see also Fan Jianhong, "Das Zhong-Yong-Prinzip (Golden Mean) im Lichte des Verhältnismässigkeitsgrundsatzes i.e.S. in der chinesischen relativen Kündigungsbeschränkung" in Volker Rieble (ed), *Festschrift für Manfred Löwisch zum 70. Geburtstag* (München: Sellier European Law Publishers, 2007) 99.

163 See Lao Tzu, *The Book of Tao and Teh* (Beijing: China Translation and Publishing Corporation, 2006) 1 at 3.

bad, beautiful and ugly, heaven and earth, or body and soul.[164] The emphasis on complementary (or oxymoronic) thinking pervades all of its chapters as exemplified by the following sentence:

> Therefore just as we take advantage of what is, we Should recognise the usefulness of what is not.[165]

These ancient lines are very similar to some written by the French philosopher Simone Weil about human needs for both the body and the soul that they are arranged "in antithetical pairs and have to combine together to form a balance", because man "requires food, but also an interval between his meals; he requires warmth and coolness, rest and exercise".[166]

In essence, the search for harmony between opposites or the solution to the apparent conflicts between opposites yoked together by apparent violence in essentially oxymoronic concepts is first no question of East or West as well as North or South. It knows no geography. Many sources from different places and times indicate the significance of the complementarity between opposites. They also show that adding complementary thinking to dualistic thinking may prove a way to alter the perception and, consequently, the understanding of complex phenomena altogether. This is perhaps the central message that oxymoronic concepts convey, which also finds reflection in the law of associations as defined by Ernst Mach as the fact that "practically each time that two different concepts are evoked together, each one of them will automatically be remembered when the other is evoked".[167] In effect, it means that notably oxymora create a web of associations desiring to connect single constituents and to combine them to a larger whole, thereby, it is hoped, expanding our perception and understanding of reality. In their functional role, essentially oxymoronic concepts can be compared to koans as their Western counterparts in the same way as dialetheism resembles the doctrine of the *chung yung*.

8.3 Art, science, law and technology: metaphors of the future?

> ***There was no distinction between art, science, and technology. It was a human activity guided by awe, curiosity, primordial quest, magic, and mystery.***[168]

In addition to language, there exists one more area of human activity which says a lot about human nature, the human mind and how it works. This area therefore

164 See also Antonio S. Cua, "Opposites as Complements: Reflections on the Significance of Tao" (1981) 31(2) *Philosophy East and West* 123.

165 Lao Tzu, *Tao Te Ching* (Beijing: Wordsworth, 1997) at 23.

166 See Simone Weil, *The Need for Roots* (London: Routledge, 2002) at 12.

167 Ernst Mach, *The Analysis of Sensations and the Relation of the Physical to the Psychical* (New York: Dover Publications, 1959) at 239 [first published in 1885].

168 Vinod Vidwan, "Expressing with Grey Cells: Indian Perspectives on New Media Arts" in Melvin L. Alexenberg (ed), *Educating Artists for the Future: Learning at the Intersections of Art, Science, Technology and Culture* (Bristol: Intellect Books, 2008) 141 at 143.

allows for insights into the deeper layers of the brain and cognition and hopefully also in how we can embrace contradictions better and tackle paradoxical problems. This area also reflects the trends of an accelerating pace of innovation and development. It usually brings drastic changes to human perception based on convergence and expresses itself in changes in language that alter our understanding of the world in terms of time and space. The same area also supports the view of deeper connections between art, science and even law. It also reveals connections between Eastern and Western philosophy, the past and the future as well as time and space in an era of the "global village". The area in question is technology. Technology has inspired many questions about its relation notably to art and science.[169] Etymologically, it even combines both as the Greek term "*technē*" is "the name not only for the activities and skills of the craftsman but also for the arts of the mind and the fine arts".[170] Additionally, *technē* also closely relates to literature by belonging to *poiēsis* ("bringing forth"), which also gives it a nature of something "poetic".[171]

Technology, combining both elements of art and science, also has a profound impact on law and vice versa. This, in particular, as both influence each other in the boost they provide to change.[172] Technology and law also mutually influence each other in terms of changes in perception, as the cinematograph and subsequent inventions like the computer and digital technologies prove. The impact of new technologies on the law has been recorded many times and is visible in parallel developments in law and technology.[173] The same can be said about the link between art and the law, which, however, is often treated separately from technology or science.[174] Less researched or understood seems to be the reverse, namely the impact of law on the development of technologies,[175] which explains why there is a general assumption of law lagging behind technology. More

169 See also David Carrier, "Editorial: The Arts and Science and Technology: Problems and Prospects" (1988) 21(4) *Leonardo* 341 and Moisei Kagan, "Art, Science and Technology in the Past, Present and Future" (1994) 27(5) *Leonardo* 409.

170 See Martin Heidegger, "On the Question of Technology" in Martin Heidegger, *Basic Writings* (London: Routledge, 1979) 311 at 318; see also C. T. Onions (ed), *The Oxford Dictionary of English Etymology* (Oxford: Clarendon Press, 1966) at 906.

171 See Heidegger, *supra* note 170 at 318.

172 See also Lyria Bennett Moses, "Agents of Change: How the Law "Copes" with Technological Change" (2011) 20(4) *Griffith Law Review* 763.

173 See *e.g.* H. Guyford Stever, "Science, Technology, and Law – A Growing Partnership" (1977) 17(3) *Jurimetrics Journal* 189, Colin B. Picker, "A View From 40,000 Feet: International Law and the Invisible Hand of Technology" (2001) 23(1) *Cardozo Law Review* 149, and Brad Sherman and Leanne Wiseman, *Copyright and the Challenge of the New* (Alphen aan den Rijn: Kluwer Law International, 2012).

174 See *e.g.* Franklin Feldman, "Reflections on Art and the Law: Old Concepts, New Values" (1987) 131(2) *Proceedings of the American Philosophical Society* 141 and John Henry Merryman, "A Course in Art and the Law" (1974) 26(4) *Journal of Legal Education* 551; see also Lee Loevinger, "Science, Technology and Law in Modern Society" (1985) 26(1) *Jurimetrics* 1.

175 But see *e.g.* Wesley A. Magat, "The Effects of Environmental Regulation on Innovation" (1979) 43(1) *Law and Contemporary Problems* 4 and Richard B. Stewart, "Regulation, Innovation, and Administrative Law: A Conceptual Framework" (1981) 69(5) *California Law Review* 1256.

complex still, law and technology may converge and merge to combine its task, namely when technological standards become or enforce regulatory norms.[176] The fundamental problem concerning the relation between law, technology and change was summarized by Judge Lachs of the International Court of Justice in a dissenting opinion to a judgment, where he wrote:

> However, the great acceleration of social and economic change, combined with that of science and technology, have confronted law with a serious challenge: one it must meet, lest it lag even farther behind events than it has been wont to do.[177]

This paragraph not only reflects the acceleration of change of everything but of science in technology as well. The acceleration of change by technology is also paralleled by related expressions in language, through notably the creation of neologisms or portmanteau words that are often oxymora. Numerous new technologies reflect the increasing convergence between different technologies or product categories, which carry the process of breeding oxymora further, as terms like "nutriceutics", "cosmeceutics", "SUVs", "artificial intelligence", "Microsoft Works", or "virtual reality" prove. New technologies also often give rise to paradoxes, as generally speaking new technologies create both new opportunities and dangers or that humans invent and use technologies to shape their lives and their lives are (in turn) shaped by technologies.[178] The so-called "technology paradox" was perhaps best characterized by Blaise Pascal's paradox of progress.[179] A more recent example would be the "Internet paradox", which was said to lie in the apparent contradiction that the Internet is "a social technology used for communication with individuals and groups, but it is associated with declines in social involvement and the psychological well-being that goes with social involvement".[180] Other technology-related paradoxes are, for instance, a "productivity paradox", which critically questions the expected positive implications of information technology (IT) on output and productivity.[181] Similar questions about the paradoxical impact of IT or computers on human creativity have been raised.[182] Other paradoxes related to IT are that we usually get a highly positive description

176 See *e.g.* Dan L. Burk, "Legal and Technical Standards in Digital Rights Management" (2005) 74(2) *Fordham Law Review* 537.

177 Cited in Manfred Lachs, "Thoughts on Science, Technology and World Law" (1992) 86(4) *The American Journal of International Law* 673 at 698.

178 See generally David Glen Mick and Susan Fournier, "Paradoxes of Technology: Consumer Cognizance, Emotions, and Coping Strategies" (1998) 25(2) *Journal of Consumer Research* 123.

179 Blaise Pascal, *The Thoughts of Blaise Pascal* (London: Kegan Paul, Trench & Co., 1885) at 57.

180 See *e.g.* Robert Kraut et al., "Internet Paradox: A Social Technology that Reduces Social Involvement and Psychological Well-Being?" (1998) 53(9) *American Psychologist* 1017 at 1029.

181 See *e.g.* Erik Brynjolfsson, "The Productivity Paradox of Information Technology" (1993) 36(12) *Communications of the ACM* 66.

182 See Steven Marc Edwards, "The Technology Paradox: Efficiency Versus Creativity" (2001) 13(2) *Creativity Research Journal* 221.

of the benefits of IT products (paradox of positive value) while we later encounter bad surprises in making use of them (paradox of negative experience).[183] Finally, it was also suggested that the incredible amounts of data collected by various information technologies are "cooked" and never entirely "neutral" or "raw", which is why it was said that "raw data" constitutes an oxymoron.[184]

The rise of essentially oxymoronic concepts in relation to technology supports the existence of close metaphorical connections between the evolution of technologies and the understanding of the mind, as technologies carry an important message about how the mind works.[185] The same was found to be true for the meaning of words and constructions and how they are used.[186] Put briefly, like language, technology is an equally strong expression of the human mind, because the mind is possibly a human's only tool to allow him to be creator of his own fate (*homo faber*).[187] This particular quality of the mind in relation to the creation of the fate or future is well exemplified by the literary works of "science fiction" of many writers like Jules Verne or H. G. Wells. Interesting to note is that this prophetic quality rooted in science fiction, likely another oxymoron, often develops from oxymoronic thoughts. For instance, Jules Verne was named a "nostalgic visionary" who "foretold the future, 'inventing' modern technology through the power of his imagination".[188] H. G. Wells did no less and was said to have initiated "future history" novels.[189]

It is imagination combined with creativity that serves as an important source of inspiration in this regard. Both also serve scientists as well. Taking the example of Peter W. Higgs who with other peers in 1964 correctly anticipated the discovery of the Higgs boson or "God particle" in 2013,[190] it is interesting to add that the discovery was also made possible by an oxymoronic method, namely a "creation from destruction" consisting in the collision of particles at high speed in the Large Hadron Collider. Another such scientist is Leon O. Chua, who in 1971 also theoretically anticipated the discovery in 2008 of a fourth physical

183 See Terri L. Griffith and Gregory B. Northcraft, "Cognitive Elements in the Implementation of New Technology: Can Less Information Provide More Benefits?" (1996) 20(1) *MIS Quarterly* 99.

184 See Lisa Gitelman and Virginia Jackson, "Introduction" in Lisa Gitelman (ed), *"Raw Data" is an Oxymoron* (Cambridge, MA: MIT Press, 2013) 1 at 2–3.

185 See Norm Friesen, "Mind and Machine: Ethical and Epistemological Implications for Research" (2010) 25(1) *Artificial Intelligence and Society* 83 at 83.

186 See Steven Pinker, *The Stuff of Thought: Language as a Window into Human Nature* (New York: Penguin, 2007) at 427.

187 See Jon R. Stone, *The Routledge Dictionary of Latin Quotations* (New York: Routledge, 2005) at 31.

188 See Timothy Unwin, "Technology and Progress in Jules Verne, Or Anticipation in Reverse" (2000) 93(1) *Journal of the Australasian Universities Language and Literature Association* 17 at 18 and 31.

189 See Patrick Parrinder, *Shadows of the Future: H. G. Wells, Science Fiction, and Prophecy* (New York: Syracuse University Press, 1995) at 3.

190 See Peter W. Higgs, "Broken Symmetries and the Masses of Gauge Bosons" (1964) 13(16) *Physical Review Letters* 508; see also Jörn Bleck-Neuhaus, *Elementare Teilchen: Von den Atomen über das Standard-Modell bis zum Higgs-Boson*, 2nd ed (Berlin: Springer, 2013) at 659 and John Alison, *The Road to Discovery: Detector Alignment, Electron Identification, Particle Misidentification, WW Physics, and the Discovery of the Higgs Boson* (Cham: Springer, 2015) at 285.

device next to the resistor, inductor and capacitor, which he called "memristor" as a portmanteau coined from memory and resistor.[191] The memristor may be an exceptional invention as it is said to revolutionize how computers will work in the future. It may actually represent a turning point in the evolution of the mind as reflected in the invention of technologies. The reason that the memristor has been hailed as a revolution is not only because it will allow us to build better, faster and more energy-efficient computers, which, for instance, instantly turn on and off without losing the data.[192] They have generated so much interest because it was suggested that they will allow us to build "creative computers", that is to say "brain-like" or "neural computers", which may provide robots with the capacities needed "to plan for the future, learn from the past and make intelligent judgements in the present".[193] This quality further confirms the identity between technology and the mind, where the former is the external expression of the latter's internal quality and perhaps inner desires. In this regard, the most interesting facet of memristors is that they will allow computers to escape the boundaries of binary codes.[194] This may be novel for computers but is already quite commonly used in other technological products, like washing machines, air conditioners or anti-lock brakes in cars, all of which use "fuzzy thinking".[195]

Binary codes in computing and digital electronics thus reflect the dualistic modes of thinking or binary logic used by humans. The way computers use binary processes like human thinking is explained by dual process theories. In this respect it is also more than coincidence that an important contribution to the development of the present computer was provided by Gottfried W. Leibniz (1646–1716) in his work on the binary system.[196] More telling is that Leibniz was inspired in his work on binary arithmetic by the ancient Chinese book of changes (*I Ching*),[197] which supports the view expressed above that oxymora and koans may perform a similar function in the mind. This again is also confirmed

191 See Leon O. Chua, "Memristor – The Missing Circuit Element" (1971) 18(5) *IEEE Transactions on Circuit Theory* 507 at 507 and Dmitri B. Strukov et al., "The Missing Memristor Found" (2008) 453(7191) *Nature* 80.

192 See Jacopo Prisco, "So Long, Transistor: How the 'Memristor' Could Revolutionize Electronics", *Cable News Network (CNN)* (26 February 2015); available at: http://edition.cnn.com/2015/02/26/tech/mci-eth-memristor/ and Makoto Itoh and Leon O. Chua, "Memristor Oscillators" (2008) 18(11) *International Journal of Bifurcation and Chaos* 3183 at 3183.

193 See Ella Gale, Ben de Lacy Costello and Andrew Adamatzky, "Does the D.C. Response of Memristors Allow Robotic Short-Term Memory and a Possible Route to Artificial Time Perception?" (2013) *IEEE International Conference on Robotics and Automation*, Karlsruhe, Germany, 6–10 May 2013; available at: http://eprints.uwe.ac.uk/19413/1/TimePerception.pdf (accessed 1 October 2017).

194 See Prisco, *supra* note 192.

195 See Kosko, *supra* note 26 at 180–190.

196 See also Martin Davis, *The Universal Computer: The Road from Leibniz to Turing* (New York: W. W. Norton, 2000) at 16 and Jerry M. Lodder, "Binary Arithmetic: From Leibniz to von Neumann" in Brian Hopkins (ed), *Resources for Teaching Discrete Mathematics: Classroom Projects, History Modules, and Articles* (Washington: The Mathematical Association of America, 2009) 169.

197 See *e.g.* E. J. Aiton and Eikoh Shimao, "Gorai Kinzō's Study of Leibniz and the I Ching Hexagrams" (1981) 28(1) *Annals of Science* 71 and James A. Ryan, "Leibniz' Binary System and Shao Yong's 'Yijing'" (1996) 46(1) *Philosophy East and West* 59.

by Leibniz being fascinated with the idea of a universal language.[198] Interestingly, digital technology may provide the platform for such common language with essentially oxymoronic concepts as the content. The development of the computer certainly is an expression of a desire to communicate via a universal tool. In this context, the idea of a universal language coincides with the claim that a common language is needed to build a global legal framework for the future.

Thus, following the invention of cinematography, the computer represents the last stage in the human evolution of the mind as reflected in technology. Computers are perhaps the external mirror of the mind, which is explained by the search for "artificial intelligence". So far, dual thinking has found expression in contested concepts which led to the invention of binary codes used in computing. Now, oxymoronic concepts seem to continue this evolutionary process but where will computers go next? Here the memristor as a tool for the creation of the next generation of computers may provide some useful insights. First, memristors can apparently transcend the binary coding and implement a fuzzy logic.[199] Moreover, fuzzy logic was mentioned as playing a central role in "computing with words".[200] Some of the main advantages of memristors have been said to lie in their high-density multilevel memory and behavioural similarity to biological synapses, which represent "a major step towards emulating the incredible processing power of biological systems".[201]

Perhaps the discovery of the memristor effectively means another major step towards the creation of artificial intelligence, the merger of humans and machines giving birth to the "cyborg", an abbreviation for "cybernetic organism", which constitutes yet another oxymoron.[202] Only time will tell but if machines are using logic, more flexibly and perhaps accurately than their creators, is it not time to rethink even the foundations of our thinking? In this regard, it has been said that we can already build machines or computers using oxymora or paradoxes, so perhaps we are indeed already accustomed to preliminary forms of oxymoronic thinking.

What, however, does this possibility mean for law and the future of law? Like technology, law too is a reflection of the human mind and can be considered both an art and a science. Both concur in their fascination with perception and the perception of the future in contrast with the past. So far, new technologies have already left their mark on law, mostly by means of legal practice

198 See Paolo Rossi, *Logic and the Art of Memory: The Quest for a Universal Language* (London: Continuum, 2000) at 173 and 176.

199 See *e.g.* Farnood Merrikh-Bayat and Saeed B. Shouraki, "Memristive Neuro-Fuzzy System" (2013) 43(1) *IEEE Transactions on Cybernetics* 269.

200 See Lotfi A. Zadeh, "Fuzzy Logic = Computing with Words" (1996) 4(2) *IEEE Transactions on Fuzzy Systems* 103 at 110.

201 See Dhireesha Kudithipudi et al., "Design of Neuromorphic Architectures with Memristors" in Robinson E. Pino (ed), *Network Science and Cybersecurity* (New York: Springer, 2014) 93 at 93.

202 See Timo Siivonen, "Cyborgs and Generic Oxymorons: The Body and Technology in William Gibson's Cyberspace Trilogy" (1996) 23(2) *Science Fiction Studies* 227.

and legal education.[203] This has not been recognized without criticism, as the following account reflects:

> Electronic techniques for rapid large-scale information handling provide important opportunities to refine legal technique. To use them well will require stringent adherence to the "logic of the machine," perhaps at the expense of some of the richness and ambiguity of legal concepts.[204]

While the statement that the impact of technology comes at the expense of the richness and ambiguity of legal concepts may be contradicted by the rise of oxymoronic language in general, it is the "logic of the machine" that draws attention. This is because when the logic of the "machine", i.e. the computer, is changing it may also be time for the realm of law to consider serious changes to logic and thinking in law.[205] Therefore, recent trends in technology may assist in preparing the way for a future role of law and the role of law in the design of the future. This last point is of utmost importance in the Anthropocene era and, particularly, if we do not want to cede the control of the future completely to machines.[206]

Regarding the present trends, a prominent position is taken by convergence in general, as reflected also in language. In technology, it concerns mainly the convergence between notably several technological subgroups, including nanotechnology, biotechnology and information and communication technologies (ICT). To these categories, the field of cognitive studies was added as bearing enormous potential in the future.[207] Perhaps the field of transport, which is closely connected with communication technologies, should also be added.[208] Jointly and through close interaction, these fields will and have already begun to drastically alter the way we live our lives. For instance, nanotechnology will alter everything we use in terms of materials, from clothes, food and cosmetics, to machines, arms and computers.[209] Biotechnology has already invaded our lives with GM food and other potential applications ranging

203 See also Peter Alldridge and Ann Mumford, "Gazing into the Future Through a VDU: Communications, Information Technology, and Law Teaching" (1998) 25(1) *Journal of Law and Society* 116 and Richard E. Susskind, *The Future of Law: Facing the Challenges of Information Technology* (Oxford: Clarendon Press, 1996).

204 See Carl F. Stover, "Technology and Law – A Look Ahead" (1963) 4(1) *MULL: Modern Uses of Logic in Law* 1 at 1.

205 See John Dewey, "Logical Method and Law" (1924) 10(1) *Cornell Law Quarterly* 17 at 27.

206 See also Ray Kurzweil, *The Age of Spiritual Machines: When Computers Exceed Human Intelligence* (New York: Viking, 1999).

207 See also Mihail C. Roco and William Sims Bainbridge (eds), *Converging Technologies for Improving Human Performance: Nanotechnology, Biotechnology, Information Technology and Cognitive Science* (Dordrecht: Springer, 2003).

208 See also Mark W. Zacher, *Governing Global Networks: International Regimes for Transportation and Communications* (Cambridge: Cambridge University Press, 1996).

209 See also Jeremy Baumberg et al., "Where is Nano Taking Us?" (2007) 3 *Nanotechnology Perceptions* 3.

from the development of new drugs and chemicals to animal and human cloning.[210] Both areas, combined into the concept "nanobiotechnology", are also likely to push this process even further.[211]

The Internet too, having gradually merged the industries of telecommunication, broadcasting, audiovisual and even printed media, is already changing our lives drastically. These technologies will continue to evolve rapidly, especially in the fields of mobile and video telephony,[212] social and other media,[213] instant messaging applications,[214] or the upgrades from 2G to 5G networks.[215] Foreshadowed by drones, transport too will continue to accelerate, both in accessibility, volume and speed, but it is too early to tell when revolutionary means of transport, like "beaming" or "teleportation" will be available to commuters and travellers alike.[216] Communication technologies will equally evolve with speech technology and machine translation improving,[217] which can be expected to have interesting effects on communication across different cultures and languages. As a whole, science and technology will continue to have an exponential impact on life in the future.[218]

In all these fields separately, considerable progress can be expected in the decades to come. What is more difficult to forecast is the arrival of a so-called "tipping point"[219] or "paradigm shift",[220] when a major game changer occurs that leaves no stone unturned and drastically alters at least some of the fundamental assumptions (like gravity or the impossibility of travelling faster than light) that we have about life. Such game changers are hard to imagine but could be of the nature of the discovery

210 See also Brian Sager, "Scenarios on the Future of Biotechnology" (2001) 68 *Technological Forecasting & Social Change* 109 at 109.

211 See Jeremy J. Ramsden, "What Is Nanotechnology?" (2005) 1 *Nanotechnology Perceptions* 3 at 14.

212 See *e.g.* H. Lacohée, N. Wakeford and I. Pearson, "A Social History of the Mobile Telephone with a View of its Future" (2003) 21(3) *BT Technology Journal* 203.

213 See *e.g.* Crystal Thies, "The Future of Social Media" in Matthew Halloran and Crystal Thies, *The Social Media Handbook for Financial Advisors: How to Use LinkedIn, Facebook and Twitter* (Hoboken: John Wiley & Sons, 2012) at 267.

214 See *e.g.* Karen Church and Rodrigo de Oliveira, "What's up with whatsapp?: comparing mobile instant messaging behaviors with traditional SMS" (2013) *Proceedings of the 15th International Conference on Human–Computer Interaction with Mobile Devices and Services* 352.

215 See also Shakil Akhtar, "Evolution of Technologies, Standards, and Deployment for 2G-5G Networks" in Margherita Pagani (ed), *Encyclopedia of Multimedia Technology and Networking*, 2nd ed (Hershey: Information Science Reference, 2008) 522.

216 See also Anton Zeilinger, "The Science-Fiction Dream of 'Beaming' Objects From Place to Place Is Now a Reality At Least For Particles of Light" (2000) 282(4) *Scientific American* 50.

217 See *e.g.* Farzad Ehsani et al., "Spoken Language Translation" in Fang Chen and Kristiina Jokinen (eds), *Speech Technology: Theory and Applications* (New York: Springer, 2010) 167 and Martin Kay, "The Proper Place of Men and Machines in Language Translation" (1997) 12(1–2) *Machine Translation* 3.

218 See also Michio Kaku, *Physics of the Future: How Science Will Shape Human Destiny and Our Daily Lives by the Year 2100* (New York: Doubleday, 2011).

219 See Malcolm Gladwell, *Blink: The Power of Thinking Without Thinking* (London: Penguin, 2005).

220 See Thomas S. Kuhn, *The Structure of Scientific Revolutions* (Chicago: The University of Chicago Press, 1996).

of alien life forms, new and inexhaustible energy resources, mind-reading or dream recording devices,[221] or insights into the nature (or nonexistence) of death, or something else unexpected and hard to imagine at this point.

In this paradoxical task, it can be expected that the computer will continue to play an important role in our scientific quest for answers and the coordination of the different areas. Computers may take the role of a "world brain". In this regard, the future computer will be required to play a role in our attempts to enhance our means of perception, that is to say, to enhance our perception in order to create more possibilities based on a so-called "augmented reality", as an intermediate between science and fiction or reality and virtual reality. The themes of recent movies, like *Lucy* (2014) or *Inception* (2010),[222] already reflect the interest of the public in possibilities of enhanced perception and augmented reality.[223] Exemplified by the cinematograph, we also see the gradual evolution of motion pictures from 2D, via 3D to 4D cinemas, which highlight an urgent desire for greater unity in the diversity of the individual senses. This desire can again be taken as a metaphor for the challenge faced at the level of global law, where different international organizations function as individual organs but lack a common switchboard or "common sense", like a global mind. This metaphor, for which oxymoronic concepts may provide the common language, may serve as the starting point for the formulation of a novel "law for the time of oxymora" (Chapter 9) to be discussed below. Having outlined general problem-solving mechanisms and possible cultural differences in the reception of contradictions, it is first necessary to inquire into the ways that law deals with oxymoronic concepts.

8.4 Law and cognition: the solution of paradoxes in law

> *From the perspective of the brain, there's a thin line between a good decision and a bad decision.*[224]

The close relation between law and the mind may be clear but is not always evident. In fact, all laws can be regarded as mental constructs. After earlier works on law and the mind, like that by Jerome Frank, novel findings in the fields of neuroscience and cognitive studies have also renewed the interest in law's connection with the mind.[225] Here, we are now concerned with the question of how

221 See *e.g.* Christian Herff et al., "Brain-to-Text: Decoding Spoken Phrases from Phone Representations in the Brain" (2015) *Frontiers in Neuroscience* 1; available at: https://www.frontiersin.org/articles/10.3389/fnins.2015.00217/full (accessed 1 October 2017) and T. Horikawa et al., "Neural Decoding of Visual Imagery During Sleep" (2013) 340(6132) *Science* 639.

222 See Christopher Nolan (dir.), *Inception* (2010), IMDB; available at: http://www.imdb.com/title/tt1375666/ (accessed 1 October 2017) and Luc Besson (dir.), *Lucy* (2014), IMDB; available at: http://www.imdb.com/title/tt2872732/ (accessed 1 October 2017).

223 See also Michael Haller, Mark Billinghurst and Bruce H. Thomas (eds), *Emerging Technologies of Augmented Reality: Interfaces and Design* (Hershey: Idea Group, 2007) and Marcus Tönnis, *Augmented Reality: Einblicke in die Erweiterte Realität* (Berlin: Springer, 2010).

224 See Jonah Lehrer, *How We Decide* (Boston: Houghton Mifflin Harcourt, 2009) at xiv.

225 See *e.g.* Semir Zeki and Oliver R. Goodenhough (eds), *Law and the Brain* (Oxford: Oxford University Press, 2004) and Steven L. Winter, *A Clearing in the Forest: Law, Life, and Mind* (Chicago: The University of Chicago Press, 2001); see also Jerome Bruner, *Minding the Law*

the law (and lawyer's mind) embraces contradictions and law proposes to solve them. As mentioned above, the present conception of law remains largely dualistic and relying on classical logic. Such a conception, it is argued, would render dialethism or fuzzy thinking in law rather useless. Indeed, the paralysis of law in the face of contradictions due to the dualistic conception has been well outlined by the French lawyer Mireille Delmas-Marty who wrote that one may argue that "the law is not fuzzy" because it is laid down in codes, strict tables of truth, which separate the right from the wrong, the legal from the illegal or the guilty from the innocent.[226] On the other hand, "if the law were fuzzy", it would no longer be law.[227] Or else, a "bias toward adopting a binary, rather than a probabilistic approach (endorsing one alternative, rather than assigning probabilities to all of them)" was found to guide our legal reasoning.[228]

Leaving aside this problem of the conception of law, which may differ in different times and places, it is important to see how law can deal with contradictions laid down in paradoxes or oxymora. As a first important statement, one can reiterate that law has one important advantage over reasoning in general when it comes to solving paradoxes or antinomies (as they are also called in law). The law can not only show that reasoning is fallacious, that the premises applied are wrong or that a conclusion can be accepted; *the law can also change the law* when such paradoxes arise. There is one more easy way out of "ignorance" for law when facing uncertainty or lack of knowledge. This way is called a "legal fiction", i.e. when the law assumes a fact to be legally true even if it may not be true in reality.

But before pondering these two approaches further, it is advisable to look more closely at paradoxes in the law or so-called "legal paradoxes". In this regard, it is important to point out that legal paradoxes largely depend on the notion of paradox, for which also exist different definitions. In this regard, a useful overview of different terminologies and classifications applied to paradoxes in the legal sphere has been provided by Oren Perez.[229] After classifying several categories of paradoxes, he concludes about the principal challenge they pose to law as follows:

> The static perspective which characterises the study of paradoxes in logic is not suited for that task because it is not sensitive to the social dynamics underlying the paradoxes of law.[230]

(Cambridge: Harvard University Press, 2002) and Lorie M. Graham and Stephen M. McJohn, "Cognition, Law, Stories" (2008) 10(1) *Minnesota Journal of Law, Science & Technology* 255.

226 See Mireille Delmas-Marty, *Le flou du droit: du code pénal aux droits de l'homme* (Paris: Presses Universitaires de France, 1986) at 11.

227 *Ibid* at 11.

228 See Giovanni Sartor, *Legal Reasoning: A Cognitive Approach to the Law* (Dordrecht: Springer, 2005) at 74–75.

229 Oren Perez, "Law in the Air: A Prologue to the World of Legal Paradoxes" in Oren Perez and Gunther Teubner (eds), *Paradoxes and Inconsistencies in the Law* (Oxford: Hart Publishing, 2006) 3 at 4–13.

230 *Ibid* at 17.

This statement brings to the fore one of the main problems related to perceptions of change and changes in perception. It also relates directly to the distinction between dialectics and dialetheism or between a static and dynamic view of the world. Again, underlying all these distinctions are dichotomies formulated on the basis of binary thinking and classical logic. It is thus noteworthy that like John Dewey calling for an "infiltration into law of a more experimental and flexible logic",[231] Oren Perez also proposes as a solution to the riddles of legal paradoxicality, the usage of "extra-logical tools".[232] This also largely resonates with critical views on the role of (classical) logic in the realm of law as expressed by other jurists interested in legal paradoxes.[233] Perhaps finding a more adequate logic, a so-called "modern legal logic",[234] that is to say, one that can "intimately relate the life of the law to the experience of all life" [235], or one that reconciles a lawyer's and a logician's truth,[236] is the way forward.

More recently, H. Patrick Glenn has outlined the limits of binary logic in his book, *The Cosmopolitan State*, which, in response to my question, he admitted can be construed as an oxymoron, particularly from a static view.[237] In the book, he convincingly lays bare how binary (as opposed to multivalent or paraconsistent) logic in law fails to fulfil the urgent needs and complex challenges of today's cosmopolitan states and societies. Elsewhere, he clarifies that multivalent logic is "that which refuses to regard the world as an endless series of dichotomies or binary choices".[238] Glenn also clarifies that while bivalent thinking has been associated with Western thinking and multivalent thinking with Hindu and other Asian thinking, multivalent thought can actually be found in all legal traditions.[239] Moreover, multivalence is an important feature within all major legal traditions and for their mutual interaction and reconciliation as well.[240]

231 See Dewey, *supra* 205 at 27.
232 See Perez, "Law in the Air: A Prologue to the World of Legal Paradoxes", *supra* note 229 at 17.
233 See *e.g.* Oliver W. Holmes, *The Common Law* (Boston: Little, Brown and Company, 1923) at 1, Benjamin N. Cardozo, *The Paradoxes of Legal Science* (New York: Columbia University Press, 1928) at 111 and 136, George P. Fletcher, "Paradoxes in Legal Thought" (1985) 85(6) *Columbia Law Review* 1263 at 1292, and Grant Gilmore, "Law, Logic and Experience" (1957) 3(1) *Howard Law Journal* 26 at 41.
234 See *e.g.* Ilmar Tammelo, "Logic as an Instrument of Legal Reasoning" (1969–1970) 10(3) *Jurimetrics Journal* 89; see generally Chaim Perelman, "What Is Legal Logic" (1968) 3(1) *Israel Law Review* 1 and Leonard G. Boonin, "Concerning the Relation of Logic to Law" (1964–1965) 17(2) *Journal of Legal Education* 155.
235 See Lee Loevinger, "An Introduction to Legal Logic" (1950) 27(4) *Indiana Law Journal* 471 at 522.
236 See Felix S. Cohen, "Field Theory and Judicial Logic" (1950) 59(2) *The Yale Law Journal* 238 at 239.
237 H. Patrick Glenn, *The Cosmopolitan State* (Oxford: Oxford University Press, 2013) at 259–276.
238 H. Patrick Glenn, "A Concept of Legal Tradition" (2008) 34(1) *Queen's Law Journal* 427 at 443.
239 See Glenn, *Legal Traditions of the World*, *supra* note 90 at 351.
240 *Ibid* at 351–360.

In fact, these complex challenges are found also to a large extent in legal paradoxes taking the form of legal conflicts, antinomies or other inconsistencies. In this regard it is important to distinguish between a legal conflict and mere legal divergence. A legal conflict was defined as a direct incompatibility that arises where "a state party to two treaties cannot simultaneously comply with its obligations under both treaties".[241] Divergence, on the other hand, was described as the case when "two law-making treaties with a number of common parties may deal with the same subject from different points of view or be applicable in different circumstances".[242] Thus it is legal conflicts that are closest to legal paradoxes. Seen from this perspective, legal paradoxes in the form of legal conflicts are antinomies,[243] their connection being outlined as follows:

> Paradoxes and antinomies, on the other hand, reflect problems of logical rather than factual consistency. To follow Quine's definitions, paradoxes are contradictions that result from overlooking an accepted canon of consistent thought. They are resolved by pointing to the fallacy that generates them. When we confront the special form of paradox called an antinomy, however, we have no such easy way out. The resolution of these more troubling contradictions requires reexamination of our fundamental premises. The solution typically represents a conceptual innovation, a new way of looking at the field of life that generates the contradiction.[244]

Thus legal conflicts in the strict sense mark a special form of legal paradoxes and the degree of conflict may vary similar to the distinct degrees of contradiction rooted in paradoxes, enantioses or oxymora. The issue of legal conflicts at the international level has become more serious given the increasing juridification and fragmentation of international law.[245] Thus, it is our dominant conception of a global legal order through the lens of the territorial nation state that hinders a flourishing life in political, economic, cultural and even legal terms. The flaw in the legal design becomes obvious by the existence of a specific category of law devoted to "international" legal conflicts. This category of law is called "conflict of laws" (or private international law). Historically, this category of law is the result of the division of the Earth into "distinct Nations, inhabiting different regions, speaking different languages, engaged in different pursuits, and attached to different forms of government".[246] The fact that conflict of laws still persists as

241 See C. Wilfred Jenks, "The Conflict of Law-Making Treaties" (1953) *British Yearbook of International Law* 401 at 425–426.

242 *Ibid* at 426.

243 See also Chaïm Perelman, "Les antinomies en droit" (1964) 18 *Dialectica* 392 at 400.

244 Fletcher, "Paradoxes in Legal Thought", *supra* note 233 at 1263 [footnotes omitted].

245 See also International Law Commission (ILC), *Fragmentation of International Law: Difficulties Arising from the Diversification and Expansion of International Law*, A/CN.4/L.682 (13 April 2006).

246 See *e.g.* Joseph Story, *Commentaries on the Conflict of Laws, Foreign and Domestic, in regard to Contracts, Rights and Remedies*, 2nd ed (London: A. Maxwell, 1841) at 1.

a category today is more the result of a flawed conception of "international law" caused by another antinomy, namely the distinction between public international and private international law.[247] The continuing separation between public international and private international law is still a major obstacle to the formulation of a truly global legal order. At the same time, the continuing distinction also proves, as outlined at the outset, that most conflicts are not an element of reality but, instead, a category and the result of the human mind and, subsequently, also of human doing.[248]

But legal conflicts caused by fragmentation are by no means limited to international law and also arise at the national level. Therefore, a cognitive change needs to be accomplished first before meaningful changes in both national and international law can materialize. But even changes in the mind often come only either by meeting with a major catastrophe, like the two World Wars or other major conflicts and cataclysms. This time, hopefully, changes in the mind will come gradually through greater awareness and better means of communication between people and governments around the world. Accepting differences and most of all contradictions, like in dialetheism, may prove a first step on a long journey. This is why creating a common language based on oxymoronic concepts can help to pave the way for new and more coherent cognitive modes of perception and reasoning to be developed. The acceptance of contradictions may provide the foundation for a more peaceful and sustainable strategy that allows the system of governance of global affairs to improve altogether.

To test the claim that cognitive changes in the form of dialetheism are required for the solution and even prevention of legal paradoxes, it is necessary to look for various solutions that have been proposed. To begin with the gallows paradox formulated by Cervantes, mentioned above,[249] the judge faces the dilemma of either hanging the man who – telling the truth – said he would be hanged, or acquitting him in the face of a lie. The solution to this paradox ends in a paradox, namely, that by taking the correct decision (acquittal) the judge creates injustice and by taking the wrong decision (hanging) would establish justice. So how to solve it? As one solution it was proposed to hang half of the man and acquit the other half, which in reality would not be feasible as it would result in the death of the man. Eventually, Cervantes himself solves the paradox by letting Sancho acquit the man due to the following reasoning:

> "See here, my good sir," said Sancho, "either I am a blockhead or this man you speak of deserves to die as much as he deserves to live and cross the bridge; for if the truth saves him, the lie equally condemns him. And this

247 See also Rostam J. Neuwirth, "International Law and the Public/Private Law Distinction" (2000) 55(4) *Zeitschrift für öffentliches Recht* 393 and Alex Mills, "Antinomies of Public and Private at the Foundations of International Investment Law and Arbitration" (2011) 14(2) *Journal of International Economic Law* 469.

248 See Negoita, *supra* note 1 at 98.

249 See in Section VII.1, Miguel de Cervantes Saavedra, *Don Quixote de la Mancha* (New York: Modern Library, 1998).

> being the case, as indeed it is, it is my opinion that you should go back and tell those gentlemen who sent you to me that, since there is as much reason for acquitting as for condemning him, they ought to let him go free, as it is always more praiseworthy to do good than to do harm. [...]
>
> "When justice was in doubt," he said, "I was to lean to the side of mercy; and I thank God that I happened to recollect it just now, for it fits this case as if made for it."[250]

Here it is the application of Chatton's anti-razor by way of an extension of reasoning to greater virtues that prompts the decision to let him go free. It is the application of principle(s) (*in dubio mitius* and *in dubio pro reo*; principles of applying the "milder law" or deciding in favour of the accused, in line with the presumption of innocence) prevailing over the strict application of the rule that decides the outcome of the case.

A similar reasoning is also at the heart of the so-called "Radbruch formula", named after the German jurist Gustav Radbruch who – in the wake of the negative experiences with the judiciary of Nazi Germany – proposed a solution to the dilemma between positive law and justice. He argued for the prevalence of justice over positive law in cases where valid laws disregard the goals of justice.[251] Here too is an extension of the existing knowledge, the taking into account of a wider set of facts or considerations.

An opposite way to solve paradoxes is to "shave off" an element in line with Ockham's razor by simply "cancelling" one of its contradicting presuppositions.[252] This also seems a way that Nicholas Rescher suggests by giving the following solution to the paradox:

> In the circumstances the tacit premiss of the situation "The law is to be obeyed: what is done should be in accordance with the law" needs to be abandoned in the case at hand precisely because this case is so constructed that there just is no possible way for the law to be obeyed. The paradox is thus dissolved by noting that it rests on the mistaken presupposition that the legal code's stipulation is a meaningful law that can and should always be obeyed.[253]

In both cases, the results obtained may be satisfactory in terms of justice being served but they are still unsatisfactory in terms of logic and the dominant mode of dualistic reasoning. The reason is that they do not alter the mode of thinking itself but merely tamper with the presumptions.

250 *Ibid* at 997.

251 See Gustav Radbruch, "Gesetzliches Unrecht und übergesetzliches Recht" (1946) 1(5) *Süddeutsche Juristen-Zeitung* 105 at 107.

252 See Mikko Yrjönsuuri, "Treatments of the Paradoxes of Self-Reference" in Dov M. Gabbay and John Woods (eds), *Handbook of the History of Logic: Mediaeval and Renaissance Logic*, vol 2 (Amsterdam: Elsevier, 2008) 579 at 581.

253 Rescher, *Paradoxes*, *supra* note 36 at 63.

Similarly, law can serve the objectives of justice better by simply preventing bad laws that lead to contradictions being adopted in the first place. Or else, if they have been adopted, they should be quickly repealed and replaced by no laws at all or at least better ones. The same amendment should also take place in case of the emergence of new facts, presented by way of neologisms in the disguise of oxymora or paradoxes, which may render the laws in force obsolete.

A more sustainable approach to legal paradoxes in the service of justice appears to lie in a change in the cognitive approach. Such change could mean the a priori acceptance of contradictions, which could be complemented by a dynamic rather than static reading of laws. Such a dynamic reading must be complemented by their more dialetheic and holistic (or contextual and teleological) rather than dialectical and atomistic (or textual) interpretation and implementation. The challenges with regard to justice in law have also been aptly summarized by the following paragraph:

> It needs to be reminded constantly that law is a means to justice, which cannot be realised in an unbending order of any authority or convention, but through a balance of considerations for the elements of order as well as its lively counterpart, chaos. Only then a productive equilibrium of stability and dynamism, of generality and specialty, and of unity and diversity can be achieved.[254]

In the pursuit of justice, it is not true that law uses or has always used dualistic reasoning and been hostile to a more inclusive or holistic mode of legal reasoning. This seems more the result of an extreme (and meanwhile obsolete) obsession with legal positivism under the pretext of a false scientific paradigm. For instance, Talmudic law avails itself of the concept of ***lifnim mishurat hadin***, which reflects the distinction between the letter and the spirit of the law or that which is "within the line of the law" and "that which goes beyond the boundaries of the law".[255] ***Lifnim mishurat hadin*** can be regarded as a judicial standard that can also be used to solve legal paradoxes. The reason is that the Talmudic legal tradition struggled with these divisions and, to produce just results, the Sages used concepts like ***lifnim mishurat hadin*** to find that which goes beyond the boundaries of the law, which meant "the use of the legal system as whole, its positive law and as well its superseded law".[256]

It seems thus that many propositions formulated in the context of dialethism, such as notably the acceptance of contradictions per se, a more dynamic mode of reasoning and more inclusive mode of logic, may better serve the role of law in the pursuit of greater justice. In this regard, accepting contradictions laid down in

254 See Emir Kaya, "Injustice as a Judicial Product: A Problematic Tendency in Legal Thinking and Practice" in Şefika Şule Erçetin and Santo Banerjee (eds), *Chaos, Complexity and Leadership* (Cham: Springer, 2013) 255 at 259.

255 Saul J. Berman, "Lifnim Mishurat Hadin (II)" (1975) 26(1–2) *Journal of Jewish Studies* 86 at 86.

256 *Ibid* at 193.

paradoxes as potentially true may be helpful.[257] This possibility is already reflected in the creeping codification of oxymoronic terms in different legal instruments, such as culture industry in international trade law, or as legal concepts in law and policy discourses, like "regulatory coopetition", "multilateralizing regionalism" as well as "a regionalization of multilateralism".

As for dialetheic reasoning in law by way of using the legal syllogism, it is the American poet Wallace Stevens who points the way for lawyers in his poem "Connoisseur of Chaos", which reads:

> A. A violent order is disorder; and
> B. A great disorder is an order. **These**
> **Two things are one.** (Pages of illustrations.)[258]

In legal practice, it means that whenever a fundamental dichotomy is encountered, the judge or decision maker is called upon, by applying the law of complementarity, to search for the best possible ways to reconcile their apparent contradiction. A first step towards their reconciliation may lie in the detection of a paradox and/or the formulation of an oxymoron. For instance, the apparent dichotomy of developing versus developed countries has been met by various paradoxes. One example is Arnold Beisser's "paradoxical theory of change", which – put briefly – states that "change occurs when one becomes what he is, not when he tries to become what he is not".[259] Another paradox is the "Lucas paradox", which found that, counter to neoclassical economic predictions, in reality capital does not flow from richer to poorer countries.[260] Similarly, their apparent differences and resulting irreconcilability, however, has been transcended by the formulation of the oxymoron of "sustainable development". Another way of reconciling the flawed distinction is to emphasize the changing nature of life, which means that every country ought to be a "developing country" as time and the world never stand still, which is why a country is never "developed" forever.[261]

The response to paradoxes arising from rigid dichotomies by new essentially oxymoronic concepts, such as oxymora, however, helps to increase the awareness about the potential intrinsic mutual relations and their possible complementarity.

257 See also Niklas Luhmann, "The Third Question: The Creative Use of Paradoxes in Law and Legal History" (1988) 15(2) *Journal of Law & Society* 153 and H. Buch, "Conception dialectique des antinomies juridiques" (1964) 18 *Dialectica* 372 at 391.

258 Wallace Stevens, *The Collected Poems of Wallace Stevens* (New York: Vintage Books, 1990) at 215.

259 Arnold Beisser, "A Paradoxical Theory of Change" in Joen Fagan and Irma Lee Shepherd (eds), *Gestalt Therapy Now: Theory, Techniques, Applications* (Palo Alto: Science and Behavior Books, 1970) 77 at 77.

260 See Robert Lucas, "Why Doesn't Capital Flow from Rich to Poor Countries?" (1990) 80(2) *American Economic Review* 92 at 92.

261 See Rostam J. Neuwirth, "Global Law and Sustainable Development: Change and the 'Developing-Developed Country' Terminology" (2016) 29(4) *European Journal of Development Research* 911.

Formulating an oxymoron does not solve a paradox, yet it has been stated that before paradoxes or antinomies can be resolved, they also need to be recognized as such.[262] Once they have been recognized, the formulation of oxymora may help their resolution as they intensify the degree of contradiction. Eventually then, at one point, the intensification of cognitive conflicts engendered by the oxymoronic concept will push open a door to a new understanding similar to koans inciting *satori*. Before this can happen, certain criteria can help to dissolve antinomies vested in paradoxes. In this regard, Noberto Bobbio lists as the most commonly used criteria in law those of time, hierarchy, and specialty between conflicting laws or norms.[263] In international law, these criteria are part of the customary rules of interpretation and are known as the hierarchical principle that the higher law (or treaty) prevails over the lower law, the *lex posterior* principle that the later law prevails over the earlier law, and the *lex specialis* principle according to which the special law prevails over the general law.[264] However, even these conflict of law solving principles may also clash with each other, which can give rise to new paradoxes. One such paradox is when there is an antinomy between the different criteria to resolve antinomies or when a criterion to resolve a conflict between criteria is missing. This is why, in the end, Noberto Bobbio concludes that the only viable criterion for the solution of a conflict between two equal criteria is the choice of the more "just" one.[265]

This last point confirms again that paradoxes usually breed paradoxes. Or else, a common feature of contradictions is their self-referential character, which ends in a loop of reasoning that is difficult to exit from. Nonetheless, the preceding paragraphs have shown that the law or lawyers' minds are quite creative in their efforts to resolve legal paradoxes. The different approaches include denial, discounting, differentiation and dialectical thinking. Lawyers may also postpone problems rooted in legal paradoxes to a distant day and try to let time solve the problem for them. Others have called for dialetheism yielding perhaps new modes of fuzzy thinking and the use of novel forms of legal logic. Such calls already resonate in lawyers formulating legally oxymoronic concepts. In sum, the vast evidence before us suggests that solutions must be sought, as George P. Fletcher put it, not only for the "deeper causes of the legal premises that guide our thinking",[266] but also simultaneously in potentially higher forms of reality. For the parallel realization of both ends, essentially oxymoronic concepts may be called on to perform an important role, as they mark a gradual extension of legal reasoning from a primarily dualistic to a more oxymoronic mode of thinking.

262 See Norberto Bobbio, "Des critères pour résoudre les antinomies" (1964) 18 *Dialectica* 237 at 237.

263 *Ibid* at 241.

264 See *e.g.* Oliver Dörr and Kirsten Schmalenbach (eds), *Vienna Convention on the Law of Treaties* (Berlin: Springer, 2012) 505.

265 Bobbio, *supra* note 262 at 258.

266 Fletcher, "Paradoxes in Legal Thought", *supra* note 233 at 1292.

They also indicate the emergence of a universal language for the global community regardless of cultural and other differences. The reason is that essentially oxymoronic concepts coupled with dialetheism formulated in the West have also proved to be tools similar to the concepts of koans and *chung yung* used in the East. In their further combination and based on a fruitful joint debate, they may thus pave the way to a common language that is urgently needed to move from a stage of theorizing to creating a truly global legal order. To elucidate this potentially constructive role, it is after pondering on oxymora *in* law that the analysis shifts to their role *for* law. It aims to try to outline the fundamental features of a future global body of laws that is united in its diversity under the term "mnemonic law".

9 Law for the time of oxymora

Mnemonic law

If two contrary actions be excited in the same subject, a change must necessarily take place in both, or in one alone, until they cease to be contrary.[1]

Law is closely related to and even dependent upon art and science. This is because both art and science provide useful insights into human nature, its principal desires and its underlying cognitive processes. The separation between art and science can also be taken as a metaphor for the separation between the left and the right hemispheres of the brain, which also represents the separation of rational thoughts from emotional feelings. They also stand for other more fundamental dichotomies applied to human nature, such as body and mind, life and death, as well as other unsolved mysteries often expressed through dichotomies. And oxymoronic language is applied to bridge and overcome the gaps created by these various separations expressed in dichotomies. A powerful argument against these separations as reflected in reductionism is that "explanation is not understanding".[2] Explanation may be a step towards understanding but it cannot replace it.

Generally, the features of human nature surface in language and other means of communication accessed by the senses. In this regard, art and science not only concur in the use of oxymoronic concepts but are also connected by creativity that transforms ideas from the world of thoughts into that of facts. Their connection is manifest also in technology, which etymologically refers to both artistic and scientific skills used creatively. Literally, creativity in the sense of connecting the ideal with the real is also an important function of law. Hence, the shift from contestation by conflict to convergence by contradiction that is reflected in language by a move from essentially contested to essentially oxymoronic concepts also affects the separate classification of the artistic and the scientific world. The impact of essentially oxymoronic concepts as a common language of and for both requires the search for novel ways for their combined consideration after centuries of mutual separation. At the same time, essentially oxymoronic concepts were also found to play an ever increasing role in law, both in action and

1 Benedict de Spinoza, *Ethics* (New York: G.P. Putnam's Sons, 1888) at 303.
2 See Erwin Chargaff, "In Dispraise of Reductionism" (1997) 47(11) *BioScience* 795 at 796.

in books. As in art and science, by virtue of their intrinsic but varying degrees of contradiction, they also "puzzle" in law. The quest for possible solutions to these contradictions has yielded several creative approaches at the level of the mind and cognition. These creative approaches, whether called "paradoxical", "fuzzy" or "oxymoronic thinking" all share a critical stance towards traditional or well-established modes of primarily dualistic thinking and classical (binary) logic. An important feature of all of them, however, is that they do not propose radically to change our thinking by replacing the older modes of thought by newer ones. In lieu, they offer continuity as they are inclusive and merely propose to expand the existing cognitive framework by another layer so as to enhance our understanding of the world around us.

With regard to the understanding of the world around us, essentially oxymoronic concepts, whether used in art, science or law or merely chitchat, carry important messages for the future. To recall briefly, oxymora and paradoxes first and foremost reflect the deficiencies in the processes underlying our perception as well as its causal cognitive modes. Most importantly, they represent a tool to express the serious challenges arising from "change". The challenge is serious as we seem to face changes even in the perception of change, viz. an acceleration of the pace with which change is perceived. The increase in the speed with which we notice change has serious repercussions for how we perceive, decide and accordingly take action. In brief, it affects the totality of how we organize life in this world. The same acceleration threatens to undermine the accuracy of concepts used to describe and make sense of reality before deciding on future actions to be taken accordingly. What is affecting every individual is also taking place collectively, as is noticeable in the challenges that change poses to the integrity of law in the sense of being able to provide certainty and predictability. In this regard, essentially oxymoronic concepts have the advantage that they allow for change, perceived as processes oscillating between two polar extremes, to be described more accurately. Thus, they take a different approach to time, as they shift the descriptive accuracy from a static to a more dynamic view. Taking the oxymoronic term of "sustainable development" as an example, it helps to address a complex global phenomenon of many facets, which hitherto has been described by the simplified (and false) distinction of "developing vs developed countries" (which logically should have been framed as "developing versus non-developing countries"). In short, oxymora allow, by stretching the time frame, to describe and communicate changes and their possible consequences better. This is why ultimately we will also need to inquire what they want to tell us about the nature of our perception of time.

Yet, this advantage of stretching the time frame of our observation is also their strong disadvantage. The reason is that oxymoronic language shocks, puzzles and creates confusion by presenting us with apparent contradictions. By old habits rooted in dual thinking modes, contradictions make us uncomfortable; they cause an irritation in our minds as they seemingly harbour uncertainty. And these cognitive modes were said to be hard to change, as they are either innate or at least "die hard".[3] Oxymora and paradoxes alike confront us with contradictions of varying degrees. In art as in mysticism, they form the basis for the expression of the ineffable. They do not express the world as it is but perhaps as it may, could or will be. Again, they indicate change. In science too, their inherent dynamism means they really expose the ephemeral nature of scientific fact or knowledge. They show how little we actually understand in scientific terms. Last but not least, in law, by blurring former distinctions laid down in traditional dichotomies they gravely challenge our sense for and belief in justice. In sum, essentially oxymoronic concepts seem to render us powerless, like a leaf floating down a river, a river that we cannot step into even once.

Facing paradoxes and oxymora, such a feeling seems justified as dictionaries define them as "contrary to received opinion", "essentially absurd", "self-contradictory" and "conflicting with preconceived notions of what is reasonable or possible".[4] In scientific language, they are described as expressing "instances where current knowledge may be deficient, and thus predictions based on such knowledge may be inconsistent with actual events or findings".[5] But these brief quotes only represent half of the truth, as both the dictionary definitions also add that they are just "seemingly absurd though perhaps really well-founded".[6] By the same token, scientists also add that they "offer powerful opportunities to test models and conceptual frameworks, and to enable true 'paradigm shifts' in certain areas of scientific inquiry".[7] These additional facets shift the focus of essentially oxymoronic concepts from the descriptions of a given status quo to one of a future potential state of affairs. This is the quality that now deserves attention and which in the area of law means to ask what lessons can be learned from the findings in the previous chapters. It also means to inquire what changes the present understanding of law and legal science needs to accept in its own sphere before it can constructively contribute to the realization of desired changes in the world.

Once the relevant changes in legal science have been accommodated, it is important to lead a constructive debate about how and through what instruments law can effectuate these desired changes. Such debate must be accompanied by a parallel process of contrasting past problems with future trends. This process is warranted if law wants to prepare for the challenges that the future will eventually bring. Ultimately, it may mean to follow closely changes in all areas of human activity in a coherent way without giving particular preference to a single area. Paradoxically, it may mean to remain open, flexible and

3 See Gabriel Segal, "Poverty of Stimulus Arguments Concerning Language and Folk Psychology" in Peter Carruthers, Stephen Laurence and Stephen Stich, *The Innate Mind: Foundations and the Future*, vol 3 (Oxford: Oxford University Press, 2008) 90 at 101.

4 See H. W. Fowler and F. G. Fowler (eds), *The Concise Oxford Dictionary of Current English* (Oxford: Clarendon Press, 1919) at 593.

5 See Narinder Kapur et al., "The Paradoxical Nature of Nature" in Narinder Kapur (ed), *The Paradoxical Brain* (Cambridge: Cambridge University Press, 2011) 1 at 1.

6 See Fowler and Fowler, *supra* note 4 at 593.

7 See Kapur et al., *supra* note 5 at 1.

dynamic if desiring to provide at least some degree of certainty and predictability. Ultimately, as proposed solutions to legal paradoxes lead to more legal paradoxes, it will also require a drastic change in the basic assumptions we have about human nature and the phenomena we perceive. This is why real, measurable changes in law and legal (as well as political) institutions require cognitive changes in the first place. This being a kind of paradox itself, like the global governance paradox, means that some changes will come from both the cognitive and the legal sphere, as both seem to be mysteriously and paradoxically linked.

As a first step taken in law, George P. Fletcher concluded that for contradictions to be avoided it is necessary to reach a "deeper understanding of the legal premises that guide our thinking".[8] In this context, essentially oxymoronic concepts may perform an important role as they may slowly trigger the cognitive and even genetic changes necessary for dissolving contradictions between dichotomies, such as nature and nurture or language and genes. These changes will manifest themselves by their increasing penetration of public, scientific and other discourses. Their effects will be felt first gradually and later suddenly. Thus, oxymoronic language is likely to have not an immediate but rather an intermediate impact, where time will be a crucial factor. Yet, it is already recommended to prepare actively for these changes before they manifest themselves. In the legal realm, this must be done through the formulation of ideas and concepts adequate for the challenges coming with these changes. Given that these challenges for law pose a conceptual challenge to the mind, it is in the sphere of law and the mind that the responses need to be sought. The intrinsic connection between law and the mind was expressed by the term "law as mnemonics".[9] Since then significant progress has been made in neuroscience, which is also manifest in various technological innovations, such as those described as "virtual reality". Therefore, it is now possible to advance the debate by designating the future of law as one of a "global mnemonic law".

9.1 Global law and mnemonics: the challenges

> *Our mind is capable of passing beyond the dividing line we have drawn for it. Beyond the pairs of opposites of which the world consists, other, new insights begin.*[10]

For law facing global challenges in the form of an increasing diversity and complexity, the concept of "mnemonic law" is proposed as a point of departure for the search for novel solutions in line with the rising interest in cognitive science.

8 George P. Fletcher, "Paradoxes in Legal Thought" (1985) 85(6) *Columbia Law Review* 1263 at 1292.

9 See Rostam J. Neuwirth, "Law as Mnemonics: The Mind as the Prime Source of Normativity" (2008) 2(1) *European Journal of Legal Studies* 143 at 151.

10 See Hermann Hesse, *Stories of Five Decades* (New York: Farrar Straus & Giroux, 1973) at 263.

The proposal is based on the observation that all laws have their origin in the mind and that there may be need to reexamine our fundamental premises.[11]

In the quest for the resolution of problems of paradoxes, mnemonics, a term derived from the Greek goddess of memory called Mnemonsyne, carries the proposition that the mind is the prime source of law and the nomos (legal universe). As such, the mind is both the root of the problems as well as the point of departure for their workable solutions. This is where mnemonics is called to play an important role. Generally, mnemonics can be defined as both the art and science of "the study and development of systems for improving and aiding the memory".[12] Arguably, this definition matches one of the primary but most difficult functions of law, namely to reconcile as the irreconcilable the past with the future. It means that law functions as a reminder of past wrongs as a tool to avoid them in the future. This function combines a twofold and closely intertwined task for law, namely to function simultaneously as a mnemonic trace of lessons learned in the past and as a mnemonic device for the realization of objectives formulated for the future.

The significance of mnemonics for law is that memory is a function central to "self-consciousness" operating through the mind served by the known and possibly also the unknown senses. A loss of memory, however, leads directly to a loss of identity.[13] By analogy, the law can be seen as the memory of the community in its pursuit of justice or other objectives.[14] Law as the memory of justice also functions through several "sense organs", including visible and invisible ones, which correspond to the distinction between known and unknown senses in humans. The legal sensors are various legal instruments (from case law to international agreements and constitutions) or legal institutions (from courts to ombudsmen and public authorities) that together systematically collect and process relevant experiences. As memory constitutes a personality, law also creates identity in the form of "legal personality", be it in the form of the constitution of a state, a multilateral organization or a company. By the same token, the loss of law's senses leads to a loss of collective memory, which – manifest in a loss of the rule of law – leads to chaos and disintegration of the legal entity concerned.

In addition to pioneering works on law and the mind by jurists like Jerome Frank, the significance of mnemonics for law is also supported by the perception of "law as a social medicine", as Pierre Lepaulle had convincingly phrased it.[15] The comparison between law and medicine is well founded, as they were both

11 Fletcher, "Paradoxes in Legal Thought", *supra* note 8 at 1263 [footnotes omitted].

12 See also Eric Partridge, *Origins: A Short Etymological Dictionary of Modern English*, 4th ed (London: Routledge, 1966) at 1991 and Angus Stevenson and Maurice Waite (eds), *Concise Oxford English Dictionary*, 12th ed (Oxford: Oxford University Press, 2011) at 918.

13 See Louis H. Stewart, *Changemakers: A Jungian Perspective on Sibling Position and the Family Atmosphere* (London: Routledge, 1992) at 122.

14 See also Peter Goodrich, *Languages of Law: From Logics of Memory to Nomadic Masks* (London: George Weidenfeld and Nicolson, 1990) at vii and 32–43.

15 Pierre Lepaulle, "The Function of Comparative Law with a Critique of Sociological Jurisprudence" (1922) 35(7) *Harvard Law Reveiw* 838 at 838.

considered an art but "claimed for themselves the status of science".[16] The shift in law's focus from the tangible to the intangible world is reflected in the growing – but still widely neglected – problem in medicine globally of mental illness.[17] It thus corresponds to trends witnessing an increasing rise of the noosphere, neuroscience or cognitive studies, to mention but a few. According to these trends of an increasing significance of the immaterial, intellectual or virtual world, law will ideally function both as a general practitioner and a psychoanalyst. By the same token, the optimal medical approach to healthcare would be a holistic therapeutic approach that combines both aspects of physical and mental health with the use of conventional and traditional medicines.[18]

The role of the mind for law has also been recognized internationally in the Constitution of UNESCO, which declares: "[T]hat since wars begin in the minds of men, it is in the minds of men that the defences of peace must be constructed".[19] The emphasis on the mind comes as little surprise to those familiar with UNESCO being the successor of the International Commission for Intellectual Cooperation created in 1921 – a quite visionary role at the time, which it should revive in the face of new threats and challenges in the global community.[20]

Ultimately, mnemonic law can also be taken as a response to the insights gained from the study of the links between law and language, as for instance reflected in the present shift from essentially contested to oxymoronic concepts. As language reflects the deeper cognitive processes, it also combines not only the past and the present but also holds the key to future trends. Moreover, the emergence of a common language for humanity has also been called the prerequisite for the establishment of a global legal order. Therefore, it is advocated that the mind offers itself as the adequate foundation on which a future legal order can be built.

Finally, a last argument for mnemonic law or the mind as the point of departure for the establishment of the future global legal order comes from a brief glimpse at some of the major global problems and challenges for their resolution. In the search for a synopsis of the most serious global problems, the Millennium

16 See Ian Maclean, "Evidence, Logic, the Rule and the Exception in Renaissance Law and Medicine" (2000) 5(3) *Early Science and Medicine* 227 at 229–230 [footnote omitted].

17 See *e.g.* Edwin Fuller Torrey and Judy Miller, *The Invisible Plague: The Rise of Mental Illness from 1750 to the Present* (New Brunswick: Rutgers University Press, 2001) and Robert Whitaker, *Anatomy of an Epidemic: Magic Bullets, Psychiatric Drugs, and the Astonishing Rise of Mental Illness in America* (New York: Crown Publishers, 2010); but see the World Health Organization (WHO), *Mental Health Action Plan 2013–2020* (Geneva: WHO, 2013).

18 See also Rostam J. Neuwirth and Alexandr Svetlicinii, "Law as a Social Medicine: Enhancing International Inter-Regime Regulatory Coopetition as a Means for the Establishment of a Global Health Governance Framework" (2015) 36 (3–4) *The Journal of Legal Medicine* 330.

19 Recital 1 of the Preamble of the *Constitution of the United Nations Educational, Scientific and Cultural Organization (UNESCO)*, signed at London on November 16, 1945, 4 U.N.T.S. 275 (entry into force: November 4, 1946).

20 See Rostam J. Neuwirth, "The UNESCO Convention and Future Technologies: 'A Journey to the Center of Cultural Law and Policymaking'" in Lilian Hanania-Richieri and Anne-Thida Nodorom (eds), *Diversity of Cultural Expressions in the Digital Era* (Buenos Aires: TESEO, 2016) 85 at 102.

Development Goals (MDGs) provide a useful starting point.[21] Formulated at the turn of the millennium, they listed eight objectives to be realized in 2015, related mostly to the alleviation of poverty as well as improvements in education and health around the world. Tellingly, while some uneven progress was made, the overall results are far from being satisfactory.[22] Thus, to try to complete what the MDGs did not achieve, the 2015 Sustainable Development Goals (SDGs) were formulated, which list 17 broad objectives for global action to be achieved by 2030.[23] The 17 areas are broader in scope than the MDGs and include goals formulated for various issues ranging from poverty, health and education, to energy, economic growth, the environment, peace and stability.[24] Looking at daily media reports also produces a similar picture of the contemporary world that is struggling with wars and violent conflicts, terrorism, environmental and health threats like global climate change, earthquakes, or pollution, poverty and hunger, exclusion and discrimination, as well as numerous economic problems, to mention but a few.

However, as selected scientific publications indicate, the main problem with a mere listing of serious global problems urgently needing immediate action is that their classification, in particular in a hierarchical ordering, is impossible. This task seems impossible because of the scientific uncertainties, the many paradoxes that govern the process of data gathering and the establishment of their respective causal links. For instance, taking perhaps the most destructive form of human behaviour, it is hard to establish and agree on what causes wars and conflicts.[25] A long scientific study of possible causes of war sums up the problem by concluding that there is no "single theory that alone can account for war as a general phenomenon" and instead there are "several islands of theory that have achieved partial validation".[26] Similar difficulties exist in the search for the causes of even a specific war or conflict.[27] It is equally difficult to establish a link between causes and their effects, such as counting the precise financial costs or human fatalities related to wars.[28] With these uncertainties surrounding the causes and effects of

21 United Nations, *Millennium Development Declaration*, General Assembly A/RES/55/2 (18 September 2000).

22 United Nations, *The Millennium Development Goals Report 2015* (New York: United Nations, 2015) at 3 and 8.

23 United Nations, *Transforming Our World: The 2030 Agenda for Sustainable Development*, General Assembly A/RES/70/1 (21 October 2015).

24 *Ibid* at 14.

25 See *e.g.* Jack S. Levy and William R. Thompson, *Causes of War* (Chichester: John Wiley & Sons, 2010) at 1–2.

26 See Greg Cashman, *What Causes War?: An Introduction to Theories of International Conflict*, 2nd ed (Lanham: Rowman & Littlefield Publishers, 2013) at 477.

27 See *e.g.* Shane Mountjoy, *Causes of the Civil War: The Differences Between the North and South* (New York: Chelsea House, 2009) at 14 and Mark Hewitson, *Germany and the Causes of the First World War* (London: Bloomsbury Academic, 2004) at 1.

28 See *e.g.* Joseph Stiglitz and Linda Nilmes, *The Three Trillion Dollar War: The True Cost of the Iraq Conflict* (London: Penguin Books, 2008) at 3–31 and Bethany Lacina and Nils Peter Gleditsch, "Monitoring Trends in Global Combat: A New Dataset of Battle Deaths" (2005) 21(2–3) *European Journal of Population* 145.

wars and conflicts, aggravated by their changing nature, it is no surprise that there is doubt about the best possible strategy to prevent them for the future.[29]

Like war,[30] other contested concepts used to classify serious global problems, such as culture,[31] poverty,[32] health,[33] environment[34] and sustainable development,[35] face similar conceptual and taxonomic challenges. Taking development as an example, it is not clear which factor is most successful in contributing to its objectives in any country or what to include or prioritize in the formulation of development policies. Is it policies related to the economy, to education, health, poverty alleviation or culture? The same troubles occupy international trade policies in their relation to other, or falsely called "non-trade", policies, as the "trade linkage debate" addresses them. Here, too, various "trade and . . ." pairs exist, but their mutual hierarchical relation (if any) is disputed, as is the principal question of whether trade should prevail over any of these "non-trade concerns". Most likely, it is all of them combined, as they are all inextricably linked. However, this poses a conceptual challenge, one that may explain why so many of them are also framed in terms of oxymoronic language.

Hence, these problems are all related to complexity, which is usually met by attempts to isolate particular areas and subject them to separate institutions, which – at the global level – is reflected in an increasing division of labour between international bodies and similar agencies. The tendency to "isolate" is also in line with the ongoing trend of specialization in science, which continues to erode the unity of science and of art. The fragmentation of politics and science is therefore mainly a conceptual problem, as can be seen from many conflicting views about competences. These conceptual conflicts surface in the different and frequently changing terminologies and classifications used to group different areas under the portfolio of a ministry. The history of the structural organization of various ministries often shows that, as a matter of fact, almost any area can be and has been linked with another since every area is somehow connected. The same can be seen at the international level, with the many overlaps in or even conflicts between the

29 See also Seyom Brown, *The Causes and Prevention of War*, 2nd ed (New York: MacMillan Education, 1994) at 247.

30 See Stanley Hauerwas, "Sacrificing the Sacrifices of War" in Linda Hogan and Dylan Lehrke (eds), *Religion and the Politics of Peace and Conflict* (Eugene: Pickwick, 2009) 83 at 87 (Fn 12).

31 See *e.g.* Lisa Harrison, Adrian Little and Edward Lock, *Politics: The Key Concepts* (London: Routledge, 2015) at 41.

32 See *e.g.* Gottfried Schweiger and Gunter Graf, *A Philosophical Examination of Social Justice and Child Poverty* (New York: Palgrave Macmillan, 2015) at 2.

33 See *e.g.* A. Edgar, "Health Care Allocation, Public Consultation and the Concept of 'Health'" (1998) 6(3) *Health Care Analysis* 193 at 197.

34 See *e.g.* John Barry, *Environment and Social Theory* (London: Routledge, 1999) at 12.

35 See *e.g.* Michael Jacobs, "Sustainable Development as a Contested Concept" in Andrew Dobson (ed), *Fairness and Futurity: Essays on Environmental Sustainability and Social Justice* (Oxford: Oxford University Press, 2002) 21 and Steve Connelly, "Mapping Sustainable Development as a Contested Concept" (2007) 12(3) *Local Environment: The International Journal of Justice and Sustainability* 259 at 260 and 262.

activities of distinct international organizations as the failed initiative of the UN to "deliver as one" shows.[36]

Therefore, the conceptual problems of finding the appropriate name for a specific area of policymaking or scientific research is really just the tip of the iceberg of much deeper problems. These problems are of a cognitive nature, rooted in the depths of the mind. Expressed by complexity, these problems become manifest as information overload, which was said to occur when "the amount of input to a system exceeds its processing capacity", which usually results in a reduction in decision quality due to the limited cognitive processing capacity by decision makers.[37]

Thus complexity may reduce the quality of our decisions and the reason given was that "if overstimulation at the sensory level increases the distortion with which we perceive reality, cognitive overstimulation interferes with our ability to 'think'".[38] Thus, the ability to think adequately is closely connected with the possible solutions to the various problems presented to us. The same connection is also reflected in the statement that "conflict is a category of man's mind, not in itself an element of reality".[39] In this regard, it is also no coincidence that the verb "isolate" is etymologically related to "island",[40] which has been used to emphasize the deficiencies in our conceptual and cognitive approaches to the complexity governing our lives at present. These deficiencies have been outlined as follows:

> No game is an island. Even so, people draw boundaries and divide the world up into many separate games. It's easy to fall into the trap of analyzing these separate games in isolation—imagining that there's no larger game. The problem is that mental boundaries aren't real boundaries—there are no real boundaries. Every game is linked to other games: a game in one place affects games elsewhere, and a game today influences games tomorrow. Even the mere anticipation of tomorrow's game influences today's.[41]

In this quote the term "game" could be replaced by any other term, such as "scientific field", "policy area", "law" as well as "problem" or "word", as everything seems to be and can be connected. Instead, we still tend to fall into the same trap

36 See United Nations High Level Panel on Coherence, *Delivering as one: Report of the High-level Panel on United Nations System-wide Coherence in the Areas of Development, Humanitarian Assistance and the Environment*, G.A. A/61/583 (9 November 2006).

37 See Cheri Speier, Joseph Valacich and Iris Vessey, "The Influence of Task Interruption on Individual Decision Making: An Information Overload Perspective" (1999) 30(2) *Decision Sciences* 337.

38 See Alvin Toffler, *Future Shock* (London: Pan Books, 1971) at 318.

39 See Constantin Virgil Negoita, "Cybernetics and Society" (1982) 11(2) *Kybernetes* 97 at 98.

40 See Ernest Klein, *A Comprehensive Etymological Dictionary of the English Language*, vol I (Amsterdam: Elsevier, 1966) at 818.

41 See Adam M. Brandenburger and Barry J. Nalebuff, *Co-opetition: A Revolution Mindset That Combines Competition and Cooperation: The Game Theory Strategy That's Changing the Game of Business* (New York: Doubleday, 1996) at 234.

of using solely analytical thinking without ever trying to synthesize the findings. It is no coincidence either that such critical reflection on our dominant approach to almost every area in life or politics comes from the authors of a book that uses an oxymoronic title. However, even a scholar of global governance has come to a similar conclusion for law and legal problems, when he writes:

> It is hard to think of a legal problem which does not cross disciplinary and national boundaries and it is common for internationalists themselves to stretch across public and private law, to teach about trade and security and development, dipping into national and comparative law as they do.[42]

The dangers related to the fragmentation of international law have also been compared to a sea of "self-contained islands of international law".[43] Thus our conception of law too suffers from the same conceptual ills, which lead to further problems resulting in antinomies, fragmentation or overregulation (also known as "deluge of norms"), to mention but a few fundamental legal problems.

Generally, today's complexity, resulting from the sum of isolated individual problems, seems to suggest that a new approach is needed, like a series of failed scientific experiments requires a change in methods. The reason is that if the question itself is wrong, it is likely to prompt wrong answers. Therefore, there is an urgent need in science and in law to realize the goal of greater coherence in order to solve problems more efficiently. In law, coherence has been found to be in vogue, but is perhaps more prominent in legal theory than in practice.[44] In law and international relations, coherence is often understood as the "effective co-operation and the avoidance of unnecessary duplication in the activities of these organizations".[45] Coherence is relevant not only for the resolution of institutional problems. It also applies to substantive legal problems as well, such as the relationship between different international treaties or laws.[46] Generally, coherence is seen as a way to overcome the negative consequences caused by an

42 See David Kennedy, "The Mystery of Global Governance" (2008) 34(3) *Ohio Northern University Law Review* 827 at 831.

43 See Joost Pauwelyn, "Bridging Fragmentation and Unity: International Law as a Universe of Inter-connected Islands" (2004) 25(4) *Michigan Journal of International Law* 903 at 904.

44 See *e.g.* Joseph Raz, "The Relevance of Coherence" (1992) 72(2) *Boston University Law Review* 273 and Aldo Schiavello, "On "Coherence" and "Law": An Analysis of Different Models" (2001) 14(2) *Ratio Juris* 233; but see United Nations High Level Panel on Coherence, *supra* note 36.

45 See Art. 86(2) Havana Charter for an International Trade Organization, UN Conference on Trade and Employment, *Havana Charter for an International Trade Organization and Final Act and Related Documents* (Havana November 21, 1947 to March 24, 1948), UN Doc ICITO/1/4/1948.

46 See *e.g.* Christian Tietje, "The Concept of Coherence in the Treaty on European Union and the Common Foreign and Security Policy" (1997) 2(2) *European Foreign Affairs Review* 211; Koen Lenaerts, "The Rule of Law and the Coherence of the Judicial System of the European Union" (2007) 44(6) *Common Market Law Review* 1625 and Thomas Cottier and Panagiotis Delimatsis (eds), *The Prospects of International Trade Regulation: From Fragmentation to Coherence* (Cambridge: Cambridge University Press, 2011).

excessive degree of fragmentation in law. To overcome these problems, there exist concepts that are synonymously used for coherence in legal discourse, such as those of integrity,[47] unity[48] or consistency.[49]

It is interesting to note that a similar terminology is also used in broader scientific discourse, where coherence is used to "evaluate and compare rival but potentially incompatible theories that account for the same set of observations".[50] More still, coherence, or at least the right kind of explanatory coherence in science, may lead to a considerable approximation of truth.[51] Interestingly, even art recognizes its significance, as it was found that "coherence, unity, form and their negations are notions that are commonly used in an evaluative manner when they appear in talk about artworks".[52] In literature, a similar desire for coherence may even constitute a fundamental theme of world literature.[53]

In law too, coherence may be regarded as precondition for an approximation of truth in the sense of justice. In science the difference between high coherence theories and low coherence theories is that the former are "those whose formulas are tightly coupled in accounting for observations, while low coherence theories contain many disjointed and isolated statements".[54] Transplanted into law, it means that, from the perspective of an approximation of justice based on truth, a high coherence legal system is superior to a low coherence system. The difference is that the latter is more fragmented and more inconsistent as opposed to the former. One expression of the role of coherence for justice in law is found in the Latin principle of "*venire contra factum proprium (non valet)*", which means that "to come against one's own fact (is not allowed)".[55] In common speech we would call a person violating this principle a hypocrite and there are numerous sayings expressing the same deeper meaning, such as "the road to hell is paved with good intentions" or in Italian "*fatti, non parole*" (deeds, not

47 See *e.g.* Ronald Dworkin, *Law's Empire* (Cambridge: Harvard University Press, 1986) at 176 and Ronald Dworkin, "Law as Interpretation" (1982) 9(1) *Critical Inquiry* 179 at 195.

48 See *e.g.* Mario Prost, *The Concept of Unity in Public International Law* (Oxford: Hart, 2012) and Denis Alland et al. (eds), *Unité et Diversité du Droit International / Unity and Diversity of International Law: Ecrits en L'honneur du Professeur Pierre-Marie Dupuy / Essays in Honour of Professor Pierre-Marie Dupuy* (Leiden: Martinus Nijhoff, 2014).

49 See *e.g.* J. M. Balkin, "Understanding Legal Understanding: The Legal Subject and the Problem of Legal Coherence" (1993) 103(1) *The Yale Law Journal* 105 at 115–116.

50 See Jason Jingshi Li, Rex Bing Hung Kwok and Norman Y. Foo, "The Coherence of Theories—Dependencies and Weights" in David Makinson, Jacek Malinowski and Heinrich Wansing (eds), *Towards Mathematical Philosophy: Papers from the Studia Logica Conference Trends in Logic IV* (New York: Springer, 2009) 297 at 297.

51 See Paul Thagard, "Coherence, Truth, and the Development of Scientific Knowledge" (2007) 74(1) *Philosophy of Science* 28 at 47.

52 See Karl Aschenbrenner, *The Concept of Coherence in Art* (Dordrecht: D. Reidel, 1985) at 3–4.

53 See Nicholas Hagger, *A New Philosophy of Literature: The Fundamental Theme and Unity of World Literature: The Vision of the Infinite and the Universalist Literary Tradition* (Hants: O-Books, 2012).

54 See Li, Kwok and Foo, *supra* note 50 at 297.

55 See Aaron X. Fellmeth and Maurice Horwitz, *Guide to Latin in International Law* (Oxford: Oxford University Press, 2009) at 290.

words). In international law, the principle means that a state may not set itself in contradiction to its own previous conduct.[56] This principle not only applies to states but also to persons. In private law, acting against one's own conduct is considered a violation of *bona fide* (good faith) and may lead to the loss of the related rights, such as those related to property, legal claims, or action for voidness.[57] In Germany, the principle's applicability has also been discussed in the context of criminal law.[58] In common law, a similar tool is the doctrine of equitable estoppel, which serves the purpose of addressing a possible inequity by "estopping" or preventing a litigant from being able to take advantage before a court of contradictory conduct that worked either to his advantage in a case or to the disadvantage of the adverse party.[59]

In summary, there are numerous fields of application for the concept of coherence and its many synonyms. Despite their inherent differences, they may have in common that they meet in the mind, as the origin of perception, cognition and consciousness. The relevance of coherence for cognition is because from perception, via the senses and subsequent cognitive processing of the data received, all future thoughts and actions derive. In fact, psychological experiments confirm the role of coherence for reasoning and decision making.[60] Coherence in the sense of cognition also plays an important role in nature, as the natural sciences indicate.[61] Cognition also does matter in law and in legal decision making, where coherence-based reasoning was found to show that the decision-making process progresses bidirectionally, which means that "premises and facts both determine conclusions and are affected by them in return".[62] But even empirical evidence suggests that emotions have an impact on our cognitive processes applied to legal decisions.[63] Similarly bias or stereotypes, which are deemed useful in cognitive terms for their tendency to simplify the world,[64] can "lead to pervasive errors in decision making by causing us to ignore important information and make

56 *Ibid.*

57 See Hans Josef Wieling, "Venire contra factum proprium und Verschulden gegen sich selbst" (1976) 176 *Archiv für die civilistische Praxis* 334 at 334.

58 See Hans-Jürgen Bruns, "Venire contra factum proprium im Strafrecht?" (1956) 11(5/6) *Juristenzeitung* 147.

59 See T. Leigh Anenson, "The Triumph of Equity: Equitable Estoppel in Modern Litigation" (2008) 27(3) *The Review of Litigation* 377 at 380; see also Gunther Kühne, "Reliance, Promissory Estoppel and Culpa in Contrahendo: A Comparative Analysis" (199) 10 *Tel Aviv University Studies in Law* 279 at 281.

60 See Dan Simon et al., "The Emergence of Coherence Over the Course of Decision Making" (2001) 27(5) *Journal of Experimental Psychology: Learning, Memory, and Cognition* 1250.

61 See *e.g.* C. W. Rietdijk, "Consciousness and the Coherence of Natural Law" (2006) 19(2) *Physics Essays* 200.

62 See Dan Simon, "A Third View of the Black Box: Cognitive Coherence in Legal Decision Making" (2004) 71(2) *The University of Chicago Law Review* 511 at 511.

63 See *e.g.* David J. Arkush, "Situating Emotion: A Critical Realist View of Emotion and Nonconscious Cognitive Processes for Law and Legal Theory" (2008) 2008(5) *Brigham Young University Law Review* 1275 at 1365.

64 See Ronald A. Farrell and Malcolm D. Holmes, "The Social and Cognitive Structure of Legal Decision-Making" (1991) 32(4) *The Sociological Quarterly* 529 at 532.

inaccurate predictions".[65] Last but not least, new information technologies, such as various online legal databases, also seriously impact cognition in the way we research and process legal information through our cognitive tools.[66]

More support for the relevance of coherence for perception, cognition and decision making, notably when facing complexity or other difficulties, comes from the field of management. Interestingly, Michael Lissack and Johan Roos state that we live in times facing a shift from a "complicated" to a "complex" world in which coherence based on the "next common sense" will help to master "the complex swirl of events and situations around us".[67] The choice of the term "common sense" points to another related problem of coherence in cognition, which is the problem of achieving coherence in perception that receives sensory data from different sense organs. Thus the term "common sense" may be understood as a coherent sense of information received from different senses, whether known or unknown. Generally, there is growing interest in greater unity or coherence between the mind, the brain and the world, known also as cognitive studies or the science of consciousness.[68]

In summary, "coherence" is perhaps the generic concept used to describe a fundamental desire of humans for "atonement", not in the religious sense of a reparation for a wrong or injury, but rather in the etymological sense of "*at-one-ment*", defined as "[t]he condition of being *at one* with others; unity of feeling, harmony, concord, agreement".[69] Using Tagore's words, coherence can thus be described as the search between endless dichotomies for "a harmony in a manner not yet dreamt of".[70] Even scientists may express such desire in the form of an integral theory of everything:

> An integral theory of everything would bring us closer to understanding the real nature of all the things that exist and evolve in space and time, whether they are atoms or galaxies or mice and men. It gives us an encompassing and yet scientific view of ourselves and of the world; a view that we very much need in these times of accelerating change and mounting disorientation.[71]

65 See Ian Weinstein. "Don't Believe Everything You Think: Cognitive Bias in Legal Decision Making" (2003) 9(2) *Clinical Law Review* 783 at 783.

66 See also Robert C. Berring, "Legal Information and the Search for Cognitive Authority" (2000) 88(6) *California Law Review* 1673 and 1675-1708.

67 See Michael Lissack and Johan Roos, *The Next Common Sense: Mastering Corporate Complexity Through Coherence* (London: Nicholas Brealey Publishing, 1999) at 1.

68 See *e.g.* G. E. R. Lloyd, *Cognitive Variations Reflections on the Unity and Diversity of the Human Mind* (Oxford: Clarendon Press, 2007) and Alfredo Pereira Jr and Dietrich Lehmann (eds), *The Unity of Mind, Brain, and World: Current Perspectives on a Science of Consciousness* (Cambridge: Cambridge University Press, 2013).

69 See Matthew Sperling, *Visionary Philology: Geoffrey Hill and the Study of Words* (Oxford: Oxford University Press, 2014) at 42.

70 Rabinandrath Tagore, "Nationalism" in Rabinandrath Tagore, *Omnibus III* (New Delhi: Rupa & Co., 2005) 1 at 7.

71 See Ervin Laszlo, *Science and the Akashic Field: An Integral Theory of Everything*, 2nd ed (Rochester: Inner Traditions, 2007) at 4.

Finally, in law, H. Patrick Glenn used the term "convivencia" for coherence or a harmonious and peaceful coexistence and even interaction between various legal systems or traditions in spite of their differences.[72] The same kind of "convivencia" is what essentially oxymoronic concepts tend to express, whereby two seemingly contradictory statements are condensed in one or more words that are united in spite of their diversity and apparent opposition. In brief, they also express the desire for greater coherence and, when understood and applied correctly, may contribute to such harmony or an approximation towards greater truth or justice. They certainly remind us of the need to build a "legal memory palace", i.e. a future global legal order that, paradoxically, is adequate for tackling the problems we tend to create ourselves.

Therefore, greater coherence in law, and legal thinking in particular, may be able to resolve many serious global problems that humanity faces. The reason is that when facing complexity, the difficulty of the task is not to identify the correct means for the solution of each single problem; instead, the difficulty lies in the solution of each single problem through a coordinated and coherent approach. Expressed differently, a single policy can only be dealt with successfully by considering the entirety of other policies simultaneously. Otherwise, in the absence of such a coherent strategy, the danger is that – paradoxically – the solution of one problem will either impede the solution of another problem or create new problems. Last but not least, the challenge that essentially oxymoronic concepts indicate for law is to find coherence first and foremost in cognitive terms. Greater cognitive coherence is what the term mnemonic law suggests for a future global legal order. In analogy to the human mind, a global mnemonic law underlying a future global legal order needs to create a seamless web of legal paths connecting all legally relevant subjects, as brain cells (neurons) are connected with each other via synaptic connections. In this regard, H. G. Wells provided a useful analogy when he spoke of a "world brain" that would, perhaps, allow for greater global cognitive coherence. Such a world brain, he described as follows:

> In a universal organisation and clarification of knowledge and ideas, in a closer synthesis of university and educational activities, in the evocation, that is, of what I have here called a World Brain, operating by an enhanced educational system through the whole body of mankind, a World Brain which will replace our multitude of unco-ordinated ganglia, our powerless miscellany of universities, research institutions, literatures with a purpose, national educational systems and the like; in that and in that alone, it is maintained, is there any clear hope of a really Competent Receiver for world affairs, any hope of an adequate directive control of the present destructive drift of world affairs.[73]

72 H. Patrick Glenn, "Com-paring" in Esin Örücü and David Nelken (eds), *Comparative Law: A Handbook* (Oxford: Hart, 2007) 91 at 92.

73 Herbert G. Wells, *World Brain* (San Bernardino: Read Books Ltd, 2016) at 16.

In similar terms, the future global legal order – if it wants to assist in tackling the most serious problems in global affairs – must seek to reduce the fragmentation of legal systems and laws, and do away with their lack of coherence. It must replace the many uncoordinated ganglia of legal norms and procedures, the powerless miscellany of international, regional and national organizations, courts and ministries and the like. This is the challenge for a global mnemonic law, which functions like a legal memory palace. Its efficient creation, however, raises the questions of how to achieve such greater coherence in global governance of the future. As a first step, it may be useful to outline the contours or basic requirements of a global legal order built on mnemonic law. Following that, it is possible to look at ways of establishing such an order in line with the fundamental message that essentially oxymoronic concepts carry, namely that contradictions and conflicts arise in the mind and that it is in the mind where their solutions have to be sought.

9.2 The contours of a global mnemonic legal order

> *[. . .] how to prove with a noncontradictory logic that the reality is contradictory?*[74]

As a result of the close analysis of a large number of essentially oxymoronic concepts in all areas of human activity, coherence and especially cognitive coherence surfaced as the principal challenge of many decision-making processes. These challenges in decision making concern individuals much like collective organs from groups, companies to states or multilateral organizations. The increasing complexity everywhere, paralleled by an unprecedented acceleration of the perception of change through time, contributes to a loss of orientation and greater uncertainty. The felt lack of certainty seems to make it more difficult for everyone everywhere to take adequate decisions allowing for an efficient planning of the future. Thus, it is important to consider the primary requirements for a global legal order of the future to build upon the following recommendations inherent to essentially oxymoronic concepts.

First and foremost, a future global legal order must be based on "dialetheism", meaning that it deals with "powerful tensions, profound contradictions, and perplexing paradoxes" (as Rosenau put it)[75] in a way that accepts not rejects them. Such acceptance requires constant efforts to enhance the understanding of human nature and to feed the findings back into the organization of life at all levels. Equally, it asks for significant efforts by our educational institutions to assist everyone in the process of acquiring the skills of "oxymoronic thinking" as a means to discern differences and dissolve contradictions by finding greater complementarity between the apparently opposite concepts expressed in numerous dichotomies. It

74 See Niklas Luhmann, "The Third Question: The Creative Use of Paradoxes in Law and Legal History" (1988) 15(2) *Journal of Law & Society* 153 at 154.

75 James N. Rosenau, "Governance in the 21st Century" (1995) 1(1) *Global Governance* 13 at 13.

does not reject bifurcation and separation as tools of analytical thinking but it does not stop there. Instead it complements them by dialetheism, i.e. the acceptance of contradictions and fuzzy logic, as a tool for holistic thinking. As a concrete example, one could name the various "trade and . . ." problems, where institutional designs and regulatory techniques need to be applied that allow for their mutual complementarity rather than their conflict. Put simply, allowing for trade in polluting or unhealthy goods and services serves neither the objectives of free trade nor those of the protection of the environment. A concrete regulatory response trying to achieve such greater complementarity is found in so-called "integration clauses" or "cross-sectional clauses". For instance, the EU's treaty framework features a general integration clause, which requires that the "Union shall ensure consistency between its policies and activities, taking all of its objectives into account".[76] In addition to this general clause, the treaties also list several specific integration clauses, such as for the environment or culture.[77]

Second, a future global legal order must be "inclusive", which means to be based on a simultaneously atomistic and holistic conception of the world. This is the challenge of coherence in general and of cognitive coherence in particular. In terms of logic, it must mean to adopt a new logic, forming a second layer of paraconsistent logic around classical binary logic. According to Glenn, such paraconsistent logic means to admit "the possibility of true contradictions in the world and providing means of dealing with them (beyond radical and definitive choice of one or the other)".[78] In practice, for law to be inclusive, it must provide equal access to all relevant data, facts, or considerations as well as, most importantly, all legal subjects. It means a legal system must be accessible for claims at all levels, the local, national, regional and global. To this end, it must also make sure that no one is barred from having her or his claim heard before a judicial tribunal or other competent legal authority, and that for every legal act an equivalent legal remedy must be made available. More concretely, it means to eliminate all barriers in terms of international competences, national boundaries, boundaries of jurisdictions or any other criterion used for discrimination or a denial of access to justice. As a simple example, one could name a person whose house has been destroyed and family members killed by a drone attack as one who needs to be given a due access to justice to claim his damages and to bring the perpetrators to justice.

Third, a global mnemonic legal order must remain "dynamic". Again this means by way of oxymoronic thinking to combine the static and the dynamic, the certain and uncertain, as it is reflected in the oxymoronic concept of a "dynamic status quo".[79] This necessity is indicated by the conceptual shifts from more static to more dynamic concepts, such as from government to governance, from litigation to arbitration, or legislation to regulation, to name but a few. In the

76 See Art. 7 TFEU, *Treaty on the Functioning of the European Union (TFEU) (consolidated version)*, (2010) O.J. C 83/01 (30 March 2010).

77 See *e.g.* Articles 8–11 and 167(4) TFEU; *ibid.*

78 See H. Patrick Glenn, *The Cosmopolitan State* (Oxford: Oxford University Press, 2013) at 267.

79 United Kingdom, *Jet2.com Ltd v. Blackpool Airport Ltd*, [2010] EWHC 3166 at para 35; see also Court of Appeal (Kuala Lumpur), *Sdn Bhd v. Radio & General Engineering Sdn Bhd*, [2005] 2 MLJ 422 at 435.

quest of law for legal certainty and predictability, as laid down in the rule of law, it often relies on science and scientific facts. In this regard, law misses the point and forgets that scientific fact is never complete. This can be seen from the many paradoxes and oxymora coined by scientific experts in their attempts to explain nature and the universe. This is why it was said that the "static perspective which characterizes the study of paradoxes in logic is not suited for that task because it is not sensitive to the social dynamics underlying the paradoxes of law".[80] At best, science and the scientific process mean that an approximation of truth like law can ideally achieve an approximation of justice. In regulatory terms, it means to remember that "crossing the lines depends on where you draw them"[81] and to redraw them when necessary so as to avoid arbitrariness of the lines proposed. This general problem often emerges as a kind of sorites paradox, as it recently did in the question of the legality of an upper limit for refugees to be admitted into Europe. Its arbitrariness and unlawfulness under a dynamic reading of the law can be exemplified by following the suggestion by Oliver Wendell Holmes of showing the arbitrariness of such strict lines of distinction by "by putting cases very near to it on one side or the other".[82] So, similar to the question of refugees, one could imagine a small town with a hospital with a total of 100 beds for patients to be treated. One day, a major disaster injures 200 people at once, would the hospital manager merely admit the first 100 victims and, beginning with the injured number 101, leave everyone else outside and medically unattended? In this regard, it is a frequently observed paradox in law that especially laws for emergency situations are always repealed precisely in the case of the emergency for which they were adopted in the first place. Just consider that ambassadors are usually recalled precisely when a diplomatic conflict erupts, or human rights are suspended in a state of national emergency.

These few examples underscore how dualistic reasoning in the form of static lines of distinctions does not work in reality. Yet, we still choose to stick to such theoretical approaches in law, as Oliver Wendell Holmes further pointed out:

> But the theory of the law is that such lines exist, because the theory of the law as to any possible conduct is that it is either lawful or unlawful. As that difference has no gradation about it, when applied to shades of conduct that are very near each other it has an arbitrary look. We like to disguise the arbitrariness, we like to save ourselves the trouble of nice and doubtful discriminations.[83]

Fourth, and related to the former precondition, a global mnemonic legal order must also remain "open". This means that the legal system of the future must

80 See Oren Perez, "Law in the Air: A Prologue to the World of Legal Paradoxes" in Oren Perez and Gunther Teubner (eds), *Paradoxes and Inconsistencies in the Law* (Oxford: Hart Publishing, 2006) 3 at 17.

81 Phrase freely adapted from the poster of the Canadian film *Kissed* (1996/97) ["Crossing the line depends on where you draw it"] directed by Lynne Stopkewich; see IMDB at http://www.imdb.com/title/tt0116783/ (accessed 1 October 2017).

82 See Oliver W. Holmes, "Law in Science and Science in Law" in Oliver W. Holmes, *The Collected Legal Papers* (New York: Harcourt, Brace and Howe, 1920) 210 at 232–233.

83 *Ibid.*

give greater recognition to the precautionary principle, meaning that it needs to proceed with greater caution, being reminiscent of the limitations imposed by insufficient scientific knowledge. It also means not discarding the "paranormal", understood in the senses of paradoxes as pointing out phenomena that go beyond the existing widely held beliefs. Examples supporting the openness of a legal system are numerous, such as the paradox that emerged from the "black hole" cases brought before courts in three different jurisdictions. In these cases judges not trained in physics were asked to settle a scientific dispute that could lead to the end of the world and the core issue of which divided even the scientific community.[84] In another case concerning an oil drilling contract, the court also discussed various paranormal activities, such as "spiritualistic communications" and, although it did not take them into consideration, still acknowledged that "the phantasm of today is so often a reality of tomorrow".[85] Or else, even the term "absolute impossibility" is relative, because what is "impossible" changes and depends partly on the current state of technology.[86] The absolute impossibility being impossible is – together with the possibility of error (both in technological and human terms) – one of the strongest arguments against the death penalty, due to its irreversible nature.

Fifth, in terms of the sanctions imposed by its various legal instruments to secure compliance, a global legal order must be "creative". This means first to balance constantly between various degrees of persuasive and coercive means of intervention, whereby the former must be the starting point and the latter the last resort (*ultima ratio*).[87] In practice, it also necessitates a good use of all regulatory techniques available. Lawmakers in particular must be reminded that not only regulatory activity (positive integration) is their main job. The fact is that deregulatory activity (negative integration) has the same importance as regulatory activity. Moreover, the dichotomous pairs of deregulation and regulation cover a range of different shades of such regulatory techniques, such as self-regulation or co-regulation, or soft law and hard law. Additionally, efforts have to be made to formulate novel regulatory concepts (e.g. regulatory coopetition) and apply novel regulatory techniques, such as various experimental regulatory tools.[88] The judicial process also knows various alternative methods of conflict resolution that start with negotiation and move via dispute prevention, mediation and arbitration to stringent methods of adjudication by litigation.[89]

84 See generally Eric E. Johnson, "The Black Hole Case: The Injunction Against the End of the World" (2009) 76(4) *Tennessee Law Review* 819.

85 See *Burchill v. Hermsmeyer*, 212 S. W. 767 at 771 (1919); see also Lee Blewett, "Psychic Phenomena and the Law" (1921) 34(6) *Harvard Law Review* 625.

86 See Guenter Treitel, *The Law of Contract* (London: Sweet & Maxwell, 2003) at 880.

87 See generally H. Patrick Glenn, "Persuasive Authority" (1987) 32(2) *McGill Law Journal* 261 at 286.

88 See *e.g.* Sofia Ranchordás, "Sunset Clauses and Experimental Regulations: Blessing or Curse for Legal Certainty?" (2015) 36(1) *Statute Law Review* 28.

89 See Albert K. Fiadjoe, *Alternative Dispute Resolution: A Developing World Perspective* (London: Cavendish, 2004) at 19–21.

Sixth, future laws must speak with a clear language. This requirement reflects the importance of the linguistic and cognitive dimension of law. Like technology or other human activities, language is one of the most important expressions of the human mind. Law is little different in this regard as can be seen by the rise of essentially oxymoronic concepts. As law primarily but not exclusively functions through written language, close attention must be paid to changes in language as indicators of changes in human nature. Moreover, laws today are too many, too long, too complex, too often void of meaning, so that even those who formulated them no longer understand their meaning (provided they ever understood it in the first place). Put briefly, it means that regulatory processes must advance in close alliance with language. Existing helpful tools to simplify laws are various methods of the repeal, consolidation or codification of laws. However, new modes for the communication of legally relevant information need to be found, just as traffic signs accompanied the rise in traffic-related laws. In summary, the principal challenge is to find ways to communicate information in ways allowing for greater cognitive coherence.

Seventh, a future global legal order must be coherent, in the sense of unity but not uniformity. Here, too, exist various nuances of methods used to achieve unity. Various legal approaches by way of comparative law include different forms of interactions between different laws or legal systems. Existing practices or tools are communication, cooperation, approximation and harmonization of laws, as well as the adoption of uniform laws. But again, it must be not forgotten that one of the strongest expressions of uniform laws is "no laws at all". The wide range of methods has also been framed by the dichotomy of regulatory diversity versus regulatory harmonization, which occasionally has been transcended by various oxymora, such as regulatory coopetition or the multilateralization of regionalism and vice versa. Coherence, in short, is a requirement to try to transcend all apparent opposites as framed by the numerous dichotomies, such as past and future, local and global, individual and collective, or legal and illegal.

Eighth, and to cut a long story short, future laws must be just or at least seek to approximate justice. What sounds trivial is the greatest challenge and, like the first element, is a matter of cognitive coherence. This is because it can be argued that the greater the input of relevant information, the wider the overall picture that is drawn, which eventually allows for an optimized approximation of justice. Therefore, it is vain to describe further the particular requirements of a future legal order in contrast with the deficiencies of the present order when each single problem is intrinsically connected with all other single problems. In practice, it means to look at all the individual constituents in isolation and the shape of their sum as a whole. This method can also be derived from the previous paragraphs, which can all be reduced to the first requirement, namely that of calling for the adoption of a greater recognition of an inclusive or oxymoronic mode of thinking as also suggested by dialetheism. For example, it means equally and without preliminary hierarchical ordering, simultaneously and coherently to apply all rules of interpretation, i.e. literal, systemic (or grammatical), historical and teleological.

As a second reason, it is equally vain to try to describe these single requirements because our linguistic and conceptual tools are inadequate. Put simply, most legal problems, whether local or global, individual or collective, merely identify the weaknesses of our present legal realities that are due to limitations in current language or, generally, an inadequate cognitive framework of conception. These limitations in linguistic and cognitive terms surface with the mushrooming of essentially oxymoronic concepts, i.e. paradoxes and oxymora in all areas, amplified further by an acceleration of change and convergence of dichotomous concepts. This is why the principal deficiencies of law today, when transformed into challenges of the future of law, seem to be of a cognitive nature in dealing with complexity. So how to change the cognition? It is almost a paradox as, for law to adapt to the future, its underlying cognition needs to change now, but how can a change in cognition be effectuated? By law or by any other means? Again the question is, what is the role played by essentially oxymoronic concepts in this regard? Answers to these problems of paradoxes are again paradoxical, pointing to conceptual difficulties in expressing them through present-day concepts, grammar, syntax or language as a whole. It means to try to say the ineffable, to utter paradoxes for the explanation of paradoxes. However, it may help to try to learn how these changes may be brought about in the future by essentially oxymoronic concepts.

9.3 The "colour of law" or cognitive coherence through legal synaesthesia

> *In like manner when two texts contradict each other, we follow the second, until a third text is found which reconciles the contradiction.*[90]

The recent rise of essentially oxymoronic concepts can be taken as a sign that complexity is increasing, that acceleration of perception of change through time is intensifying and that our current cognitive modes of processing data by primarily binary thinking or logic are inadequate. To address this sign more efficiently, cognitive coherence should be the top priority in attempts to tackle the fundamental crisis that humanity is presently facing. For future law to meet this crisis, by, for instance, reforming the present institutional frameworks applied throughout the world, both globally and locally, *à la longue* paradigm shifts both in how we interpret change (mind the change) and how we respond to it (change the mind) in cognitive terms seem inevitable. At this point, we may only speculate how to interpret the role of essentially oxymoronic concepts for the future of human evolution. So far, we have merely restated or summarized the explicit or implicit criticism these rhetorical figures provide for the present scientific method, in art, for law and for our lifestyle. Yet, the rising number of paradoxes and oxymora seems to form an invisible bond between all these

90 See David Instone Brewer, *Techniques and Assumptions in Jewish Exegesis before 70 CE* (Tübingen: J. C. B. Mohr, 1992) at 228.

separate areas. They perhaps indicate the beginning of a common language of cognition, needed for humanity to solve the global governance paradox, or, as Pierre Teilhard de Chardin wrote, to meet the "urgency of forming a single body coextensive with itself".[91] Taken a step further, essentially oxymoronic concepts may indicate the beginning of a global legal order that – as global mnemonic law – is built like a vast legal memory palace in line with the human mind, or its ability to think, imagine and create. Ultimately, this question will raise a profound problem of human nature, namely whether there is free will or not. Before that, however, other important questions need to be addressed, namely whether language in general as well as oxymoronic concepts in particular will affect not only the way we think but also the way we biologically evolve through genes. In short, is there a possible link between nature and nurture or other fundamental dichotomies, like life and death, which strongly influence our decisions and actions and have also shaped the designs of the numerous legal systems around the world, both past and present.

It is interesting to recall that words may be capable of affecting the brain.[92] Such a possible link between cognition and genetics was also described as follows:

> New organs of cognition arise. [. . .] As humans have evolved biologically, so, too, has human consciousness evolved. Moreover, that evolution continues on our own day, and its future remains open.[93]

Perhaps, there is even a parallel or a bi-directional influence between consciousness and genes in a sense that cognitive changes also trigger biological changes in evolution and vice versa. Their mutual relation is like the chicken-and-egg paradox. Here too, the mystery lies in the perception of change and our conceptualization of time and space. In this regard, it has also been said that the "questions we ask, as well as the answers we are willing to accept, reflect our temper of mind".[94] Leaving this subject aside for a moment, as it continues to be the subject of scientific controversy, it is interesting to note that there have been people in the past, like Jules Verne or H. G. Wells, who were "nostalgic visionaries" or "mad geniuses" and, in this quality were able to anticipate quite accurately later developments. The reason may be that they managed to decode the past and present signs accessible at their time. As path dependency suggests, the future is already, at least partially, immanent in both the past and the present. This is why a vigilant observer may be able to glimpse behind the revolving door leading from an infinite present to the future. Today, too, many people are

91 See Pierre Teilhard de Chardin, *Activation of Energy* (San Diego: A Harvest Book, 1978) at 15.

92 See also Andrew Newberg and Mark Robert Waldman, *Words Can Change Your Brain: 12 Conversation Strategies to Build Trust, Resolve Conflict, and Increase Intimacy* (New York: Plume, 2013) at 3.

93 See Arthur Zajonc, *Catching the Light: The Entwined History of Light and Mind* (Oxford: Oxford University Press, 1993) at 184 and 185.

94 *Ibid* at 38.

devoting their energies to the reading of contemporary signs to predict future trends.[95] So do governmental and intergovernmental agencies and individuals in their different capacities. In fact, caught in the perception of time following a unilinear direction, we are all forcibly concerned with the future, whether we like it or not.

Interestingly, sometimes possible signs for future developments seem hidden in those places where one is least likely to look for them. In the search for greater cognitive coherence, this may be the case with synaesthesia. Put simply, it means a form of coherent perception based on the unity of senses or "neurological blending of the senses".[96] The meaning of "unity of the senses" has been explained as follows:

> The unity of the senses reveals itself in a variety of ways: in sensory processes, where the psychophysical behavior of different senses shows marked similarities; in perceptual processes, where different senses provide common information about the world and where characteristics of sensory experience resemble one another; and in cognitive processes, where *verbal metaphors* describe or suggest similarities among sensory phenomena.[97]

Interestingly, it has also been said that the many different senses have genetically evolved from one single "primitive sense" with no responsiveness to external stimulation.[98] This is different in the case of more senses, as it is characterized by synaesthesia, which is defined as "a condition in which stimulation of one sense generates a simultaneous sensation in another".[99] It means that persons capable of such sensations, namely synaesthetes, can hear colours, feel sounds or taste shapes. There are at least fifty different forms of synaesthesia:

> Most common are **grapheme-color synesthesia**, in which a person sees colors when viewing letters, numbers, or words (i.e., graphemes) on a printed page, and **time-space synesthesia**, in which a person experiences months, days, hours, and other units of time as occupying specific spatial locations around him or her (e.g., January is 308 to the left of midline). Rarer types include **mirror-touch synesthesia**, in which a person watching

95 See *e.g.* Ervin Laszlo and Judah Bierman (eds), *Goals in a Global Community: The Original Background Papers for Goals for Mankind: A Report to the Club of Rome* (New York: Pergamon Press, 1977), Ervin Laszlo, *VISION 2020: Reordering Chaos for Global Survival* (Yverdon: Gordon and Breach, 2005), Jacque Fresco, *Designing the Future* (Venus: The Venus Project, 2007) and Jacques Attali, *A Brief History of the Future: A Brave and Controversial Look at the Twenty-First Century* (2011).

96 See Gary R. VandenBos (ed), *APA Dictionary of Psychology*, 2nd ed. (Washington: American Psychological Association, 2015) at 1060.

97 See Lawrence E. Marks, *The Unity of the Senses. Interrelations Among the Modalities* (New York: Academic Press, 1978), at 182 [*Italics* added].

98 *Ibid.*

99 See VandenBos, *supra* note 96 at 1060.

> another individual being touched feels a tactile sensation on his or her own body, and **lexical-gustatory synesthesia** (or **word-gustatory synesthesia** or **word-taste synesthesia**), in which individuals experience flavors when they hear certain words.[100]

It is also interesting to point out that synaesthesia may play an important role of the function in the enhancement of memory. The story told by Aleksandr R. Luria of a young man who had limitless memory and later worked as a mnemonist shows that his outstanding memory was based on synaesthesia.[101] There are many more analogies that can be drawn between cognitive coherence and coherence in legal terms. For example, synaesthetic modes of perception are also described by people who have taken psychedelic or hallucinogenic drugs like lysergic acid diethylamide, better known as LSD.[102] Recently a study made visible the effects of LSD on the human brain using fMRI (functional Magnetic Resonance Imaging), which showed an increased global connectivity.[103] Accordingly, LSD has the effect of simultaneously activating and connecting several parts of the brain which are not usually connected. The study's results showed that LSD selectively expands global connectivity in the brain, which means an increased global integration by inflating – temporarily – the level of communication between normally distinct brain networks.[104] The increased global integration of the senses drastically alters perception altogether, i.e. has radical effects on how we perceive the most fundamental aspects of reality. Compared with mystical experiences, these alterations in perception become manifest, for instance, in an experience of an undifferentiated unity and a sense of timelessness through the transcendence of time and space.[105] Other perceptual boundaries that seemingly become blurred are those between the self and the environment.[106]

The writer Aldous Huxley, who experimented with such psychedelic drugs, even came to the following conclusion about the brain's hidden potentials:

> Each person is at each moment capable of remembering all that has ever happened to him and of perceiving everything that is happening everywhere in the universe. The function of the brain and nervous system is to protect us from being overwhelmed and confused by this mass of largely useless and

100 *Ibid*; see also Richard E. Cytowic, *Synesthesia: A Union of the Senses*, 2nd ed (Cambridge: MIT Press, 2002) at 17 [emphasis in original].

101 See Aleksandr R. Luria, *The Mind of a Mnemonist: A Little Book About a Vast Memory* (Cambridge: Harvard University Press, 1968).

102 David Matsumoto (ed), *The Cambridge Dictionary of Psychology* (Cambridge: Cambridge University Press, 2009) at 533.

103 See Enzo Tagliazucchi et al., "Increased Global Functional Connectivity Correlates with LSD-Induced Ego Dissolution" (2016) 26(8) *Current Biology* 1043.

104 *Ibid.*

105 See Walter N. Pahnke and William A. Richards, "Implications of LSD and Experimental Mysticism" (1966) 5(3) *Journal of Religion and Health* 175 at 177–180.

106 See Tagliazucchi et al., *supra* note 103.

> irrelevant knowledge, by shutting out most of what we should otherwise perceive or remember at any moment, and leaving only that very small and special selection which is likely to be practically useful.[107]

Of course, here "global" does not refer to the ordinary meaning of the term (i.e. planet Earth) but specific parts in the brain (i.e. a sub-cortical structure of the brain). In the brain, "global connectivity" describes whole brain network properties that host the capacity for cognitive control that are used for the solution of "most problems of everyday life requir[ing] effective control of thought and behavior".[108] In this regard, it is similar to the kind of "global connectivity" that seems to be needed for a more efficient governance of global affairs from a legal perspective. It is a global connectivity expressed in terms of a coherent global legal order or else a global constitution. This analogy of global connectivity in law and psychology supports a conception of law as mnemonic law. In this regard, the quote above also supports the comparison between synaesthesia and the comparative method in law, which aims for lawyers to "*see their subject as a whole*".[109]

What lawyers "see", however, also depends largely on what they admit as evidence. This marks another close analogy between law and the senses, an area which has gained some modest attention recently.[110] It is interesting to note that the law has hardly ever questioned the number of senses, which is usually put at five.[111] Moreover, it seems that law is favouring a hierarchy of the senses, clearly giving priority to sight over other senses (legal ocularcentrism).[112] This is also reflected in terms like "evidence", which derives from Latin "to see" (*videre*) or expressions like "in the eyes of the law" (and not the nose or ear of the law).[113] It is also noteworthy that, as a result, the expression "oral evidence" is perhaps oxymoronic but certainly synaesthetic because it combines sensations of both sight and sound. More synaesthetic associations with the law surface in colourful expressions, like "black-letter law", "red tape", or "greening the law", that link colours with the law. Other terms also combine the written and the spoken as well as unspoken, such as "oral law", "silent"

107 See Aldous Huxley, *Doors of Perception* (New York: Harper, 1954), cited in Ronald Wesley Neufeldt, *Karma and Rebirth: Post Classical Developments* (New Delhi: Sri Satguru Publications, 1986) at 266.

108 See Michael W. Cole et al., "Global Connectivity of Prefrontal Cortex Predicts Cognitive Control and Intelligence" (2012) 32(26) *The Journal of Neuroscience* 8988 at 8988.

109 See Arthur K. Kuhn, "The Function of the Comparative Method in Legal History and Philosophy" (1939) 13(3) *Tulane Law Review* 350 at 361 [*Italics* added].

110 See Lionel Bently and Leo Flynn (eds), *Law and the Senses: Sensational Jurisprudence* (London: Pluto Press, 1996).

111 See Lionel Bently, "Introduction" in Lionel Bently and Leo Flynn (eds), *Law and the Senses: Sensational Jurisprudence* (London: Pluto Press, 1996) 1 at 2–3.

112 *Ibid* at 7–8.

113 *Ibid* at 4–6.

and "mute law".[114] To distinguish hard and soft law also means to bring in a haptic reference to the law, like the expression that the "law stinks"[115] which contains an olfactory element. In sum, there are lots of aspects in the law that relate to and depend on the different senses and most likely even some unknown or subconsciously used ones. Most interesting, it was said that the reason for law not questioning its own senses was due to the law's acceptance of "Cartesian dualism" as the dominant conception, as law associated itself purely with reason.[116] Thus, it is another sign that the challenge of oxymoronic language to a dualistic reasoning is also opening the doors for a greater communication and synergy between the senses.

As in law, synaesthesia also plays an important role in language. This is where essentially oxymoronic concepts come into play as well. For the change in language, mainly through neologisms or semantic change, an important regularity for the English language was observed (which is also likely to apply to other languages). This regularity has been outlined as follows:

> One of the most common types of metaphoric transfer in all languages is synaesthesia—the transfer of a lexeme from one sensory area to another: ***dull colors, brilliant sounds, sharp tastes, sour music*** etc.[117]

These examples immediately invite associations with oxymoronic concepts. Their resemblance lies in the challenge of coherence, between either opposite terms or different senses. Interestingly, various aspects of poetic language, as found in neologisms, oxymora or other rhetorical figures, were found to be "themselves constrained by cognitive principles".[118] If this is true, can the reverse not also apply, namely that poetic language shapes cognitive processes and eventually also biological features, such as the brain?

Seen from such an angle, essentially oxymoronic concepts can be regarded as functioning like "verbal LSD". The important difference between the two is that essentially oxymoronic concepts are not illegal and do not unleash their effect on cognition immediately and merely temporarily like LSD does. Instead, they unfold their effect gradually but then permanently alter our mode of perception – even to the extent where one day all distinctions expressed in dichotomies may be transcended, eventually to vanish completely.

114 See Marianne Constable, *Just Silences: The Limits and Possibilities of Modern Law* (Princeton: Princeton University Press, 2005) and Rodolfo Sacco, "Mute Law" (1995) 43(3) *The American Journal of Comparative Law* 455.

115 See Marjorie Crowder Briggs, "The Verdict is Hilarious" (1985) 2(3) *Compleat Lawyer* 44 at 44.

116 See Bently, *supra* note 111 at 3.

117 See Joseph M. Williams, "Synaesthetic Adjectives: A Possible Law of Semantic Change" (1976) 52(2) *Language* 461 at 463.

118 See Yeshayahu Shen and Michael Cohen, "How Come Silence is Sweet but Sweetness is not Silent: A Cognitive Account of Directionality in Poetic Synaesthesia" (1998) 7(2) *Language and Literature* 123 at 124.

The synaesthetic effect of oxymora has also been observed by the law of associations, which Ernst Mach explained as follows:

> It is well known that a very prominent position is given, in psychology, to the laws of association. These laws can be reduced to a single law, which consists in saying that if two contents of consciousness, *A* and *B*, have once appeared simultaneously, one of them, when it arises, will evoke the other. And in fact it is much easier to understand physical life when we have recognized the constant recurrence of this fundamental feature.[119]

The law of association thus functions like a bridge between two different or possibly also opposite concepts (or sensations). As synaesthesia connects two or more sensory modalities, oxymora may at least inseparably connect two opposite or antagonistic concepts and thereby pave the way towards greater "global connectivity" through cognitive coherence in both the psychological and legal sense. They may also serve as a means to express the strong desire for such coherence in terms of harmony between apparently conflicting or contradictory concepts. This desire was summed up by Erich Fromm in the following paragraph:

> The deepest yearning of human beings seems to be a constellation in which the two poles (motherliness and fatherliness, female and male, mercy and justice, feeling and thought, nature and intellect) are united in a synthesis, in which *both sides of the polarity lose their antagonism* and, instead, *color each other.*[120]

It is also interesting to note in this quote the metaphorical use of "colour", as it is characteristic for synaesthetes. Another metaphor for the expression of this desire for coherence between the senses at least, is provided in the book *Of Human Bondage* by William Somerset Maugham, where he wrote: "Money is like a sixth sense without which you cannot make a complete use of the other five".[121] This allusion to a unity of senses may, at least in part, explain the strong appeal money has for human beings. Strangely, "money", the function which was also compared to the role of blood circulating in a human body, also serves as a way to measure the changing pace of life in terms of time perception.[122]

In turn, the comparison of money with a sixth sense also means that the five senses alone cannot be fully used without a sixth sense combining all other individual senses regardless of their number. But this raises the question about

119 Ernst Mach, *The Analysis of Sensations and the Relation of the Physical to the Psychical* (New York: Dover Publications, 1959) at 239.

120 Erich Fromm, *To Have or To Be?* (New York: Continuum, 1997) at 119 [*Italics* added].

121 See William Somerset Maugham, *Of Human Bondage* (New York: Garden City, 1915) at 304.

122 See Georg Simmel, "The Pace of Life and the Money Economy" in Hartmut Rosa and William E. Scheuerman (eds), *High-Speed Society: Social Acceleration, Power and Modernity* (University Park: Pennsylvania State University Press, 2009) 41–56.

the nature and location of this combined or "common sense". Interestingly an old Hindu epic, the *Bhagavad Gītā*, defines the sixth sense – depending on the English translation – as either consisting in the heart[123] or the mind.[124] But even the location of the mind in the brain is not clear, as the scope of the brain remains difficult to assert considering theories talking about four brains.[125] What speaks for such an extended scope of the brain to include also the solar plexus as an abdominal brain is that it would transcend the dichotomy of rational thought and emotional feeling, as it is captured by the notion of "emotional intelligence".

There exist also various meanings attributed to the notion of "common sense".[126] Generally, we define it as "normal understanding". Similar to Aristotle's "*sensus communis*" taken as a "mental faculty that takes data provided by the five senses and integrates them into unified perceptions",[127] here it is more understood as a sense constituted by the sum of the other individual senses, or else an additional sense to those we already use that will complement all other senses. The fact is that we all rely on the different senses, sometimes alone and sometimes in combination. We have also seen problems that arise from conflicts between the senses, such as in the case of pilots experiencing spatial disorientation where what they "feel" is different from what they "see" on a plane's instruments.[128] Eating foodstuffs like "stinky tofu" or the smelly durian fruit may also send – via the olfactory (smell) and gustatory (taste) senses – contradictory signals to the mind. Sceptics may try to answer the following question, namely which of the two nonsense words "*takete*" or "*malumma*" refers to a round and which to a sharp-edged visual form?[129] The answer may be obvious and shows that, in addition to our visual sense applied to extract meaning from letters, we also take sounds into account.

Another case of integrated sensory perceptions is found in our daily replies to the mere question "How are you?". Sincere or not, our response is usually determined by the sum of bodily sensations determining whether we feel fine or

123 See John Cockburn Thomson (trans.), *The Bhagavad-Gītā, Or, A Discourse Between Kṛiṣhṇa and Arjuna on Divine Matters* (Hertford: Stephen Austin, 1855) at 102 (Fn 17) ("[. . .] the senses, which have the heart as sixth.").

124 See Christopher Key Chapple (ed), *The Bhagavad Gītā (Twenty-fifth-Anniversary Edition)* (Albany: State University of New York Press, 2009) at 596 ("[. . .] mind, the sixth, and the (other) senses [. . .].").

125 See Theron Q. Dumont, *The Solar Plexus: The Abdominal Brain* (Chicago: Advanced Thought Publishing, 1920) at 1–9.

126 See *e.g.* Radu J. Bogdan (ed), *Mind and Common Sense: Philosophical Essays on Commonsense Psychology* (Cambridge: Cambridge University Press, 1991).

127 See VandenBos, *supra* note 96 at 966; see also Simon Kemp and Garth J. O. Fletcher, "The Medieval Theory of the Inner Senses" (1993) 106(4) *The American Journal of Psychology* 559 at 567–568.

128 See Federal Aviation Administration (FAA), *Spatial Disorientation*, at 8; available at: http://www.faa.gov/pilots/safety/pilotsafetybrochures/media/SpatialD.pdf (accessed 1 October 2017).

129 See Heikki Piha, "Intuition: A Bridge to the Coenesthetic World of Experience" (2005) 53(1) *Journal of the American Psychoanalytic Association* 23 at 34.

unwell, happy or unhappy, tired or energetic. This blend of different bodily sensations is also called "coenesthesia" (or cenesthesia).[130] Similar to synaesthesia, it has also been equated with the sixth sense, as follows:

> The word "coenaesthesis" indicates the total inner perception that we have of our organism. Beside the five senses by means of which we perceive the outside world our coenaesthesis is a kind of sixth sense by means of which our organism perceives itself in its ensemble.[131]

Thus, we do already integrate different sensory data into a more coherent set of data but we seem to face difficulties in making sense of them all the time. This is probably related to the distinctions made by dual process theories or between thinking fast and slow. This difficulty can be tested by the reader trying to answer quickly the question posed by Aleksandr R. Luria:

> There were two books on a shelf, each 400 pages long. A bookworm gnawed through from the first page of the first volume to the last page of the second. How many pages did he gnaw through?[132]

Every year I conduct this experiment with my students and the most frequent answer is 800, i.e. the 400 pages of volume I plus the 400 pages of volume II. The reason is that – in contrast to an integrated mode of perception – we tend to judge the question based on how we read through a book and not how we visually perceive it when it is placed on a shelf in the usual way as specified in the paragraph.[133]

Ideally, therefore, in life and in law, we are able to make sense out of information that we need to judge for future actions to be taken, based on an integrated mode of sensory perception, i.e. in short a "common sense", for which synaesthesia may help to point the way. In this regard, it is possible to speak not of a paradox but of hypocrisy if we call athletes "stars" because they excel in a sport (like Roger Federer in tennis), while we treat synaesthetes as "patients" suffering from a kind of mental disorder because they possess particular sensory skills that most other people may also possess but are not aware or make no use of. Instead, we should take their experiences seriously and carefully assess what lessons can be learned from them for perception in general and the impact of the senses on the law in particular.[134]

130 See VandenBos, *supra* note 96 at 167.

131 See Hubert Benoit, *Zen and the Psychology of Transformation: The Supreme Doctrine* (Rochester: Inner Traditions International, 1990) at 81 (Fn 1).

132 Luria, *supra* note 101 at 100.

133 The correct answer is that he only gnaws through the two bindings alone; *ibid.*

134 See also Noam Sagiv, "Synesthesia in Perspective" in Lynn C. Robertson and Noam Sagiv (eds), *Synesthesia: Perspectives from Cognitive Neuroscience* (Oxford: Oxford University Press, 2005) 3.

The numerous contradictory problems communicated via rising numbers of essentially oxymoronic concepts especially suggest that there is a need to seek possibilities for greater "global connectivity" in the neuroscientific and legal sense. Greater connectivity may warrant new modes of more coherence-based reasoning using all sensory channels of information. There already exists evidence that oxymoronic thinking is common to all of us, which was restated as follows:

> Most generally, the psychological evidence shows that people can make immediate sense out of novel oxymoronic statements. We easily interpret these contradictory phrases because of our conceptual ability to understand incongruent events and experiences.[135]

It was also found that we do "have an ability to take contradictory, paradoxical stances toward people and events".[136] Usually, abilities can be refined and enhanced. Such paradoxical problem-solving skills are already available and are likely to increase in demand in the near future. So how then can these skills be enhanced and put to use for the establishment of a global legal framework adequate for the challenges in the governance of global affairs?

9.4 Law and the language of the future: from instinct, via intellect to intuition

> *The universe is full of magical things patiently waiting for our wits to grow sharper.*[137]

Language is changing constantly with the perception of change as perhaps the only constant. Recently, essentially oxymoronic concepts, often converging opposite or seemingly unrelated concepts, were found to be on the rise in an era of accelerated perception of change. Oxymoronic language thus directly challenges the dualistic conception of perception as it is based on contrast effects between two extreme poles. From this challenge derive many serious problems that originate from the contradictions that pop up everywhere in the form of oxymora, enantioses or paradoxes, which create the impression of an increasing complexity. Paradoxically, essentially oxymoronic concepts appear to be both the cause and the response of these problems. The reason is that they first create or at least make us aware of these contradictions and, second, provide a better descriptive tool for dealing with the complexity arising from the blurring of lines of distinction

135 See Raymond W. Gibbs, *The Poetics of Mind: Figurative Thought Language and Understanding* (New York: Cambridge University Press, 1994) at 397.

136 See Raymond W. Gibbs Jr. and Lydia R. Kearney, "When Parting is Such Sweet Sorrow: The Comprehension and Appreciation of Oxymora" (1994) 23(1) *Journal of Psycholinguistic Research* 75 at 75.

137 Eden Phillpotts, *A Shadow Passes* (London: Cecil Palmer & Hayward, 1918) at 19.

due to an acceleration of perception, like that experienced when watching single frames of a motion picture. In this process of an accelerated perception there exist strong constraints, which – if a dichotomy is permitted – are grounded in both biological as well as cognitive reasons, or to use the analogy of computers, in both our human software and hardware. The two seem, however, linked by a paradox, namely that even words may shape our genes from which our organs develop. Possibly, essentially oxymoronic concepts function as the programming language that enhances our software and requires improvements to the hardware as well. Put briefly, it seems – as Oren Perez rightly proposed – that "our problem does not lie in the paradox, but in a certain logical and anti-paradoxical state of the mind which has become prevalent".[138]

This raises the question of how the problems caused by contradictions can be overcome. In this respect, we can take note of many different responses, one of which is the faster semantic change of language through neologisms, which often proceeds by means of synaesthetic adjectives, i.e. adjectives referring to sensory experiences. Synaesthesia seems in this regard to be able to provide relief in times of great complexity, as it makes better use of all available (both known and unknown) senses by connecting and integrating them into one "common sense" that is sometimes referred to as a "sixth sense". We already rely on synaesthetic or coenesthetic experiences but most of the time we are not aware of it. We can also see this tendency through the emergence of new communication technologies, such as email or texting. These new technologies have radically transformed the way we write and, in the future, they may also lead to a greater convergence between written and spoken language.[139] Moreover, they increase in the more "iconic" nature of language, as we can see in the form of icons, ideograms, emoticons or emojis, like smileys, on our technological communication devices. These new abbreviated forms of communication seem to be gradually introducing more elements of character-based languages, like Chinese, into alphabet-based languages, like English. In short, they tend towards convergence of pictures and letters, like Rene Magritte's *Ceci n'est pas une pipe*, which synaesthetically challenges our perception. This may have the advantage of conveying more information in a shorter time, as is captured by the idiom "a picture is worth a thousand words".

On the other hand, a reverse trend of alphabet-based languages influencing character-based languages may also be taking place in parallel, which may be visible in the change of the direction of writing in China, in 1955, from vertical (beginning on the right side) to horizontal writing (left to right).[140] Yet, despite some obvious differences between Chinese and European languages,

138 Oren Perez, "The Institutionalisation of Inconsistency: From Fluid Concepts to Random Walk" in Owen Perez and Gunther Teubner (eds), *Paradoxes and Inconsistencies in the Law* (Oxford: Hart Publishing, 2006) 119 at 143.

139 See Naomi S. Baron, *Alphabet to Email: How Written English Evolved and Where It's Heading* (London: Routledge, 2000) at 7–8 and 269.

140 See Jerry Norman, *Chinese* (Cambridge: Cambridge University Press, 1988) at 80.

the cognitive processes seem to be universal.[141] Even though the universal origin of languages remains in doubt,[142] it is interesting to note that mysteriously humanity has developed scripts – perhaps in alignment with the planet's shape – in all directions both vertically and horizontally as well as from left to right and right to left.[143]

Even law, as it heavily relies on written and spoken language, needs to adapt to these changes. But law too faces a synaesthetic challenge, meaning that it needs to rethink "legal ocularcentrism" or the dominant reliance on sight as the source of sensory perception. As the term "oral evidence" and other legal oxymora suggest, law too must find more oxymoronic expressions in both language and underlying cognitive processes related to legal thinking and reasoning. In line with linguistic and technological manifestations, law too must embrace the acceleration of perception and other drastic changes by expanding its sources in all directions. As a first step, it must give up the exclusive or at least consciously dominant use of dualistic reasoning. In fact, law is in most instances less rational than it pretends; it uses more magical terms than it would like to admit.[144] Law uses synaesthetic sources based on intuition but later tends to justify decisions rendered based on complicated (pseudo-)rational arguments.

It is therefore advocated that to deal successfully with the present problems related to faster change and complexity, law must break free from the dualistic chains and classical logic it has been put in. To dissolve the many contradictions, we must "reach a deeper understanding of the legal premises that guide our thinking".[145] In this regard, we must also critically, especially in legal education, question some of the basic assumptions, like those put forward by Max Rheinstein, when he wrote that in law, thinking without concepts like thinking without thoughts is impossible, as is "to make music without tones, to talk without sounds, or to see without images".[146] What, I wonder, would, for instance, John Cage having composed *4'33"* without a single tone, Rodolfo Sacco talking about "mute law", or a synaesthete seeing music in colours, have to say about that?

In other words, the issue is not to deny the role of language of thoughts, but one can question what we mean by "thinking" and how it relates to logic and underlying cognitive processes fed by an unknown number of senses as well as

141 See *e.g.* Xiaolin Zhou, Zheng Ye and Him Cheung and Hsuan-Chih Chen, "Processing the Chinese Language" (2009) 24(7/8) *Language and Cognitive Processes* 929 at 938.

142 See generally Jean Aitchison, "Lifting the Veil: Uncovering Language Origin" in Piet van Sterkenburg (ed), *Unity and Diversity of Languages* (Amsterdam: John Benjamins Publishing Company, 2008) 17.

143 See Omniglot: The Online Encyclopedia of Writing Systems & Language, *Writing Direction Index*; available at: http://www.omniglot.com/writing/direction.htm (accessed 1 October 2017).

144 Jerome Frank, *Law and the Modern Mind* (New Brunswick: Transaction Publishers, 2009) at 68.

145 Fletcher, "Paradoxes in Legal Thought", *supra* note 8 at 1292.

146 Max Rheinstein, "Education for Legal Craftsmanship" (1945) 30(3) *Iowa Law Review* 408 at 415.

our theories about the functioning of the brain. Apparently we can also think without words and in images instead.[147] The most important question is how we can decipher the code hidden in the numerous essentially oxymoronic concepts and what kind of thinking is best adapted to deal with the cognitive challenges that derive from them. The most pressing problems concern the limitations that language based on dualistic reasoning and binary logic impose. In addition to concepts like "dialetheism", "oxymoronic thinking" or "fuzzy logic", other useful concepts to consider are those of "intuition" or "intuitive thinking". The value of intuition for our daily life is priceless although few recognize it as such. Intuition is closely related to synaesthesia or coenesthesia and provides a better orientation in a complex world. Its possible contribution to a better understanding of the contradictions inherent in essentially oxymoronic concepts as well as their dissolution in an integrated mode of perception that allows for more coherent actions to be taken seems of even greater value. So if we apply intuition based on synaesthesia to daily routine actions, why not also try to make conscious use of it for law and the design of a future global legal order?

The link between law and intuition is less than obvious. It is almost paradoxical, as, on the one hand, "for much of history, laws were passed and cases decided with little more than intuitive knowledge about how the mind works", and on the other, "psychological intuitions were present at the dawn of law, but the interdisciplinary venture is in its teens".[148] In dealing with complex or contradictory problems, law usually applies as heuristics a rational method of problem solving that relies on bifurcation, i.e. a mode of dualistic thinking and binary logic. The reasons for this simplification have been given as follows:

> For many legal problems, finding the absolutely best solution to a problem (i.e., optimization) is out of reach. The problem is too complex, information is scarce and contradictory, too many players are involved with dissimilar goals, or time is pressing and the world uncertain.[149]

Again we can see complexity and contradiction, as addressed by oxymoronic language, as the principal challenges to law, which should perhaps be complemented by the serious problem of greater uncertainty due to an accelerated perception of change.[150] For this reason, it is necessary to look out for ways to adopt a better mode of legal thinking, more appropriate logic underlying legal reasoning, and,

147 See *e.g.* James J. Gibson, "The Information Available in Pictures" (1971) 4(1) *Leonardo* 27 at 34; see also Rudolf Arnheim, "A Plea for Visual Thinking" (1980) 6(3) *Critical Inquiry* 489.

148 See Christoph Engel and Gerd Gigerenzer, "Law and Heuristics: An Interdisciplinary Venture" in Gerd Gigerenzer and Christoph Engel (eds), *Heuristics and the Law* (Cambridge: The MIT Press, 2006) 1 at 1.

149 See Gerd Gigerenzer, "Heuristics" in Gerd Gigerenzer and Christoph Engel (eds), *Heuristics and the Law* (Cambridge: The MIT Press, 2006) 17 at 17.

150 On decision making in view of uncertainty in general, see also Amos Tversky and Daniel Kahneman, "Judgment under Uncertainty: Heuristics and Biases" (1974) 185(4157) *Science* 1124.

most of all, cognitive ways of dealing with the information glut and confusion between the senses manifest in a lack of coherence in perception and actions. To improve legal reasoning and with it generally the quality of decision making, it has been proposed to complement it by methods of cognitive heuristics as applied in other scientific disciplines, such as psychology.[151] A better way of legal heuristic processing may be found in intuition or intuitive thinking.[152]

The fact is that – next to daily activities – the value of intuition and intuitive thinking has been recognized in various contexts, such as notably in medicine[153] and economics,[154] as well as in both science[155] and art[156] in general. In all these fields as well as in law, the main problem related to intuition is to "recognize" its powers and perils or to distinguish true from false intuition.[157] In this regard, a true intuition can be defined as an insight or an action that is confirmed by later events whereas the false intuition is not. For example, if intuitively I decide to call off an overtaking manoeuvre on a tricky road and then suddenly I see a car coming out of a side street, it worked, whereas in the contrary example it has not worked and cannot be called intuition. Intuition, in a true sense, would be a sense superior to instinct and intellect and fit within the higher order of the universe. However, this question leads back to the dichotomy of free will and determinism, which currently evades our understanding. In this book, intuition is understood as a higher form of cognitive processing, using an integrated sense (common sense or "sixth" sense), which has a higher chance of being in accordance with the laws of nature and is therefore more reliable. Whereas, when intuition errs, it was not intuition but a hunch or gut feeling gone wrong. The importance is that if we already use intuition, even in an occasionally erroneous way, it does not mean that we cannot improve its use. It can also mean that we may develop a new way of thinking, which may – at least – be more efficient in the way we use facts to estimate the consequences.[158] This may prove to be

151 See *e.g.* Leeanne Sharp, "Cognitive Heuristics and Law: An Interdisciplinary Approach To Better Judicial Decision-Making" (1995) 20 *Bulletin of the Australian Society of Legal Philosophy* 71 at 71, Engel and Gigerenzer, "Law and Heuristics: An Interdisciplinary Venture", *supra* note 148 at 1 and Tilmann Betsch, "The Nature of Intuition and Its Neglect in Research on Judgment and Decision Making" in Henning Plessner, Cornelia Betsch, Tilmann Betsch (eds), *Intuition in Judgment and Decision Making* (New York: Lawrence Erlbaum Associates, 2008) 3 at 8–9.

152 See Henning Plessner, Cornelia Betsch, Tilmann Betsch (eds), *Intuition in Judgment and Decision Making* (New York: Lawrence Erlbaum Associates, 2008) at viii–ix.

153 See *e.g.* Mark Quirk, *Intuition and Metacognition in Medical Education: Keys to Developing Expertise* (New York: Springer, 2006).

154 See *e.g.* Roger Frantz, *Two Minds: Intuition and Analysis in the History of Economic Thought* (New York: Springer, 2005).

155 See *e.g.* Frederick Grinnell, *Everyday Practice of Science: Where Intuition and Passion Meet Objectivity and Logic* (Oxford: Oxford University Press, 2009).

156 See *e.g.* Louis Arnaud Reid, "Intuition and Art" (1981) 15(3) *The Journal of Aesthetic Education* 27.

157 See also David G. Myers, *Intuition Its Powers and Perils* (New Haven: Yale University Press, 2002).

158 See also Jonathan Baron, *Judgment Misguided: Intuition and Error in Public Decision Making* (New York: Oxford University Press, 1998) at 201.

necessary in times of greater contradiction, complexity and faster change. Especially a faster pace of change suggests that the law of cause and effect (karma), i.e. the time gap between what we reap and what we sowed will become shorter and shorter. It may mean that which may have taken years or even different lives to materialize, may now become visible in a few days, hours or seconds. This can be called "instant karma", to use the title of John Lennon's song from 1970, when he sings, "Instant Karma's gonna get you, gonna knock you right on the head". In allusion to the prohibition of acting against one's own conduct (*venire contra factum proprium*), from a synaesthetic perspective, "instant karma" can be understood to mean "*non venire contra sensum proprium (non valet)*" or that to come against one's own sense is not allowed.

To avoid painful experiences of instant karma by misjudging information as received through various senses, trying to learn or cultivate the right kind of intuition can perhaps be of great use, even if a rational approach may have some limitations, like aporetics mentioned before. This is because "rational intuition"[159] or "intuition as a method" itself is considered an oxymoron.[160] Similar to dialetheism or accepting contradictions in principle, again a first useful step may consist in scientifically taking intuition seriously as a valuable tool for decision making, especially in the context of a better coordination of sensations originating from different sources. Like musical education perhaps,[161] it means to combine rationality and intuition, thought and emotion, sight and hearing, smell and taste, body and soul, and to integrate all of them into one single "common sense". It means to gain a deeper insight, a meaning of intuition which can be derived from its etymological origin deriving from Latin *intueri*, which means "to look inside". More broadly, it can also be understood as a new sense, which allows us to "gain insight", i.e. a deeper understanding of any phenomenon's constitution, simultaneously revealing the shape as a whole and each single constituent separately.

The connection between intuition and the senses is outlined in an article by Heikki Piha, in which he calls intuition a "bridge to the coenesthetic world of experience".[162] He defines intuition as "an integrated mode of archaic coenesthetic thinking" and "preconscious nondiscursive thinking process [that] is needed in creativity, as well as less conspicuously in countless everyday activities".[163] Intuition is also deemed useful in its capacity to deal "immediately with various rationally indistinct phenomena, such as forms, shades, and multidimensionality,

159 See generally Barbara S. Held and Lisa M. Osbeck, *Rational Intuition: Philosophical Roots, Scientific Investigations* (Cambridge: Cambridge University Press, 2014).

160 See *e.g.* Lee Nam-In, "The Crisis of Modern Society and Critical Rationality" in Thomas Nenon and Philip Blosser (eds), *Advancing Phenomenology: Essays in Honor of Lester Embree* (New York: Springer, 2010) 235 at 245 and Lawrence Krader, "On Method of Noetics" in Cyrill Levitt (ed), *Noetics: The Science of Thinking and Knowing* (New York: Peter Lang, 2010) 229–241 at 234.

161 See Keith Swanwick, *Musical Knowledge: Intuition, Analysis and Music Education* (London: Routledge, 1994).

162 Piha, *supra* note 129.

163 *Ibid* at 23.

regardless of the boundaries between sensory modalities".[164] It was also suggested that intuition may be cultivated through "talent, training and experience".[165] But of greatest relevance for oxymora and paradoxes is that intuition is a bridge that transcends dichotomies or particularly boundaries between the different senses, between thoughts and emotions,[166] between science and art, between left brain and right brain, or the two systems I and II underlying dual process theories,[167] or possibly between time and space.

These synergic qualities were also outlined by Anton Ehrenzweig when he linked intuitive thinking, also called "seeing together", as the "search for the unification of the incompatible" and the possible creation of "order in chaos".[168] Interesting for oxymoronic concepts, he continues by stating that in "true intuition the normal differentiation of time and space is suspended and events and objects can freely interpenetrate".[169] This is again remarkable as time and space was also mentioned as disappearing in mystical or drug-related experiences.

Another interesting boundary that becomes dissolved is the one between the self and the other, as is the case with empathy or "mirror-touch synaesthesia". It has also been said that even though empathy and intuition are not the same, intuitive understanding may be based upon information provided by empathic responses.[170] The reference to empathy is also of interest, as it was linked to the "hidden paradox of human history", by which Jeremy Rifkin refers to the tragicomic observation that "we are beginning to glimpse the prospect of global emphatic consciousness [when] we find ourselves close to our own extinction".[171]

As for the precise relation of intuition to instinct and intellect in human evolution, intuitive human capacities were qualified as "rudimentary derivatives of phylogenetically earlier instinctive functions".[172] Perhaps instinct, intellect and intuition form a chain in human evolution as we perceive it in linear mode. This entire question may be vain, if – based on intuition – we eventually transcend the perception of time and space as separate entities as then there will be no real beginning or end. Perhaps, like in the movie *The Matrix*, sensations of *déjà vu*, of synchronicity, or of the famous "law of the series"[173] are intuitively received

164 *Ibid.*

165 *Ibid* at 27.

166 See *e.g.* Nico H. Frijda, Antony S. R. Manstead and Sacha Bem (eds), *Emotions and Beliefs: How Feelings Influence Thoughts* (Cambridge: Cambridge University Press, 2000).

167 See also James T. McLaughlin, "Primary and Secondary Process in the Context of Cerebral Hemispheric Specialization" (1978) 47(2) *Psychoanalytic Quarterly* 237.

168 Anton Ehrenzweig, *The Hidden Order of Art* (Berkeley: University of California Press, 1967) at 132.

169 *Ibid.*

170 See Piha, *supra* note 129 at 28.

171 Jeremy Rifkin, *The Empathic Civilization: The Race to Global Consciousness in a World in Crisis* (New York: Jeremy P. Tarcher, 2009) at 25.

172 See Piha, *supra* note 129 at 39.

173 See Paul Kammerer, *Das Gesetz der Serie: Eine Lehre von den Wiederholungen im Leben und im Weltgeschehen* (Stuttgart: Deutsche Verlags-Anstalt, 1919).

indicators for a dimension beyond time and space in the way we perceive and understand it at present.

What speaks for the idea that essentially oxymoronic concepts gradually breed a new sense, a more synaesthetic, integrated or common sense that will allow us to tackle contradictions better, is that they inspire more intuitive thinking. This is why it is interesting that "intuition" is said to form "a bridge to the grammar of the primary process, whose structure is far from primitive, though it is of archaic origin".[174] More so, it was specified that "intuitive thinking takes place in an area where the primary and secondary processes are integrated with each other without conflict or hierarchical juxtaposition".[175]

In conclusion, if we permit ourselves to stop thinking in dualistic and linear terms for a while, essentially oxymoronic concepts will deliver the following message as the central rhetorical devices of the language of the future that will also determine the function of law:

To begin with, essentially oxymoronic concepts will continue to rise in number as paradoxes and oxymora are found to breed more of their kind. The headache they will cause in view of many "powerful tensions, profound contradictions, and perplexing paradoxes", will lead to novel ways of thinking and reasoning, which will – perhaps based on new technologies – enhance our perception of reality to transform our understanding further. In parallel with these efforts, a new integrated "sense organ" may gradually develop but abruptly enter into operation similar to the experiences described by koans. This will work with the forces of evolution, which has always progressed by both nature and nurture. The role of oxymora and paradoxes in such cognetic process was compared to the relation between computer hard- and software, or applied to humans, as one of a "neuro-linguistic-genetic programming tool". But oxymoronic language is not the only factor – the growing appeal of meditation as non-dual awareness,[176] yoga,[177] as well as other creative activities, whether in science, in art, in the economy or in law, will work as further catalysts of this process.

In this process of shaping the cognitive and genetic conditions of humans, dialetheism or the mere acceptance of contradictions in a paraconsistent logic marks an important step on the path of the golden mean (*chung yung*). Acceptance will come automatically, as one is unable to remain in one extreme for long. And for the unwilling, instant karma produced by the acceleration of everything will provide both immediate sanctions in the forms of gratification or punishment. Essentially oxymoronic concepts will stimulate intuitive thinking, function like a "verbal LSD", which will increase the global connectivity of the brain, bridging the left and right hemispheres, the dual processes associated with them. Perhaps,

174 See Piha, *supra* note 129 at 46.

175 *Ibid.*

176 See also Zoran Josipovic, "Neural Correlates of Nondual Awareness in Meditation" (2014) 1307(1) *Annals of the New York Academy of Sciences* 9.

177 See also R. C. Mohan, *The Essence of Yoga* (New Delhi: Penguin Ananda, 1977) at 184 ("Because one cannot remain on one extreme for long").

the "bridge" built by intuition may awaken the so-called "third eye" or "third ear", which will perhaps originate from somewhere near the pineal gland.[178]

Parallel to the emergence of a common sense, language will change further based on neologisms and semantic change. Eventually, it will create a common language, which is needed for a global legal order to be established. Such a common language may not be entirely verbal or rely on letters – it will be a cognitive language. Corresponding to novel synaesthetic skills, it may combine different features of communication, including images, body language and perhaps telepathy. Already, the future of language has been outlined in the following lines:

> Language is merely a tool we use to translate our thoughts. In the future, we won't need to code thoughts into language – we will uniformly send symbols and ideas and concepts without speaking . . . in the future, speech will be what baby talk is today.[179]

In fact, it is not only children who have access to the undifferentiated, non-verbal mode of thinking.[180] So, too, do grown-ups but their senses generally have become caught up in the constraints imposed by schools rigidly teaching language, grammar, syntax and other topics. It is interesting to note that even the Bible contains a passage where a stronger sense of coenaesthesia in children, which becomes weakened in later age, is mentioned as follows:

> When I was a child, I spake as a child, I understood as a child, I thought as a child; but when I became a man, I put away childish things.
> For now we see through a glass, darkly; but then face to face: now I know in part; but then shall I know even as also I am known.[181]

The same phenomenon was also observed in child psychology by Jean Piaget and expressed through the following paradox:

> Here, we are at once confronted with a paradoxical fact: compared with ourselves, the child is both closer to immediate observation and further removed from reality.[182]

This reflects that greater partial knowledge acquired by a dominantly analytical mode of thinking comes at a price for a better holistic understanding of the whole.

178 See Williams, *supra* note 117 at 463.

179 See Mark Andrejevic, *Infoglut: How Too Much Information Is Changing the Way We Think and Know* (New York: Routledge, 2013) at 77–78.

180 See Piha, *supra* note 129 at 35; see generally William S. Condon and Louis W. Sander, "Synchrony Demonstrated between Movements of the Neonate and Adult Speech" (1974) 45(2) *Child Development* 456.

181 Corinthians 13:11–12; *The Holy Bible, Containing the Old and New Testaments* (London: G. E. Eyre and W. Spottiswoode, 1849).

182 Jean Piaget, *The Child's Conception of Physical Causality* (London: Routledge, 1999) at 253 [first published in 1930].

Finally, what do these potential evolutionary trends hold for the future of law or the quest for a global legal order? In this quest mnemonic law based on legal synaesthesia provides a useful metaphor for the search for greater "global connectivity" in terms of greater coherence in global governance. The reason is that greater global connectivity will naturally develop from our newly acquired cognitive abilities as law has since time immemorial. Moreover, the realities linked to economic globalization and the growing threat provided by global problems in the Anthropocene era will also do their part. Ultimately, the newly acquired cognitive tools will make new perceptions possible, and a common legal global order will be established based on them. In this sense, it is hoped that various political institutions or single persons, like the prime ministers of countries, the Secretary General of the UN and other functional units, will act as true organs of an "integrated sense". It means they will help to secure greater coherence in law and policy making and to "deliver as one" in all matters pertaining to global governance. Legal education and more multidisciplinary research in matters pertaining to "law and mind" still need to be encouraged so as to prevent the "hidden paradox of human history" tipping towards the extinction of humanity. Or, formulated in less pessimistic terms, the due preparation of our cognitive tools may be able to prevent unnecessary suffering of people around the world, which delays progress in areas that really do matter in terms of human evolution. For such progress to materialize, it is deemed indispensable to build a global legal order in analogy to the mind of humanity, i.e. an order of global mnemonic law, a law in and for the time of oxymora.

10 Concluding remarks

Dualism is the chief "idol": let us free ourselves from it.[1]

Essentially oxymoronic concepts denote a category of rhetorical devices that includes oxymora, enantioses (or contradictions in terms) as well as paradoxes. This category was coined in homage to Walter B. Gallie's article on "essentially contested concepts", in which he pointed out the frequent misunderstandings and disputes that come with most generic concepts, like art, democracy, morality or the rule of law. In fact, essentially contested concepts point to a much deeper obsession of human beings with "contest", "competition" or "conflict", whether they occur in debates, sports, politics or war. The external manifestation of the nature of contest is matched by an internal cognitive process based on dualistic thinking and supported by a binary logic, whereby two opposite thoughts compete for victory. With evolution continuing at an apparently accelerated pace of change in time and in space, the traditional dualistic mode of thinking and binary logic is coming under increased pressure. This happens for the simple reason that when change accelerates, the oscillation between opposites as underlying contrast effects necessary to perceive change in the first place leads to a blurring of the lines of distinctions. This is well exemplified by the invention of cinematography, which literally set still pictures in motion (stasis in motion). When the former well-established lines of distinctions between opposite concepts become blurred, the complexity seems to increase as well. With greater complexity in times of faster change perception, the possibility of contradictions and inconsistencies appears to increase as well. This is the main reason why oxymora and paradoxes are proliferating around us, because they provide a more accurate description of the "dynamic status quo" that we live in. At the same time, they also highlight the instance where our current scientific knowledge is insufficient. Paradoxically, but not surprisingly, they affect the way we perceive, think and act. They tend to induce the need for more holistic and dynamic thinking, summarized as "oxymoronic thinking". Through these qualities

1 Peter D. Ouspensky, *Tertium Organum: The Third Canon of Thought – A Key to the Enigmas of the World*, 2nd ed (New York: Alfred A. Knopf, 1922) at 266.

they also hold the key to the future, as they inspire creative ideas or new discoveries, which may be able to transcend the boundaries imposed by the past or bias and uncritical assumptions.

The "creative" quality of essentially oxymoronic concepts has been used since time immemorial in art, magic or mysticism as the forerunners of today's concept of science. Recently, even our strictest conception of science has seen their role increase in practically all scientific disciplines from A to Z. In this regard, the examples of oxymoronic concepts in art and science revealed more than a coincidental terminological overlap between the two areas, which – regrettably – had become separated in the course of time. In this regard the poem "The Fable of the Bees" finds expression in economics by the "paradox of thrift", as much as Ovid's phrase "my plentie makes me poore" in the Easterlin paradox. It is by the same means that the principle of the pursuit of happiness in law relates to the paradox of happiness in philosophy, or the oxymoron "free jazz" in music to that of the "free market" in political economy. Additionally, through creative marketing strategies and technological convergence, oxymora and paradoxes are now also a fixed part of daily discourse, as we eat gourmet pizza and drink iced tea before we drive our SUVs to nearby cinemas to watch movies like *True Lies.* Similarly, the same oxymoronic language perplexes individuals in their daily decisions as they do at the global and local level in the form of numerous unsolved problems addressed by the glocal governance debate in the quest for global justice. In sum, the noticeable changes in language suggest, as a wider trend, a general shift from a paradigm of contestation and conflict to one of contradiction and convergence; a shift that was also recognized by Charles Handy in the title of his book, *The Age of Paradox.*[2]

Given the trends of overregulation and a creeping juridification, the sheer and still growing number of oxymoronic concepts in all areas of life also means they are playing an increasing role in law. Under the heading "Law in the Time of Oxymora" in this book, this trend in law was confirmed by the analysis of their significance in both law in action and law in books. In law, oxymora especially were used to show how they clash with a dominant conception of justice in terms of bifurcation of dualistic thinking between antagonistic concepts, like guilty and innocent, right and wrong, or legal and illegal, to mention but a few. Numerous oxymora formulated by judges, like "pure law", "just fraud" or "welcome sexual harassment", match the number of those coined in scholarly writings, which range from a paradox of constitutionalism to the oxymoron of "regulatory coopetition". Moreover, these concepts often match or resemble the terminology coined by poets and follow the wider trend of the ever faster changes in language, mainly through neologisms and semantic change.

As in science, in law too these oxymoronic concepts reveal the weaknesses and deficiencies rooted in our current understanding and dualistic conception of perception and cognition. It also clashes with the uncritical belief in the undoubted

2 See Charles Handy, *The Age of Paradox* (Boston: Harvard Business School Press, 1995).

principal value of binary logic or a Western scientific paradigm that relies more on analysis than synthesis, on atomistic rather than holistic thinking. The frequent distinction between Eastern and Western philosophy, logic or thinking merely reflects the limitations of dualistic thinking that is based largely on an attitude of *divide and rule*. This attitude, however, is not one that can be tied down in geographical terms. There have been many in the West who have cultivated a more balanced or holistic approach, but they have often been ridiculed, oppressed or even killed for their scientific discoveries or mere ideas. The dichotomies between East and West or North and South indicate that we do not face a geographical problem but a conceptual one, namely one where we fail to see the unity in diversity. More so still, we fail to see that we are oxymora and that – paradoxically – we are full of contradictions both biologically and cognitively. This misconception is a general problem that dominates not only many scientific disciplines but our mindset as well. It finds expression in the attempts to separate woman from man, the left from the right brain, genetics from cognition, or life from death. The same divided mind also separates state from state or international organization from international organization, as well as different legal disciplines from each other, causing a further fragmentation of laws that is detrimental to the cause of the rule of law and global justice.

Gradually, however, we are forced to realize the value inherent in these contradictions, given the accelerating pace at which we perceive changes. The reason is that the acceleration of everything leads to a greater state of uncertainty, insecurity and unpredictability when we apply our traditional mode of thinking. Essentially oxymoronic concepts function like a mirror of our deficiencies rooted in dualistic thinking and in the binary logic taught in schools and universities. For a while still science may progress more by funerals than by reason and logic, as Dean Radin wrote.[3] But the process launched by essentially oxymoronic concepts in art, as the language of the future a long time ago, will be unstoppable in science, in law and everywhere else. Ironically, the many essentially oxymoronic concepts not only display our deficiencies in dualistic thinking against the backdrop of so many logical dilemmas or seemingly unsolvable problems, but – in line with their contradictory nature – also hold at least the key to their transcendence and solution. They are providing the links between all apparent opposites as framed in innumerable dichotomies. Equally, they are at the same time the *Gestalt* (shape) as a whole as well as the sum of its single constituent parts, like a melody and its tones. By linking nature to nurture, word to gene and thought to deed, they, most importantly, are building a "bridge" between our different senses leading to a synaesthetic sensation increasing the overall global connectivity in the brain as manifest in intuitive thinking. Thus, various attempts to elaborate heuristic methods for the successful management of paradoxes or oxymora, such as paradoxical thinking, fuzzy logic or dialetheism are merely the beginning, the forerunners, of a major change in cognition. This major change in cognition will happen

3 See Dean Radin, *The Noetic Universe* (London: Corgi Books, 2009) at xxi.

neither gradually nor smoothly. It will gradually develop but then erupt suddenly like a volcano that has lain dormant for aeons and then erupts. Artistic creativity, scientific discovery or the study of koans, as the Eastern oxymora, all testify to such dynamics described by and inherent in essentially oxymoronic concepts.

Until the moment for such a cognitive "eruption" arrives, we can still try to foster the sustainable development of ourselves and the world around us. This is where law is called upon to play a constructive role. Internally, law is a mirror of our mind, which through memory gives us identity. Externally, law is the manifestation of humanity's collective memory that, like technology, tells us a lot about our destiny. As our perception of change continues to accelerate, it will increase the contact points between individuals, states and international organizations. It will increase the overall complexity. At the same time, it will also bind together, in ever shorter cycles of time, the links between cause and effect, creating an instant and efficient sanctioning mechanism that may be called "instant karma". These dynamics need to be understood and translated into a coherent and consistent framework for a global legal order. It is framework of greater "global connectivity" in both cognitive and geographic terms that can be built on the notion of "global mnemonic law" as the expression of the origin of law in the mind of humans. It is also the creative power of law that is equal to that of essentially oxymoronic concepts, which should, therefore, join forces in laying the foundations for a new chapter of life on Earth, which will be written as a constitution for a more just, efficient and sustainable mode of global governance. This new chapter opens with two paradoxically related steps that everyone can take, first, to accept the contradictions inherent in paradoxes, enantioses or oxymora as being possibly true (dialetheism) and, second, to free oneself from the "chief idol of dualism".[4] These steps taken, there may lie a world beyond dichotomies, such as time and space, where the obsolete thinking modes will end and new interesting insights will begin.

4 Ouspensky, *supra* note 1 at 266.

11 Epilogue

A new era of light

This was some time a paradox, but now the time gives it proof.[1]

In the end, it remains to return to the riddle mentioned in the Prologue and reveal the hiding place of the light that was taken from humanity and which casts a shadow over the destiny of human evolution. As the reader may have guessed but without further suspense, the heated discussion mentioned in the old allegory regarding the human quest for "light" ends with one member of the conclave suggesting as the final hiding place the following location:

> Let us hide the stolen jewel of man's divinity within himself, for there he will never look for it.[2]

It seems that humans have already started to look for it within but still we can neither locate it precisely within the human body nor know what to expect from it. At least for the possible precise location, the paradoxical brain or, in cognitive terms, the mind as the origin of a common, integrated or synaesthetic sense that is capable of making sense of the many senses, appears to provide a plausible point of departure. As for what we can expect from the quest for light being successful, we can at least gather a growing number of fragments from all areas of life that seem to begin to form a coherent picture. The many fragments are found in a growing number of oxymora and paradoxes that suggest the necessity to free ourselves from the "idol of dualism" which currently imposes strong limitations in our present mindset. In this regard, oxymoronic thinking and paraconsistent or fuzzy logic such as dialethism seem to provide a cognitive cure. In other words, accepting contradictions as being possibly true can help us to discover a more profound truth in the sense of Niels Bohr's understanding that an ordinary

1 William Shakespeare, *Hamlet, Prince of Denmark: A Tragedy* (Leipzig: Theodor Thomas, 1857) at 100.

2 Foster Bailey, *The Spirit of Masonry*, 3rd ed (New York: Lucis Publishing, 1979) at 107.

truth is a statement whose opposite is a falsehood, whereas "a profound truth is a statement whose opposite is also a profound truth".[3]

One such profound truth that indirectly surfaced from the many paradoxes and oxymora presented throughout this book is the paradox of free will and fate, i.e. the question of whether we freely choose our actions based on conscious decisions or are walking on a predetermined path towards a fixed and unchangeable goal. In this sense, it is also expressed by the oxymoron of "constant change", or that change is the only constant in life. In this regard, it seems that essentially oxymoronic concepts are mysteriously tied to the perception of an accelerating pace of change, by both describing it and also possibly causing it. Usually, the prime unit we use to measure "change" is time. What exactly the concept "time" refers to remains paradoxical as it surfaces in the grandfather paradox. Yet, time is still paradoxical even when it is measured by way of its mysterious relation to space, as indicated by the oxymoron "spacetime" that combines them into a single continuum. In the end, all three concepts – time, space and motion – appear somewhat mysteriously linked in our attempts to measure "change" in a three-dimensional system.[4] In this regard, it is no coincidence that the notion "dimension" etymologically derives from the Latin word "*dimensio*", which means "a measuring". Gradually, in response to the acceleration of the perception of change, both our perception and understanding of time and other measuring units are changing.[5] Or else, it was said that "time management" is an oxymoron, as time is a constant and that all you can change is yourself.[6] In sum, perhaps the dimensions as a whole are changing.

Why is time and the underlying three-dimensional system important for essentially oxymoronic concepts? A possible answer may lie in the mysterious ability of time to "heal all wounds", even those perhaps caused by contradictions inherent in oxymora and paradoxes. One prominent example is the court facing a paradox in the decision between Protagoras and Euathlus in their rhetorical feud over tuition fees, where the final judgment leaves the question undecided and defers the cause to a very distant future time. Shakespeare too supports the thesis underlying this book in the sense that the perplexing because apparent contradictions that characterize essentially oxymoronic concepts will eventually be true. In this phenomenal question lies the scientific uncertainty about the nature of change measured in time, space and motion. From the limited understanding of the three-dimensional framework many problems are derived that – framed

3 See Frank Wilczek, *The Lightness of Being: Mass, Ether, and the Unification of Forces* (New York: Basic Books, 2008) at 11.

4 See also Joseph Mazur, *The Motion Paradox: The 2,500-Year-Old Puzzle Behind All the Mysteries of Time and Space* (New York: Dutton, 2007) and R. M. Sainsbury, *Paradoxes*, 3rd ed (Cambridge: Cambridge University Press, 2009) at 4-21.

5 See *e.g.* Philip Zimbardo and John Boyd, *The Time Paradox: The New Psychology of Time That Will Change Your Life* (New York: Free Press, 2008).

6 See Maynard Rolston, *Time Management Is an Oxymoron: Learn How to Get More Done in Less Time* (Leawood: Leathers Publishing, 2001) at 86.

as dichotomies – cannot be answered in a satisfactory way. To mention but a few, these are: the present understanding of the relations between past and future, life and death or free will and fate. For a long time, humans have been fascinated by these questions and made efforts to arrive at a deeper understanding under many different concepts. One concept, the fourth dimension, can be invoked as a useful point of departure of the world that lies beyond the present scientific paradigm. And it is to the discovery of this world that essentially oxymoronic concepts seem to work, as they have been said to serve "to test models and conceptual frameworks, and to enable true 'paradigm shifts' in certain areas of scientific inquiry".[7] In short, essentially oxymoronic concepts may be the language indicating and paving the way to the future discovery of another dimension looming behind the one we currently perceive as reality.

If most contradictions can be dissolved by time, is it then possible that time itself is the fourth dimension? Possible answers, however, depend on a number of other unknown factors and even in the present third dimension, classifications must, as a lawyer wrote, "be provisional, for forms run into one another".[8] For instance, it has also been suggested that the mind be classified as a fourth dimension, which would mean that time would be moved up to the fifth dimension.[9] Perhaps the question is completely vain, as it is possible that, once we perceive the fourth dimension, "there should be time no longer", as the Book of Revelation reveals.[10] Furthermore, it seems impossible to judge by standards of the third dimension those prevalent in the fourth, let alone the fifth, dimension; it appears vain to try to express the ineffable. In this regard, Peter D. Ouspensky identified the following problem:

> Furthermore, and most important, our ignorance of things in themselves does not depend upon our *insufficient knowledge*, but is due to the fact that by means of sensuous perception we cannot know the world correctly *at all*.[11]

We recall, however, that essentially oxymoronic concepts have been qualified as rhetorical figures that are capable of expressing "the superior power of the experience, the ineffability of the experienced".[12] They are, like art, the language of future possibilities. A good example of art's contribution to the understanding

7 See Narinder Kapur et al., "The Paradoxical Nature of Nature" in Narinder Kapur (ed), *The Paradoxical Brain* (Cambridge: Cambridge University Press, 2011) 1 at 1.

8 Benjamin N. Cardozo, "Law and Literature" (1939) 48(3) *Yale Law Journal* 489 (first published in 1925) at 493.

9 See Marc Seifer and Stanley Krippner, *Transcending the Speed of Light: Consciousness, Quantum Physics, and the Fifth Dimension* (Rochester: Inner Traditions, 2008) at 77.

10 Revelation 10:6; *The Holy Bible, Containing the Old and New Testaments* (London: G.E Eyre and W. Spottiswoode, 1849).

11 See Peter D. Ouspensky, *Tertium Organum: The Third Canon of Thought – A Key to the Enigmas of the World*, 2nd ed (New York: Alfred A. Knopf, 1922) at 17.

12 See Alois M. Haas, *Sermo mysticus: Studien zu Theologie und Sprache der deutschen Mystik* (Freiburg: Universitätsverlag, 1989) at 27–28 [translation from German by author].

of the fourth dimension is found in Marcel Duchamp's painting entitled *Nu descendant un escalier n° 2* (Nude Descending a Staircase, No. 2) from 1912, which gives a visual taste of what a fourth dimension may look like. We have also seen evidence of their potential impact on perception and cognition in the case of synaesthesia, which also reveals a common element between time and mind:

> If there is any attribute that truly deserves to be called a common sensible, any attribute of objects or events that really can manifest itself through *all* of the senses, it is time. Duration is unquestionably universal.[13]

The link between the senses and the fourth dimension is described in the following paragraph:

> Is it not more than possible, is it not more than probable, that there is a Fourth Dimension to which our eyes have not been opened, and that our so-called dead are living in this world, and that through our own development communication with them will come; that this new world is all around and about us, and is a world of an infinite variety of color and sound; that it is nature's great vacation ground; that we enter it at so-called death; that in reality there is neither birth nor death, but that dying is but the passing into a larger life, and birth and effort to express externally some of the wonder and glory of that which we now call the Undiscovered Country; that in this Fourth Dimension all other dimensions exist but varying in degree and not in kind; that length, breadth, and thickness exist as much as they do in our three dimensional worlds, but that we are not able to see them or know them because the rate of vibration is so high that the physical eye and ear are incapable of seeing and hearing; that it is only when both are disclosed to the outer eye that we apprehend what may be termed an inner vision, and an inner hearing?[14]

Many more have dedicated their minds in time and in space to the fourth dimension over the past century, bringing interesting insights into a world to be discovered.[15] They largely complement what the innumerable essentially oxymoronic concepts reveal as well. For the time being, and until our wits grow sharper,[16] we can only try to understand the existing ones in their whole and to

13 See Lawrence E. Marks, *The Unity of the Senses. Interrelations Among the Modalities* (New York: Academic Press, 1978) at 32.

14 See Charles Brodie Patterson, *A New Heaven and a New Earth or the Way to Life Eternal (Thought Studies of the Fourth Dimension)* (New York: Thomas Y. Crowell, 1909) at 90–91.

15 See *e.g.* Charles H. Hinton, *A New Era of Thought* (London: Swan Sonnenschein & Co., 1888) at 84; Charles H. Hinton, *The Fourth Dimension* (London: Swan Sonnenschein & Co., 1901), E. H. Neville, *The Fourth Dimension* (Cambridge: Cambridge University Press, 1921), Ouspensky, *supra* note 11, Tony Robbin, *Shadows of Reality: The Fourth Dimension in Relativity, Cubism, and Modern Thought* (New Haven: Yale University Press, 2006) and Stephen Leon Lipscomb, *Art Meets Mathematics in the Fourth Dimension*, 2nd ed (Cham: Springer, 2014).

16 See Eden Phillpotts, *A Shadow Passes* (London: Cecil Palmer & Hayward, 1918) at 19.

coin new ones as an expression of the approximation of truth resulting from our relentless efforts to search for the light. That these past efforts have been fruitful can be seen from the many pieces that have been discovered that now need to be put and sensed together to form a coherent picture as a whole.

With relation to the role of law in this search, as metaphorically described by the notion of mnemonic law, the combined consideration of the many dichotomies that dominate law and life need to be approached by the acceptance of contradictions, by the combined consideration of the principles of *coincidentia oppositorum* (coincidence of opposites) and *contraria sunt complementa* (opposites are complementary). By doing so law may be able to find a new role and help to solve another paradox, that of free will and fate. A possible solution to this paradox can be formulated as a question, namely whether it is possible to determine the future by creating it. The concept that puts this question into practice is the "self-fulfilling prophecy", a phrase coined by Robert Merton. He defined it as being "in the beginning, a *false* definition of the situation evoking a new behavior which makes the originally false conception come *true*". From this perspective, a self-fulfilling prophecy strongly resembles the dictionary definitions of oxymora and paradoxes, as carrying disturbing contradictions that "may in fact be true".[17] But the analogy can also be extended to law, where its normative power can help to create a situation that is deemed desirable. In this regard, it is necessary to point out an interesting aspect of the concept of fate, as also known by the term "*kismet*". Kismet derives from the Arabic word "*quisma*", which is related to the verb "divide" and means "that which is apportioned".[18] Thus, fate can be understood to mean that because we are merely aware of a part of reality, because of the many divisions that we have drawn up, we do not get to see the full picture.

It is just because we cannot see the cause (like the film projector behind us in a cinema) that the images on the screen appear as reality to us. By the same token, it is the misperception of reality that makes us believe that life is governed by fate, because we cannot see and understand all the causes that create the many effects we notice. In such a situation, it is clear that what may be determined by fate already appears to us as free will and, likewise, what appears to us as free will appears as fate. Such a feeling of awe in view of the paradox of free will and fate, or "want and will", is well reflected in the following anonymous saying:

> I asked for strength and God gave me difficulties to make me strong.
> I asked for wisdom and God gave me problems to solve.
> I asked for prosperity and God gave me brawn and brains to work.
> I asked for courage and God gave me dangers to overcome.
> I asked for patience and God placed me in situations where I was forced to wait.
> I asked for love and God gave me troubled people to help.

17 See Catherine Soanes and Angus Stevenson (eds), *Concise Oxford English Dictionary*, 11th ed (Oxford: Oxford University Press, 2008) at 1037.

18 See Muhammad Asad, *The Road to Mecca* (New Delhi: Islamic Books Service, 2004) at 32.

I asked for favours and God gave me opportunities.
I asked for everything so I could enjoy life.
Instead, He gave me life so I could enjoy everything.
I received nothing I wanted, I received everything I needed.[19]

The truth, however, as the discovery of a fourth dimension of mind and/or time may reveal eventually is that they are not opposites but complementaries, like a dream and reality. Their connection is today captured by the oxymoron of "virtual reality" but in the past was expressed by the saying that "a man is only shown [in a dream what emanates] from the thoughts of his heart".[20] This is but one more contradiction that time, or a new understanding of time in a fourth dimension, may prove true. Many more proofs are likely to follow, and sooner rather than later, given the accelerating pace of change.

Until proof has come, we can nonetheless make constructive use of the many insights gained from essentially oxymoronic concepts by applying them to the field of global law and policymaking. One of them is to monitor closely cognitive processes as they shape the formulation and formation of laws and policies, as the notion of mnemonic law suggests. It also means further efforts to locate the seat of light in humans themselves, which means, as Jack M. Balking wrote, that "we can no longer remain content to imagine law's nature exterior to us; we must search for the nature of the law within".[21] We need to use this insight to prepare law effectively for the future, perhaps for a future in a fourth dimension where even reality in the sense of the laws of nature (or at least the way we perceive them through our senses) have been changed drastically. For the time being, it means to prepare and handle better the consequences of an accelerated oscillation between opposites, captured by the increasing usage of essentially oxymoronic concepts that characterize life and law in the time of oxymora. This is necessary due to the limitations in human perception based on a fragmented set of isolated senses, which also characterizes the external world. As long as this condition prevails, the term "global justice" will be understood as an oxymoron in the form of "just injustice" (in the double sense of "just" and "merely" injustice). Paradoxically, once global justice has been established it will no longer be seen as a contradiction. Eventually, in a moment in time where time itself has ended, it will give proof to the realization that there never has been JUSTICE, nor is, nor will there ever be! It is more likely that – as essentially oxymoronic concepts pointing to the existence of a higher cognitive dimension indicate – there ***JUST-IS***!

19 Anonymous or also attributed to the Sufi teacher Hazrat Ianyet Khan (1882–1927); see Peter L. Johnston, *The Eagle's Way: The Importance of Love in Healthcare* (Bloomington: Balboa Press, 2012) at 201 [*Italics* added].

20 See Abraham Cohen, *The Babylonian Talmūd: Tractate Berākōt* (Cambridge: Cambridge University Press, 1921) at 363 (55b).

21 J. M. Balkin, "Understanding Legal Understanding: The Legal Subject and the Problem of Legal Coherence" (1993) 103(1) *The Yale Law Journal* 105 at 176.

Index

For Product Safety Concerns and Information please contact our
EU representative GPSR@taylorandfrancis.com Taylor & Francis
Verlag GmbH, Kaufingerstraße 24, 80331 München, Germany